bioso   ogy

This book is designed to bring criminology into the 21st century by showing how leading criminologists have integrated aspects of the biological sciences into their discipline. These authors cover both behavioral and molecular genetics, epigenetics, evolutionary biology, and neuroscience, and apply them to various correlates of crime such as age, race, and gender. There are also chapters on substance abuse, psychopathy, career criminals, testosterone, and treatment. While not dismissing traditional ideas about these topics, the authors of these chapters show how biosocial concepts add to, complement, and strengthen those ideas. The book is uniquely valuable in that it brings together many of the leading figures in biosocial criminology to illustrate how the major issues and concerns of criminologists cannot be adequately addressed without understanding their genetic, hormonal, neurological, and evolutionary bases.

Anthony Walsh (Ph.D. Bowling Green State University) is Professor of Criminal Justice at Boise State University, Idaho. He is the author or editor of more than twenty books and scores of articles and essays on the interplay of biological, social, and cultural factors involving crime and criminality. He is author of the text *Biosocial Criminology: Introduction and Integration*. http://cja.boisestate.edu/walsh.htm

Kevin M. Beaver (Ph.D. University of Cincinnati) is Assistant Professor in the College of Criminology and Criminal Justice at Florida State University, Tallahassee. He teaches courses on biosocial criminology and genetic/biological correlates of offending. He is the author of more than forty scholarly works.

CRIMINOLOGY AND JUSTICE STUDIES SERIES

Edited by **Chester Britt**, *Northeastern University*, **Shaun L. Gabbidon**, *Penn State Harrisburg*, and **Nancy Rodriguez**, *Arizona State University*

Criminology and Justice Studies seeks to publish brief and longer length manuscripts that will innovate intellectually and stylistically. Our goal is to publish works that model the best scholarship and thinking in the field today, but in a style that connects that scholarship to a wider audience of advanced undergraduates, the general public, as well as beginning graduate students. Topics the series will include, but are not limited to, are the causes and consequences of crime, the globalization of crime, crime control policy (domestic and international), crime prevention, organizational approaches to the study of the criminal justice system, decision-making in the criminal justice system, terrorism and homeland security, and immigration and crime.

Books in the Series

Published:

Community Policing in America by Jeremy M. Wilson
Criminal Justice Theory edited by David E. Duffee and Edward R. Maguire
Criminological Perspectives on Race and Crime by Shaun L. Gabbidon
Race, Law and American Society: 1607 to Present by Gloria J. Browne-Marshall
Biosocial Criminology edited by Anthony Walsh and Kevin M. Beaver

Forthcoming:

Not Just History: Lynching in the 21st Century by Kathryn Russell-Brown and Amanda
  Moras
White Collar Crime and Opportunity by Michael Benson and Sally Simpson
White Crime in America by Shaun L. Gabbidon
Crime and the Lifecourse by Michael Benson and Alex Piquero
The New Criminal Justice edited by John Klofas, Natalie Kroovand Hipple, and Edmund J.
  McGarrell

biosocial
criminology

new directions in theory and research

edited by

anthony walsh and
kevin m. beaver

Routledge
Taylor & Francis Group

NEW YORK AND LONDON

First published 2009
by Routledge
270 Madison Ave, New York, NY 10016

Simultaneously published in the UK
by Routledge
2 Park Square, Milton Park, Abingdon, Oxon OX14 4RN

Routledge is an imprint of the Taylor & Francis Group, an informa business

Typeset in Minion by
Swales & Willis Ltd, Exeter, Devon
Printed and bound in the United States of America on acid-free paper by
Edwards Brothers, Inc.

Library of Congress Cataloging-in-Publication Data
Contemporary biosocial criminality / edited by Anthony Walsh and Kevin M. Beaver.
p. cm.
Includes bibliographical references.
1. Criminology.   2. Criminal behaviour—Physiological aspects.   3. Criminal behaviour—Genetic aspects.   4. Human beings—Effect of environment on.   5. Sociobiology.
6. Environmental psychology.   I. Walsh, Anthony, 1941–   II. Beaver, Kevin M.
HV6025.C616 2008
364.2′4—dc22

2008013700

ISBN10: 0–415–98943–4 (hbk)
ISBN10: 0–415–98944–2 (pbk)
ISBN10: 0–203–92991–8 (ebk)

ISBN13: 978–0–415–98943–5 (hbk)
ISBN13: 978–0–415–98944–2 (pbk)
ISBN13: 978–0–203–92991–9 (ebk)

Dedication

This book is dedicated to my wife, Grace, my parents, Lawrence and Winifred, my sons, Robert and Michael, and my grandchildren, Robbie, Ryan, Mikey, Randy, and Stevie.

Anthony Walsh

This book is dedicated to my beautiful wife, Shonna, my two precious children, Brooke and Jackson, and my loving parents, Jack and Joan.

Kevin M. Beaver

Contents

List of Illustrations

Figures

Tables

Boxes

Contributors

Kevin M. Beaver is an Assistant Professor in the College of Criminology and Criminal Justice at Florida State University. He received his doctoral degree and his master's degree in criminal justice from the University of Cincinnati. His current research examines the biosocial and genetic underpinnings to serious violent behavior.

Danielle Boisvert, M.S., Ph.D. candidate, received her bachelor's degree in biology from the University of Western Ontario and her master's degree in forensic sciences from the George Washington University. She is currently a doctoral candidate in the Division of Criminal Justice at the University of Cincinnati. Her teaching and research interests include biosocial criminology, life-course criminology, and early intervention.

Anne Campbell is Professor of Psychology at Durham University in England. Her current research takes an evolutionary approach to gender differences in aggression and violence, a topic on which she has written a book entitled *A Mind of Her Own: The Evolutionary Psychology of Women*. She spent several years at Rutgers School of Criminal Justice where she did field research on female gang membership in New York City.

Kim Dietrich received his Ph.D. in developmental neuropsychology from Wayne State University in 1980. He has published widely on the effects of environmental chemicals on child health and development. He is currently director of the Division of Epidemiology and Biostatistics at the University of Cincinnati College of Medicine and Academic Health Center.

Matt DeLisi (Ph.D., University of Colorado, 2000) is Associate Professor in the Department of Sociology and Coordinator of Criminal Justice Studies at Iowa State University. Professor DeLisi's current research focuses on the genetic underpinnings of antisocial behavior.

Satoshi Kanazawa is Reader in Management at the London School of

Economics and Political Science. His work on evolutionary psychology and intelligence research has appeared in peer-reviewed journals in all of the social sciences (psychology, sociology, political science, economics, and anthropology) and in biology. He is the coauthor (with the late Alan S. Miller) of *Why Beautiful People Have More Daughters* (Penguin 2007).

Allan Mazur is a sociologist and engineer, and is Professor of Public affairs in the Maxwell School at Syracuse University, and a Fellow of the American Association for the Advancement of Science. He is author or coauthor of over 150 academic articles and eight books, most recently *Implausible Beliefs in the Bible, Astrology, and UFOs* (Transaction 2007). Mazur does research on social aspects of science, technology and environment, and on biological aspects of sociology.

M. Douglas Ris, Ph.D., is a Board-Certified Clinical Neuropsychologist (ABCN/ABPP), Director of the Neuropsychology Program at Cincinnati Children's Hospital Medical Center, and Professor of Pediatrics, University of Cincinnati College of Medicine. He received his Ph.D. in Clinical Psychology from Wayne State University in 1982 and completed clinical internships at Henry Ford Hospital, and Michigan State University College of Human Medicine. Dr. Ris's research has been sponsored by the National Institute of Environmental Health Sciences and the National Cancer Institute. He has published on a wide variety of conditions affecting the central nervous system in children including environmental toxicants, cancer and brain tumors, sickle cell disease, and traumatic brain injury.

Matthew Robinson received his Ph.D. in criminology and criminal justice from Florida State University in 1997. His areas of expertise include criminological theory, crime prevention, capital punishment, the war on drugs, and social justice. He is the author/coauthor of eight books and over 70 articles and book chapters. Robinson has been Board Member and President of the Southern Criminal Justice Association (SCJA).

Michael G. Vaughn, Ph.D., received his doctoral degree from Washington University in St. Louis and is currently Assistant Professor in the School of Social Work, University of Pittsburgh. His interdisciplinary research has appeared in such journals as *Addictive Behaviors, American Journal of Psychiatry, Drug and Alcohol Dependence, Criminal Justice and Behavior, Behavioral Sciences and the Law, Youth Violence and Juvenile Justice, Journal of Emotional and Behavioral Disorders,* and *Social Work Research*. In addition to several projects examining adolescent substance abuse, self-regulation, and violence, he is developing and testing a general biosocial theoretical model for research and intervention applications.

Anthony Walsh received his Ph.D. in criminology from Bowling Green University, Ohio in 1983. He has field experience in both law enforcement and corrections, and teaches criminology, law, and statistics at Boise State University, Idaho. He is the author, coauthor, editor, or coeditor of 20 books and over 100 journal articles. His primary interest is in the integration of the biological and social sciences in the development of a truly scientific criminology.

Richard P. Wiebe received his J.D. from the University of Buffalo in 1983 and his Ph.D. in psychology from the University of Arizona in 1998. He practiced law for 10 years, including 4 years as a legal services attorney specializing in family law. He is currently coordinator of the criminal justice program at Fitchburg (MA) State College. His publications have centered on the delinquent and criminal personality, adolescent risk behaviors, behavior genetics, and person–environment interactions.

John Paul Wright received his Ph.D. from the University of Cincinnati, Ohio, in 1996. He has published widely on the development of criminal behavior with an emphasis on genetic and biological factors associated with violent conduct. His work spans several disciplines, including criminology, molecular and behavioral genetics, and evolutionary theory. He seeks to unite these disciplines under a broad biosocial criminology framework.

Foreword

Criminology and Justice Studies offers works that make both intellectual and stylistic innovations in the study of crime and criminal justice. The goal of the series is to publish works that model the best scholarship and thinking in the criminology and criminal justice field today, but in a style that connects that scholarship to a wider audience including advanced undergraduates, graduate students, and the general public. The works in this series help fill the gap between academic monographs and encyclopedic textbooks by making innovative scholarship accessible to a large audience without the superficiality of many texts.

  Biosocial Criminology presents research on the intersection of biology and criminology in a way that will be accessible to a wide range of readers. Anthony Walsh and Kevin Beaver have compiled a series of challenging, compelling, and thoughtful essays on the application of biosocial approaches to the study of criminal behavior. The biosocial approach offers a way of understanding criminal behavior through the interaction of the biological characteristics of human organisms with the social and cultural environments in which they are located. Following a general overview of the various ways the biosocial approach to human behavior can be used to understand criminal behavior, the essays in this collection focus on applying the approach to explain the basic correlates of crime and the implications for crime prevention efforts. *Biosocial Criminology* is the first book in criminology and criminal justice to provide a thorough assessment of current research on the multiple ways that biological and social factors are linked with one another as causes of crime that is in a format accessible and understandable to a broad range of readers.

Preface

Sociological criminology was the reigning paradigm that guided the study of crime in the 20th century. I was, and remain, a proud member of this paradigm. I was raised, so to speak, as a strain theorist, schooled at Columbia University by Robert Merton and by Richard Cloward, my cherished mentor. In a true Kuhnian sense, this paradigm has helped my career to flourish, furnishing both empirical puzzles to solve and opportunities to author books chronicling the diverse theories that have arisen under its umbrella. Others have built careers in a similar fashion.

Beyond the personal advantage it has afforded many of us, sociological criminology was an important intellectual enterprise. It was shaped by two periods of social turmoil in the century: the rapid urbanization and depression of the century's first four decades and the socio-political transformation that emerged from the 1960s and lives with us in the baby boom generation even today. The theories nourished by these social contexts forced attention on fundamental transformations that restructured the social landscape. Scholars witnessed the effects of mass movements of the population, disorganized communities where vice activities flourished, sudden and widespread poverty, widening forms of inequality, the repression and then liberation of civil rights, and on and on. It would have been foolish to believe that none of this made a difference.

Adherents to sociological criminology were justifiably suspicious of those claiming that the roots of crime lay within individuals. The biology used was clumsy and the data collected hopelessly flawed. More disquieting, biology was rarely used as a universal theory of behavior but as an explanation for the supposed waywardness of the poor, the epileptic, the immigrant, the Jew, and the black. In today's more antiseptic times, cleansed of the perniciously biased commentary that once was so comfortably expressed in polite circles, we cannot feel on a gut level how awful this theorizing was. Biological models not only happily justified eugenics but also did not bother to mask the racist, sexist, and classicist ideology that informed them. It was this genre of thinking that helped to justify the Holocaust.

Sociological criminology thus removed us from the simplistic notion that crime was due to human defect. It liberated us from the idea that offenders were evil by nature and beyond redemption. It forced us to confront that social arrangements were not the natural product of good and bad bodies but intimately shaped by power, politics, and social advantage. Most of all, it stopped us from the facile view that society, in its many manifestations, could be absolved of any responsibility in the origins of crime. Since the 1980s, its advocates have stood firm against the absurd "get tough" movement that has been needlessly repressive and based on a crude view of human choice.

Although I have trumpeted its value, I am equally persuaded that sociological criminology has exhausted itself as a guide for future study on the origins of crime. It is a paradigm for the previous century, not the current one. Let me hasten to say that I do not see the demise of sociological criminology on the immediate horizon. Its status in the discipline is still near-hegemonic. The current generation of scholars is being socialized into its tenets—though, I suspect, imperfectly. But the seeds of its partial demise—of its foundation cracking—are at hand. The paradigm suffers two fundamental problems.

First, it ignores too much that we know matters. Biology is no longer clumsy. Science, theory, and technology from other fields make it impossible to ignore that we are in the midst of a revolution in knowledge that will unlock secrets about human nature and the human mind. The rise of developmental or life-course criminology—especially Terrie Moffitt's work on neuropsychological deficits—made looking at biology respectable. Development, after all, does not commence in adolescence as many sociological theories implicitly assume; it starts in the womb. But this is only the beginning. As more biologically informed research appears, the theoretical predictions of the sociological paradigm will be revealed as limited, if not misspecified in important ways. Eventually, it will become commonplace to ask: How can any theory that ignores the human body be complete?

Second, sociological criminology has usefully deconstructed conservative get tough views, but it has not constructed much useful knowledge about how to save offenders from a life in crime. Despite good intentions and heartfelt beliefs, its advocates have developed scarce pragmatic advice on how to lessen the misery that crime brings into the lives of its perpetrators and their victims. The problem, I believe, is that sociological criminology simply starts too far away from the offender. It specifies root causes that are not mutable, given existing socio-political arrangements. This perspective thus ignores the insights from correctional rehabilitation that change occurs up close and in person by transforming thoughts and choices. Life-course studies show the same thing. It is the spouse or the boss that restructures lives and reshapes cognitions. The advantage to biologically informed perspectives is that they start inside the person and work outward. It is hard to become too divorced from keeping a close eye on the ways in which offenders lead their lives.

I should caution, however, that the weakness of sociological criminology does not mean that its demise is ensured. My sense is that it has grown stale (do we really need another test of self-control theory?) and ineffectual in directing public policy. But if biology is to be the foundation of 21st-century criminology, it will have to surmount important challenges. Three tasks seem most pressing. First, its advocates will have to educate fellow criminologists about the new paradigm. Ideas will have to be made accessible and understandable. Second, its advocates will have to relinquish their antagonism toward sociology and instead create a broader, more powerful paradigm that encompasses rather than dismisses the social. And, third, its advocates will have to show how the new paradigm rejects its repressive heritage and instead opens up important vistas for progressive crime policies. Yes, I believe in objective truth. But from a normative vantage point, I also believe that the goal of science should be to use empirically grounded understanding to improve the human condition.

Fortunately, *Biosocial Criminology* makes important strides in these directions. It strikes me as a criminological Wal-Mart, offering under one cover a primer on virtually every aspect of biology and crime. It not only educates but also is persuasive in showing the power of this new paradigm. It respects as well the social, revealing how separating the biological from the sociological is, in many respects, a false and unhelpful dichotomy. And it begins to explore how a biosocial approach can illuminate the importance of intervening early in individuals' lives, often by preventing their exposure to toxic and unhealthy environments.

Biosocial Criminology, in short, is a book that should grace the shelf of every student of crime. For sociological criminologists skeptical that biology matters, it provides an excursion through the frontiers of biosocial theory and research. Even if not transformed, the travelers on this trip should return home with a new respect for emerging insights. For those less wed to old ways of thinking, the experience may be more profound. The lessons taught will not be learned in standard criminology textbooks or courses. There is a good chance that *Biosocial Criminology* thus will leave the reader brimming with fresh ideas and with prospects for pursuing richer and perhaps more exciting research enterprises. If so, *Biosocial Criminology* will have served its purpose of laying one of the cornerstones in the foundation for a new paradigm capable of guiding criminology in the 21st century.

Francis T. Cullen
University of Cincinnati

Acknowledgments

We would first of all like to thank executive editor Stephen Rutter for his faith in this project from the beginning. Thanks also for the commitment of his very able assistant, Beatrice Schraa. This tireless team kept up a most useful three-way dialog between authors, publisher, and a parade of excellent reviewers. Our copyeditor, Helen Baxter, spotted every errant comma, dangling participle, missing reference and misspelled word in the manuscript, for which we are truly thankful, and our Production Editor, Sarah Stone, made sure everything went quickly and smoothly thereafter.

We are also most grateful for the reviewers who spent considerable time providing us with the benefit of their expertise during the writing/rewriting phase of the text's production. Trying to please so many individuals is difficult, but it is ultimately satisfying and one that undoubtedly made the book better than it would otherwise have been. These expert criminologists were Chris L. Gibson, Ph.D. and Stephen G. Tibbetts, Ph.D.

Anthony Walsh would like to acknowledge the love and support of his most wonderful and drop-dead gorgeous wife, Grace Jean. Grace's love and support has sustained me for so long that I cannot imagine life without her; she is a real treasure and the center of my universe.

Kevin M. Beaver would like to acknowledge the unwavering support of his wife, Shonna, and the constant love and affection of his children, Brooke and Jackson. Without them, my life would lack meaning and purpose.

Part I

An Overview of the Biosocial Approach

The aim of this book is to convince the reader of the desirability of linking criminology with biology. Why should criminologists concern themselves with linking their discipline with one associated with illiberal politics by many social scientists? There are numerous scientific and practical reasons for doing so outlined in this book, but a short answer will suffice for now. Over 10 years ago a review of the behavior genetic literature led the reviewer to state that behavior genetics studies often reach the same conclusions about social problems that "left-leaning sociologists" do (Herbert, 1997:80). Why then should we burden ourselves with a body of literature telling us the same thing that sociology supposedly does? Herbert provides the short answer again by pointing out that the conclusions arrived at by behavior geneticists were arrived at using "infinitely more sophisticated tools." These "infinitely more sophisticated tools" (theories, models, methodologies, concepts, instruments) developed by behavior geneticists (as well as by the other disciplines such as neuroscience, molecular genetics, and evolutionary biology represented in this book) can be brought to bear on the concepts and assumptions of traditional criminological theories as quality control devices that will help us to separate the considerable wheat in criminology from the also quite considerable chaff.

Additionally, because biosocial approaches include both biological and environmental risk factors, they are "more likely to refine social policies to better specification of environmental factors than to divert funds from environmental prevention strategies" (Morley & Hall, 2003).

The first part of this book introduces biosocial criminology via brief overviews of the three major approaches to it: genetics, evolutionary biology, and neuroscience. The first chapter, written by coeditors Anthony Walsh and Kevin Beaver, provides an overall introduction to the field and claims that sociological criminology has gone as far as it can go, and that the only real pathway to progress is the one taken by other sciences. The pathway these other sciences have taken has been to ally themselves with the more fundamental sciences and integrate all the relevant knowledge those sciences had to offer. For instance, most chemists in the 19th century were opposed to the intrusion of the physicists' atomic theory of matter into their discipline in much the same way that sociological criminologists have opposed the intrusion of biology into criminology. Similarly, a significant number of early and mid-20th century biologists were opposed to the intrusion of molecular chemistry into biology, the phenomena of which one biologist claimed should be explained only by other biological facts (Woodger, 1948). Today, all chemists learn physics and all biologists learn chemistry. Any claim that they need not would be met with incredulity by today's chemists and biologists. We hope for the day when criminologists will be similarly puzzled with the suggestion that they need not study biology to participate in the criminological enterprise.

In Chapter 2, Anthony Walsh introduces genetics and how it is useful to criminologists. He explains how behavior geneticists are able to tease apart genetic and environmental variance in phenotypic (observable) traits while at the same time emphasizing that genes and the environment always operated in tandem to produce any trait or behavior. His primary concern is to allay the fears of some that to allow that genes can influence behavior is to open the floodgates to determinism and reductionism, as well as concerns about racism, sexism, and classism. He shows that all of these concerns are unfounded. All scientists seeking causes are determinists, but they are not fatalists, as those who charge determinism seem to imply. As for reductionism, seeking to understand a phenomenon at a more fundamental is the way science has typically progressed.

Seeking to understand why some groups commit more (or less) antisocial acts than others, or perhaps the genetics behind occupational success, may be construed by some as engaging in racism, sexism, and classism. There is nothing anyone can do to convince such people that science must take us where it takes us, regardless of its potential to offend some. With padlocks on the scientific mind, we would still think that the sun revolves around the earth and that humans are nearer to angels than to chimpanzees. The bad news that humans were not the center of the universe and were just a few genes away from chimps was deeply offensive to many people, but we are, for the most part, over all that now as we have come to accept reality.

In Chapter 3, Kevin Beaver provides an overview of molecular genetics. This review of molecular genetics is very important because very few criminologists have any real understanding of what genes are and how they operate. Beaver also provides lay explanations of the three ways that genes can cause phenotypic variation (i.e., **OGOD [one gene, one disorder]**,

polygenic, and **pleiotropy**). An understanding of molecular genetics can go a long way in dispelling the fears many criminologists have that to admit genes into the causal picture is to surrender to fatalism. Genes are nothing but snippets of DNA that code for the manufacture of proteins such as hormones and neurotransmitters. These proteins facilitate and modulate our behavior, but they do not "cause" it. Indeed, the more we know about genetics the more we realize how important the environment is.

If criminologists come to realize that genes are turned on and off in response to environmental events, then surely they will be less reluctant to utilize genetic information in their studies. It is becoming increasingly easy to do so with the advent of technology that allows us to go directly to the DNA. If we as criminologists don't get our fingers into this particular pie we will forfeit the study of criminal behavior to the hungrier practitioners of other sciences, who have been breathing down our necks for a long time now.

Chapter 4, by John Wright and his colleagues, introduces readers to the amazing world of the brain. They first provide the needed introduction to major brain areas and their function and to the brain imaging technologies such as PET, MRI, and fMRI allowing for in vivo assessment of brain structure and function. These imaging techniques have resulted in an explosion of new information on the brain over the past three decades. The brain is where genetic dispositions and environmental experiences are integrated, and thus the basics of neuroscience must become part of every criminologist's repertoire. Although we are a long way from fully understanding the brain, we cannot ignore what is known that is relevant to criminology. Robinson (2004:72) goes as far as to say that any theory of behavior "is logically incomplete if it does not discuss the role of the brain."

The insights criminologists can derive from the neurosciences will not only buttress our traditional theories, but may also strengthen our claims for preventive *environmental* intervention. The primary message in neuroscience is that a cause can be "biological" without being "genetic" because the brain may be compromised by a variety of environmental insults. Abuse and neglect during the early years of life has particularly deleterious effects on the brain, which will impact much of the behavior of the developing organism. Neuroscience, along with genetics, is able to give us a more precise understanding of why socioeconomic status has the influence on behavior that it does, and that is far more useful than appealing to the "ghosts in the machine," as Wright and colleagues put it.

Likewise, low self-control theory has had a major impact in criminology without the discipline having any kind of firm hand on the origins of self-control. For most criminologists, self-control (and any other trait) is the result of differential socialization. However, Wright, et al. make it abundantly clear that the scientific data clearly and consistently indicate that self-control is housed in the **frontal** and **prefrontal cortex**, that it is strongly influenced by genetic factors expressed in the brain, and that it involves a complex, dynamic balancing of limbic and cortical functioning. Genetics and neuroscience can thus provide criminology with a solid foundation for, and a more sophisticated understanding of, many of its central concepts.

In Chapter 5, Satoshi Kanazawa takes us through what evolutionary psychology has to offer criminology. Whereas genetics and neuroscience explain proximate "how" causal mechanisms (e.g., "Testosterone energizes male competition for mating opportunities and is aided by amygdala functioning that is less responsive to fear cues than it is in females"), evolutionary psychology asks ultimate-level "why" mechanisms (e.g., "Why do males have so much more testosterone than females, and why is the male amygdala less responsive to fear?"). In other words, it seeks to understand the adaptive function of a mechanism in terms of its survival and reproductive value. Evolutionary approaches are fundamentally environmental in that they describe how environments, through natural selection, have shaped the behavior of organisms as they adapt to their environments, and how environmental inputs are needed for the emergence of behavior.

Kanazawa examines crime from an evolutionary standpoint. Note that his discussion of status and intelligence can inform traditional criminological theories for which those concepts are central. Kanazawa is basically asking why the actions we currently define as criminal are part of the human behavioral repertoire; what evolutionarily relevant purpose did (and still do) they serve? He is not saying that natural selection preserved genetic material dedicated to carjacking, robbing banks, jimmying locks, or manipulating the stock market. Rather, the traits underlying these actions were selected to assist a male to gain more copulation opportunities than the next male. The sum of these traits leads their possessors to greater mating success. This is called mating effort (the proportion of total reproductive effort allotted to acquiring sexual partners), which is the opposite to parenting effort (the proportion of total reproductive effort invested in rearing offspring).

David Rowe (2002:62–63) provides a thumbnail sketch of the traits useful in supporting extreme mating effort to the detriment of parenting effort:

> A strong sexual drive and attraction to novelty of new sexual partners is clearly one component of mating effort. An ability to appear charming and superficially interested in women while courting them would be useful. The

emotional attachment, however, must be an insincere one, to prevent emotional bonding to a girlfriend or spouse. The cad may be aggressive, to coerce sex from partly willing partners and to deter rival men. He feels little remorse about lying or cheating. Impulsivity could be advantageous in a cad because mating decisions must be made quickly and without prolonged deliberation; the unconscious aim is many partners, not a high-quality partner.

Note that these are the same traits that prove useful in pursuing criminal activities. The most useful traits underlying parenting effort, by the same token, are the prosocial traits of empathy, altruism, nurturance, and intelligence. Thus, the main point of the evolutionary psychology approach to crime is that although the traits mentioned by Rowe were designed by natural selection to facilitate mating effort, they are also useful in gaining non-sexual resources by illegitimate means once they are in place.

References

Herbert, W. (1997). The politics of biology. *U.S. News & World Report*, 21 April, 72–80.

Morley, K. & W. Hall (2003). Is there a genetic susceptibility to engage in criminal acts? *Trends and Issues in Crime and Criminal Justice*. Australian Institute of Criminology, October:1–10.

Robinson, M. (2004). *Why crime? An integrated systems theory of antisocial behavior.* Upper Saddle River, NJ: Prentice-Hall.

Rowe, D. (2002). *Biology and crime.* Los Angeles: Roxbury.

Woodger, J. (1948). *Biological principles.* London: Routledge & Kegan Paul.

1

Introduction to Biosocial Criminology

Anthony Walsh and Kevin M. Beaver

Introduction

Trying to get to the core (if indeed there is a core) of the crime problem is an extraordinarily difficult, complex, but exciting enterprise. Many criminologists have taken their spades to it, but they have barely cracked the mantle, never mind approached the core. Thomas Bernard (2002) has made the point that decades of criminological research has not yielded the accumulation of "taken for granted" knowledge that is the hallmark of any discipline claiming to be a science. The problem has been not with the tenacity with which they have dug, but with the instruments that they have used and with their stubborn refusal to accept any help proffered by the more fundamental sciences.

The Biosocial Approach is Integrative

The **biosocial** approach to criminology, by way of contrast, gratefully accepts this help, and integrates relevant data, concepts, and methods from the biological sciences into traditional criminological approaches. As little as 25 years ago any positive mention of biology in a criminologist's work was an invitation to hostile derision. This situation existed because most criminologists were (and are) sociologically trained (Walsh & Ellis, 2004), and sociology possesses "a conceptual scheme that explicitly den[ies] the claims of other disciplines potentially interested in crime" (Gottfredson & Hirschi, 1990:70). Most criminologists are also poorly trained in biology and few have the interest or inclination to rectify the situation and thus cling to the biology-free theories that were in vogue when they were graduate students. This is a pity, for as sociologist Matthew Robinson (2004: ix–x) has pointed out: "[T]he biological sciences have made more progress in advancing our understanding about behavior in the last 10 years than sociology has made in the past 50 years." In response to the explosive advances in biological knowledge, however, a growing number of criminologists have come to realize that if they are to capture the dynamic nature of criminal behavior they must span multiple levels of analysis and thus multiple disciplines.

Society may "prepare the stage for crime," as sociologically oriented criminologists like to point out, but the crime is committed by flesh and blood human beings with brains, genes, **hormones**, and an evolutionary history. We therefore have to get beyond trying to understand the behavior of these human beings as if they were disembodied spirits blown hither and thither by environmental winds. Biosocial criminology recognizes the tremendous role the environment plays in all aspects of human life, but it also recognizes that environments act on diverse human materials. There is a pithy old adage that points out: "The heat that melts the butter hardens the egg." In a nutshell, that is what biosocial criminology is all about: how similar environments have different effects on different people, and vice versa.

The Biosocial Approach is Developmental

Biosocial criminology is also developmental. Whereas many criminological theories are static in that they imply that criminal behavior is self-perpetuating and continuous once initiated, biosocial theories are dynamic. They emphasize that individuals develop along different pathways, and as they develop factors that were previously meaningful to them (e.g., acceptance by antisocial peers) no longer are, and factors that previously meant little to them (e.g., marriage and a career) suddenly become meaningful. But biosocial theories go beyond merely noting social turning points over the life-course: they attempt to explain why they are turning points, why they are meaningful at certain life junctures and not at others, and why individuals are differentially affected by them.

By *developmental* we do not mean the kind of **preformationism** that Sampson and Laub (2005) accuse developmental theories of adhering to. Preformationism implies a latent predetermined form waiting only for a developmental process to make it apparent, like dough waiting for the oven to bake it into a loaf. To say someone or someone's theoretical perspective is "preformationist" is to substitute an old and gentle metaphysical term for the more modern accusatory and hostile "genetic determinist." The metaphysical opposite of preformationism is **epigenesis** (not to be confused with the modern usage of the term **epigenetics** by geneticists), which insists on the efficacy of environmental plasticity to mold individuals in ways not supposedly predestined by their genes.

We are not going to play the nature–nurture game. Biosocial theorists are developmental in the sense that they believe genes set us on particular developmental trajectories, but they are aware that the vagaries of the environment can send those trajectories askew. We also are developmentalist enough to take issue with Sampson and Laub's (2005) implication that childhood experiences deserve no special place in the pantheon of behavioral causes. Our earliest years, when the brain is most pliable, chisels neural networks in ways that are not easily altered. Later experiences (Sampson and Laub's "turning points") have a weaker influence on the developing person because their influence is channeled along the neural pathways laid down during childhood: Is the person intelligent and conscientious enough to take advantage of this opportunity? Is the job seen as a new beginning or as an opportunity for illegitimate exploitation? Will he love and care for the woman he marries or will he abuse her and abandon her and the children? And so on it goes.

In sum, the authors of the chapters in this book believe that the biological sciences have a bounty of treasures to offer criminology and that criminology should seek theoretical integration with them. *Any* trait, characteristic, or behavior of *any* living thing is *always* the result of biological factors interacting with environmental factors (Cartwright, 2000), which is why we call modern biologically informed criminology *biosocial* rather than *biological*. As the variety of chapters in this book attest, there is no single biological approach to the study of criminal behavior any more than there is a single environmental approach. The three broad biological approaches to the study of human behavior represented here are the genetic, evolutionary, and neuroscience approaches. These approaches employ different theories and methods and work with different levels of analysis, but their principles are conceptually consistent across all three levels. Not only are they consistent (i.e., non-contradictory) across approaches, they are all so "environment friendly" that we may well call them "biologically informed environmental approaches." We begin with an introduction to the genetic approach.

Genetics and Criminal Behavior

Genetic approaches to understanding criminal behavior included in this book include behavior (or behavioral) genetics, molecular genetics, and epigenetics. **Behavior genetics** is the application of quantitative genetics to the study of human personality, characteristics, and behavior. It explores the relative contributions of heredity and environment to variance in quantitative measures of phenotypical (observable and measurable) traits and behaviors such as **IQ**, extroversion, and delinquency. Behavior geneticists are interested in much the same sort of issues as other behavioral scientists, but they employ different research designs and operate with different assumptions.

The central concept of behavior genetics is **heritability**—the extent to which variation in measured phenotypic traits is genetically influenced. The extent to which traits *are not* heritable is a measure of environmental influences on them. All human traits have been found to be heritable to some extent, with traits associated with criminality (IQ, impulsiveness, conduct disorder, sensation seeking, empathy, and so forth) being moderately to strongly influenced by genes (Rutter, 2007). However, a major drawback of heritability studies is that they require special samples of pairs of individuals of known genetic relationship (identical and fraternal twins, siblings, adopted children, and so on) in order to compute heritability coefficients. Such samples are difficult to come by and usually consist of white middle-class individuals (Chapter 2 provides more information on these and other concepts in behavior genetics).

Heritability only informs us about the extent to which genes are implicated in a trait of interest in a particular population at a particular time; they cannot tell us which genes. For this we need molecular genetics. Today there are a number of exceptionally ambitious longitudinal studies carried out over decades in concert with medical and biological scientists, such as the National Youth Survey (Menard & Mihalic, 2001), the Dunedin Multidisciplinary Health and Development Study (Moffitt, 1993), and the National Longitudinal Study of Adolescent Health Study (Udry, 2003). These studies are able to gather a wealth of genetic data (as well as other biological measures) using DNA from cheek swabs. Now that we can go right to the DNA we no longer have to rely on the special samples needed to compute heritability coefficients. Chapter 3 provides a primer on molecular genetics and the criminological studies based on this approach.

The third genetic approach is epigenetics, an approach that is in its infancy. Epigenetics is the study of how environmental factors (both the internal environment of the organism and its external environment) can change gene function without altering DNA sequences. These factors operate by either preventing genes from issuing instructions to manufacture its protein or by making it easier for them to do so. Almost all the epigenetic work to date has been conducted with animals in experimental conditions. These studies have shown how environmental features such as maternal nurturance can alter genetic production of brain chemicals in positive directions. Epigenetics may be viewed as a modern scientific synthesis of the old preformationist and epigeneticist positions. Epigenetics is discussed at greater length in Chapter 2.

What are Genes and do they Signify Fatalism?

According to evolutionary biologist, Richard Dawkins (1982:13), genes have a "sinister, juggernaut-like reputation," among social scientists. A juggernaut is an inexorable force that crushes everything in its path. To the extent that social scientists think of genes in this way, it is reasonable for them to believe that if any problematic behavior such as substance abuse or criminal behavior is said to have genetic underpinnings, it is fixed and immutable. A short step from this belief is to dredge up Lombroso's atavism, Galton's eugenics, Hitler's Holocaust, and all the other usual clichéd arguments as if cruelty, genocide, and immoral and nutty ideas about disvalued groups did not exist before Gregor Mendel opened the genetic Pandora's Box. We must not let either censors or bigots define scientific agendas for us. Their fears about the "demon" biology can be alleviated by learning something about it. As Bryan Vila pointed out: "[B]iological findings can be used for racist or eugenic ends only if we allow perpetuation of the ignorance that underpins these arguments" (1994:329).

Human beings have a tendency to think in either/or terms about most things, particularly about human behavior. The nature vs. nurture dichotomy ("if genetic, then not environmental; if environmental, then not genetic") has bedeviled the human sciences for so long that it has grown rank. We know of no biologist or biosocial criminologist with the slightest doubt that it is the silliest of fictions to oppose nature to nurture. They are two sides of the same coin; the heads and tails of the existence of every living thing.

The genes underlying most human traits (especially those of interest to criminologists) do not follow simple dominant/recessive rules. The offspring of tall and short human parents are usually of intermediate height, and the offspring of dark- and light-skinned parents typically have an intermediate skin color. In other words, dominant and recessive traits blend their traits in the phenotype. These traits are also polygenic, meaning that they are produced by complexes of coordinated genes each having minor additive effects.

It is imperative to understand that genes do not code for any kind of behavior, feeling, or emotion; there is no neat cryptography by which certain kinds of gene build certain kinds of brain, which in turn produce certain kinds of behavior. A **gene** is simply a segment of **deoxyribonucleic acid (DNA)** that codes for the amino acid sequence of a protein (**enzyme**s, hormones, or cell structure proteins). Several of these gene products have a lot to do with how we behave or feel, but they do not *cause* us to behave or feel one way or another, they *facilitate* our behavior and our feelings. These substances produce tendencies or dispositions to respond to the environments in one way rather than in another. Even this might be too deterministic. It might be better yet to think of genes as modulators of how we respond to the environment, since the gene products that facilitate behavior and emotions are produced in response to environmental stimuli.

Think of the gene/environment relationship in terms of the relationship between a heating and cooling system and temperature. A thermostat senses when the temperature in the house is above or below the temperature at which it was set, and when it does it activates the furnace or air conditioner to restore the house temperature to the comfort level desired by its inhabitants. Likewise, human sensory "thermostats" (the afferent nerves in the eyes, ears, skin, etc. that carry impulses toward the central nervous system) transmit information about the state of the environment to our inner processing devices. We can think of the nucleus of our cells sitting and waiting to instruct its DNA to unwind and transcribe itself into a slice of **messenger RNA (mRNA)** as the furnace or air conditioner. When it receives information from the environment requiring attention, it kicks on and sends its mRNA into the protein-building factory in the cell outside the nucleus. These instructions are in the form of triplets of chemical "letter" (the bases adenine, cytosine, thymine, and guanine) called codons. **Transfer RNA (tRNA)** "reads" the coded message and picks up and transports the appropriate anticodons (sets of bases that complement the codons on the mRNA) to the mRNA strand where they are slotted into place by molecules of ribosomal RNA. When this is complete we have a protein that will help the organism to respond effectively to the environmental challenge (see Chapter 3 for more about this process).

Just as information from the environment activates the furnace or air conditioner, so information from the environment activates the genetic machinery. Far from people being slaves to juggernaut genes, genes are at the beck and call of people as they meet environmental challenges. The protein manufactured depends on the nature of the challenge. If the challenge is something requiring a conscious decision, such as whether to fight or to flee, several different proteins may be manufactured to facilitate the response the person decides on. Genes are not little homunculi pulling strings in our heads and determining the directions of our lives; rather they help us to get there once the direction has been decided. This is not to say that variability in genetic **polymorphisms** (different forms a gene might take) does not bias us in certain directions, doing so weakly or strongly at different stages of development and within different environmental contexts. Differential responses to environmental challenges may be most proximally determined by the person's subjective appraisal of a situation, but that appraisal depends on a causal chain involving prior learning, enduring personal traits, developmental history, genetic inheritance, and the evolutionary history of the species.

Evolutionary Psychology

Evolutionary psychology seeks to explain human behavior with reference to human evolutionary history. Criminologists operating within an evolutionary framework investigate how behaviors we call criminal may have been adaptive in ancestral environments. When exploring the behavioral repertoire of any species the first question evolutionists ask is: "What is the adaptive significance of this particular behavior?" If asking about violence, for example, they want to know how violence was adaptive in evolutionary environments, what its function is, and what environmental circumstances are likely to evoke it.

Evolutionary psychology complements genetics because it informs us how the genes of interest came to be present in the first place. There are two important differences between the two disciplines: (1) genetics looks for what makes people different, evolutionary psychology focuses on what makes them the same; and (2) evolutionary psychology looks at ultimate-level "why" questions (what evolutionary problem did this behavioral mechanism evolve to solve?), and geneticists look at proximate-level "how" questions (to what extent is this behavioral mechanism influenced by genes in this population at this time; and what genes are involved?).

Because evolutionary psychologists seek to provide ultimate-level explanations, it does not mean that they consider culture and the present context of behavior unimportant. Evolutionary psychologists simply ask us to remember that "psychology underlies culture and society, and biological evolution underlies psychology" (Barkow, 1992:635). It is true that the fine nuances of life as subjectively experienced are lost as we move from proximate- to ultimate-level explanations, but ultimate-level explanations seek to complement, not supplant, proximate explanations. We now briefly describe some important evolutionary concepts important for criminology.

Natural Selection

Although the idea that life evolved naturally had been around since at least the time of Plato, it was Charles Darwin who first organized the evidence into a scientific theory, a theory that has stood the test of time, requiring only a few minor modifications. Darwin's basic point was that populations of plants and animals grow until they strain the ability of the environment to support all members. The production of excess off-spring results in a struggle for existence in which only the "fittest" survive.

Darwin also noted that individual organisms within populations exhibit a considerable degree of *variation* with respect to traits and characteristics (color, size, alertness, speed, aggressiveness, cunning, disease resistance, etc.). Certain trait variants gave their possessors an edge in the struggle for survival in prevailing environmental conditions such that they would be more likely than those not possessing them to survive and reproduce, thus passing the edge on to future generations. The trait variant selected is selected because it best "fit" its possessors into the environmental conditions existing *at the time*; at other times the trait may not confer an advantage. Darwin called this process of selecting the "fittest" **natural selection**, because it is nature (the environment) that "selects" the favorable variants and preserves them in later generations.

The differential reproductive success of genotypes is what natural selection is all about. Natural selection is the engine and organizer of evolution because it continuously adjusts populations to their environments. Biologists call these adjustments **adaptations**. Adaptations may be anatomical, physiological, or behavioral. An adaptation is some species characteristic that arose and promoted its own frequency via an extended period of selection. The sum of these adaptations is human nature in its most fundamental form, but culture tweaks this universal human nature in many and varied ways.

It is important not to fall into the trap of thinking that traits are selected *in order* to make organisms more adapted to their environments. Such thinking implies purpose. Evolution has no "purpose," it cannot look into the future to divine some plan for optimal adaptation of organisms. Natural selection is a trial and error process. Environmental conditions set evolution on a particular adaptive trajectory, but if environments change, former adaptations may become maladaptive and may even drive a species into extinction.

Today's evolutionary theory is a synthesis of the theory of natural selection and genetics (the so-called *modern synthesis*). The synthesis filled in many blanks in Darwin's theory. In addition to understanding the genetic source of trait variation, we now view evolution as changes in the genetic composition of a population from generation to generation, and reserve the term *fittest* to mean the most prolific reproducers. The most reproductively successful organisms leave behind the largest number of offspring, and hence the greatest number of genes. The genes underlying whatever anatomical, physiological, or behavioral traits that contributed to reproductive success will thus be found more frequently in subsequent generations. For the behavioral scientist, this boils down to the powerful idea that to the degree a particular type of behavior is prevalent in a population today, that behavior is likely to have contributed to the reproductive success of our ancestors. The particular behavior in question may be morally repulsive and in need of cultural constraints, but it is "natural" (the product of nature) rather than pathological.

Such a statement (the "naturalness" of some immoral behaviors) highlights the uncommon logic of evolutionary thinking and makes its acceptance difficult. Evolutionary theory is not shy about revealing the dark side of human nature when it states that reproductive success is the ultimate goal of all life, and lays bare our aggressiveness, deceptiveness, and selfishness as evolved strategies that have proved useful in pursuing it. It is not pleasant to think of ourselves in this light, and some of us would rather burn the message than listen to it. But other more positive human characteristics such as altruism, nurturance, and empathy have also evolved because they equipped us with parental and social skills. Having offspring does little to perpetuate parental genes if those offspring do not themselves survive to reproductive age among caring and trustworthy others. If *Homo sapiens* is to be defined by any one characteristic, it is that it is a social species anxious to cooperate and engage in mutual aid. But it is those among us who refuse to sign on to the social contract—the cheats and the exploiters—who interest criminologists; vice, not virtue, is criminology's stock in trade.

Chance alterations of the genome occur all the time via mutations, and the vast majority of them are disadvantageous and are soon culled from the gene pool. Evolutionary psychologists do not assume that everything that is currently useful is an adaptation. All functional features of organisms need not be adaptations per se, but rather features that have been co-opted by features that are adaptations and have gone along for the ride. Adaptations are not optimal solutions to all evolutionarily relevant problems. Natural selection is a mindless algorithmic process; it does not have the luxury of foresight or access to comparative models; it can only work with the genetic variation existing at the time a given environmental problem presents itself. Neither can natural selection anticipate the future. Behavior that was adaptive in the past may not be today, or may even be maladaptive, and behaviors that may be adaptive (fitness promoting) today may not be adaptations in the sense that they have an evolutionary history (Barkow, 2006; Walsh & Beaver, 2008). To claim that something is an adaptation is to make a claim about the past, not the present, and definitely not about the future.

Evolution and Human Motivation

One common misunderstanding of evolutionary logic is that behavior is *directly* and consciously motivated by concerns of reproductive success.

mating effort, they are also useful in gaining non-sexual resources via illegitimate means (Quinsey, 2002; Walsh, 2006).

Conversely, traits that facilitate parenting effort underlie other forms of prosocial activity: "[C]rime can be identified with the behaviors that tend to promote mating effort and noncrime with those that tend to promote parenting effort" (Rowe, 1996:270). Because female reproductive success hinges more on parenting effort than mating effort, females have evolved greater strength of the traits that facilitate it (e.g., empathy and altruism), and weaker strength of the traits unfavorable to it (e.g., aggressiveness, dominance seeking) than males. Evolutionary biologists claim that sex-based differences in parental investment are the ultimate causes of gender behavioral differences (Mascaro, et al., 2002; see also Campbell, Chapter 6, this volume). Of course, both sexes engage in both mating and parenting strategies, and both follow a mixed mating strategy at different times. It is only claimed that mating behavior is more typical of males and parenting effort is more typical of females.

Empirical research supports the notion that an excessive concentration on mating effort is linked to criminal behavior. A review of 51 studies relating number of sex partners to criminal behavior found 50 of them to be positive, and, in another review of 31 studies, it was found that age of onset of sexual behavior was negatively related to criminal behavior (the earlier the age of onset, the greater the criminal activity) in all 31 (Ellis & Walsh, 2000). A British cohort study found that the most antisocial 10 percent of males in the cohort fathered 27 percent of the children (Jaffee, et al., 2003), and a recent molecular genetic study found the same genes that were significantly related to number of sexual partners were also significantly related to antisocial behavior (Beaver, et al., 2008). Finally, anthropologists tell us that there are striking differences in behavior between members of cultures that emphasize either parenting versus mating strategies. Males in cultures emphasizing mating effort the world over exhibit behaviors (low-level parental care, hypermasculinity, transient bonding, etc.) considered antisocial in western societies (Ember & Ember, 1998).

The Neurosciences

The neurosciences encompass several interrelated disciplines that examine the anatomy, physiology, and chemistry of the brain to explore the degree to which observed brain variations are correlated with a variety of physical, psychological, and behavioral syndromes, including criminality. Toward this end, neuroscientists use a variety of devices ranging from electroencephalograms (EEGs) to sophisticated **neuroimaging techniques** such as **magnetic resonance imaging (MRI)**, functional magnetic resonance imaging (fMRI), **positron emission tomography (PET)**, and **single photon emission computed tomography (SPECT)**. These techniques reveal either the structure (gross anatomy) or the functioning (the processing of information) of the brain. These techniques have revealed many of the brain's secrets, but the secret most welcomed by social sciences from neurosciences is the same as that which comes from the genomic and evolutionary sciences—we are designed to be exquisitely responsive to the environments we find ourselves in.

Criminologists do not have to be experts in neuroscience anymore than they have to become experts in genetics or evolutionary biology to understand what neuroscience can do for us. Thankfully, we only have to learn a few rudimentary facts about anatomical brain structures and how they function, and about a very limited number of neurotransmitters. There are a number of ways of dividing up the brain, but in terms of evolutionary sequence the brain's three main divisions are the **reptilian system**, the oldest and most primitive part; the **limbic system**, the emotional center of the brain which evolved along with maternal care; and the **neocortex**, the latest evolutionary addition, the rational, thinking part of the brain. Among the major brain structures and their functions to be encountered and more fully explained in later chapters are the following:

Amygdala: Part of the limbic system; plays a primary role in the processing and memory of emotions, and is especially implicated in fear conditioning.

Cingulate gyrus: Part of the limbic system involved with emotion formation and processing, learning, and memory.

Neurotransmitters: These are chemical messengers that shunt information across neural networks. The most important of these transmitters for criminologists to understand are **dopamine, serotonin**, and norepinephrine.

Nucleus accumbens: Part of the limbic system; plays an important role in the experience of pleasure and strongly implicated in addictions of all kinds.

Prefrontal cortex: Part of the neocortex; the seat of evaluation and judgment of thoughts and emotions.

Reticular activating system: Part of the reptilian system; the "gateway" system of cortical arousal.

The Brain's Responsiveness to the Environment

Regardless of whether the stimulus for any behavior arises from within the person or from the person's environment, that stimulus is necessarily funneled through the brain for evaluation before a response is emitted. Although the brain is only about 2 percent of body mass, it consumes 20 percent of the body's energy as it perceives, evaluates, and responds to its environment (Shore, 1997). This marvel of evolutionary design is the chief executive officer of all that we think, feel, and do. The human brain accomplishes all that it does via intricate networks of about 100 billion communicating **neurons** sorted into systems of domain-specific neural modules. The evolutionarily more primitive parts of the brain (the brain stem) come "hardwired" at birth, but the development of the higher brain areas (the cerebral cortex) depends to a great extent on environmental "software" downloaded after birth in response to experience.

Of course, the genes must specify the architecture of the brain and manufacture all of the necessary substances to keep it running in the same way for everyone (50 to 60 percent of all human genes are believed to be involved in the development of the brain [Shore, 1997]); it is the patterns of interconnections of the brain wiring that is downloaded by environmental experience. Because many neural connections reflect experience, in many ways the environment shapes the brain in its own image. Genes carry an immense amount of information, but they are far too few in number to completely specify the trillions of connections the billions of neurons will eventually make with one another. If only genes were responsible for specifying neural connections, we would be hardwired drones unable to adapt to novel situations, and our human environments are much too complex for hardwired brains.

Neuroscientists distinguish between two brain developmental processes: **experience expected** and **experience dependent** (Edelman, 1992). Experience-expected development relies on mechanisms that are hardwired to "expect" exposure to certain environmental experiences. These mechanisms reflect the phylogenic history of the species. Experience-dependent mechanisms reflect the malleability or plasticity (the ability of the brain to calibrate itself to the environment) of the individual brain. To put it another way, every member of a species inherits species-typical brain structures and functions that are produced by a common species gene pool, but individuals vary in brain functioning as their genes interact with the environments they encounter to construct those brains (Depue & Collins, 1999; Pinel, 2003).

The experience-expected process, furthermore, reminds us that the human mind is not a blank slate that must learn everything through experience; it is fertile with built-in assumptions about the nature of the species-relevant environments that it will encounter. We attend to some kinds of information more readily than to others because we possess such inbuilt assumptions. This selectivity reflects evolved neural preparedness to capture and incorporate environmental information that is vital to normal development. Natural selection has recognized that certain developmental processes and abilities such as sight, speech, depth perception, affectionate bonds, certain fears and aversions, mobility, and sexual maturation are vital, and has provided mechanisms designed to take advantage of experiences occurring naturally within the normal range of human environments to activate them at appropriate junctures across the life course.

Pre-experiential brain organization frames our experiences so that we will respond consistently, stereotypically, and adaptively to vital stimuli. Natural selection has removed heritable variation for these processes making them stable across all members of a species. The upshot is that all animals (including humans) have decision-making algorithms crafted by natural selection to perceive and sort stimuli into positive and negative categories according to their potential for harming or assisting them in their survival and reproductive goals and to respond to them accordingly. We make these selections and respond so automatically that the process is often referred to as "instinctual," which is exactly what it is.

Whereas the neural wiring involved in experience-expected development is identical across the human species, experience-dependent brain wiring varies depending on the kinds of physical, social, and cultural environment individuals encounter. It is not an exaggeration to say that "experience-dependent processes are central to understanding personality as a dynamic developmental construct that involves the collaboration of genetic and environmental influences across the lifespan" (Depue & Collins, 1999:507). Although brain plasticity is greatest in infancy and early childhood, a certain degree is maintained throughout the lifespan so that every time we experience or learn something, we shape and reshape the nervous system in ways that could never have been preprogrammed. The message neuroscience has for us is that the experiences we encounter strongly influence the patterns of our neural connections, and thus the content of our subsequent experiences (Pinel, 2003).

All this means that neural network connections are continually being built and selected for retention or elimination in use-dependent fashion. That is, selection is governed by the strength (defined in terms of the emotional content of the experience) and frequency of experience in a process that has been termed **neural Darwinism** by Nobel Prize winner, Gerald Edelman (1992). The process of neural Darwinism helps us to understand in *physical* (not just psychological) terms how events with strong emotional content experienced with some frequency come to form a person's behavioral patterns. A pattern of behavior of particular interest to criminologists is violent behavior.

Violence and the Brain

Neural networks that are most stimulated during the earliest years when the brain is more pliable biases the selection process (Seth & Baars, 2005). This is why early bonding and attachment are so vital to human beings, and why abuse and neglect of children is so injurious; experience is *physically* captured by the brain in ontogenetic time just as adaptive behavior is physically captured by the genome in phylogenetic time. Chronic stress resulting from abuse/neglect can produce neuron death via the production of stress hormones, high levels of which lead to cognitive, motor, and social development delays (Schore, 2001).

Anyone doubting the primacy of childhood experiences over later experiences should mark the neuroscience truism as stated by Perry and Pollard (1998:36, emphasis added): "Experience in adults *alters* the *organized* brain, but in infants and children it *organizes* the *developing* brain." Because neural pathways laid down early in life are more resistant to elimination than pathways laid down later in life, brains organized by stressful and traumatic events tend to relay subsequent events along the same neural pathways. A brain organized by negative events is ripe for antisocial behavior because established neural pathways are activated with less provocation than is required to engage less established pathways. The stability of neural pathways established in early childhood relative to those established later in life is why we took issue with Sampson and Laub's (2005) dismissal of the prime importance of early childhood for understanding many kinds of subsequent behavioral outcome. Sampson and Laub are completely correct, however, in their assertion that early experience does not have to doom children to enduring difficulties because the nature–nurture interplay is a constant source of development and change across the life-course.

If children's brains develop in violent environments, they expect hostility from others and behave accordingly. By doing so, they invite the very hostility they are on guard for, thus confirming their beliefs that the world is a dangerous and violent place, thus setting in motion a vicious circle of negative expectations and confirmations (Niehoff, 2003; Volavka, 2002). Children in our inner cities witness violence on an almost daily basis. For instance, 33 percent of inner city Chicago schoolchildren said they had witnessed a homicide and 66 percent a serious assault (Osofsky, 1995). Witnessing and experiencing violence on a consistent basis gouges the lesson on the neural circuitry that the world is a hostile place in which one must be prepared to protect one's interests by violent means if necessary.

This is not to say that violence is irrational and maladaptive; it is more rational in some environments than in others. Having a reputation for violence would have been an asset in evolutionary environments in which you couldn't call 911 when someone was threatening you because others would be aware of your reputation. Even in today's environments where one is expected to take care of one's own beefs, violence or credible threats of violence works to let any potential challenger know that it would be in his best interests to avoid you and your resources and look elsewhere. All this is why a "bad ass" reputation is so valued in so-called subcultures, why those with such a reputation are always looking for opportunities to validate it, and why it is craved to such an extent that: "Many inner city young men . . . will risk their lives to attain it" (Anderson, 1994:89).

Natural selection has provided us with the ability to switch to a violence mode quickly when we have reason to believe that things we value may be taken from us. Such a switch is most useful today in disorganized neighborhoods in which a tradition of settling one's own quarrels without involving the authorities is entrenched; that is, in neighborhoods in which social institutions that control, shape, and sublimate violent tendencies are absent or enfeebled. Natural selection has favored flexibility over fixity of human behavior, which is why behaving violently is very much contingent on environmental instigation. The evolutionary point of view shares the neuroscience point of view that the major long-term factor in violence instigation is how much violence a person has been exposed to in the past. As Gaulin and Burney (2001:83) explain, when many acts of violence are observed: "[T]here is a feedback effect; each violent act observed makes observers feel more at risk and therefore more likely to resort to preemptive violence themselves."

Reward Dominance and Prefrontal Dysfunction Theories

Reward dominance theory is a neurological theory based on the proposition that behavior is regulated by two opposing mechanisms, the **behavioral activating system** (BAS) and the **behavioral inhibition system** (BIS). The BAS is associated with the neurotransmitter dopamine and with pleasure areas in the brain, most notably the nucleus accumbens (Gove & Wilmoth, 2003). The BIS is associated with serotonin and with brain structures that govern memory (Goldsmith & Davidson, 2004). Dopamine facilitates appetitive goal-directed behavior and serotonin generally modulates or inhibits behavior (Depue & Collins, 1999).

The BAS is sensitive to reward and can be likened to an accelerator motivating a person to seek rewarding experiences. The BIS is sensitive to threats of punishment and can be likened to a brake that stops a person from going too far too fast. A normal BAS combined with a faulty BIS, or vice versa, leads to an impulsive person with a "craving brain" that can lead him or her into all sorts of physical, social, moral and legal difficulties, by becoming addicted to pleasures such as food, gambling, sex, alcohol, drugs, and even risky endeavors such as crime (Gove & Wilmoth, 2003; Ruden, 1997).

While the normal brain state is to be more or less equally sensitive to both reward and punishment (in state of dopamine/serotonin balance), in some people one system dominates the other. The theory asserts that criminals, especially chronic criminals and psychopaths, have a dominant BAS, which tends to make them overly sensitive to reward cues and relatively insensitive to punishment cues (Franken, et al., 2005). Reward dominance theory provides us with hard physical evidence relating to the concepts of sensation seeking, impulsiveness, and low self-control, concepts that figure strongly in much current criminological thinking, because each of these traits is underlain by either a sticky accelerator (high dopamine) or faulty brakes (low serotonin).

A third system of behavior control is the **flight/fight system** (FFS) which is chemically under the control of epinephrine (adrenaline). The FFS is part of the autonomic nervous system that mobilizes the body for vigorous action in response to threats by pumping out epinephrine. Fear and anxiety at the chemical level is epinephrine shouting its warning: "Attention, danger ahead; take action to avoid!" Having a weak FFS (low epinephrine) that whispers rather than shouts its warning combined with a BAS (high dopamine) screams to "Go get it," and a BIS (low serotonin) too feeble to object, is obviously very useful when pursuing all kinds of criminal and antisocial activity.

Another neurologically specific theory of criminal behavior is **prefrontal dysfunction theory**. As already mentioned, the prefrontal cortex (PFC) is responsible for a number of functions such as making moral judgments, planning, analyzing, synthesizing, and modulating emotions. The PFC provides us with knowledge about how other people see and think about us, thus moving us to adjust our behavior to consider their needs, concerns, and expectations of us. These PFC functions are collectively referred to as *executive functions* (Fishbein, 2001), and are clearly involved in prosocial behavior. If the PFC is compromised in some way, the result is often antisocial behavior.

Brain imaging studies consistently find links between PFC activity and impulsive criminal behavior. A PET study comparing impulsive murderers with murderers whose crimes were planned found that the former showed significantly lower PFC and higher limbic system activity (indicative of emotional arousal) than the latter and other control subjects (Raine, et al., 1998). It is important to note that these findings relate to acts of impulsive reactive violence, not planned proactive violence. Cauffman, et al. (2005) combined reward dominance and PFC dysfunctions theories in a large-scale study of incarcerated and non-incarcerated youths in California and found that seriously delinquent offenders have lower resting heart rates (indicative of low fear and thus low FFS functioning) and performed poorly relative to non-delinquents on various cognitive functions performed by the PFC.

Other studies have combined brain imaging and genetics to arrive at interesting conclusions which strongly support these two theories (Davidson, et al., 2000; Yacubian, et al., 2007). Such studies typically assess reward system activation in the brain using fMRI brain scans and then correlate variation in activation with variation in dopamine-regulating polymorphisms. Neurogenomic studies sometimes correlate the response patterns with behaviorally relevant traits of interest to criminologists such as sensation seeking, impulsiveness, and addiction. The integration of the brain and genomic sciences, and their attention to the behavioral concerns of criminology should be extremely gratifying to all criminologists concerned with the future of their discipline.

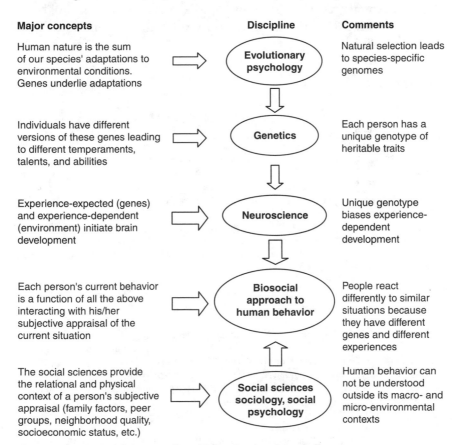

Figure 1.1 Biosocial Approach to Behavior in a Nutshell.

The Biosocial Approach in a Nutshell

Figure 1.1 provides a "nutshell" model of the biosocial approach to human behavior. It names the disciplines that contribute to the biosocial approach, identifies some major concepts from them, and provides commentary on each. The figure tells us that we must look at all levels of explanation—from the social to the genetic, and from the distant evolutionary to the most immediate situation—if we wish to understand human behavior. Our evolutionary history has provided us with the same species-specific human nature, which is underlain by genes. However, these genes come in different versions (polymorphisms) that provide each person with a unique genotype, which lead to different temperaments and trait variation. Genotypical differences are modified by developmental histories. Nature and nurture combine to produce personality, variations which lead individuals to seek and/or be exposed to different situations and experiences. These situations and experiences further mold each person's ongoing development as they interpret and respond to them in their own way.

References

Alcock, J. (2001). *Animal behavior: an evolutionary approach*, 6th edn. Sunderland, MA: Sinauer Associates.

Anderson, E. (1994). The code of the streets. *The Atlantic Monthly*, 5:81–94.

Barkow, J. (1992). Beneath new culture is an old psychology: gossip and social stratification. In Barkow, J., L. Cosmides, & J. Tooby (Eds.). *The adapted mind: evolutionary psychology and the generation of culture*. New York: Oxford University Press.

Barkow, J. (2006). *Missing the revolution: Darwinism for social scientists*. Oxford: Oxford University Press.

Beaver, K., J. Wright, & A. Walsh (2008). A gene-based evolutionary explanation for the association between criminal involvement and number of sex partners. *Social Biology*, forthcoming.

Bernard, T. (2002). Twenty years of testing theories: what have we learned and why? In Cote, S. (Ed.). *Criminological theories*. Thousand Oaks, CA: Sage.

Cartwright, J. (2000). *Evolution and human behavior*. Cambridge, MA: MIT Press.

Cauffman, E., L. Steinberg, & A. Piquero (2005). Psychological, neuropsychological and physiological correlates of serious antisocial behavior in adolescence: the role of self-control. *Criminology*, 43:133–175.

Daly, M. & M. Wilson (1988). *Homicide*. New York: Aldine De Gruyter.

Davidson, R. K. Putnam, & C. Larson (2000). Dysfunction in the neural circuitry of emotion regulation—a possible prelude to violence. *Science*, 289:591–594.

Dawkins, R. (1982). *The extended phenotype*. Oxford: Oxford University Press.

Depue, R. & P. Collins (1999). Neurobiology of the structure of personality: dopamine, facilitation of incentive motivation, and extraversion. *Behavioral and Brain Sciences*, 22:491–569.

Edelman, G. (1992). *Bright air, brilliant fire*. New York: Basic Books.

Ellis, L. & A. Walsh (2000). *Criminology: a global perspective*. Boston: Allyn & Bacon.

Ember, M. & C. Ember (1998). Facts of violence. *Anthropology Newsletter*, October:14–15.

Fishbein, D. (2001). *Biobehavioral perspective in criminology*. Belmont, CA: Wadsworth.

Fisher, H. (1998). Lust, attraction, and attachment in mammalian reproduction. *Human Nature*, 9:23–52.

Franken, I., P. Muris & E. Rassin (2005). Psychometric properties of the Dutch BIS/BAS scales. *Journal of Psychopathology and Behavioral Assessment*, 27:25–30.

Gaulin, S. & D. McBurney (2001). *Psychology: an evolutionary approach*. Upper Saddle River, NJ: Prentice-Hall.

Geary, D. (2000). Evolution and proximate expression of human paternal investment. *Psychological Bulletin*, 126:55–77.

Goldsmith, H. & R. Davidson (2004). Disambiguating the components of emotion regulation. *Child Development*, 75:361–365.

Gottfredson, M. & T. Hirschi (1990). *A general theory of crime*. Stanford, CA: Stanford University Press.

Gove, W. & C. Wilmoth (2003). The neurophysioogy of motivation and habitual criminal behavior. In Walsh, A. & L. Ellis (Eds.). *Biosocial criminology: challenging environmentalism's supremacy*. Hauppauge, NY: Nova Science Publishers.

Jaffee, S., T. Moffitt, A. Caspi, & A. Taylor (2003). Life with (or without) father: the benefits of living with two biological parents depend on the father's antisocial behavior. *Child Development*, 74:109–126.

Kenrick, D. & J. Simpson (1997). Why social psychology and evolutionary psychology need one another. In Simpson, J. & D. Kenrick (Eds.), *Evolutionary social psychology*. Mahwah, NJ: Lawrence Erlbaum Associates, Inc.

Mascaro, S., K. Korb & A. Nicholson (2002) A life investigation of parental investment in reproductive strategies. In *ALIFE VIII—Proc. of the 8th International Conference on the Simulation and Synthesis of Living Systems*:358–361.

Menard, S. & S. Mihalic (2001). The tripartite conceptual framework in adolescence in adolescence and adulthood: evidence from a national sample. *Journal of Drug Issues*, 31:905–940.

Moffitt, T. (1993). Adolescent-limited and life-course-persistent antisocial behavior: a developmental taxonomy. *Psychological Review*, 100:674–701.

Niehoff, D. (2003). A vicious circle: the neurobiological foundations of violent behavior. *Modern Psychoanalysis*, 28:235–245.

Osofsky, J. (1995). The effects of exposure to violence on young children. *American Psychologist*, 50:782–788.

Perry, B. & R. Pollard (1998). Homeostasis, stress, trauma, and adaptation: a neurodevelopmental view of childhood trauma. *Child and Adolescent Psychiatric Clinics of America*, 7:33–51.

Pinel, J. (2003). *Biopsychology*, 5th edn. Boston: Allyn & Bacon.

Plomin, R., J. Defries, I. Craig, & P. McGuffin (2003). Behavioral genomics. In Plomin, R., J. Defries, I. Craig, & P. McGuffin (Eds.). *Behavioral genetics in the postgenomic era*. Washington, DC: American Psychological Association.

Quinsey, V. (2002). Evolutionary theory and criminal behavior. *Legal and Criminological Psychology*, 7:1–14.

Raine, A., T. Lencz, S. Buhrle, L. LaCasse, & P. Colletti (2000). Reduced prefrontal gray matter volume and reduced autonomic activity in antisocial personality disorder. *Archives of General Psychiatry*, 57:119–127.

Restak, R. (2001). *The secret life of the brain*. New York: Dana Press/Joseph Henry Press.

Robinson, M. (2004). Why crime: an integrated systems theory of antisocial behavior. Upper Saddle River, NJ: Prentice-Hall.

Rowe, D. (1996). An adaptive strategy theory of crime and delinquency. In Hawkins, J. (Ed.). *Delinquency and crime: current theories*. Cambridge: Cambridge University Press.

Rowe, D. (2002). *Biology and crime*. Los Angeles: Roxbury.

Ruden, R. (1997). *The craving brain: the biobalance approach to controlling addictions*. New York: HarperCollins.

Rutter, M. (2007). Gene-environment interdependence. *Developmental Science*, 10:12–18.

Sampson, R. & J. Laub (2005). A life-course view of the development of crime. *American Academy of Political & Social Sciences*, 602:12–45.

Schore, A. (2001). The effects of early emotional trauma on right brain development, affect regulation, and infant mental health. *Infant Mental Health Journal*, 22:201–269.

Seth, A. & B. Baars (2005). Neural Darwinism and consciousness. *Consciousness and Cognition*, 14:140–168.

Shore, R. (1997). *Rethinking the brain: new insights into early development.* New York: Families and Work Institute.

Tooby, J. (1999). The view from the president's table: the most testable concept in biology. *Human Behavior and Evolution Society Newsletter,* 8:1–6.

Udry, J. R. (2003). *The National Longitudinal Study of Adolescent Health (Add Health).* Chapel Hill, NC: Carolina Population Center, University of North Carolina at Chapel Hill.

Vila, B. (1994). A general paradigm for understanding criminal behavior: extending evolutionary ecological theory. *Criminology,* 32:311–358.

Volavka, J. (2002). *Neurobiology of violence,* 2nd edn. Washington, DC: American Psychiatric Publishing.

Walsh, A. (2006). Evolutionary psychology and criminal behavior. In Barkow, J. (Ed.). *Missing the revolution.* Oxford: Oxford University Press.

Walsh, A. & K. Beaver (2008). The promise of evolutionary psychology for criminology: the examples of gender and age. In Duntley, J. & T. Shackleford (Eds.). *Evolutionary forensic psychology.* Oxford: Oxford University Press.

Walsh, A. & L. Ellis (2004). Ideology: criminology's Achilles' heel? *Quarterly Journal of Ideology* 27:1–25.

Yacubian, J. T., K. Sommer, J. Schroeder, R. Glascher, B. Kalisch, D. Leuenberger, et al. (2007). Gene–gene interaction associated with neural reward sensitivity. *Proceedings of the National Academy of Sciences,* 104:8125–8130.

2

Criminal Behavior from Heritability to Epigenetics: How Genetics Clarifies the Role of the Environment

Anthony Walsh

Biosocial approaches include looking at the contribution of genetic variation to phenotypic variation in criminal behavior, which is unacceptable to many sociologically trained criminologists as reductionist. Perhaps the two biggest fears about reductionism are that it privileges biological mechanisms at the expense of environmental factors as explanations of criminality, and that mechanistic accounts ignore context and thus the *meaning* of situations and things. I argue that reductionist accounts augment and strengthen, not compete with, holistic accounts, and that paradoxically they more forcefully underline the importance of the environment than do accounts that only emphasize the environment.

Reductionism is the process of examining a complex phenomenon at a more fundamental level. For the most part, sociologists have been inveterate antireductionists since the appearance of Durkheim's famous dictum that the cause of social facts "should be sought among the social facts preceding it" (1982:110). Most modern sociologists are more thoroughgoing "social factists" than Durkheim was, having interpreted the dictum as an authoritative disavowal of other sources of human behavior rather than as a statement defining the initial boundaries of their discipline (Udry, 1995). Durkheim himself was less parochial about nonsocial causes of human behavior than his latter-day disciples: "From the fact that crime is a phenomenon of normal sociology, it does not follow that that the criminal is an individual normally constituted from the biological and psychological points of view" (1982:106), and wrote of the "criminal character" as a person who has diverged "from the collective [social] type" (1982:101).

To explain something we have to discover its causes, and to discover its causes we have to look at its constituent parts. We can never discover the causes of something by looking up the hierarchy at the larger things of which it is a part. Descriptive observation is only the first step in characterizing the phenomenon one is studying, but some never go beyond this.

For instance, criminologists often make claims that such variables as age or gender *explain* a certain amount of variance in antisocial behavior. Age and gender are certainly predictors of antisocial behavior, but identifying young males as more prone to antisocial behavior than females or older males is a descriptive statement, not an explanation. What we would like to know is *why* young males everywhere and always are more prone to antisocial behavior than females and older males. To do this requires proximal genetic and neurohormonal explanations of age and sex differences, and ultimate evolutionary explanations of why they exist in the first place.

It is true that there are times when holistic accounts are more coherent than reductionist accounts, and that the interaction of the individual elements of a system (atoms, molecules, cells, people) produce effects not readily predictable a priori from their constituent parts. Fluctuating crime rates cannot be explained by appealing to genes and hormones; explanations for crime rates require traditional sociological, political, and economic explanations. It is also true that propositions about biological entities such as genes, hormones, and neurons do not contain terms that define the most important aspects of the human condition (e.g., love, justice, morality) at their most meaningful level. What biological entities do is identify and elucidate mechanisms underlying these abstractions. Only when mechanisms are discovered and understood can we begin to reasonably understand scientifically the holistic phenomena they underlie.

However, we must be careful that we do not lose *meaning* as an essential component to understanding behavior by an overemphasis on mechanistic accounts. I would condemn what Daniel Dennett (1995:82) calls a "greedy reductionist" (a person who skips over several layers of higher complexity in a rush to fasten everything securely to a supposedly solid foundation) just as surely as I would a naive antireductionist. Nonetheless, science has made its greatest strides when it has picked apart wholes to examine the parts to gain a better understanding of the wholes they constitute. As Matt Ridley (2003:163), the heavyweight champion of nature *via* nurture has opined: "Reductionism takes nothing from the whole; it adds new layers of wonder to the experience."

The natural and physical sciences accept reductionist and holistic accounts as complementary, not as zero-sum competitors. Holistic descriptions of phenomena existed in the natural sciences long before their underlying mechanisms were discovered and elucidated. Holistic theories are not abandoned when reductionist theories arrive as long as they maintain consistency with them. Cell biologists are aware that they are dealing at some level with atoms, but they also know that there are properties of the cell that cannot be easily deduced from those particles a priori. Biologists understand the atomic structure of the cell, but they also require functional explanations of the whole cell, and how cells fit together into networks to form the organism. Useful observations and hypotheses go in both directions in the hard sciences, such as from quarks to the cosmos in physics and from nucleotides to ecological systems in biology.

A typical social scientist's annoyance with reductionist explanations is exemplified by Jerome Miller's ironic appeal for further reductionism to rescue him from them: "If there *is* a criminal gene, or a combination thereof, let us *see it* or them—not a factor analysis or artificial constructs like *g*, but in a microscope."[1] If we can't show Miller genes "for" criminality under a microscope, then he declares that "it might be well for political scientists, mathematicians, and 'behavior geneticists' to hold their tongues, and their pens" (1996:210). This tough statement displays ignorance about how science is conducted and about the operating principles of psychometrics and behavior genetics, the discipline he places in sneer quotes.

No biosocial scientist has ever expressed the nonsensical notion that there are genes "for" crime, so Miller knows that we won't find such creatures by rummaging around among our chromosomes. Genes are recipes for making proteins; they are not "for" crime or "for" any of the traits that make crime more probable. Genes said in shorthand to be "for" something unwelcome (alcoholism, schizophrenia, etc.) are typically rare alleles (alternate forms of a gene), mutations, or gene regulatory aberration. As indicated in Chapter 1, evolutionary logic avers that genes that increase the probability of criminal behavior were selected to assist male mating effort. Once the mechanisms underlying traits useful to mating effort are in place, however, they can serve purposes other than those for which they were designed. These traits are normally distributed around a population mean and tend to be associated with antisocial behavior only if the secretion patterns of the gene products underlying them depart too radically from the mean or the person possesses receptors that are hyper- or hypo-receptive to them (Moffitt, 2005).

If physical and natural scientists had insisted that explanations must always focus on whole systems and not on their component parts and if they had the flat and censorious perspective displayed by some social scientists, they would not have made the spectacular gains that they have. Take the concept of the atom, for instance. Although the idea has been around at least since Democritus (460–370 BCE), our modern conception of it is derived from John Dalton in 1805. Dalton arrived at his notion of the atom from observing that there are some substances (oxygen, sulfur, iron, etc.) that could not be broken down, and therefore such substances were "elementary." He intuited that these elements had their own peculiar kinds of atom, and although he could not see them he did not hold his tongue or his pen because the atomic notion (the ancient idea that atoms are the smallest irreducible part of a substance) had heuristic qualities that enabled him to provide a rudimentary explanation of his observations.

From then on chemists began to systemize these elements, and, in 1869, Dmitri Mendeleev arranged them in his famous periodic table according to their atomic (still unseen) number, which proved invaluable to chemistry theorizing (Knight, 1992). Throughout the 19th and into the 20th century scientists debated whether atoms really existed or were simply a useful idea. In a manner reminiscent of many modern sociologists' attitude toward biology, a significant number of chemists, fearful of the intrusion of physics into their discipline, even tried to get the whole atomic idea banished (Walsh, 1997). Albert Einstein's mathematical treatment based on the kinetic theory of matter put paid to the debate for most scientists in 1905 when he explained the erratic jiggling of pollen grains suspended in water observed through a microscope (Brownian motion) as the random movement of atoms. But we still could not see atoms until the invention of the scanning tunneling microscope in 1981, which made it possible to photograph them, and thus to finally see them.

Heritability and What it Tells us about the Environment

Our ideas about the relationship of genes to human behavior has proceeded like this, beginning with Francis Galton, the first person to systematically study heredity and human behavior. Much like Dalton, Galton intuited that an unseen "something" accounted for greater similarity of traits observed as we move along the continuum from unrelated pairs of individuals to monozygotic twins. With the concept of the gene (which appeared in 1909, 2 years before Galton's death) as the agent of transmission of traits from parent to offspring to work with, scientists began to look for differences in quantitative traits among people with various degrees of genetic relatedness. Heritability estimates are a way of doing this. If correlations between pairs of individuals on a given trait did not increase systematically with increases in genetic relatedness, heritability coefficients (h^2) significantly different from zero could not be calculated.

Like Brownian motion observations, a heritability coefficient does not enable us to see what is underlying it. We see only that the degree of genetic sharing and the degree of phenotypic similarity are correlated. In fact, we consistently observe that it makes little difference in terms of phenotypic similarity in cognitive and personality traits whether monozygotic (MZ) twins are reared together or apart, and that MZ twins reared apart are far more similar on these traits than are dizygotic (DZ) twins reared together (Wong, et al., 2005). Today, every imaginable trait and characteristic has been found across all cultures to be heritable to some extent (Rutter, 2007). As an indirect measure of genetic affects, heritability does not inform us of causal mechanisms, but it would require the most bizarre of assumptions to conclude that genes had no affect on the ways humans think and act in the light of such consistently found and highly robust evidence.

Heritability and Environmentality

At the same time that behavior geneticists provide information about the genetic underpinnings of human traits and characteristics, they are also providing the best possible evidence for the importance of the environment (Plomin, 2000). As Baker, et al. (2006:44) put it: "[T]he more we know about genetics of behavior, the more important the environment appears to be." Heritability coefficients for most traits related to antisocial behavior are typically in the .20 to .80 range, and for antisocial behavior itself, two meta-analyses concluded that they are in the .40 to .58 range (Miles & Carey, 1997; Rhee & Waldman, 2002), with h^2 being higher in adult than in juvenile populations because of the high base rate of juvenile offending. Because $1 - h^2 = $ **environmentality** (c^2), environmental factors must account for between 40 and 60 percent of the variance in antisocial behavior, although just like h^2, c^2 does not inform us of what these factors are.[2]

The practice of apportioning variance gives rise to the notion that genes and environments are separate entities as expressed in phenotypes, and to questions about whether genes or environment is more important in this or that trait. This is like asking if hydrogen or oxygen is more important to rain or if width or length is more important to the rectangular garden it falls on. Because it takes two hydrogen atoms for every oxygen atom in a raindrop, or because the length of the garden is twice that of the width does not mean that one is more important than the other. Without the two components working together we have only two gases and two lines, not rain and rectangles. Genes and environments are separate entities as are hydrogen and oxygen, and can be analyzed as such, but when they have worked their magic and produced a phenotype they are no more separable than hydrogen and oxygen are when talking about the water they produce. David Lykken (1995:85) put it more colorfully when he wrote that without an environment our genotypes would create "nothing more than a damp spot on the carpet."

Heritability provides only an index of *actualized* genetic effects in a population in a particular environment at a particular time, and whatever the unactualized potential may be it cannot be inferred from h^2 (Bronfenbrenner & Ceci, 1994). Different environments provide different opportunities for genetic potential to be realized. For instance, disadvantaged environments suppress the expression of genes associated with prosocial traits such as IQ and permit the expression of genes associated with antisocial traits such as aggression. Advantaged environments operate on the genes in the opposite direction. Intelligence is like a flower—it needs cultivating to grow. In disadvantaged families, parents are typically unwilling or unable to tap the intellectual potential of their children or provide them with the tools (proper nutrition, books, personal mentoring) and thus it does not flower. By the same token, aggression is like a weed. It will flourish without proper care and attention given to the preventative monitoring of children's behavior, i.e., doing nothing allows it to grow. In advantaged environments, parents typically strive to cultivate the flower of intelligence and uproot the weed of aggression. Thus, heritability coefficients for IQ and aggression should be higher in advantaged than in disadvantaged environments.

This is what we see. Rowe, et al. (1999) found heritability coefficients for IQ of .74 and .26 in advantaged and disadvantaged environments, respectively, and Turkheimer and colleagues (2003) found heritability coefficients for IQ of .72 and .10 in advantaged and disadvantaged environments, respectively. Similarly, Rowe, et al. (1999) found a higher heritability coefficient (0.65) for aggression among adolescents who were one standard deviation above the mean on a measure of family and school "warmth" than on adolescents one standard deviation below the mean (0.13). Most of the variance in both IQ and aggression in disadvantaged environments is accounted for by non-shared environment rather than by shared environment.

Shared (or common) environment refers to the environment experienced by children reared in the same family (parental SES, religion, values and attitudes, parenting style, family size, intactness of home, and neighborhood) and assumed to make them similar. **Non-shared (or unique) environment** refers to environmental experiences that make children from the same family different. Non-shared environment can be familial or extra-familial. Familial non-shared variables include gender, birth order, perinatal trauma, illness, and parental favoritism. Extra-familial non-shared factors include having different peer groups and teachers, experiencing a different, time-dependent, culture, and any other idiosyncratic experiences.

Various environmental features may sometimes be considered either shared or non-shared. For instance, parenting style may not be uniform for all siblings, and may be more a function of the evocative style of each child than anything else. This is supported by studies showing that monozygotic twins *reared apart* assess their affective experiences with their different adoptive parents significantly more similarly than dizygotic twins *reared together* (Plomin & Bergeman, 1991). These findings indicate that just as there is environmental mediation of genetic effects, there is genetic mediation of environmental effects.

One of the most consistent findings is that shared environmental effects on cognitive and personality traits, although moderate during childhood, disappear almost completely in adulthood. This is *not* to say that parents have no effect on children apart from the genes they provide them with. Parental effects on their adult children's attitudes, values, behavior, and choice of leisure activities and professions do not necessarily disappear, although they are surely confounded with genetic effects. It is only averred that parental effects on personality and cognitive traits that made siblings somewhat similar while they shared a home fail to survive after the period of common rearing. The non-shared features of the environment appear to be much more salient with respect to the formation of an individual's personality and cognitive traits. Genetic effects on personality and cognitive traits, however, continue to increase throughout the lifespan (McGue, et al., 1993).

The more advantaged and egalitarian the environment the more genes assert themselves (high h^2); the more disadvantaged and unequal the environment the less genes will assert themselves (low h^2). Higher heritability coefficients found in advantaged environments does not mean that environmental influences are less important there than they are in disadvantaged environments. Paradoxically, environmental influences may be more important in the case of some traits. High h^2 simply means that environmental *variation* is less important to phenotypic *variation* in accounting for the correlations between pairs of individuals than genetic variation. In the case of aggression, it means a stronger genetic "dose" is required for its expression in advantaged environments precisely because the environmental controls militating against its expression are so strong. Likewise, low h^2 in disadvantaged environments is telling us that individuals have roughly similar correlations between their IQ (or aggression) scores regardless of how genetically similar they are. This tells us that the environment is suppressing genetic actualization of IQ while encouraging the expression of aggression even among those with a genetic inclination to avoid it.

The fact that heritability coefficients are higher for quantitative than for qualitative traits also bears mentioning. Quantitative traits always require the shared operation of more genes than qualitative traits, which means that there is no direct genetic route from genes to any quantitative trait such as IQ and aggression. Criminality, for instance, is a quantitative variable that is itself an amalgam of other quantitative variables such as negative emotionality, impulsiveness, egoism, low empathy, sensation seeking, and many others traits that make a person less than desirable as a friend, mate, or employee. Thus heritability coefficients computed "for" criminality are actually capturing a wide variety of correlated sub-traits just as Spearman's g is capturing a range of different but correlated cognitive abilities.

Gene/Environment Correlation and Interaction

It is a central tenet of evolutionary biology that all living things are designed to be responsive to their environments. Genes, organisms, and environments form a complex interacting whole; if we miss the interaction the whole thing evaporates and we are reduced to chasing ghosts. In the process of these three-way interactions, individuals create micro-environments by their purposeful activities. The environments people create will be attuned (correlated with) their genetic proclivities since it is not reasonable that people would create environments at odds with their genetic inclinations.

Concepts such as **gene/environment correlation (rGE)** and **gene/environment interaction (G × E)** have yielded enormous benefits to our understanding of the environment's role in shaping behavior. The rGE concept means that genotypes and the environments they find themselves in are not random with respect to one another. For good or bad, parents provide their offspring with genes for traits and environments conducive to their expression (passive rGE). The constant interplay between genes and environments informs us of how what may initially be only a small genetic affect for a trait snowballs into large phenotypic affects as we select and create environments compatible with our genetic propensities and as others react to us on the same basis. Differential environmental exposure results in a multiplier effect on the phenotype (Dickens & Flynn, 2001), and can be captured by the old saying that "miseries multiply and advantages aggregate." The multiplier effect reinforces what we said earlier about a high h^2 not implying the lack of environmental effects, but rather the opposite.

G × E is about differential sensitivity to the environment based on genotype and is captured by the saying "the heat that melts the butter hardens the egg." Because genes affect differential *exposure* to environmental risks via active rGE and differential *susceptibility* to environmental risks via G × E, both processes are always operating and difficult to untangle. In other words, because people self-select into different environments on the basis of their genetic preferences (active rGE), those who seek out a particular environment (say, association with delinquent peers) will be more susceptible to its influence (G × E) than will those there by happenstance. Once in contact with a criminogenic environment, the environment may have unique causal effects of its own on future anti-social behavior by foreclosing on opportunities to forge prosocial bonds and on finding other prosocial opportunities.

Studies of rGE and antisocial behavior tend to focus on parenting practices evoked by the behavior of adopted children (evocative rGE). Antisocial behavior of birth parents serves as the genetic predictor, and parenting serves as one dependent variable and children's aggressive and conduct disordered behavior as the other (Ge, et al., 1996; O'Connor, et al., 1998; Riggins-Caspers, et al., 2003). In all studies, adopted children at genetic risk for antisocial behavior consistently received more negative (harsh/abusive/neglectful) parenting from their adoptive parents than did children not at genetic risk. In each case negative parenting was seen as parental reaction (evocative rGE) to the behavior of their adopted children (Moffitt, 2005).

G × E studies typically examine the effects of aversive home environments (marital discord, divorce/separation, substance abuse, neglect/abuse) on adoptees who are and who are not at genetic risk for antisocial behavior, again indexed by antisocial behavior of birth parent or parents (Cadoret, et al., 1995; Riggins-Caspers, et al., 2003). Adverse home environments lead to significant increases in antisocial behavior for adoptees at genetic risk, but not for adoptees without such risk. Genes and environments operating in tandem (interacting) were required to produce significant antisocial behavior, while neither was powerful enough to produce it independent of the other. That is, children genetically at risk for antisocial behavior reared in positive family environments did not display antisocial behavior, and children not at genetic risk did not become antisocial in adverse family environments.

Figure 2.1 illustrates passive, evocative, and active gene/environment correlation and gene × environment interaction. Note that whatever type of rGE is operating (evocative and active frequently overlap), G × E is always operating simultaneously.

Figure 2.2 illustrates the intimate interaction with individual criminal propensities with the environments they find themselves in. The horizontal line represents individual propensity for criminal behavior from low to high and the vertical line represents environmental instigation to crime from low to high. Person A has high criminal propensity and will cross the criminal threshold at almost any level of environmental instigation; and will seek out and create criminal opportunities (active rGE). Person B has low criminal propensities and will only cross the threshold from law-abiding behavior to criminal behavior under strong environmental instigation. Such a person may be someone taking advantage of the chaos caused by some natural disaster by stealing food or other resources, or a business executive faced with the opportunity to make millions

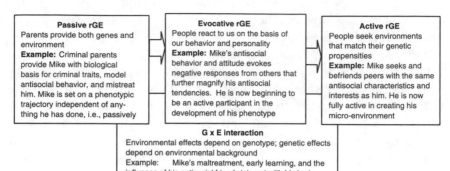

Passive rGE
Parents provide both genes and environment
Example: Criminal parents provide Mike with biological basis for criminal traits, model antisocial behavior, and mistreat him. Mike is set on a phenotypic trajectory independent of anything he has done, i.e., passively

Evocative rGE
People react to us on the basis of our behavior and personality
Example: Mike's antisocial behavior and attitude evokes negative responses from others that further magnify his antisocial tendencies. He is now beginning to be an active participant in the development of his phenotype

Active rGE
People seek environments that match their genetic propensities
Example: Mike seeks and befriends peers with the same antisocial characteristics and interests as him. He is now fully active in creating his micro-environment

G x E interaction
Environmental effects depend on genotype; genetic effects depend on environmental background
Example: Mike's maltreatment, early learning, and the influence of his antisocial friends interact with his brain that is reward dominant (high dopamine and/or low serotonin). He becomes addicted to alcohol, drugs, and the excitement of criminal behavior. (See Chapter 1)

Figure 2.1 Illustrating Passive, Evocative, and Active rGE and G × E Interaction.

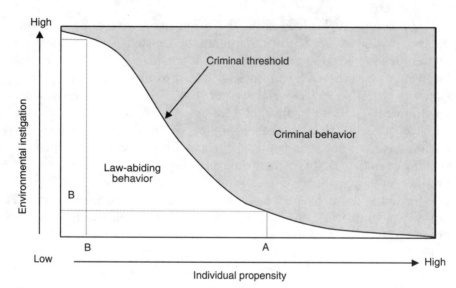

Figure 2.2 Environment/Individual Interaction and Criminal Behavior Threshold.

through stock manipulations. Each of these normally law abiding people under high environmental instigation has taken advantage of opportunities for personal gain that have minimal probabilities of apprehension and punishment attached to them. Most individuals will be somewhere between the extremes, of course, and so will most environments.

Molecular Genetics

Unfortunately, behavior genetic studies show only that "something genetic" is operating and generally consider environmental effects to be those effects "left over" after the "something genetic" explained all that it could. In other words, such studies do not tell us what genes are involved or what the environmental influences are. Environmental effects are always amenable to identification measurement (albeit imperfectly) because we need little more technology than eyes, paper, pencil, willing subjects, and a computer, but identifying the precise genes involved had to wait until the late 20th century and the advances in molecular genetics.

Biosocial criminologists may now go beyond computing heritability coefficients that only index that "something genetic" is going on and into the causal world of molecular genetics. Molecular genetics, the study of the molecular structure and function of genes, is the next step in the bottom-up search for the genetic contribution to the causes of behavior. Molecular genetics may rely on heritability studies as the first step because they are the first indication that genes for the proteins underlying the trait in question exist (i.e., h^2 significantly greater than zero repeatedly detected). One of the problems with behavior genetic research is that it requires difficult-to-obtain special samples (twins or adoptees) in order to calculate heritability coefficients, but advances in technology have made it possible to go straight to the DNA itself. DNA can be collected and analyzed from each sampled individual through cheek saliva swabs for about $10 each. After sampling the DNA, researchers may correlate gene variants already identified with a trait, or search for multiple candidate genes that may be associated with a quantitative trait via **quantitative trait loci (QTL) mapping.**

A QTL is a locus of closely linked polymorphic genes the alleles of which are thought to affect variance of targeted quantitative traits such as intelligence or impulsiveness (Brodkin & Nestler, 1998). QTLs are detected using either linkage analysis (shared DNA markers among family members) or allelic association (correlations within a population between an allele and the trait of interest). Each QTL may have small effect sizes, but multiple QTLs may be identified and combined into a QTL "set" as genetic risk factors much like various environmental factors are aggregated into environmental risk factors (Plomin & Asbury, 2005). QLT risk sets in combination with environmental risk sets determine the level at which the trait(s) in question (say impulsiveness and anger) is/are expressed.

After QTLs are identified, the next step is to identify the exact genes within them affecting the quantitative trait. The level of the challenge involved depends on the number of genes contained on a particular locus as well as the complexity of the traits being examined. Some QTLs for complex traits have effect sizes of only 1 percent or less with a probability of .01 (Butcher, et al., 2004), making the idea of QTL sets a very good idea indeed. For instance, a recent genome-wide search found 29 genetic markers out of 374 examined for the comorbidity of conduct disorder and vulnerability to substance dependence (Stallings, et al., 2005).

QTL sets can be combined with environmental risk sets in bottom-up–top-down fashion to arrive at better understanding of trait expression (Plomin, 2000). However, it bears emphasizing that having discovered QTLs related to some trait or capacity means only that we have abstracted one causal route from a complex system of possible routes, not an expressway that takes us unerringly straight from genes to behavior. There is no direct route from genes to nontrivial behavior, only winding detour-ridden backroads.

As previously noted, in past G × E studies both G and E were usually latent or at least G was. A growing number of modern studies, however, have been conducted in which both G and E were specifically identified. Perhaps the most cited of these studies so far is the longitudinal cohort study of Caspi and his colleagues (2002). In this study, the measured environmental risk was verified child maltreatment and the identified genetic risk was the **monoamine oxidase A (MAOA)** polymorphism. (This study and others like it are examined in detail in Chapter 3.)

Epigenetics: The Third Wave

Additional nuances on the interplay of nature and nurture are provided by the burgeoning science of epigenetics, the "third wave" of genetics. Epigenetics is putting a whole new face on the meaning of G × E. The prefix "epi" means *on* or in *addition to*, and epigenetics literally means on or in addition to the genes. Conceptually, epigenetics is "any process that alters gene activity without changing the DNA sequence" (Weinhold, 2006:163). Epigenetic modifications affect the ability of the DNA code to be read and translated into proteins. They make the code accessible or inaccessible or increases or decreases the level of protein products and thus the reaction range of a gene (Gottlieb, 2007). DNA itself only specifies for transcription into messenger RNA (mRNA) which itself has to be translated by transfer RNA (tRNA) and assembled by ribosomal RNA (rRNA). The genes of interest to behavioral scientists are switched on and off by signals from the organism's internal chemical environment and/or by its external physical and social environment according to the challenges it faces. There are some genes that may be shaped by protracted internal or external environmental events so that they are permanently turned on or off by less than the normal environmental instigation required to do so, or even in the absence of such instigation. This is what is meant by the alteration of gene activity, and thus the phenotype, without altering its DNA sequence.

The epigenetic regulation of genetic activity is accomplished by two main processes: DNA methylation and histone acetylation, although there are a number of others. **Acetylation** involves a groups of atoms called an acetyl group (CH_3CO) attaching itself to histones (the protein cores around which the DNA is wrapped) which has the effect of "loosening" or "relaxing" them, which increases the likelihood of genetic expression. Conversely, deacetylation has the opposite effect (Lopez-Rangel & Lewis, 2006).

DNA **methylation** occurs when an enzyme called DNA methyltransferase attaches a group of atoms called a methyl group (CH_3) to a cytosine base (one of the four "letters" of DNA) which prevents the translation of DNA into mRNA, and hence the protein the gene codes for is not manufactured (Corwin, 2004). To grossly simplify with a criminal justice metaphor, acetylation is a mechanism that aids and abets gene expression while methylation arrests it. Both of these processes may occur spontaneously, but mostly in response to various internal and external signals, and the resulting regulatory alterations are heritable (thus changes occurring in one generation are passed onto the next without altering DNA sequences) but reversible (Lopez-Rangel & Lewis, 2006). At the cellular level epigenetics encompasses the old Lamarkian notion of the inheritance of acquired characteristics since epigenetic modifications have been shown to be passed down across generations (Holliday, 2006).

Epigenetics is leading to the idea of genomic plasticity in somatic time similar to the idea of neural plasticity. Neural plasticity is developmental because it allows for novel responses as the brain is physically calibrated to environmental events. Epigeneticists propose that the genome is likewise calibrated by assimilating environmental events into it, although they are not proposing that the genome possesses the level of plasticity that the brain does (Pigliucci, et al., 2006). Put otherwise, epigenetics provides the software by which organisms respond genetically to their environments without having to change the DNA hardware.

But what does all this have to do with criminology? The truth is that we do not know at this juncture because epigenetics itself is only in its infancy. However, there are many quite suggestive lines of evidence that may open up whole new vistas for criminologists. For instance, a number of mental health researchers have been looking into the epigenetic regulation of serotonin and dopamine receptors in the etiology of schizophrenia and bipolar disorder (Petronis & Gottesman, 2000). A person having an identical twin with schizophrenia will have about a 50 percent probability of developing schizophrenia compared with a 1 percent probability in the general population. While this is indicative of a large genetic effect, given that MZ twins share 100 percent of their genes, the concordance rate is low. The search for specific genes that predispose individuals to major psychosis has not been productive, and the search for environmental effects even less so. The search has now shifted to looking for epigenetics as a possible answer to both the etiology of psychopathology and the relatively high discordance rates found between genetically identical individuals (Crow, 2007).

One study of phenotypic discordance for a number of traits among healthy MZ twins found that MZ twin pairs are virtually epigenetically indistinguishable in early life. As twins got older they diverged considerably epigenetically, with 50-year-old twin pairs averaging four times the epigenetic differences than 3-year-old twin pairs (Fraga, et al., 2005). This indicates that epigenetic alterations accumulate and occur throughout life. These twins were reared together, so they shared both 100 percent of their genes and 100 percent of their rearing environment. Thus, epigenetic alterations have to be attributed to unique environmental (each twin's molecular or external environment) events or to stochastic events. It would be a mistake, however, to attribute phenotypic differences (e.g., schizophrenic/non-schizophrenic) among MZ twins to the usual socio-cultural environmental factors that mainstream social scientists study (Wong, et al., 2005). For the biologist *environment* means everything not transmitted by the DNA.

The Epigenetics of Nurturing

An important environmental variable that behavioral scientists study is nurturing because nurturing has long been viewed as critical for the healthy development of children and the establishment of social bonds. The highly dependent human infant is adapted to crave contact stimuli from loving and supportive caretakers as the expected evolutionary environment of the species. If children do not receive what their neurological and endocrine structures demand they are vulnerable to a variety of social, emotional, and behavioral difficulties, as many animal and human studies have demonstrated (Glaser, 2000).

Being lab scientists, epigeneticists can manipulate both genes and environments at will to arrive at cause/effect conclusions with a great deal more confidence than behavioral scientists can. A study by Weaver and his colleagues (2004) zeroed in on the molecular bases and behavioral consequences of different levels of maternal care among rats. Maternal solicitude varies greatly among rat mothers just as it does among human mothers, with the level of rodent nurturing indexed by the level of pup licking and grooming (LG) and arch-back nursing (ABN). Examining high- and low-level nurtured pups as adults, it was noted that offspring resemble their mothers with respect to temperament and behavior.

Offspring of high LG/ABN mothers had lower hypothalamic-pituitary-adrenocortical (HPA) axis responses to stress (as well as a number of other behaviors such as better memory and learning abilities) and were generally more socially adept than offspring of low LG/ABN mothers.

A portion of the pups of each litter from each inbred stain was then cross-fostered (high LG/ABN mothers fostering pups born to low LG/ABN mothers, and vice versa) to determine how much of this mother/offspring correlation is attributable to shared genes and how much can be attributed to the nurturing experience. It was found that in adulthood cross-fostered pups exhibited temperaments and behaviors resembling more their adopted mother rather than their biological mother, indicating that early nurturing experiences have a profound impact on adult patterns of rat behavior. The next step was to identify the precise mechanisms involved.

Examining the epigenetic profiles of the high and low LG/ABN pups researchers found a number of significant differences. High LG/ABN reduces methylation of glucocorticoid receptor (GRs) genes, the genes that determine the number of hippocampal GRs an animal will have, and high levels of GRs means the animal will have greater control of HPA stress responses. GRs modulate the expression of a variety of neuronal genes and are vital to neuronal homeostasis, and thus to mental health. Pups nurtured by high LG/ABN mothers (regardless of biological relationship) showed significantly greater acetylation of a nerve growth factor in the hippocampus. Administering a drug called trichostatin to adult rats nurtured by low LG/ABN mothers negated epigenetic changes and resulted in their stress responses being indistinguishable from adults that had been nurtured by high LG/ABN mothers. Thus epigenetic effects can be pharmacologically reversed.

Implications for Criminology

Can we extrapolate these data to humans? Animal models have often proved pivotal to our understanding of all sorts of human physical and psychological problems. Once a biological mechanism has been demonstrated in one species, it is almost always found to be applicable to others (Ridley, 2003). Nature is parsimonious: it does not create an entire new genome every time species branch off from the ancestral line. The lab mouse has been the medical and biological scientists' best friend for decades because mice share about 99 percent of their genome with humans (Mouse Genome Sequencing Consortium, 2002). Of course, this does not mean that every gene will have precisely the same effect on mice and humans: having 99 percent shared DNA does not mean having 99 percent identical genetic functioning. Mice pups develop far more rapidly than human babies, and their "critical periods" for incorporating experience-expected events into their neurogenomic machinery are far shorter (Hensch, 2004). For instance, the epigenetic differences occurring as a function of maternal behavior in the study conducted by Weaver, et al. (2004) occurred only in the first week of life, after which maternal behavior had no obvious effects.

The area to which extrapolation of epigenegic data to humans is most likely to apply is early developmental processes (Rutter, 2007). For instance, one study looked at Russian and Romanian orphans who had been in orphanages an average of 16.6 months before being fostered to American middle-class families for an average of 34.6 months (Wismer Fries, et al., 2005). Compared with a control group of American children reared by their biological parents but matched on other important criteria, the fostered children showed significantly lower base levels of the **neuropeptides** (a class of chemicals that function as neurotransmitters or hormones that play roles in information processing) vasopressin and oxytocin (the so-called "cuddle chemicals"). They also showed significantly lower levels of them after experimental interaction with their mothers, which normally increases neuropeptide levels. These results reveal mechanisms that may account for the well documented fact that children reared without frequent tactile comfort become vulnerable to difficulties in forming secure relationships with caregivers and forming social bonds in the wider society. Of course, this outcome is not inevitable since idiosyncratic genetic, epigenetic, and experiential processes will create many individual differences with respect to these outcomes (a small proportion of the adoptees in this study actually had oxytocin levels higher than the average of the control group).

No one contends that stress is unequivocally bad; stress is a normal and necessary part of life. Individuals who experience average levels of stress during childhood most likely possess brains so calibrated as to better navigate the travails of life as adults than those who have been assiduously protected from almost all stress (Meaney, 2001). It is protracted and toxic stress which does the real damage to vital behavioral regulatory regions such as the amygdalae and hippocampi. Most intriguing is that the potential adaptive advantage of stress reaction as a protector against engaging in antisocial behavior. A number of studies have shown that individuals raised in criminogenic environments who remain free of their criminogenic influences are shy, timid, and evidence hyperactive autonomic nervous system (ANS) arousal under conditions of threat (Boyce, et al., 2001; Lacourse, et al., 2006). Such youths are also less likely to commit antisocial acts than youths reared in non-criminogenic environments with hyporeactive ANS arousal (Brennan, et al., 1997). In fact, greatly reduced ANS response to stressors is one of the best predictors of anti-social behavior that we have across races, classes, and genders (Raine, et al., 1997; Walsh, 2002).

We do not know the full range of cognitive, personality, and behavioral traits that may be subjected to epigenetic alteration, much less epigenetic inheritance. A number of scientists working in the field are making statements in the popular media indicating that the field may have profound meaning for human development and behavior. For instance, in a popular science piece the author (Watters, 2006:75) quotes leading epigeneticist Michael Meaney as saying: "We're beginning to draw cause-and-effect arrows between social and economic macrovariables down to the level of the child's brain." The same piece then quotes Lawrence Harper on epigenetic inheritance saying: "If you have a generation of poor people who suffer from bad nutrition, it may take two or three generations for that population to recover from that hardship and reach its full potential." To the extent that epigenetic effects in humans operate across generations, they may well be the answer to the seemingly intractable 15-point IQ mean difference between white and black populations. It is too early in the epigenetic game to go much beyond speculation, but for my money the possibilities are about as exciting and intriguing as anything that has come along in the behavioral sciences in the past 50 years.

Conclusion

The concepts, methods, and research I have addressed here are reductionist in the sense that ever lower levels of scientific investigation were needed to discover mechanisms, but in another sense they are the antithesis of reductionism since they have enabled researchers to unite the only two sources of human phenotypic variation there are: genes and environments. They have helped to simultaneously look bottom up and top down at the same time, and that is *quintessentially* holistic. As Matt Ridley (2003:6) wrote about unwarranted fears about genes:

> Genes are not puppet masters, nor blueprints. They may direct the construction of the body and brain in the womb, but they set about dismantling and rebuilding what they have made almost at once in response to experience. They are both the cause and consequence of our actions. Somehow the adherents of the "nurture" side of the argument have scared themselves silly at the power and inevitability of genes, and missed then greatest lesson of all: the genes are on our side.

We are much more than "disposable vehicles," mere temporary care-takers of our immortal genes. Genes are at our beck and call, constantly

Dennett, D. (1995). *Darwin's dangerous idea: evolution and the meanings of life*. New York: Simon & Schuster.

Dickens, W. & J. Flynn (2001). Heritability estimates versus large environmental effects: the IQ paradox resolved. *Psychological Review*, 108:346–349.

Durkheim, É. (1982). *Rules of sociological method*. New York: Free Press.

Fraga, M., E. Ballestar, M. Paz, S. Ropero, F. Setien, M. Ballestar, et al. (2005). Epigenetic differences arise during the lifetime of monozygotic twins. *Proceedings of the National Academy of Sciences*, 102:10604–10609.

Friedman, D. (2006). Stress and the architecture of the brain. National Scientific Council on the Developing Child: Perspectives. http://www.developingchild.net.

Ge, X., R. Conger, R. Cadoret, J. Neiderhiser, W. Yates, E. Troughton, et al. (1996). The developmental interface between nature and nurture: a mutual influence model of child antisocial behavior and parent behaviors. *Developmental Psychology*, 32:574–589.

Glaser, D. (2000). Child abuse and neglect and the brain–a review. *Journal of Child Psychology and Psychiatry*, 41:97–116.

Gottfredson, M. & T. Hirschi (1990). *A general theory of crime*. Stanford, CA: Stanford University Press.

Gottlieb, G. (2007). Probabilistic epigenesis. *Developmental Science*, 10(1):1–11.

Hensch, T. (2004). Critical period regulation. *Annual Review of Neuroscience*, 27:549–579.

Holliday, R. (2006). Epigenetics: a historical review. *Epigenetics*, 1–2:76–80.

Jablonka, E. & M. Lamb (2002). The changing concept of epigenetics. *Annals of the New York Academy of Sciences*, 981:82–96.

Jensen, A. (1998). *The g factor*. Westport, CT: Praeger.

Knight, D. (1992). *Ideas in chemistry: a history of the science*. New Brunswick, NJ: Rutgers University Press/Knopf.

Kumar, A., K. Choi, W. Renthal, N. Tsankova, D. Theobold, H. Truong, et al. (2005). Chromatin modeling is a key mechanism underlying cocaine-induced plasticity in striatum. *Neuron*, 48:303–314.

Lacourse, E., D. Nagin, F. Vitaro, S. Cote, L. Arsenault, & R. Tremblay (2006). Prediction of early-onset peer group affiliation. *Archives of General Psychiatry*, 63:526–568.

Lopez-Rangel, E. & M. Lewis (2006). Loud and clear evidence for gene silencing by epigenetic mechanisms in autism spectrum and related neurodevelopmental disorders. *Clinical Genetics*, 69:21–25.

Lykken, D. (1995). *The antisocial personalities*. Hillsdale, NJ: Lawrence Erlbaum Associates, Inc.

McGue, M., T. Bouchard, W. Iacono, & D. Lykken (1993). Behavioral genetics of cognitive ability: a lifespan perspective. In Plomin, R. & G. McClearn (Eds.). *Nature, nurture, and psychology*. Washington, DC: American Psychological Association.

Meaney, M. (2001). Maternal care, gene expression, and the transmission of individual differences in stress reactivity across generations. *Annul Review of Neuroscience*, 24:1161–1192.

Meyer-Lindenberg, J., B. Buckholtz, B. Kolachana, A. Hariri, L. Pezawas, G. Blasi, et al. (2006). Neural mechanisms of genetic risk for impulsivity in violence in humans. *Proceedings of the National Academy of Sciences*, 103:6269–6274.

Miles, D. & G. Carey (1997). Genetic and environmental architecture of human aggression. *Journal of Personality and Social Psychology*, 72: 207–217.

Miller, J. (1996). *Search and destroy: African American males in the criminal justice system*. Cambridge: Cambridge University Press.

Moffitt, T. (2005). The new look of behavioral genetics in developmental psychopathology: gene–environment interplay in antisocial behavior. *Psychological Bulletin*, 131:533–554.

Mouse Genome Sequencing Consortium. (2002). Initial sequencing and comparative analysis of the mouse genome. *Nature* 420:520–562.

O'Connor, T., K. Deater-Deckard, D. Fulker, M. Rutter, & R. Plomin (1998). Genotype–environment correlations in late childhood and early adolescence: antisocial behavioral problems and coercive parenting. *Developmental Psychology*, 34:970–981.

Petronis, A. & I. Gottesman (2000). Psychiatric epigenetics: a new focus for the new century. *Molecular Psychiatry*, 5:342–346.

Pigliucci, M., C. Murren, & C. Schlichting (2006). Phenotypic plasticity and evolution by genetic assimilation. *Journal of Experimental Biology*, 209:2362–2367.

Plomin, R. (2000). Behavioural genetics in the 21st century. *International Journal of Behavioral Development*, 24:30–34.

Plomin, R. & K. Asbury (2005). Nature and nurture: genetic and environmental influences on behavior. *The Annals of the American Academy of Political and Social Science*, 600:86–98.

Plomin, R. & C. Bergeman (1991). The nature of nurture: genetic influences on "environmental" measures. *Behavioral and Brain Sciences*, 14:373–427.

Raine, A., H. Venables, & S. Mednick (1997). Low resting heart rate at age 3 years predisposes to aggression at age 11 years: evidence from the Mauritius Child Health Project. *Journal of the American Academy of Child and Adolescent Psychiatry*, 36:1457–1464.

Rhee, S. & I. Waldman (2002). Genetic and environmental influences on antisocial behavior: a meta-analysis of twin and adoption studies. *Psychological Bulletin*, 128:490–529.

Ridley, M. (2003). *Nature via nurture: genes, experience and what makes us human*. New York: HarperCollins.

Riggins-Caspers, K. R., J. Cadoret, J. Knutson, & D. Langbehn (2003). Biology–environment interaction and evocative biology–environment correlation: contributions of harsh discipline and parental psychopathology to problem adolescent behaviors. *Behavior Genetics*, 33:205–220.

Rowe, D., K. Jacobson, & E. Van den Oord (1999). Genetic and environmental influences on vocabulary IQ: parents' education level as moderator. *Child Development*, 70:1151–1162.

Rutter, M. (2007). Gene–environment interdependence. *Developmental Science*, 10:12–18.

Stallings, M., R. Corely, B. Dennhey, J. Hewwitt, K. Krauter, J. Lessem, et al. (2005). A genome-wide search for quantitative trait loci that influence antisocial drug dependence in adolescence. *Archives of General Psychiatry*, 62:1042–1051.

Sternberg, R. (1983). How much gall is too much gall? A review of frames of the mind: the theory of multiple intelligences. *Contemporary Education Review*, 2:220–221.

Turkheimer, E., A. Haley, M. Waldron, B. D'Onofrio, & I. Gottesman (2003). Socioeconomic status modifies heritability of IQ in young children. *Psychological Science*, 14:623–628.

Udry, J. R. (1995). Sociology and biology: what biology do sociologists need to know? *Social Forces*, 73:1267–1278.

Walsh, A. (1997). Methodological individualism and vertical integration in the social sciences. *Behavior and Philosophy*, 25:121–136.

Walsh, A. (2002). *Biosocial criminology: introduction and integration*. Cincinnati, OH: Anderson.

Walsh, A. & K. Beaver (forthcoming). The promise of evolutionary psychology for criminology: the examples of gender and age. In Duntley, J. & T. Shackleford (Eds.). *Evolutionary forensic psychology*. Oxford: Oxford University Press.

Warr, M. (2002). *Companions in crime: the social aspects of criminal conduct*. Cambridge: Cambridge University Press.

Watters, E. (2006). DNA is not destiny. *Discover: Science, Technology and the Future*. November.

Weaver, I., N. Cervoni, F. Champagne, A. D'Alessio, S. Sharma, J. Seckl, et al. (2004). Epigenetic programming by maternal behavior. *Nature Neuroscience*, 7:847–854.

Weinhold, B. (2006). Epigenetics: the science of change. *Environmental Health Perspectives*, 114:161–167.

Wismer Fries, A. T. Ziegler, J. Kurian, S. Jacoris, & S. Pollak (2005). Early experience in humans is associated with changes in neuropeptides critical for regulating social behavior. *Proceedings of the National Academy of Sciences*, 102:17237–17240.

Wong, A., I. Gottesman, & A. Petronis (2005). Phenotypic differences in genetically identical organisms: the epigenetic perspective. *Human Molecular Genetics*, 14:11–18.

3

Molecular Genetics and Crime

Kevin M. Beaver

In 1990 an international cast of scientists set out on the mission to identify the entire set of human genes and to sequence all of the nucleotide bases found in deoxyribonucleic acid (DNA). This long and arduous task of mapping the human **genome** was known as the Human Genome Project (HGP). The promise that the HGP held for science and medicine was profound. Once the HGP was completed, researchers would be provided with a large amount of information that could be used to examine the genetic underpinnings to a range of phenotypes including mental illnesses, terminal diseases, different types of psychopathology, and antisocial behavior, among others. Thirteen years after its inception, the HGP was completed and the end result was one of the most significant accomplishments in the history of scientific research: the human genome—and its three billion nucleotide base pairs—was successfully mapped.

At the outset of the HGP, geneticists estimated that there were approximately 150,000 genes comprising the human genome. Today that estimate has been reduced substantially with the most recent figures suggesting that there are between 20,000 and 25,000 human genes. The sequencing of the human genome, however, was only the first step towards understanding the precise ways in which genes are related to human development and normal life functioning. For example, much remains unknown about the particular functions that each gene performs and how different genetic variants translate into phenotypic variation. Even in the face of these uncertainties an impressive line of genetic literature has linked specific genes to a broad array of disorders such as **attention deficit hyperactivity disorder (ADHD)**, depression, alcoholism, and even anorexia and bulimia. But perhaps the most intriguing genetic findings come from an emerging line of quantitative research that has identified particular genes that are associated with criminality, aggression, and serious violence.

This chapter is designed to provide an overview to the molecular genetics of crime. Toward this end, the chapter is divided into two sections. Given that many criminologists are unfamiliar with human genetics, the first half of the chapter will introduce the basic concepts and terminology of genetic research. The second half of the chapter will review some of the literature that has examined the effects that genetic polymorphisms have on antisocial and criminal phenotypes. The ways in which genes and the environment interact to produce behaviors will also be discussed.

Introduction to Genetics

DNA is a chemical code found in the nucleus of every cell except red blood cells and contains the genetic recipe needed for all living organisms to form, develop, and live. Each person inherits a unique and distinctive genetic code transcribed into their DNA and human variation is reflected in person-to-person differences in DNA. For example, the information encoded into DNA determines almost every observable physical feature from hair color and eye color to skin pigment and blood type. It would be a mistake, however, to assume that DNA is only responsible for creating variation in physical attributes. Many non-physical **phenotypes**, such as shyness, impulsivity, and intelligence, are also partially influenced by DNA, as the discussion of heritability in the previous chapter made clear. Before proceeding to an explanation of how DNA creates phenotypic variation, some additional background about DNA and human genetics must first be presented.

One of the most recognizable scientific discoveries of the 20th century is the double-helix structure of DNA. DNA consists of two genetic fibers, each known as a polynucleotide. As Figure 3.1 reveals, the two polynucleotides are twisted around each other to form a double helix. Nucleotide bases are aligned along the backbone of each polynucleotide. The nucleotide bases making up DNA come in four different variants: adenine, thymine, cytosine, and guanine. Each nucleotide base is usually referred to by a one-letter label, where adenine → A, thymine → T, cytosine → C, and guanine → G. The two polynucleotides are joined together by the nucleotides of one polynucleotide bonding with the nucleotides of the opposite polynucleotide. The bonding of base pairs, however, is not a haphazard occurrence, but instead always follows a straightforward and structured process: A can only pair with T, T can only pair with A, C can only pair with G, and G can only pair with C. So imagine the following hypothetical sequence of nucleotides for one polynucleotide:

AACCTAGCGTTAACTTAT

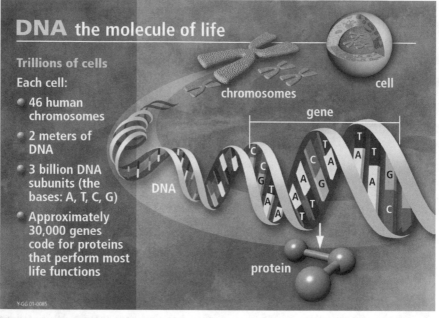

Figure 3.1 Structure of DNA.

Source: U.S. Department of Energy Human Genome Project (2001). Retrieved from http://www.ornl.gov/hgmis

The sequence of nucleotides for the complementary polynucleotide is easily deducible by applying the base pair-bonding rules reviewed earlier. The arrangement of nucleotides for the complementary strand of DNA would be:

TTGGATCGCAATTGAATA

As shown in Figure 3.1, the bonding together of nucleotides from one strand of DNA to the complementary strand of DNA holds the two poly-nucleotides together in the form of a double helix. Of course, the example presented earlier is extremely simplified using only 18 base pairs, but keep in mind this same process is at work for the roughly three billion base pairs found in human DNA.

At various points along the polynucleotides, contiguous base pairs operate in coordination to perform specialized functions. These groups of adjacent base pairs working together are called genes. Suppose the following sequence of base pairs made up a section of DNA:

CTTAGC**CTACGGAAA**TAC
GAATCG**GATGCCTTT**ATG

In this example, if the bold-typed base pairs were identified as working in concert to carry out a particular task, they would be considered a gene. Note that, by convention, only one sequence of base pairs (i.e., one poly-nucleotide) from a gene is usually presented because the complementary sequence of nucleotides is somewhat redundant. As a result, all the pro-ceeding examples only provide the base pairs for one strand of DNA. The example just presented would thus become:

CTTAGC**CTACGGAAA**TAC

News and media outlets are punctuated with headlines proclaiming that scientists have discovered a gene *for* X (e.g., a lethal illness) or a gene *for* Y (e.g., a personality trait). Actually, however, genes are not *for* anything; rather they "only" contain the genetic information needed to code for the production of proteins. **Proteins** are complex molecules that are essential to life and that perform a wealth of duties for the body. For instance, they form the structure of cells, they supply the body with energy, they are responsible for eye and hair color, and they produce antibodies that are needed to fight off infectious bacteria.

Proteins are created by joining together chains of amino acids. Genes code for the synthesis of amino acids through sequences of three contigu-ous nucleotide bases. The tri-nucleotide sequence, TGG, for instance, produces the amino acid tryptophan. The three contiguous nucleotides that code for the manufacturing of amino acids (e.g., TGG) are called codons. The 20 different amino acids are each synthesized by a distinctive three-letter sequence of nucleotide bases. Some amino acids are produced by more than one codon, but each codon can only produce one amino acid. The amino acid isoleucine, for example, can be coded for by three different codons (i.e., ATT, ATC, and ATA), but the codon TGG only codes for tryptophan. We will revisit the interrelationships among genes, pro-teins, and codons momentarily.

Although the primary function of genes is to code for protein production, about 90 percent of the human genome is considered non-coding, leaving only about 10 percent of the human genome to syn-thesize proteins. The coding regions of a gene are called **exons**, and the non-coding regions of a gene are called **introns**. Introns and exons are intermittently interspersed among one another along the entire genome. Even though the average gene is comprised of about 3,000 nucleo-tide base pairs, only about 1,200 of them code for the creation of proteins.

Although genes code for protein synthesis, they do not directly manu-facture the proteins. Rather, genes contain the *instructions* needed for the appropriate protein to be produced. The way in which the genetic code

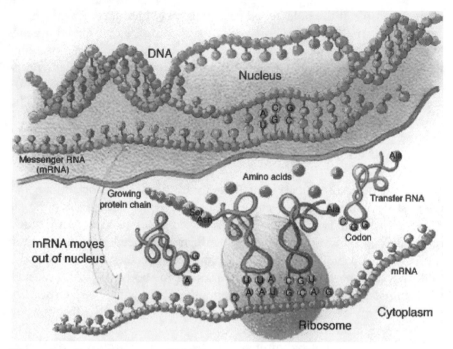

Figure 3.2 Central Dogma of Biology.

Source: U.S. Department of Energy Human Genome Project (2001). Retrieved from http:// www.ornl.gov/hgmis

(i.e., DNA) is converted into proteins is known as the **central dogma of molecular biology.** The central dogma is comprised of two stages: transcription and translation. Figure 3.2 illustrates the process of transcription and translation. As shown in the top panel of Figure 3.2, during transcription a gene duplicates itself onto a new molecule called ribonucleic acid (RNA). Only those base pairs that comprise the duplicated gene are included on RNA and the nucleotides on RNA code for the production of amino acids that will eventually create the protein specified by the gene.

RNA differs from DNA in at least three important ways. First, once the gene is duplicated the non-coding regions of the gene (i.e., introns) are deleted in a process knowing as splicing. RNA thus only retains the important protein-coding regions (i.e., exons) of the gene. Splicing transforms RNA into messenger RNA (mRNA). Second, instead of being double-stranded like DNA, RNA is comprised of only a single strand of nucleotides. Third, the genetic alphabet differs by one letter between DNA and RNA. Remember that DNA uses an alphabet containing the letters A, C, G, and T. Like DNA, RNA also includes the letters A, C, and G in its genetic alphabet. Unlike DNA, RNA uses the nucleotide urcacil (U) instead of thymine (T). The process of transcription converts the DNA code (A, C, G, and T) into the new RNA language (A, C, G, and U). Once DNA has been duplicated and transcribed onto mRNA, mRNA leaves the cell nucleus and migrates into the cytoplasm.

The second step in the central dogma of biology is called translation and is depicted in the bottom panel of Figure 3.2. Each tri-nucleotide sequence of mRNA (i.e., a codon) carries the information needed to make one amino acid. In order for the genetic code to be translated into a protein, the codons must be read by a ribosome, which is a protein-producing machine. For this to occur, mRNA locates a ribosome in the cell's cytoplasm and attaches to it. It is here, at the ribosome, where the appropriate protein will be synthesized. The ribosome reads the genetic material and along with another type of RNA—transfer RNA (tRNA)—the appropriate amino acid is produced. Once manufactured the amino acid is linked with other amino acids to form what is known as a poly-peptide chain. The protein is created once all of the necessary amino acids are linked to the growing chain of peptides. Proteins on average consist of approximately 400 amino acids (Rowe, 2002) and each polypeptide chain corresponds to a unique protein.

To summarize, DNA is a four-letter genetic code that contains around 20,000 to 25,000 genes. Every person inherits a different arrangement of base pair sequences in their DNA and thus all people (except monozygotic twins) are genetically unique. This genetic variation is important because different genotypes produce different proteins and different proteins translate into human phenotypic variation—including variation in the propensity to engage in antisocial behaviors. To understand why there is variation in genetic predispositions for antisocial behavior, it is first essential to present a discussion of how genetic variation is created.

Human Genetic Variation

Genes are located on threadlike structures called **chromosomes** (see Figure 3.1). Barring any chromosomal abnormalities, all people inherit 23 pairs of chromosomes: one pair is inherited maternally and the other pair is inherited paternally. One pair of chromosomes, called the **sex chromosomes**, is sex determining; females inherit two X chromosomes and males inherit an X chromosome and a Y chromosome. The 22 non-sex-determining chromosomes are referred to as **autosomes**, and autosomes are distinguished from each other by using numbers (i.e., chromosome # 1–22). The autosomes are ordered in descending size, such that the largest autosome is chromosome 1 and the smallest autosome is chromosome 22. Every gene occupies a specific location—also called a genetic locus—on a particular chromosome. The HGP was largely responsible for mapping each gene to a particular locus on a particular chromosome. For example, a gene responsible for the transportation of dopamine (DAT1) is always found on chromosome 5 (i.e., the fifth largest autosome).

All genes located on the autosomes are made up of two different copies: one copy of the gene is located on the maternal chromosome and one copy of the gene is located on the paternal chromosome. Genes that are located on the sex chromosomes, however, are not necessarily comprised of two copies. Males have only one X chromosome and only one Y chromosome so males inherit a single copy of all genes located on the sex chromosomes. Of course, females have two copies of each gene found on the X chromosome because they inherit two X chromosomes.

Most genes, regardless of whether they are located on an autosome or a sex chromosome, are only available in a single form. That is to say, all people inherit the same two copies of the gene because there is only one type available in the population. These genes do not vary from person to person and are responsible for why genetically healthy people are very similar to one another (e.g., having two arms, two legs, one nose, etc.). But for a small minority of all genes, there are at least two alternative forms of the gene in existence. These alternative copies of a gene are called **alleles**. When there are at least two alleles that can be inherited for a gene, the gene is called a genetic polymorphism. The genes that determine eye color, for example, would be considered polymorphisms because they vary from person to person and this genetic variation corresponds to variation in eye color. Most alleles, however, are not functionally different from one another and all alleles of a genetic polymorphism code for the synthesis of the same protein. But for some polymorphisms different alleles can code for the production of different proteins or for the production of non-functioning or suboptimal proteins.

To help explain in greater clarity the inheritance of alleles, an example using a hypothetical gene that determines temper will next be presented. Before proceeding, it is important to note that in reality multiple genes interact with each other and with the environment to create most phenotypes, including temper. For ease of presentation, however, let us pretend that one gene determines temper. Suppose that there are two different alleles for the hypothetical temper gene, where **A** = the bad temper allele and **a** = the no-temper allele. Let us also suppose that the mother has **Aa** for the bad temper gene (i.e., one bad temper allele and one no-temper allele) and the father has **AA** for the bad temper gene (i.e., two bad temper alleles). Any offspring produced by this pair of mates has the opportunity to inherit one of two different combinations of alleles: **AA** or **Aa** (the ordering of alleles is unimportant so **aA** and **Aa** are the same). In the case of **AA**, the offspring would have a bad temper because they inherited two bad temper alleles whereas if they had inherited **Aa** they would have a moderate temper. Note that the other allelic arrangement of **aa** is not possible because the father's bad temper gene has two bad temper alleles (i.e., **AA**). When polymorphic genes are made up of the same allele, such as **AA** in this example, the gene is said to be homozygous. When polymorphic genes are made up two different alleles, such as **Aa** in this example, the gene is said to be heterozygous.

Most traits, especially those relevant to criminology (e.g., low self-control), are not categorical, but are continuous. So how would a single gene with just two alleles account for variation along a trait continuum? Remember that most phenotypes are created by a multifactorial arrangement of multiple genes. If this example were expanded to two genes, each with two alleles, then the temper phenotype could begin to take on more intermediate values. As the number of genes that influence a phenotype increase, the continuum of phenotypic values also increases exponentially. Mix the genetic effects in with the environmental effects and a very detailed and specific phenotypic continuum is created.

Before turning to a discussion of how genes can affect antisocial phenotypes, let us first examine more closely genetic polymorphisms and genetic variation. Keep in mind that genes are stretches of DNA that work collaboratively to manufacture a protein. But in what ways do genes vary, and what distinguishes one allele (e.g., the **A** allele in the previous example) from another allele (e.g., the **a** allele in that example)? There are, in general, three different overarching types of genetic polymorphism that result in genetic variation. The first genetic polymorphism is known as a **single nucleotide polymorphism (SNP)**. SNPs are the most frequently occurring genetic polymorphism. They arise about once in every 100 to 300 base pairs and account for approximately 90 percent of all polymorphisms. Most SNPs are nonfunctional and do not affect cellular operations. In an SNP, a difference in just one nucleotide base is what differentiates one allele from another allele. Take, for example, the following sequence of part of a hypothetical gene in Person 1:

TCACCTTGGA**A**TGGGCTA

Compare the sequence of nucleotide bases with the following sequence in the same hypothetical gene in Person 2:

TCACCTTGGA**GTG**GGCTA

Of the 18 nucleotides, 17 of them are identical between the two people. The difference is that the 10th nucleotide, which is in bold and underlined, in Person 1 is A, while it is G in Person 2. The difference of one letter may not seem too important, but, in this case, the amino acid produced by the tri-nucleotide sequence ATG in Person 1 would be methionine, while the amino acid produced by the codon GTG in Person 2 would be valine (e.g., in the catechol-O-methyltransferase gene). It has been estimated that about 85 percent of the genetic causes of most disorders are attributable to SNPs (Plomin, et al., 2001).

Microsatellites are the second type of genetic polymorphisms and allelic differences in microsatellites arise because the alleles differ from each other in terms of their end-to-end length: that is, one allele is longer (or shorter) than the others. At certain places along a section of gene, a small number of contiguous nucleotide bases (usually less than four base pairs) may be repeated a different number of times. The more times the sequence of nucleotides is repeated, the longer the allele. The tetra-nucleotide sequence, TTGAn, for example, could be repeated n number of times, where an allele with $n = 3$ repeats would be shorter than an allele with $n = 8$ repeats. In microsatellites, the number of times the nucleotides can be repeated varies drastically, but some base pair sequences may be repeated more than a thousand times. Compare the following repeat sequences for TTA in the following two alleles of a hypothetical gene:

TGGATA**TTA**TTA**TTA**TTA**TTA**TTA
TGGATA**TTA**TTA**TTA**

In the top allele, TTA is repeated seven times, while in the bottom allele TTA is repeated only three times. So, in microsatellites, the number of repeat sequences is what distinguishes one allele from another.

The third and final type of genetic polymorphisms is referred to as **minisatellites**. Minisatellites are very similar to microsatellites in that they both have a section of DNA that is repeated a number of different times. For microsatellites, the number of base pairs included in the repeat sequence is relatively small, typically fewer than four base nucleotides. The repeat sequences in minisatellites, in contrast, are comprised of 20 or more nucleotide base pairs that can be repeated 100 times (Carey, 2003). A dopamine receptor gene (DRD4), for example, has a 48 base pair sequence that can be repeated up to eight times. Minisatellites are often referred to as VNTRs—that is, variable number of tandem repeats. Just remember that the main difference between microsatellites and minisatellites is the number of nucleotides that make up the repeat sequence.

How Genes can Directly Cause Phenotypic Variation

Not counting interactions with the environment or interactions with other genes, there are three ways in which genetic polymorphisms can *directly* cause phenotypic variation. First, one gene can be the sole cause of a particular phenotype. Nearly 1,200 diseases, such as cystic fibrosis, sickle-cell anemia, Huntington's disease, and fragile-X syndrome, are caused by a single gene. Geneticists refer to the one-to-one correspondence between the inheritance of a specific gene and the development of a particular phenotype by the acronym OGOD (one gene, one disorder). OGODs can either be due to recessive patterns of inheritance (e.g., fragile-X syndrome) or dominant patterns of inheritance (e.g., achondroplasia).

Genetic researchers recognize that complex traits, such as self-control or impulsivity, are not caused by a single gene. Instead a more realistic view, and one held by biosocial criminologists, is that phenotypes, including antisocial phenotypes, are partially the result of multiple genes working in unison, a process known as a polygenic effect. ADHD, aggression, and shyness are all considered polygenic phenotypes because multiple genes have been linked to their development. For polygenetic phenotypes, genes work in a probabilistic fashion where certain alleles—known as risk alleles—confer an increased risk of developing the particular phenotype. The more risk alleles inherited, the greater the risk of displaying the phenotype. In most cases, however, the possession of one allele is neither a necessary nor a sufficient condition for a phenotype to surface—the allele is only a risk factor. Most behaviors and personality traits are polygenic phenotypes.

The third and final way that a gene can influence phenotypic variation is through pleiotropic effects. Pleiotropy describes the genetic influences of a single gene on multiple phenotypic traits. For instance, variants of a dopamine transporter gene (DAT1) have been linked to schizoid/avoidant behaviors, generalized anxiety disorders, alcohol consumption, and ADHD (Gill, et al., 1997; Rowe, et al., 1998). Likewise, the gene that causes phenylketonuria (PKU) reduces tyronise, increases phenylalanine, causes hair to lighten, and is responsible for a number of other physiological changes. Some biosocial criminological research findings also underscore the importance of pleiotropic effects. This line of inquiry has revealed that some of the most robust correlates to criminal behaviors (e.g., low self-control, delinquent peers, and number of sex partners) share a common genetic pathway; that is, the same genetic factors that are associated with development of criminal behaviors are also responsible for the development of crime correlates (Beaver, et al., 2008a; Beaver, et al., 2008b).

At this point, an important digression is necessary. OGODs, polygenic effects, and pleiotropic effects all capture different processes by which genes can directly affect phenotypes. An emerging line of biosocial research, however, has pointed at the likelihood that genes oftentimes only have effects when paired to certain environments. Behavioral geneticists refer to this interplay between genes and the environment as a gene x environment interaction (G × E). Most research examining the effects that certain genes have on phenotypes has failed to take into account G × E effects. As a result, the literature that will be reviewed in this chapter will be drawn mainly from molecular genetic research, not from G × E studies. Where relevant, the results of G × E studies will be discussed.

Neurotransmitters

Most of the genetic polymorphisms that have been found to have effects on antisocial phenotypes are implicated in the regulation of neuro-transmitters. So before we can move into a discussion of these genetic polymorphisms, we first need to present a brief overview of how neuro-transmitters work and what they do. Neurotransmitters aid in the com-munication among neurons, which are nerve cells located in the brain. Neurons are made up of two types of neuronal branch: dendrites and axons. Dendrites are connected to the cell nucleus and receive incoming messages from other neurons. Axons, in contrast, send messages to other neurons. For neurons to communicate with each other, a message must move down an axon where it meets up with the dendrite of another neuron. The information is then passed from axon to dendrite where the information travels along the dendrite until, finally, it is transferred to the cell's axon. This process of a message flowing from axon to dendrite to axon to dendrite is repeated until the message reaches its ultimate destination.

It might seem as if neurons are physically wired together, where the axon of one neuron is joined to the dendrite of another neuron. Actually, in fact, there is a small gap that exists between axons and dendrites. This gap is referred to as a *synaptic gap*, a synaptic cleft, or, more frequently, a **synapse**. So how do axons and dendrites communicate with each other if there is a gap separating them? At the end of each axon, near the synapse, are compartments called vesicles where neurotransmitters are housed. When an axon of one neuron (i.e., the presynaptic neuron) needs to relay a message to a dendrite of another neuron (i.e., the postsynaptic neuron), a series of chemical and electrical reactions occur and the appropriate neurotransmitters are released from vesicles where they bridge the synapse and lock into receptors on the dendrite. The dendrite then reads the message from the neurotransmitter where it is processed and transmitted on to other neurons using this same process.

After the neurotransmitter has locked into the postsynaptic neuron and delivered the message, it needs to be removed from the synapse. This is accomplished in two different ways. First, the presynaptic neuron may reabsorb the neurotransmitters by releasing a transporter protein. Transporter proteins purge neurotransmitters from the synapse by capturing them and returning them to the presynaptic neuron. The elimination of neurotransmitters via transporter proteins is called reuptake, and the process of reuptake is vital to maintaining normal levels of neurotransmitters. When something interferes with reuptake, or when the transporter protein is inefficient or suboptimal, then neurotransmitter levels may be altered.

The second way that neurotransmitters are removed from the synaptic gap is through enzymatic degradation. Enzymes are proteins that accelerate chemical reactions, and in the degradation process, they are released into the synapse where they metabolize (break down) neurotransmitters. Similar to reuptake, these neurotransmitter-destroying enzymes are particularly important to modulating neurotransmitter levels. Reuptake and enzymatic degradation are not mutually exclusive, but instead work in tandem to sweep the synapses of neurotransmitters.

Candidate Genes for Antisocial Phenotypes

Neurotransmitters are thus important biochemicals that allow neurons to communicate with each other. Just as significant is that levels of neurotransmitters have been found to be associated with numerous phenotypes, ranging from depression and psychosis to aggression and anxiety (Niehoff, 1999; Raine, 1993). But what brings about variation in neurotransmitter levels? Levels of neurotransmitters are determined partially by environmental forces and partially by genetic factors. The death of a family member or a longtime friend, being startled by a snake, and engaging in sexual intercourse are examples of environmental stimuli that can cause neurotransmitter concentrations to ebb and flow. In this case, biochemical changes occur in response to environmental conditions.

In addition to environmental effects on neurotransmitters, certain genetic polymorphisms also have partial control over neurotransmitter levels. A number of genes associated with the modulation of neurotransmitters are functional polymorphisms, where different alleles code for the production of proteins that function differentially. Depending on which alleles are inherited will determine which proteins are produced, and which proteins are produced will determine, along with environmental conditions, neurotransmitter levels. Given that different concentrations of neurotransmitters have been linked to a number of antisocial phenotypes, it should not be too surprising that neurotransmitter-related genes are some of the most promising polymorphisms thought to be implicated in the etiology of violent, aggressive, and criminal behaviors. Although not exhaustive, the current review focuses on three different groups of genetic polymorphisms—dopaminergic polymorphisms, serotonergic polymorphisms, and enzymatic degradation polymorphisms—and how they affect antisocial phenotypes.

Dopaminergic Polymorphisms

Dopamine is an excitatory neurotransmitter that is found in the brain and is an integral part of the pleasure/reward system of the human body. The release of dopamine increases postsynaptic neuronal activity and is accompanied by intense euphoric feelings. The pleasurable effects that result from eating, sexual intercourse, and sleeping are due, in large part, to the release of dopamine. However, when dopamine levels deviate from what is considered normal—whether they are too high or too low—a host of problems can ensue. Psychosis, schizophrenia, Parkinson's disease, anorexia, bulimia, mania, and depression have all been linked to aberrant dopamine levels. Of particular importance are the effects that dopamine has on antisocial phenotypes. Researchers have hypothesized that high levels of dopamine should be associated with increased involvement in aggressive, violent, and impulsive behaviors.

Empirical evidence flowing from both human and animal studies has provided some support in favor of this hypothesis (Niehoff, 1999; Raine, 1993); however, it should be noted that the evidence is far from conclusive. Some studies have failed to detect a statistically significant association between dopamine levels and antisocial behaviors and some research has reported a negative association between levels of dopamine and aggressive conduct (for a review of studies, see Raine, 1993). What this may mean is that the relationship between dopamine and antisocial behavior is curvilinear, where both high and low levels of dopamine are contributing factors to misconduct. Regardless, the results of these studies implicate dopamine levels in the development of aggression and thus point toward the potential importance of dopaminergic genes in the study of crime and aggression.

The dopamine transporter gene (DAT1) is a dopaminergic polymorphism that is located on chromosome 5 and that codes for the production of the dopamine transporter protein (DAT). DAT1 is a polymorphic gene that contains a variable number of tandem repeats (i.e., a minisatellite) that can be repeated between three and eleven times. So some individuals inherit the DAT1 gene with a section of DNA repeated three times (i.e., the 3-repeat allele), some people inherit the DAT1 gene with a section of DNA repeated four times (i.e., the 4-repeat allele) and so on and so forth all the way to the 11-repeat allele. Genetic research has revealed that the different DAT1 alleles affect genetic expression, with the 10-repeat allele corresponding to the highest level of expression (Fuke, et al., 2001;

Michelhaugh, et al., 2001). What this could mean is that "the 10-R allele of the DAT1 gene may be associated with a dopamine transporter that is abnormally efficient at the re-uptake process" (Swanson, et al., 2000:24).

Perhaps as a result, carriers of the 10-repeat allele are at greater risk for developing an array of antisocial phenotypes. Table 3.1 contains a summary of the effects that the different genetic polymorphisms have on different antisocial outcomes. While not an exhaustive review of the literature, the table highlights some key findings for each of polymorphisms. As can be seen in the top row of the table, the 10-repeat allele of the DAT1 gene has been found to increase the risk of developing ADHD (Gill, et al., 1997) and to increase the likelihood of becoming a pathological gambler (Comings, et al., 2001).

Most germane to biosocial criminology, however, are the studies reporting a link between DAT1 and crime/delinquency. Recently Guo and his colleagues (2007) analyzed data from the National Longitudinal Study of Adolescent Health (Add Health) to examine the effect that DAT1 had on violent delinquency during adolescence and young adulthood. The results of their analysis revealed that the 10-repeat allele had statistically significant and consistent effects on the measures of serious and violent delinquency. In a follow-up study, Beaver, et al. (2008) also employed the Add Health data to examine the effects of DAT1. Using a different analytical strategy and a somewhat different measure of serious violence, their results mirrored those reported by Guo, et al. (2007). Taken together, these studies provide initial evidence linking variants of DAT1 to violent aggression and criminal behaviors.

In addition to DAT1, another dopaminergic polymorphism—the dopamine D2 receptor gene (DRD2)—has also been singled out as a potentially important gene in the genesis of antisocial phenotypes. DRD2 has been mapped to chromosome 11 and codes for the production of the D2 receptor protein. Dopamine receptors, including the D2 receptor, facilitate the binding of neurotransmitters to postsynaptic neurons. The DRD2 gene has an SNP that results in two alleles: the minor A1 allele and the major A2 allele. Carriers of the A1 allele have been found to have fewer D2 dopamine receptors (Berman & Noble, 1995; Noble, et al., 1991), decreased D2 binding (Thompson, et al., 1997), and reduced brain glucose metabolism (Noble, et al., 1997).

The A1 allele of DRD2 is considered the risk allele because it is associated with a number of different maladaptive outcomes. Empirical research, for example, has found that the A1 allele increases the likelihood of alcoholism (Uhl, et al., 1993), gambling (Comings, et al., 2001), and polysubstance abuse (Munafo, et al., 2007), all of which are highly comorbid with antisocial phenotypes.

Findings gleaned from two studies, however, stand out as particularly

Table 3.1 Genetic Polymorphisms Associated with Antisocial Phenotypes

Polymorphism	Abbreviation	Risk allele	Antisocial phenotypes
Dopaminergic polymorphisms			
Dopamine transporter gene	DAT1	10-repeat (10R) allele	ADHD; criminal behavior; gambling; violent delinquency
Dopamine D2 receptor gene	DRD2	A1 allele	Alcoholism; antisocial personality disorder; gambling; impulsivity; polysubstance use; victimization; violent delinquency
Dopamine D4 receptor gene	DRD4	7-repeat (7R) allele	ADHD; conduct disorder; externalizing behaviors; gambling; novelty seeking
Serotonergic polymorphism			
Serotonin transporter gene	5-HTTLPR	short (S) allele	ADHD; aggression; alcohol consumption; conduct disorder; nicotine dependence; physical violent behavior
Enzymatic degradation polymorphisms			
Catechol-O-methyltransferase gene	COMT	Met allele	Aggressive behavior; aggressive personality traits; violence
Monoamine oxidase A gene	MAOA	low activity alleles	Aggressive behavior; conduct disorder; violent behavior

relevant to biosocial criminology. First, and similar to the results garnered for DAT1, the analysis conducted by Guo and his colleagues (2007) revealed that the A1 allele of DRD2 was associated with increased involvement in serious violent delinquency among respondents from the Add Health study. Second, another study analyzing the Add Health found that the A1 allele conferred a greater risk of being the victim of a violent crime (Beaver, et al., 2007). However, this effect was only observed for white males who had relatively few delinquent friends; there was no association between the A1 allele and victimization for females, for black males, or for white males with high concentrations of antisocial peers. This finding of an interaction between DRD2 and delinquent peers draws attention to the importance of G × Es in the creation of adolescent victimization.

A line of research has also identified another dopamine receptor gene—the dopamine D4 receptor gene (DRD4)—as potentially important to various types of psychopathology. DRD4 is a highly polymorphic gene found on chromosome 11 and that codes for the synthesis of the D4 dopamine receptor protein. The DRD4 polymorphism contains a 48-base pair sequence that can be repeated between two and eleven times (i.e., a minisatellite), where each repeat sequence corresponds to a different allele (Chang, et al., 1996; Lichter, et al., 1993). Although the exact functional significance of the DRD4 polymorphism is not well understood, there is some evidence consistent with the possibility that the 7-repeat allele encodes a receptor that is subsensitive to dopamine (Asghari, et al., 1995; Van Craenenbroeck, et al., 2005).

Importantly, the 7-repeat allele has also been identified as the risk allele for a range of different antisocial phenotypes. ADHD (Faraone, et al., 2001), pathological gambling (Comings, et al., 2001), and high scores on the personality trait of **novelty seeking** (Noble, et al., 1998) are all more common in carriers of the 7-repeat allele. Although there are not any studies that have examined whether variants of the DRD4 gene are associated with criminal or delinquent outcomes, two studies do have direct bearing on this topic. The first study, conducted by Rowe, et al. (2001), examined whether DRD4 was associated with retrospective reports of conduct disorder. Analysis of the sample of n = 42 adult males revealed that males who possessed the 7-repeat allele had more conduct disorder symptoms.

In the second study, Bakermans-Kranenburg and van IJzendoorn (2006) tested for a G × E between DRD4 and maternal insensitivity in the prediction of externalizing problem behaviors in young children. Their analysis revealed a significant G × E, where maternal insensitivity interacted with the 7-repeat allele to produce a sixfold increase in externalizing problem behaviors. What is the relevance of these two studies to biosocial criminology? Conduct disorder (CD) and early-life problem behaviors are precursors to serious delinquent involvement during adolescence and criminal behaviors during adulthood. The 7-repeat allele, therefore, may have its effects on later life crime and delinquency by setting an individual onto an antisocial pathway very early in life. Likewise, given the high comorbidity between CD, **oppositional defiant disorder (ODD)**, and violence it is very well possible that the findings reported by Rowe and his colleagues (2001) and by Bakermans-Kranenburg and van IJzendoorn (2006) would extend to other closely related phenotypes, such as criminal and delinquent behaviors.

Serotonergic Polymorphism

Serotonin is a neurotransmitter with inhibitory properties that modulates behaviors and serves as the body's natural brake system. When serotonin is released in the brain, neuronal activity is reduced and, as a consequence, innate drives, including aggressive tendencies and primitive impulses, are dampened. As a result, biosocial researchers have posited that low levels of serotonin should be associated with a greater involvement in antisocial behaviors (Raine, 1993). Although far from conclusive, there is a line of evidence to support this proposition (Clarke, et al., 1999; Lidberg, et al., 1985). Even more telling is that two meta-analyses revealed that low serotonin concentrations were significantly associated with an increased risk of antisocial and violent phenotypes (Moore, et al., 2002; Raine, 1993). These results hint at the possibility that polymorphisms that are partially responsible for determining serotonin levels may also be associated with antisocial behaviors.

The most studied polymorphism of the serotonergic system, at least as it relates to behavioral phenotypes, is the serotonin transporter promoter polymorphism (5-HTTLPR). The serotonin transporter gene is located on chromosome 17 and codes for the production of the serotonin transporter protein. The serotonin transporter protein terminates serotonin activity in the synapse through the process of reuptake. A variable 44-base pair insertion/deletion (i.e., a minisatellite) in the 5-HTTLPR makes for two alleles: a long (L) allele and a short (S) allele. This polymorphism has been found to affect the expression of the serotonin transporter protein, where carriers of the short allele have reduced reuptake activity (Lesch, et al., 1996). What this may mean is that the short allele codes for a transporter protein that is not as efficient at removing serotonin from the synapse and thus is not as effective at modulating synaptic serotonergic activity.

Geneticists have conducted an extensive amount of research on the effects of 5-HTTLPR and found that the short allele is associated with an increased risk of displaying antisocial phenotypes. Carriers of the short allele are more likely to report ADHD symptoms (Cadoret, et al., 2003), are more likely to consume large quantities of alcohol (Herman, et al., 2003), are more likely to become dependent on nicotine (Munafo, et al., 2005), and are more likely to have CD as a child (Cadoret, et al., 2003). A number of studies have also directly examined whether the short allele relates to physical violent aggression. For example, studies by Beitchman and associates (2006) and by Haberstick and colleagues (2006) revealed that the short allele increased the risk of displaying aggression during childhood, while a study by Retz, et al. (2004) found that the short allele was more prevalent among violent offenders compared to nonviolent offenders. Similar results were reported in a sample of Chinese males, where carriers of the short allele were disproportionately over-involved in acts of extreme violence (Liao, et al., 2004).

Lastly, Reif, et al. (2007) tested for a G × E between the short allele of 5-HTTLPR and an adverse childhood environment in the creation of violent behavior. The results of their analysis provided support in favor of the G × E, where the short allele was only associated with violence for individuals exposed to a criminogenic home environment during childhood. Those individuals who possessed the short allele but who were not subjected to an adverse upbringing were no more likely to become violent than those individuals homozygous for the long allele. These findings once again underscore the importance of working from a biosocial perspective where the dual effects of genes and the environment are examined simultaneously.

Enzymatic Degradation Polymorphisms

The last two polymorphisms that will be discussed code for the production of enzymes that are involved in the inactivation of neurotransmitters. The first, **catechol-O-methyltransferase (COMT)**, is found on chromosome 22 and is responsible for manufacturing the COMT enzyme, which metabolizes catecholamines, such as dopamine, epinephrine, and norepinephrine. The COMT polymorphism is an SNP where one allele contains a codon (ATG) that codes for the amino acid methionine (i.e., the Met allele). In contrast, the other allele contains a codon (GTG; note that G replaces A in the first nucleotide) that produces the amino acid valine (i.e., the Val allele). There is a functional difference between these two alleles, where the Met allele is linked with reduced COMT enzymatic activity. This is particularly important because the COMT enzyme synthesizes catecholamines, and catecholamines are thought to be positively associated with antisocial behavior. As a result, the Met allele is considered the risk allele because it is associated with lowered enzymatic activity, which, in turn, is associated with increased levels of catecholamines.

Researchers examining the effects of the COMT polymorphism have found that the Met allele is associated with aggressive personality traits (Rujescu, et al., 2003) and with aggressive and violent behaviors (Volavka, et al., 2004). For example, among a sample of schizophrenics, Kotler, et al. (1999) found that the Met allele was more prevalent among schizophrenics who committed homicidal behaviors than among a sample of controls. Other studies have reported strikingly similar results where the Met allele is associated with violent behaviors (Jones, et al., 2001; Lachman, et al., 1998). It is important to point out that the nexus between the Met allele and violence has been primarily observed in samples comprised of schizophrenics. Whether the findings would be generalizable to the larger population of non-schizophrenics is an open empirical question.

The second enzymatic degradation polymorphism associated with antisocial phenotypes is the monoamine oxidase A (MAOA) gene. The MAOA gene is located on the X chromosome and is responsible for producing the MAOA enzyme that metabolizes monoamine neurotransmitters, including dopamine and serotonin. A 30-base pair VNTR (i.e., a minisatellite) in the promoter region of the gene is what gives rise to the polymorphism. Although the number of repeat sequences ranges between two repeats and five repeats, the alleles are typically pooled to form two groups. One group of alleles is associated with low MAOA activity, whereas the other group of alleles is associated with high MAOA activity.

Since the low activity alleles are not as efficient as the high activity alleles at metabolizing neurotransmitters, researchers have hypothesized that the low activity alleles are the risk alleles for antisocial phenotypes. Studies examining the effects of MAOA on criminal behaviors have provided inconclusive results, with some studies showing no main effect (e.g., Caspi, et al., 2002; Haberstick, et al., 2005) and others revealing that the low functioning allele is associated with low levels of aggression (e.g., Manuck, et al., 2000).

Perhaps even more interesting, and maybe even more important, are the effects of the MAOA polymorphism when paired to criminogenic environments—that is, a G × E. In one of the most significant studies to test for G × E effects on violence, Caspi and his colleagues (2002) examined the interaction between MAOA and childhood maltreatment on antisocial behavior in adult males from the Dunedin Multidisciplinary Health and Development Study. Their analysis revealed that the MAOA polymorphism did not have a statistically significant main effect on any measures of antisocial behavior. What they did find, however, was that the low activity allele increased antisocial behaviors for respondents who had been maltreated as a child. In other words, the effect of the MAOA polymorphism interacted with an environmental stimuli—childhood maltreatment. To put this finding into perspective, although only 12 percent of the sample had the low activity allele *and* were maltreated as a child, this small subsample of males accounted for 44 percent of convictions for violence. Follow-up studies have attempted to replicate this G × E, with mixed results (Foley, et al., 2004; Haberstick, et al., 2005). Even so, a recent meta-analysis indicated that the interaction between MAOA and maltreatment was a statistically significant predictor of antisocial behaviors across studies (Kim-Cohen, et al., 2006).

Conclusion

This chapter provided a brief introduction to human genetics and discussed some of the genetic polymorphisms associated with antisocial phenotypes. The available molecular genetic and behavioral genetic evidence suggests that the propensity to engage in violence, aggression, and criminal acts is partially transcribed into each person's suite of genes. How genes ultimately are responsible for predisposing to antisocial behavior still remains something of a mystery. Although the polymorphisms reviewed here work on systems of neurotransmitters, a small line of research—known as imaging genetics—has also begun to use neuroimaging techniques to link the alleles of these genes to variation in brain circuitry. Differences in amygdala functioning, prefrontal cortex activity, orbitofrontal volume, and gray matter volume depend, in part, on which alleles are inherited for MAOA, COMT, and 5-HTTLPR (Canli, et al., 2005; Meyer-Lindenberg, et al., 2006). This is not to say that environmental effects are unimportant; research has revealed beyond a doubt that criminogenic and stressful environments can—and indeed do—have detrimental and lasting effects on the brain (Pine, 2003). The key for criminology, then, is to unpack the ways in which genes, the environment, and the brain interface to produce undesirable behaviors. Although daunting, such an accomplishment would result in a rich and powerful biosocial explanation of antisocial conduct.

References

Asghari, V., S. Sanyal, S. Buchwaldt, A. Paterson, V. Jovanovic, & H. H. M. Van Tol (1995). Modulation of intracellular cyclic AMP levels by different human dopamine D4 receptor variants. *Journal of Neurochemistry*, 65:1157–1165.

Bakermans-Kranenburg, M. J. & M. H. van IJzendoorn (2006). Gene-environment interaction of the dopamine D4 receptor (DRD4) and observed maternal insensitivity predicting externalizing behavior in preschoolers. *Developmental Psychobiology*, 48:406–409.

Beaver, K. M., J. P. Wright, & M. DeLisi (2008a). Gene–environment interplay and delinquent involvement. Unpublished manuscript.

Beaver, K. M., J. P. Wright, & A. Walsh, A. (2008b). A gene-based evolutionary explanation for the association between criminal involvement and number of sex partners. *Social Biology*.

Beaver, K. M., J. P. Wright, M. DeLisi, L. E. Daigle, M. L. Swatt, & C. L. Gibson (2007). Evidence of a gene X environment interaction in the creation of victimization: results from a longitudinal sample of adolescents. *International Journal of Offender Therapy and Comparative Criminology*, 51:620–645.

Beitchman, J. H., L. Baldassarra, H. Mik, V. De Luca, N. King, D. Bender, et al. (2006). Serotonin transporter polymorphisms and persistent, pervasive childhood aggression. *American Journal of Psychiatry*, 163:1103–1105.

Berman, S. M. & E. P. Noble (1995). Reduced visuospatial performance in children with the D2 dopamine receptor A1 allele. *Behavior Genetics*, 25:45–58.

Cadoret, R. J., D. Langbehn, K. Caspers, E. P. Troughton, R. Yucuis, H. K. Sandhu et al. (2003). Associations of the serotonin transporter promoter polymorphism with aggressivity, attention deficit, and conduct disorder in an adoptee population. *Comprehensive Psychiatry*, 44:88–101.

Canli, T., K. Omura, B. W. Haas, A. Fallgatter, R. T. Constable, & K. P. Lesch (2005). Beyond affect: a role for genetic variation of the serotonin transporter in neural activation during a cognitive attention task. *Proceedings of the National Academy of Sciences*, 102:12224–12229.

Carey, G. (2003). *Human genetics for the social sciences*. Thousand Oaks, CA: Sage.

Caspi, A., J. McClay, T. E. Moffitt, J. Mill, J. Martin, I. W. Craig., et al. (2002). Role of genotype in the cycle of violence in maltreated children. *Science*, 297:851–854.

Chang, F.-M., J. R. Kidd, K. J. Livak, A. J. Pakstis, & K. K. Kidd (1996). The world-wide distribution of allele frequencies at the human dopamine D4 receptor locus. *Human Genetics*, 98:91–101.

Clarke, R. A., D. L. Murphy, & J. N. Constantino (1999). Serotonin and externalizing behavior in young children. *Psychiatry Research*, 86:29–40.

Comings, D. E., R. Gade-Andavolu, N. Gonzalez, S. Wu, D. Muhleman, & C. Chen, et al. (2001). The additive effect of neurotransmitter genes in pathological gambling. *Clinical Genetics*, 60:107–116.

Faraone, S. V., A. E. Doyle, E. Mick, & J. Biederman, J. (2001). Meta-analysis of the association between the 7-repeat allele of the dopamine D4 receptor gene and attention deficit hyperactivity disorder. *American Journal of Psychiatry*, 158:1052–1057.

Foley, D. L., L. J. Eaves, B. Wormley, J. L. Silberg, H. H. Maes, J. Kuhn, et al. (2004). Childhood adversity, monoamine oxidase A genotype, and risk for conduct disorder. *Archives of General Psychiatry*, 61:738–744.

Fuke, S., S. Suo, N. Takahashi, H. Koike, N. Sasagawa, & S. Ishiura (2001). The VNTR polymorphism of the human dopamine transporter (DAT1) gene affects gene expression. *The Pharmacogenomics Journal*, 1:152–156.

Gill, M., G. Daly, S. Heron, Z. Hawi, & M. Fitzgerald (1997). Confirmation of association between attention deficit hyperactivity disorder and a dopamine transporter polymorphism. *Molecular Psychiatry*, 2:311–313.

Guo, G., M. E. Roettger, & J. C. Shih (2007). Contributions of the DAT1 and DRD2 genes to serious and violent delinquency among adolescents and young adults. *Human Genetics*, 121:125–136.

Haberstick, B. C., A. Smolen, & J. K. Hewitt (2006). Family-based association test of the 5HTTLPR and aggressive behavior in a general population sample of children. *Biological Psychiatry*, 59:836–843.

Haberstick, B. C., J. M. Lessem, C. J. Hopfer, A. Smolen, M. A. Ehringer, D. Timberlake, et al. (2005). Monoamine oxidase A (MAOA) and antisocial behaviors in the presence of childhood and adolescent maltreatment. *American Journal of Medical Genetics Part B (Neuropsychiatric Genetics)*, 135B:59–64.

Herman, A. I., J. W. Philbeck, N. L. Vasilopoulos, & P. B. Depetrillo (2003). Serotonin transporter promoter polymorphism and differences in alcohol consumption behaviour in a college student population. *Alcohol and Alcoholism*, 38:446–449.

Hu, X.-Z., R. H. Lipsky, G. Zhu, L. A. Akhtar, J. Taubman, B. D. Greenberg, et al. (2006). Serotonin transporter promoter gain-of-function genotypes are linked to obsessive-compulsive disorder. *American Journal of Human Genetics*, 78:815–826.

Jones, G., S. Zammit, N. Norton, M. L. Hamshere, S. J. Jones, C. Milham, et al. (2001). Aggressive behaviour in patients with schizophrenia is associated with catechol-O-methyltransferase genotype. *British Journal of Psychiatry*, 179:351–355.

Kim-Cohen, J., A. Caspi, A. Taylor, B. Williams, R. Newcombe, I. W. Craig, et al. (2006). MAOA, maltreatment, and gene-environment interaction predicting children's mental health: new evidence and a meta-analysis. *Molecular Psychiatry*, 11:903–913.

Kotler, M., P. Barak, H. Cohen, I. E. Averbuch, A. Grinshpoon, I. Gritsenko, et al. (1999). Homicidal behavior in schizophrenia associated with a genetic polymorphism determining low COMT activity. *American Journal of Medical Genetics*, 88:628–633.

Lachman, H. M., K. A. Nolan, P. Mohr, T. Saito, & J. Volavka (1998). Association between catechol O-methyltransferase genotype and violence in schizophrenia and schizoaffective disorder. *American Journal of Psychiatry*, 155:835–837.

Lesch, K.-P., D. Bengel, A. Heils, S. Z. Sabol, B. D. Greenberg, S. Petri, et al. (1996). Association of anxiety-related traits with a polymorphism in the serotonin transporter gene regulatory region. *Science*, 274:1527–1531.

Liao, D. L., C. J. Hong, H. L. Shih, & S. J. Tsai (2004). Possible association between serotonin transporter promoter region polymorphism and extremely violent crime in Chinese males. *Neuropsychobiology*, 50:284–287.

Lichter, J. B., C. L. Barr, J. L. Kennedy, H. H. M. Van Tol, K. K. Kidd, & K. J. Livak (1993). A hypervariable segment in the human dopamine receptor D4 (DRD4) gene. *Human Molecular Genetics*, 2:767–773.

Lidberg, L., J. R. Tuck, M. Asberg, G. P. Scalia-Tomba, L. & Bertillson, L. (1985). Homicide, suicide, and CSF 5-HIAA. *Acta Psychiatrica Scandinavica*, 71:230–236.

Manuck, S. B., J. D. Flory, R. E. Ferrell, J. J. Mann, & M. F. Muldoon (2000). A regulatory polymorphism of the monoamine oxidase-A gene may be associated with variability in aggression, impulsivity, and central nervous system serotonergic responsivity. *Psychiatry Research*, 95:9–23.

Meyer-Lindenberg, A., J. W. Buckholtz, B. Kolachana, A. R. Hariri, L. Pezawas, G. Blasi, et al. (2006). Neural mechanisms of genetic risk for impulsivity and violence in humans. *Proceedings of the National Academy of Sciences*, 103:6269–6274.

Michelhaugh, S. K., C. Fiskerstrand, E. Lovejoy, M. J. Bannon, & J. P. Quinn (2001). The dopamine transporter gene (SLC6A3) variable number of tandem repeats domain enhances transcription in dopamine neurons. *Journal of Neurochemistry*, 79:1033–1038.

Moore, T. M., A. Scarpa, & A. Raine (2002). A meta-analysis of serotonin metabolite 5-HIAA and antisocial behavior. *Aggressive Behavior*, 28:299–316.

Munafo, M. R., I. J. Matheson, & J. Flint (2007). Association of the DRD2 gene Taq1A polymorphism and alcoholism: a meta-analysis of case-control studies and evidence of publication bias. *Molecular Psychiatry*, 12:454–461.

Munafo, M. R., K. Roberts, E. C. Johnstone, R. T. Walton, & P. L. Yudkin (2005). Association of serotonin transporter gene polymorphism with nicotine dependence: no evidence of an interaction with trait neuroticism. *Personality and Individual Differences*, 38:843–850.

Niehoff, D. (1999). *The biology of violence: how understanding the brain, behavior, and environment can break the vicious circle of violence*. New York: Free Press.

Noble, E. P., K. Blum, T. Ritchie, A. Montgomery, & P. J. Sheridan (1991). Allelic association of the D2 dopamine receptor gene with receptor binding characteristics in alcoholism. *Archives of General Psychiatry*, 48:648–654.

Noble, E. P., L. A. Gottschalk, J. H. Fallon, T. Ritchie, & J. C. Wu (1997). D2 dopamine polymorphism and brain regional glucose metabolism. *American Journal of Medical Genetics*, 74:762–166.

Noble, E. P., T. Z. Ozkaragoz, T. L. Ritchie, X. Zhuang, T. R. Belin, & R. S. Sparkes (1998). D2 and D4 dopamine receptor polymorphisms and personality. *American Journal of Medical Genetics*, 81:257–267.

Pine, D. S. (2003). Developmental psychobiology and response to threats: relevance to trauma in children and adolescents. *Biological Psychiatry*, 53:796–808.

Plomin, R., J. Defries, I. Craig, & P. McGuffin (2001). *Behavioral genetics*, 4th edn. New York: Worth Publishers.

Raine, A. (1993). *The psychopathology of crime: criminal behavior as a clinical disorder*. San Diego, CA: Academic Press.

Reif, A., M. Rosler, C. M. Freitag, M. Schneider, A. Eujen, C. Kissling, et al. (2007). Nature and nurture predispose to violent behavior: serotonergic genes and adverse childhood environment. *Neuropsychopharmacology*, 32:2375–2383.

Retz, W., P. Retz-Junginger, T. Supprian, J. Thome, & M. Rosler (2004). Association of serotonin transporter promoter gene polymorphism with violence: relation with personality disorders, impulsivity, and childhood ADHD psychopathology. *Behavioral Sciences and the Law*, 22:415–425.

Rowe, D. C. (2002). *Biology and crime*. Los Angeles: Roxbury.

Rowe, D. C., C. Stever, D. Chase, S. Sherman, A. Abramowitz, & I. D. Waldman (2001). Two dopamine genes related to reports of childhood retrospective inattention and conduct disorder symptoms. *Molecular Psychiatry*, 6:429–433.

Rowe, D. C., C. Stever, J. M. C. Gard, H. H. Cleveland, M. L. Sanders, A. Abramowitz, et al. (1998). The relation of the dopamine transporter gene (DAT1) to symptoms of internalizing disorders in children. *Behavior Genetics*, 28:215–225.

Rujescu, D., I. Giegling, A. Gietl, A. M. Hartmann, & H.-J. Moller (2003). A functional single nucleotide polymorphism (V158M) in the COMT gene is associated with aggressive personality traits. *Biological Psychiatry*, 54:34–39.

Swanson, J. M., P. Flodman, J. Kennedy, M. A. Spence, R. Moyzis, S. Schuck, et al. (2000). Dopamine genes and ADHD. *Neuroscience and Biobehavioral Reviews*, 24:21–25.

Thompson, J., N. Thomas, A. Singleton, M. Piggott, S. Lloyd, E. K. Perry, et al. (1997). D2 dopamine receptor gene (DRD2) Taq1 A polymorphism: reduced dopamine D2 receptor binding in the human striatum with the A1 allele. *Pharmacogenetics*, 7:479–484.

Uhl, G. R., A. M. Persico, & S. S. Smith (1992). Current excitement with dopamine receptor gene alleles in substance abuse. *Archives of General Psychiatry*, 49:157–160.

Van Craenenbroeck, K., S. D. Clark, M. J. Cox, J. N. Oak, F. Liu, & H. H. M. Van Tol (2005). Folding efficiency is rate-limiting in dopamine D4 receptor biogenesis. *Journal 1of Biological Chemistry*, 280:19350–19357.

Volavka, J., R. Bilder, & K. Nolan (2004). Catecholamines and aggression: the role of COMT and MAO polymorphisms. *Annals of the New York Academy of Sciences*, 1036:393–398.

4

The Ghost in the Machine and Criminal Behavior: Criminology for the 21st Century

John Paul Wright, Danielle Boisvert, Kim Dietrich, and M. Douglas Ris

"The history of science," Goldberg (2001:46) tells us, "is replete with false starts." Nowhere is this more obvious than in the study of serious criminal behavior. While theories of demonic possession have given way to more empirically oriented views of serious criminal conduct, many contemporary sociological perspectives remain just a step or two away from invoking the supernatural. Indeed, sociological criminology sometimes parallels the "intelligent design" perspective. This perspective views an invisible force as responsible for the organization of life on earth. Preachers refer to this force as God, to sociologists it is referred to as "environment," "stratification," "culture," or "socialization." Like God, these factors are omnipotent and beyond reproach.

The reasons for this situation are complex but hinge on the lack of recognition, if not outright rejection, of the "ghost in the machine" (Koestler, 1968). Of course the ghost we are referring to is the brain and its biological and genetic subsystems. Contemporary students of crime may find it odd that a science of human behavior eschews looking into the machinery of the mind. The question that emerges, obviously, is why? We offer three possible explanations. First, many sociological theories of crime require a fundamental belief about the nature of human action. Behavior, assume most social theories of crime, is the product of *external* socializing influences, such as parental efforts, peer groups, and neighborhoods. Second, many sociological theories of crime require adherence to "knowledge" that has limited, if any, scientific support. Postmodernist perspectives and many feminist theories of criminal involvement come immediately to mind. Postmodern and feminist perspectives are often antiscientific but it is worth noting that virtually every other social theory of crime is at best marginally supported by empirical evidence. Still, advocates of specific theories regularly flaunt their strengths with little consideration given to their reflection of reality. Finally, virtually all social theories of human misbehavior seek to exclude and to vilify bodies of knowledge that challenge basic sociological tenets. Sound biological and genetic findings rarely make their way into top criminology journals. Worse yet, individual researchers who conduct research in this area are often subject to speculation about their motives (are they racist or sexist),[1] their political orientations (are they liberal or conservative), and their character (are they "nice" people).

Just as Goldberg (2001) warns us of the problem of "false starts," he also offers a solution. Prior findings need not be wholly rejected, states Goldberg, but modified by the inclusion of other evidence. It is here, at the intersection between biology and social behavior, where we find hope that the study of serious criminal behavior can be pried from sociological purists. In this chapter, we argue that any theory of individual or group behavior that omits an understanding of the brain is a priori misspecified, if not wholly wrong. More importantly, we also argue that an understanding of the brain and its connection to criminal behavior *highlights* the importance of the immediate social environment because of the environment's links to healthy brain development. Far from being "dangerous" or "reductionistic," knowledge of brain structure and functioning can, in some ways, contribute to sociological theories, while in other ways it can provide the basis for the elimination of faddish and foolish theories of crime (Walsh, 2000, 2002).

Brain Basics

Much of the brain's development is ontogenic—that is, it occurs according to evolved genetic code. Of our 20,000 to 25,000 genes, over 60 percent code for the brain. The human brain accounts for 2 percent of an average person's total body weight, but it consumes roughly 10 times the amount of glucose as the rest of the body's organs, and roughly 20 percent of the body's oxygen intake (Robinson, 2004).

The human brain is a marvel of evolution. Weighing in at approximately three pounds, this organ processes all sensory input through a complex web of 100 billion nerve cells, called neurons, that "connect" individually to 1,000 to 10,000 other neurons. That is approximately 10^{16}, or 100,000,000,000,000,000, or one-hundred quadrillion connections. There are between 10 to 50 times more **glial cells**, which maintain neurons, than neurons and approximately 150,000 to 180,000 kilometers (between 93,205.6 miles to 111,846.8 miles) of nerve fibers in the brain. It has also been estimated that males have ~22.8 billion neocortical neurons while females have ~19.3 billion neocortical neurons, which may help to explain why males have larger brains than females (Pakkenberg & Gundersen, 1997).

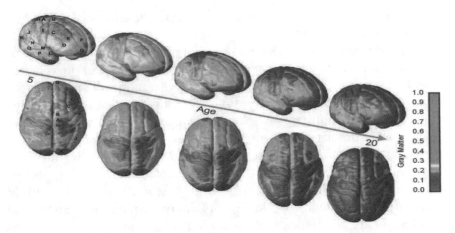

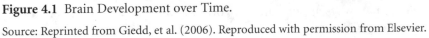

Figure 4.1 Brain Development over Time.

Source: Reprinted from Giedd, et al. (2006). Reproduced with permission from Elsevier.

This level of complexity is not achieved overnight. Indeed, claims that the brain reaches maturation between the ages of 8 and 10 (Gottfredson & Hirschi, 1990) have been proved to be incorrect. Recent research, presented in Figure 4.1, has revealed that it takes over 20 years for the brain to mature fully. Research by Gogtay, et al. (2004), for example, used anatomical magnetic resonance imaging (MRI) to scan the brains of 13 healthy individuals, aged 4 to 21. They scanned subjects every 2 years for 8 to 10 years and found that brain development occurs in an ordered fashion. Lower ordered structures, such as those that control vision and movement, mature prior to the more complex cerebral structures. As lower order structures mature they become more integrated into the upper level structures. Upper level structures, which house "executive functions" or higher order thought processes, are the last parts of the brain to mature.

Other studies have also shown that the human brain undergoes two critical periods of development. The first occurs from conception until the onset of puberty. During this period the brain is in a constant state of expansion. It will increase in cranial volume from ~350 to 400 grams at birth to between 1,300 to 1,400 grams by adolescence. The brain is also strongly linked to its immediate social environment. For instance, the brain of an average 2 year old is at least twice as active as a brain of a 40 year old. Part of this is due to the fact that most events that occur in a toddler's life are novel. Novel situations and events force the brain to expend energy. The brain has to assimilate new information, it has to store that information into memory, it has to process the emotional connotations of that information, and it has to derive new and effective behavioral approaches in reaction to the novel situation. Indeed, a child's brain will assimilate new social information at a rate unparalleled for the rest of his/ her life-course (Karr-Morse & Wiley, 1997).

Young children, however, have an overabundance of synaptic pathways. Since the brain consumes energy, it follows a form of evolutionary selection. In a process known as *synaptic pruning*, the brain will scale back the number of synaptic pathways over time. The pathways that will be eliminated are generally those that were not adequately stimulated. Those that remain were stimulated and will likely endure. This process, described by Hebbs' axiom (neurons that fire together wire together), draws attention to the interconnection between the environment and the development of a healthy brain. In short, the more the brain is stimulated, the more likely it will develop normally. While fewer pathways remain over time, those that remain are more efficient in processing and transferring information. Synaptic pathways are not the only brain component to be systematically eliminated. Current estimates indicate that the average person loses 85,000 neocortical neurons per day, or one per second (Pakkenberg & Gunderson, 1997).

The second period of development occurs with the onset of puberty. Puberty initiates a range of hormonal, physical, and brain changes. The most obvious change occurs when axons, which send information away from the body of the neuron to awaiting dendrites, myelinate. Myelin is a fatty substance that will eventually surround axons in the outer cortices of the brain and speeds the transmission of electrical signals across neurons. "Gray matter" reflects neurons that have not been myelinated, while "white matter" are neurons that have undergone myelination. Research by Gogtay, et al. (2004) and Giedd (2004) has shown that myelination occurs rapidly during adolescence. This process is visually presented in Figure 4.1. Moreover, myelination proceeds from the posterior of the brain to the anterior—or from back to front. This is important because the executive functions are housed in structures located in the **frontal lobes** (Giedd, 2004; Giedd, et al., 1999). While it remains unknown whether the changes in the adolescent brain correspond to behavioral changes, there is strong reason to suspect that maturational patterns correspond well with increased cognitive and behavioral sophistication. This may be why, for instance, the majority of adolescents and young adults "age out" of criminal and devious behavior.

Brain development begins shortly after conception. The first part of the fetal brain to develop is the **brainstem** and lower brain. This part of the brain regulates all autonomic, life essential activities, such as breathing and cardiac rhythm. At the top of the brainstem sits the recticular activating system (RAS). The RAS acts as a filter of information and as a guide— sending information to other parts of the brain. Eysenck (1964) maintains that the RAS, which extends into the deep limbic structures of the brain, is heavily implicated in personality differences related to criminal conduct. A RAS that filters too much sensory input is thought to be associated with an extraverted personality, while a RAS that allows the free flow of sensory input is associated with an introverted personality. According to several studies, extraversion, indicated by being socially gregarious and risk taking, is positively correlated with criminal behavior (Hindelang, 1971; Listwan, et al., 2007).

The next major division of the brain to develop is referred to collectively as the limbic system. The limbic system is composed of several complex structures, such as the amygdala, the **hippocampus**, the **hypothalamus** and **thalamus**, and the cingulate gyrus. It is this collection of interrelated structures that is responsible for the regulation of hormones through the **endocrine system**, especially testosterone in men and estrogen in women, the control of long-term and short-term memory, and the sensations that we label as emotions. All emotions are evolved biochemically induced states that originate in the limbic system and affect the **central nervous system (CNS)** and the **autonomic nervous system (ANS)**.

The limbic system is deeply implicated in violent behavior. Rage, impulsive anger, lust, and other excitory emotions originate in the amygdala. This input moves to the **basal nuclei** and is then threaded to the **orbital frontal cortex**, which houses information about the immediate social context. According to Davidson, et al. (2000:594), "too much or too little activation of the amygdala may give rise to either excessive negative affect or decreased sensitivity to social cues that regulate emotions, respectively."

The final part of the brain to develop is the "thinking part" of the brain, called the cortex. The cortex sits atop the limbic structures, is deeply connected to these structures, and provides humans the ability to plan for the future, the ability to control initial emotional impulses, and the ability to employ rational or quasi-rational decision making. The speech and language parts of the brain, known as **Wernike's and Broca's areas**, are also located in the neocortex. It is the neocortex that makes humans unique.

There are between 10 to 20 billion neurons in the cerebral cortex. In the frontal cortex, these neurons are connected by over 60,000 miles of synaptic connections. The cortex composes 77 percent of the human brain and appears to be more susceptible to environmental insult. This is particularly true for males, who also tend to show greater deficits in the functioning of the frontal cortex. Deficits in frontal cortex metabolism, especially the orbital frontal and ventrolateral prefrontal cortex in the left hemisphere, appear to be strongly correlated with a lack of self-control. Limited self-control is a consistent and substantive predictor of crime as well as a range of analogous behaviors (Cauffman, et al., 2005; Schoepfer & Piquero, 2006; Wright & Beaver, 2005).

The frontal cortex is critical to adaptive human behavior. While all sensory input is channeled first to the limbic system, the limbic system is under constant monitoring by the cortex. The cortex has the ability to "override" limbic system impulses and to route information to the motor cortex and to the language centers. When an environmental stimulus is present, say in the form of a threat, it can produce very strong emotions. When encountered, the limbic system may prepare the body for aggressive action. Given the situation a normally functional cortex may intervene or modify the limbic impulses. Individuals with deficits in orbital frontal, ventrolateral, and dorsolateral cortex, however, may be less able to control or to modify these limbic impulses. The result may be life-saving aggression, in the form of self-defense, or life-ending behavior, in the form of murder.

Brain Structure and Functioning is Related to Antisocial and Criminal Behavior

Research on the brain and its relationship to aggressive and antisocial behavior has made significant advancements over the years. While early studies focused on indirect measures of brain dysfunction through psychophysiological and neuropsychological assessments, advanced neuroimaging techniques are now widely available. These newer techniques provide a better representation of both the structural and functional properties of the brain. Specifically, the structure of the brain can be assessed using either **computerized tomography (CT)** or magnetic resonance imaging (MRI), while the functioning of the brain can be evaluated using positron emission tomography (PET) or single photon emission computed tomography (SPECT). Collectively, these imaging procedures allow researchers insights into the operation and structure of the brain never before realized.

Computerized Tomography (CT)

CT was first developed in the early 1970s by Hounsfeild and Cormack. Using X-rays, CT provides a two-dimensional representation of the brain's structure. Several studies have examined the relationship between brain structure and antisocial behavior using computerized tomography. While some studies have found structural brain differences between offender groups, especially in the frontal lobes (Hucker, et al., 1986, 1988; Wong, et al., 1994, 1990) others have not (Herzberg & Fenwick, 1988; Langevin, et al., 1987, 1988, 1989a, 1989b).

The studies just above have focused primarily on two types of offender: the sexual offender and the aggressive offender. Of the studies that compared sex offenders to non-sex offenders, the results have been mixed. Studies that reported significant differences between sexual offenders and non-sexual offenders have mainly reported greater **temporal lobe** abnormalities in sexual offenders (Hucker, et al., 1986, 1988; Wright, et al., 1990). For example, one of the first studies conducted in this area compared CT scans of 39 male pedophiles to the scans of 14 property offenders (Hucker, et al., 1986). The results revealed that 52 percent of the pedophiles had structural abnormalities in the frontal lobes, compared to only 17 percent of the property offenders. The most frequent abnormality detected in pedophiles was the dilation of the anterior temporal horns of the lateral ventricles. In another study conducted by Hucker, et al. (1988), abnormalities in the right temporal horn were detected in 41 percent of the sadistic sexual offenders compared to 11 percent of the nonsadistic offenders and 13 percent of the control group. Other studies have found no differences in CT data between sexual offenders and non-sexual offenders (Langevin, et al., 1988, 1989a, 1989b).

In addition to comparing sex offenders to non-sex offenders, researchers have also examined structural brain differences between aggressive offenders, such as murderers, to non-aggressive offenders, such as property offenders (Herzberg & Fenwick, 1988; Langevin, et al., 1987). For example, a retrospective study conducted by Wong, et al. (1994) found that of the most violent maximum-security mental hospital patients, 41 percent had structural abnormalities, such as dilated temporal horn and/ or a smaller sized temporal lobe, compared to only 2.4 percent and 6.7 percent of the least and moderate violent groups, respectively. By way of contrast, no significant differences were reported between CT scans of 14 aggressive patients with temporal lobe epilepsy compared to 17 nonaggressive temporal lobe epileptics (Herzberg & Fenwick, 1988). Langevin, et al. (1987) also found no significant difference in CT abnormality rates between three groups of offenders (18 murderers, 21 assaulters, and 16 property offenders). Overall, the results obtained from CT studies have provided mixed results in regards to structural brain differences between offender groups. This inexpensive imaging technique, however, is now being replaced by a more sophisticated technique known as magnetic resonance imaging.

Magnetic Resonance Imaging (MRI)

While CT uses X-rays, which is a known carcinogen, MRI relies on magnetism and radiofrequency radiation. Computer software also allows for the transformation of an MRI scan into a three-dimensional illustration of the brain. MRIs are now often used in assessing the relationship between brain structure and violence among a variety of populations, such as murderers (Sakuta & Fukushima, 1998), mentally disordered offenders (Aigner, et al., 2000; Tonkonogy, 1991), temporal lobe epileptics (van Elst, et al., 2000; Woermann, et al., 2000), repeat violent offenders (Wong, et al., 1997), and patients with **antisocial personality disorder** (Raine, et al., 2000).

Sakuta and Fukushima (1998) compared MRI scans from 52 violent murderers to those from 17 nonviolent murderers. The results revealed significantly higher structural brain abnormalities, especially in the temporal lobes, in the violent murderers (50%) compared to the nonviolent murderers (13%). The relationship between brain structure and aggression has also been assessed among mentally disordered offenders. Aigner, et al. (2000) separated a group of 82 mentally ill male prisoners into two categories: high-violent offenders and low-violent offenders. The MRI scans revealed abnormalities in 65.5 percent of the high-violent offenders compared to 16.6 percent of the low-violent offenders. Interestingly, abnormalities in the temporal region alone were found exclusively in high-violent sexually sadistic offenders while cortical **atrophy** was only detected in the high-violent offender group.

Another population of interest is that of those people diagnosed with antisocial personality disorder. An MRI study conducted by Raine, et al. (2000) revealed that individuals diagnosed with antisocial personality disorder showed an 11 percent reduction in prefrontal **gray matter** volume compared to a nonclinical control group, a substance abuse group, and a psychiatric control group. Woermann, et al. (2000) found similar results in their study of patients with temporal lobe epilepsy (TLE). They performed MRIs on 24 violent TLE patients, 24 nonviolent TLE patients, and 35 control subjects. The analyses revealed that compared to the nonviolent TLE patients and the control group, TLE patients with a history of violence had decreased gray matter, especially in the left frontal lobe. Overall, MRI studies demonstrate that abnormalities in the brain, especially dysfunction in the frontal and temporal lobes, are associated with aggressive and violent behaviors.

Positron Emission Tomography (PET)

In addition to examining the structure of the brain, researchers are also interested in studying the functional properties of the brain. Positron emission tomography is a technique often used in order to measure the metabolic activity in different areas of the brain. Numerous studies have used this sophisticated technique in order to study the relationship between brain functioning and violent behavior among criminals, such as murderers and sexual sadists (Garnett, et al., 1988; Raine, et al., 1994, 1997, 1998a, 1998b) as well as psychiatric patients, such as those diagnosed with personality disorders (Goyer et al., 1994; Volkow & Tancredi, 1987; Volkow, et al., 1995).

A leading expert in the area of brain functioning and its relationship to violent behavior is Adrian Raine. In 1994, Raine and his colleagues compared the glucose metabolism in 22 murderers to that of 22 control subjects matched on age and gender. Compared to the control group, the murderers had significantly lower **glucose** metabolism in both the medial and lateral cortices. These researchers then expanded their study in 1997 by including 41 murderers and 41 matched control subjects. The PET scans revealed that, similar to their previous findings, murderers had reduced glucose metabolism in both the medial and lateral prefrontal cortical areas. Additional analyses also revealed that murderers had reduced glucose metabolism in the **posterior parietal cortex** and the **corpus callosum**. Murderers also showed left-sided reduction in activity in the amygdala, thalamus, and the medial temporal gyrus compared to the control group. Raine, et al. (1998a) also compared PET scans between affective murderers (N = 9), predatory murderers (N = 15), and matched controls (N = 41). In relation to comparisons, the affective murderers and the predatory murderers both had higher right hemisphere subcortical functioning and lower prefrontal to subcortical ratios in the right hemisphere. The two groups of murderers differed, however, in their levels of prefrontal functioning. Specifically, the affective murderers demonstrated reduced activity in the prefrontal region compared to the other groups while the prefrontal activity in predatory murderers did not significantly differ from comparisons.

In addition to studying a criminal population, such as murderers, researchers also examine psychiatric patients in order to determine the association between brain functioning and violent behavior. Studies comparing PET scans from violent psychiatric patients to those from nonviolent psychiatric patients reveal that violent patients generally have increased blood flow and metabolic disruptions in the left temporal lobe (Volkow & Tancredi, 1987), reduced functioning in the medial temporal and prefrontal cortices (Volkow, et al., 1995), and decreased metabolism in the orbitofrontal cortex (Goyer, et al., 1994). Overall, these PET studies demonstrate that dysfunction in several areas of the brain is associated with aggressive and violent behavior. Another technique used to assess the functional properties of the brain is the single photon emission tomography.

Single Photon Emission Computed Tomography (SPECT)

Similar to PET, SPECT is used to assess the brain's functional properties. The main objectives of PET and SPECT are to measure glucose metabolism in the brain and to examine the **regional cerebral blood flow (RCBF)**. Although SPECT is a less sophisticated neuroimaging technique compared to PET, its relatively low cost and rapid results make it a desirable instrument. Several studies assessing the relationship between brain functioning and violent and antisocial behavior have relied on SPECT (Amen, et al., 1996; Goethals, et al., 2005; Graber, et al., 1982; Hendricks, et al., 1988; Hirono, et al., 2000; Kuruoglu, et al., 1996).

For example, a study conducted by Goethals, et al. (2005) found that patients (N = 37) diagnosed with either borderline personality disorder or antisocial personality disorder had significantly reduced RCBF in the right lateral temporal cortex and the polar and ventrolateral parts of the right prefrontal cortex compared to 34 healthy control subjects. Also, Hirono, et al. (2000) prospectively assessed patients with dementia who were either aggressive (N = 10) or nonaggressive (N = 10). SPECT scans revealed that aggressive dementia patients had reduced functioning in the left anterior temporal cortex, right superior parietal cortex, and in the bilateral dorsolateral frontal cortex. In an additional study conducted by Kuruoglu, et al. (1996), SPECT scans from 40 alcoholics, 15 of whom were diagnosed with antisocial personality disorder, were compared to those from 10 healthy matched controls. The results revealed a significant reduction in frontal functioning in alcoholic patients compared to the control group. Among the alcoholics who were diagnosed with antisocial personality disorder, there was significant dysfunction in the anterior frontal cortex as well as low blood flow in the right parietal and left temporal regions.

Although most SPECT studies have relied on scans from psychiatrically disordered patients, pedophiles and sexual sadists have also demonstrated reduced regional cerebral blood flow, particularly in the frontal areas (Garnett, et al., 1988; Graber, et al., 1982). Overall, the results from the SPECT studies reveal that there is a strong association between brain functioning, measured by glucose metabolism and regional cerebral blood flow, and violent and antisocial behavior.

The cumulative evidence from the neuroimaging studies, using CT, MRI, PET, and/or SPECT, reveals a strong relationship between brain structure and functioning with aggressive and other antisocial behaviors. As advancement in neuroimaging continues, it will become increasingly easier to pinpoint the structural and functional abnormalities in the brain that are associated with various behavioral problems.

Criminology for the 21st Century

We began this chapter by criticizing sociological criminology for its exclusion of neuroscience in general, and biology and genetics specifically. We believe substantial insights into the development and maintenance of criminal propensity can be gained from the consilience, or the uniting, of neuroscience and sociology (Walsh, 2000, 2002; Walsh & Ellis, 2003; Wilson, 1998). We also agree with Kanazawa (2004:372) that "the claim that social sciences are not part of biology . . . may be as peculiar and unnecessary as the establishment of hydrogenology, the study of hydrogen apart from and incompatible with physics." From our perspective, criminology must embrace and incorporate findings from fields with parallel interests in human development and antisocial behavior. We envision a *biosocial* criminology, which is interdisciplinary and attempts to integrate social and biological research.

Sociological criminology, as we mentioned earlier, has nothing to fear from the incorporation of neuroscience. Indeed, neuroscientific methods and findings provide at least three key insights that can increase greater sociological understanding into human behavior and development. First, neuroscience offers "hard" evidence of the origins of human traits and instincts. Unlike social theories that attribute human differences to distal socialization variables, neuroscience shows precisely where these differences are housed and provides irrefutable evidence of their origins. Take, for example, Gottfredson and Hirschi's (1990) theory of low self-control. Clearly, low self-control, or the inability to plan, to control emotional impulses, and the tendency to act on the spur of the moment, is related to a host of criminal and non-criminal but deleterious life outcomes (Pratt and Cullen, 2000). Neuroscience long ago classified these abilities as executive functions—or higher order thought processes that vary across humans.

Gottfredson and Hirschi attribute the origins of low self-control to parenting and hypothesize that levels of self-control are set between the ages of 8 and 10. They also openly exclude any possibility that genetic factors influence or cause self-control. However, self-control, and its parent concept of impulsivity, has been studied extensively by neuroscientists. *All* scientific data indicate that self-control is housed in the frontal and prefrontal cortex (Barkley, 1997a, 1997b, 1998; Baron-Cohen, 2003), that self-control is strongly influenced by genetic factors expressed in the brain (Congdon & Canli, 2005; Meyer-Lindenberg, et al., 2006), and that self-control involves a complex, dynamic balancing of limbic and cortical functioning. In one of the most persuasive studies, Meyer-Lindenberg and his colleagues (2006) genotyped a sample of 97 subjects, categorizing the sample by MAO-A allele length (efficiency). They then subjected these subjects to MRI scans of their brain. Their results graphically depict how the brains of these individuals varied based on allelic differences in the MAO-A enzyme. Meyer-Lindenberg, et al. found significant reductions in gray matter volume in the cingulate gyrus, the amygdala, and the hypothalamus. They also found that carriers of the short version of the MAO allele had less connection between the orbitalfrontal cortex and the amygdala, which is critical for emotion expression and regulation, and they found that, *in men only*, inhibitory control was significantly reduced by deficient activation of the **dorsal anterior cingulate**.

Clearly, Gottfredson and Hirschi are incorrect about the location of self-control. Moreover, it also appears that they are incorrect in their hypothesis linking parenting behavior to the development of self-control. As other studies have found, there are clear reasons to suspect that parenting influences, outside of the passive transfer of nuclear material, have little to do with levels of offspring self-control (Beaver & Wright, 2005; Harris, 1995, 1998; Rowe, 1994; Wright & Beaver, 2005).

Second, one of the most basic but critical limitations of environmentally pure explanations of criminal behavior hinges on individual variation. Humans, it seems, react to and are affected differentially by environmental stimuli (Caspi & Moffitt, 2006; Caspi, et al., 2004; Jaffee, et al., 2005; Kim-Cohen, et al., 2006; Rutter, et al., 2006). It is well known, for instance, that early environmental deprivation, neglect, and abuse are risk factors for later behavioral pathology (Widom, 1989). However, it is also well known that not all kids, or even the majority of youth, exposed to these risk factors develop serious behavior problems. For the most part, humans are highly resistant to even the most pronounced environmental stresses.

Individual variation to stressful environments has been well documented. Individuals respond differentially to child abuse (see Kim-Cohen, et al., 2006; see also Chapter 3, this volume) to economic deprivation, to bullying victimization, and to life stress (Arseneault, et al., 2006; Bricker, et al., 2006; Caspi, et al., 2003; Jaffee, et al., 2004a, 2004b; Kim-Cohen, et al., 2004). For the most part, humans are not susceptible to the deleterious influences of a range of difficult and taxing social conditions.

Finally, social influences are capable of altering brain structure and function above and beyond ontogenic development. Evidence for this can be garnered from studies of Romanian orphans, infants and children exposed to some of the most depriving and neglectful social conditions possible. After the collapse of the Nicolas Ceauşescu's dictatorial government, pictures of thousands of children in dilapidated state institutions emerged. These children, products of policies that required women to give birth and relinquish control of their offspring to the state, lived and developed in filthy environments barren of human contact and care.

Many of these orphans were eventually adopted by parents in the United States and Canada.

At the time of adoption, the majority of orphans were undernourished and were substantially delayed in their physical growth. In one study, one-half of the sample scored at or below the third percentile in height, weight, and developmental quotient (Rutter, 1996). There were impressive gains in physical and social functioning over time, however, depending on the orphan's age of entrance into the orphanage. The older the orphan at the time of his entrance into the orphanage, the better the long-term results. While the catch-up in development has been called "impressive," many orphans retain problems in the regulation of their conduct. Orphans who entered the orphanages prior to the age of 2 tended to suffer from hyper-activity, ADHD, and impulsiveness at unusually high rates (Fisher, et al., 1997; O'Conner, et al., 2000; Wilson, 2003).

This set of findings illustrates well the problem of attributing environ-mental deprivation to behavioral maladjustment. If deprivation causes or promotes behavioral maladaptation, it has to do so through its influence on the central nervous system. To evaluate this likelihood, Chugani, et al. (2001) imaged the brains of adopted orphans. Their results confirmed that orphans suffered from mild cognitive impairment and had prob-lems with behavior, impulsiveness, and maintaining attention. Orphans showed decreased glucose metabolism in the orbital frontal cortex, in the amygdala, the hippocampus, the brain stem, and the temporal cortex. Further evidence was provided by the MRI study conducted by Eluvathingal, et al. (2006), which found evidence consistent with environmentally induced structural alterations to the human brain, par-ticularly the **uncinate fasciculus**, which connects various regions of the brain to one another.

The union between the social and biological sciences is already taking place and will inevitably affect the field of criminology. Our discipline can little afford its continued allegiance to an ideology that systematically excludes hard scientific fact in favor of what is tantamount to fictional storytelling. Bringing biology into the equation of criminal conduct elu-cidates more clearly how and why certain social influences have an effect on the development of specific individuals as well as how and why other individuals remain immune to the same social factors. Far from being "reductionistic," as is so often alleged by our sociological brethren, incorporation of biology and brain sciences will highlight and expand the linkages between neurons and neighborhoods. The evidence pre-sented in this chapter is one small step in that direction; the evidence presented in this book, however, represents a potential leap into the 21st century.

Note

1. As we wrote this chapter, Nobel laureate, and co-discoverer of DNA, James Watson, was terminated from his position at the Cold Springs Harbor Laboratory where his name enshrines the Watson School of Biological Sciences. He was removed for his remarks about varying evolutionary pathways that may have lead to IQ differences between races. We have yet to hear of a sociologist or any other scholar removed from an academic position for passing off ideology as scientific fact. Open, scientific discourse is necessary if science is to progress. We dedicate this paper to Watson and to others who have suffered at the cross of political correctness (JPW).

References

Aigner, M., R. Eher, S. Fruehwald, P. Frottier, K. Gutierrez-Labos, & S. M. Dwyer (2000). Brain abnormalities and violent behavior. *Journal of Psychology and Human Sexuality*, 11:57–64.

Amen, D. G., M. Stubblefield, B. Carmichael, & R. Thisted (1996). Brain SPECT findings and aggressiveness. *Annals of Clinical Psychiatry*, 8:129–137.

Arseneault, L., E. Walsh, K. Trzesniewski, R. Newcombe, A. Caspi, & T. E. Moffitt (2006). Bullying victimization uniquely contributes to adjustment problems in young children: a nationally representative cohort study. *Pediatrics*, 118:130–138.

Barkley, R. A. (1997a). *ADHD and the nature of self-control*. New York: Guilford Press.

Barkley, R. A. (1997b). Behavioral inhibition, sustained attention, and executive functions: constructing a unifying theory of ADHD. *Psychological Bulletin*, 121:65–94.

Barkley, R. A. (1998). *Attention-deficit hyperactivity disorder*. New York: Scientific American, Inc.

Baron-Cohen, S. (2003). *The essential difference: The truth about the male and female brain*. New York: Perseus Books Group.

Beaver, K. M. & J. P. Wright (2005). Evaluating the effects of birth complications on low self-control in a sample of twins. *International Journal of Offender Therapy and Comparative Criminology*, 49:450–471.

Bricker, J. B., M. C. Stallings, R. P. Corley, S. J. Wadsworth, A. Bryan, & D. S. Timberlake (2006). Genetic and environmental influences on age at sexual initiation in the Colorado Adoption Project. *Behavior Genetics*, 36:820–832.

Caspi, A. & T. E. Moffitt (2006). Gene—environment interactions in psychiatry: joining forces with neuroscience. *Nature Reviews Neuroscience*, 7:583–590.

Caspi, A., J. McClay, T. E. Moffitt, J. Mill, J. Martin, & I. W. Craig (2002). Role of genotype in the cycle of violence in maltreated children. *Science*, 297:851–854.

Caspi, A., T. E. Moffitt, J. Morgan, M. Rutter, A. Taylor, L. Arseneault, et al. (2004). Maternal expressed emotion predicts children's antisocial behavior problems: using monozygotic-twin differences to identify environmental effects on behavioral development. *Developmental Psychology*, 40:149–161.

Caspi, A., K. Sugden, T. E. Moffitt, A. Taylor, I. W. Craig, H. Harrington, et al. (2003). Influence of life stress on depression: moderation by a polymorphism in the 5-HTT gene. *Science*, 301:386–389.

Cauffman, E., L. Steinberg, & A. R. Piquero (2005). Psychological, neuropsychological and physiological correlates of serious antisocial behavior in adolescence: the role of self-control. *Criminology*, 43:133–175.

Chugani, H. T., M. E. Behen, O. Muzik, C. Juhasz, F. Nagy, & D. C. Chugani (2001). Local brain functional activity following early deprivation: a study of postinstitutionalized Romanian orphans. *NeuroImage*, 14:1290–301.

Congdon, E. & T. Canli (2005). The endophenotype of impulsivity: reaching consilience through behavioral, genetic, and neuroimaging approaches. *Behavioral and Cognitive Neuroscience Reviews*, 4:262–281.

Davidson, R. J., K. M. Putnam, & C. L. Larson (2000). Dysfunction in the neural circuitry of emotion regulation—a possible prelude to violence. *Science*, 28:591–594.

Eluvathingal, T. J., H. T. Chugani, M. E. Behen, C. Juhasz, O. Muzik, M. Maqbool, et al. (2006).

Abnormal brain connectivity in children after early severe socio-emotional deprivation: a diffusion tensor imaging study. *Pediatrics*, 117:2093–2100.

Eysenck, H. J. (1964). *Crime and personality*. Boston, MA: Houghton-Mifflin.

Fisher, L., E. W. Ames, K. Chisholm, & L. Savoie (1997). Problems reported by parents of Romanian orphans adopted to British Columbia. *International Journal of Behavioral Development*, 20:67–82.

Garnett, E. S., C. Nahmias, G. Wortzman, R. Langevin, & R. Dickey (1988). Positron emission tomography and sexual arousal in a sadist and two controls. *Annals of Sex Research*, 1:387–399.

Giedd, J. N. (2004). Structural magnetic resonance imaging of the adolescent brain. *Annals of the New York Academy of Sciences*, 1021:77–85.

Giedd, J. N., Clasen, L. S., Lenroot, R., Greenstein, D., Wallace, G. L., & Ordaz, S. (2006). Puberty-related influences on brain development. *Molecular and Cellular Endocrinology*, 254–255:154–162.

Giedd, J. N., J. Blumenthal, N. O. Jeffries, F. X. Castellanos, H. Liu, A. Zijdenbos, et al. (1999). Brain development during childhood and adolescence: a longitudinal MRI study. *Nature Neuroscience*, 2:861–863.

Goethals, I., K. Audenaert, F. Jacobs, F. Van den Eynde, K. Bernagie, A. Kolindou, et al. (2005). Brain perfusion SPECT in impulsivity-related personality disorders. *Behavioural Brain Research*, 157:187–192.

Gogtay, N., J. N. Giedd, L. Lusk, K. M. Hayashi, D. Greenstein, A. C. Vaituzis, et al. (2004). Dynamic mapping of human cortical development during childhood through early adulthood. *Proceedings of the National Academy of Sciences of the United States of America*, 101:8174–8179.

Goldberg, E. (2001). *The executive brain: frontal lobes and the civilized mind*. New York: Oxford University Press.

Gottfredson, M. R. & T. Hirschi (1990). *A general theory of crime*. Stanford, CA: Stanford University Press.

Goyer, P. F., P.J. Andreason, W. E. Semple, A. H. Clayton, A. C. King, B. A. Compton-Toth, et al. (1994). Positron-emission tomography and personality disorders. *Neuropsychopharmacology*, 10:21–28.

Graber, B., K. Hartmann, J. A. Coffman, C. J. Huey, & C. J. Golden (1982). Brain damage among mentally disordered offenders. *Journal of Forensic Science*, 27:125–134.

Harris, J. R. (1995). Where is the child's environment? A group socialization theory of development. *Psychological Review*, 102:458–489.

Harris, J. R. (1998). *The nurture assumption: why children turn out the way they do*. New York: Free Press.

Hendricks, S. E., D. F. Fitzpatrick, K. Hartmann, M. A. Quaife, R. A. Stratbucker, & B. Graber (1988). Brain structure and function in sexual molesters of children and adolescents. *Journal of Clinical Psychiatry*, 49:108–112.

Herzberg, J. L. & P. B. C. Fenwick (1988). The aetiology of aggression in temporal lobe epilepsy. *British Journal of Psychiatry*, 153:50–55.

Hindelang, M. J. (1971). Extroversion, neuroticism, and self-reported delinquent involvement. *Journal of Research in Crime and Delinquency*, 8:23–31.

Hirono, N., M. S. Mega, I. D. Dinov, F. Mishkin, & J. L. Cummings (2000). Left frontotemporal hypoperfusion is associated with aggression in patients with dementia. *Archives of Neurology*, 57:861–866.

Hucker, S., R. Langevin, G. Wortzman, J. Bain, L. Handy, J. Chambers, et al. (1986). Neuropsychological impairment in pedophiles. *Canadian Journal of Behavioral Science*, 18:440–448.

Hucker, S., R. Langevin, G. Wortzman, R. Dickey, J. Bain, L. Handy, et al. (1988). Cerebral damage and dysfunction in sexually aggressive men. *Annals of Sex Research*, 1:33–47.

Jaffee, S. R., A. Caspi, T. E. Moffitt, & A. Taylor (2004a). Physical maltreatment victim to antisocial child: evidence of an environmentally mediated process. *Journal of Abnormal Psychology*, 113:44–55.

Jaffee, S. R., A. Caspi, T. E. Moffitt, M. Polo-Tomas, T. S. Price, & A. Taylor (2004b). The limits of child effects: evidence for genetically mediated child effects on corporal punishment but not on physical maltreatment. *Developmental Psychology*, 40:1047–1058.

Jaffee, S. R., A. Caspi, T. E. Moffitt, K. A. Dodge, M. Rutter, A. Taylor, et al. (2005). Nature X nurture: genetic vulnerabilities interact with physical maltreatment to promote conduct problems. *Development and Psychopathology*, 17:67–84.

Kanazawa, S. (2004). Social sciences are branches of biology. *Socio-Economic Review*, 2:371–390.

Karr-Morse, R. & M. S. Wiley (1997). *Ghosts from the nursery: Tracing the roots of violence*. New York: Atlantic Monthly Press.

Kim-Cohen, J., T. E. Moffitt, A. Caspi, & A. Taylor (2004). Genetic and environmental processes in young children's resilience and vulnerability to socioeconomic deprivation. *Child Development*, 75:651–668.

Kim-Cohen, J., A. Caspi, A. Taylor, B. Williams, R. Newcombe, I. W. Craig, et al. (2006). MAOA, maltreatment, and gene–environment interaction predicting children's mental health: new evidence and a meta-analysis. *Molecular Psychiatry*, 11:903–913.

Koestler, A. (1968). *The ghost in the machine*. London: Picador Books.

Kuruoglu, A. C., Z. Arikan, G. Vural, M. Karatas, M. Arac, M., & E. Isik (1996). Single photon emission computerized tomography in chronic alcoholism: antisocial personality disorder may be associated with decreased frontal perfusion. *British Journal of Psychiatry*, 169:348–354.

Langevin, R., M. Ben-Aron, G. Wortzman, R. Dickey, & L. Handy (1987). Brain damage, diagnosis, and substance abuse among violent offenders. *Behavioral Sciences and the Law*, 5:77–94.

Langevin, R., G. Wortzman, P. Wright, & L. Handy (1989a). Studies of brain damage and dysfunction in sex offenders. *Annals of Sex Research*, 2:163–179.

Langevin, R., R. A. Lang, G. Wortzman, R. R. Frenzel, & P. Wright (1989b). An examination of brain damage and dysfunction in genital exhibitionists. *Annals of Sex Research*, 2:77–94.

Langevin, R., G. Wortzman, R. Dickey, P. Wright, & L. Handy (1988). Neuropsychological impairment in incest offenders. *Annals of Sex Research*, 1:401–415.

Listwan, S. J., P. Van Voorhis, & P. N. Ritchey (2007). Personality, criminal behavior, and risk assessment: implications for theory and practice. *Criminal Justice and Behavior*, 34:60–75.

Meyer-Lindenberg, A., J. W. Buckhoitz, B. Kolachana, A. R. Haririt, L. Pezawas, G. Blasi, et al. (2006). Neural mechanisms of genetic risk for impulsivity and violence in humans. *Proceedings of the National Academy of Sciences of the United States of America*, 103:6269–6274.

O'Conner, T. G., M. Rutter, C. Beckett, L. Keaveney, & J. M. Kreppner (2000). The English and Romanian Adoptees study team. The effects of global severe privation on cognitive competence: extension and longitudinal follow-up. *Child Development*, 71:376–390.

Pakkenberg, B. & H. J. G. Gundersen (1997). Neocortical neuron number in humans: effect of sex and age. *The Journal of Comparative Neurology*, 384:312–320.

Pratt, T. C. & F. T Cullen (2000). The empirical status of Gottfredson and Hirschi's general theory of crime: a meta-analysis. *Criminology*, 38:931–964.

Raine, A., M. S. Buchsbaum, & L. LaCasse (1997). Brain abnormalities in murderers indicated by positron emission tomography. *Biological Psychiatry*, 42:495–508.

Raine, A., T. Lencz, S. Bihrle, L. LaCasse, & P. Colletti (2000). Reduced prefrontal gray matter volume and reduced autonomic activity in antisocial personality disorder. *Archives of General Psychiatry*, 57:119–127.

Raine, A., M. S. Buchsbaum, J. Stanley, S. Lottenberg, L. Abel, & J. Stoddard (1994). Selective reductions in prefrontal glucose metabolism in murderers. *Society of Biological Psychiatry*, 36:365–373.

Raine, A., J. R. Meloy, S. Bihrle, J. Stoddard, L. LaCasse, & M. S. Buchsbaum (1998a). Reduced prefrontal and increased subcortical brain functioning assessed using positron emission tomography in predatory and affective murderers. *Behavioral Sciences and Law*, 16:319–332.

Raine, A., J. Stoddard, S. Bihrle, & M. Buchsbaum (1998b). Prefrontal glucose deficits in murderers lacking psychosocial deprivation. *Neuropsychiatry, Neuropsychology, and Behavioral Neurology*, 11:1–7.

Robinson, M. B. (2004). *Why crime? An integrated systems theory of antisocial behavior*. Upper Saddle River, NJ: Prentice-Hall.

Rowe, D. C. (1994). *The limits of family influence: genes, experience, and behavior*. New York: Guilford Press.

Rutter, M. (1996). Romanian orphans adopted early overcome deprivation. *The Brown University Child and Adolescent Behavior Letter*, 12:1–3.

Rutter, M., T. E. Moffitt, & A. Caspi (2006). Gene–environment interplay and psychopathology: multiple varieties but real effects. *Journal of Child Psychology and Psychiatry*, 47:226–261.

Sakuta, A. & A. Fukushima (1998). A study on abnormal findings pertaining to the brain in criminals. *International Medical Journal*, 5:283–292.

Schoepfer, A. & A. R. Piquero (2006). Self-control, moral beliefs, and criminal activity. *Deviant Behavior*, 27:51–71.

Tonkonogy, J. M. (1991). Violence and temporal lobe lesion: head CT and MRI data. *Journal of Neuropsychiatry and Clinical Neurosciences*, 3:189–196.

Van Elst, L. T., F. G. Woermann, L. Lemieux, P. J. Thompson, & M. R. Trimble (2000). Affective aggression in patients with temporal lobe epilepsy: a quantitative MRI study of the amygdala. *Brain*, 123:234–243.

Volkow, N. D. & L. Tancredi (1987). Neural substrates of violent behavior: a preliminary study with positron emission tomography. *British Journal of Psychiatry*, 151:668–673.

Volkow, N. D., L. R. Tancredi, C. Grant, H. Gillespie, A. Valentine, N. Mullani, et al. (1995). Brain glucose metabolism in violent psychiatric patients: a preliminary study. *Psychiatry Research: Neuroimaging*, 61:243–253.

Walsh, A. (2000). Behavior genetics and anomie/strain theory. *Criminology*, 38:1075–1107.

Walsh, A. (2002). *Biosocial criminology: introduction and integration.* Cincinnati, OH: Anderson Publishing.

Walsh, A. & L. Ellis (2003). *Biosocial criminology: challenging environmentalism's supremacy.* Hauppauge, NY: Nova Science Publishers.

Widom, C. S. (1989). Child abuse, neglect, and violent criminal behavior. *Criminology*, 27:251–271.

Wilson, E. O. (1998). *Consilience: the unity of knowledge.* New York: Alfred A. Knopf.

Wilson, S. L. (2003). Post-institutionalization: the effects of early deprivation on development of Romanian adoptees. *Child and Adolescent Social Work Journal*, 20:473–483.

Woermann, F. G., L. Tebartz van Elst, M. J. Koepp, S. L. Free, P. J. Thompson, M. R. Trimble, et al. (2000). Reduction of frontal neocortical gray matter associated with affective aggression in patients with temporal lobe epilepsy: an objective voxel by voxel analysis of automatically segmented MRI. *Journal of Neurology, Neurosurgery, and Psychiatry*, 68:162–169.

Wong, M., P. Fenwick, G. Fenton, J. Lumsden, M. Maisey, & J. Stevens (1997). Repetitive and non-repetitive violent offending behavior in male patients in a maximum security mental hospital: clinical and neuroimaging findings. *Medicine, Science, and the Law*, 37:150–160.

Wong, M. T. H., J. Lumsden, G. W. Fenton, & P. B. C. Fenwick (1994). Electroencephalography, computed tomography and violence ratings of male patients in a maximum-security mental hospital. *Acta Psychiatrica Scandinavica*, 90:97–101.

Wright, J. P. & K. M. Beaver (2005). Do parents matter in creating self-control in their children? A genetically informed test of Gottfredson and Hirschi's theory of low self-control. *Criminology*, 43:1169–1202.

Wright, P., J. Nobrega, R. Langevin, & G. Wortzman (1990). Brain density and symmetry in pedophilic and sexually aggressive offenders. *Annals of Sex Research*, 3:319–328.

5

Evolutionary Psychology and Crime

Satoshi Kanazawa

Evolutionary psychology is the study of universal human nature, or the sex-specific male human nature and female human nature. **Human nature** consists of domain-specific evolved psychological mechanisms. A **psychological mechanism** is an information-processing procedure or "decision rule" which evolution by natural and sexual selection has equipped humans to possess in order to solve an **adaptive problem** (problem of survival or reproduction). Unlike decision rules in decision theory or game theory, however, psychological mechanisms mostly operate behind our conscious thinking. Evolved psychological mechanisms produce values and preferences, which actors then pursue within their constraints; they also engender emotions (Kanazawa, 2001).

Figure 5.1 presents the basic theoretical structure of evolutionary psychology. Some adaptive problem during the course of human evolutionary history has led to the evolution of psychological mechanisms through natural and sexual selection. Natural selection refers to the process of differential survival; sexual selection refers to the process of differential reproductive success.[1] Individuals who possess certain psychological mechanisms live longer (because the psychological mechanisms help them survive) and reproduce more successfully (because the psychological mechanisms help them find and keep mates). Those with such psychological mechanisms outreproduce those without them in each generation,

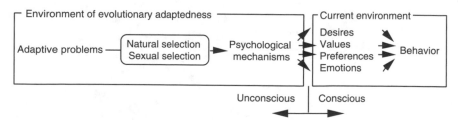

Figure 5.1 Basic Theoretical Structure of Evolutionary Psychology.

and more and more individuals come to possess the psychological mechanisms generation after generation. Eventually, all individuals come to possess them, and they become part of universal (species-typical) human nature. Because men and women often faced different selection pressures through the course of evolution, especially in the area of sexual selection, men and women often have distinct evolved psychological mechanisms, and hence separate male and female human natures. Beyond the sex differences, however, evolved psychological mechanisms, and hence human nature they comprise, are species-typical, shared by all members of the species. Evolved psychological mechanisms then engender desires, values, preferences, emotions, and other internal states which serve as the proximate causes of behavior.

From an evolutionary psychological perspective, the ultimate (albeit unconscious) function of all biological organisms, including humans, is to increase reproductive success. We are designed to reproduce by evolution by natural and sexual selection. The fact that many of us do not think that is the ultimate function of our existence or that some of us choose not to reproduce is immaterial. We are not privy to the evolutionary logic behind our design, and, no matter what we choose to do in our own lifetimes, we are all descended from those who chose to reproduce, and we are *disproportionately* descended from those who attained *disproportionate* reproductive success. Twelve children inherit the psychological mechanisms of someone who had 12 children, but only one child inherits those of someone who had only one child. And none of us inherited our psychological mechanisms from our ancestors who remained childless. Whether we like it or not, whether we know it or not, reproductive success, creating as many copies of our genes as possible, is the ultimate purpose of life for all living creatures, and humans are no exception in nature. Everything else, even survival, is a means toward reproductive success.

Male sexual jealousy is an example of an evolved psychological mechanism (Daly, et al., 1982). Because gestation in human and most other mammalian species occurs inside the female body, males of these species can never be certain of the paternity of their mates' offspring, while females are always certain of their maternity. In other words, the possibility of cuckoldry exists only for males. Men who are cuckolded and invest their limited resources in the genetic offspring of another man end up wasting these resources, and their genes will not be represented in the next generation. Men therefore have a strong reproductive interest in making sure that they will not be cuckolded, while women do not share this interest. Accordingly, men have been selected to possess a psychological mechanism that makes them extremely jealous at even the remotest possibility of their mate's sexual infidelity. The psychological mechanism of sexual jealousy attenuates men's adaptive problem of paternity uncertainty. The same psychological mechanism often leads to men's attempt at mate guarding, in order to minimize the possibility of their mate's sexual contact with other men, sometimes with violent and tragic consequences.

I must here emphasize two important principles of evolutionary psychology. First, and to reiterate, *evolved psychological mechanisms mostly operate unconsciously*. Humans (just like members of other species) are not always privy to the evolutionary logic behind our psychological mechanisms. We are, however, aware of the desires, values, preferences, and emotions that our psychological mechanisms engender in us (as Figure 5.1 indicates), and we consciously and rationally set about to pursue these goals within our constraints (Kanazawa, 2001).

Second, *evolved psychological mechanisms need only be adaptive in the environment in which they evolved, called the environment of evolutionary adaptedness or the ancestral environment.* For the most part, the environment of evolutionary adaptedness refers to the African savanna during the Pleistocene epoch about 1.6 million to 10,000 years ago.[2] To the extent that our current environment is radically different from the ancestral environment, our evolved psychological mechanisms might produce maladaptive behavior. Recall the example of male sexual jealousy as an evolved psychological mechanism. It solved the adaptive problem of successful reproduction in the ancestral environment by allowing men who possessed it to maximize paternity certainty and minimize the possibility of cuckoldry. The sexual jealousy was therefore adaptive *in the ancestral environment*. However, sex and reproduction are often separated in the current environment. There is an abundance of reliable methods of birth control in industrial societies, and many married women use the birth control pill. For these women, sexual infidelity does not lead to childbirth, and their mates will not have to waste their resources on someone else's genetic offspring. In other words, the original adaptive problem no longer exists; men whose wives are on the pill can never be cuckolded. However, men still possess the same psychological mechanisms to make them jealous at the possibility of their mate's sexual infidelity and to compel them to guard their mate to minimize the possibility of cuckoldry. *No man would ever be comforted by the fact that his adulterous wife was on the pill at the time of her sexual infidelity.*

Further, because our environment is so vastly different from the ancestral environment, we now face a curious situation where those who behave according to the dictates of the evolved psychological mechanism are often *worse off* in terms of survival or reproductive success. Extreme forms of mate guarding, such as violence against mates or romantic rivals, are felonies in most industrial nations. Incarceration, and consequent physical separation from their mates, to which such violence can lead, does everything to *reduce* the reproductive success of the men. Uncritically following the emotions and desires engendered in us by our evolved psychological mechanisms often leads to maladaptive behavior in the current environment.

Evolutionary Psychological Perspective on Crime

In their comprehensive study of homicide from an evolutionary psychological perspective, Daly and Wilson (1988:137–161) note that humans throughout their evolutionary history were effectively polygynous. Even in nominally monogamous societies, such as the United States, many men practice serial **polygyny**, through a sequence of divorce and remarriage; in other words, they can have multiple wives, not simultaneously, but sequentially, and thereby exclude other men from access to these women during their reproductive years. Only societies that prohibit simultaneous polygyny, divorce, and extramarital affairs are strictly monogamous, and no human society falls into this category.

In a polygynous breeding system, some males monopolize reproductive access to all females while other males are left out; in such a system, some males do not get to reproduce at all while almost all females do. This inequality of reproductive success (or fitness variance) between males and females makes males of species with polygynous breeding systems (such as humans) highly competitive, in their effort not to be left out of the reproductive game. This intrasexual competition among men leads to a high level of violence among them, and the large number of homicides between men (compared to the number of homicides between women or between the sexes) is a direct result of this intrasexual competition and violence.

In particular, Daly and Wilson (1988:123–136) note that most homicides between men originate from what Wolfgang (1958) calls "trivial altercations." A typical homicide begins as a fight about trivial matters of honor, status, and reputation between men (such as when one man insults another). Fights escalate because neither is willing to back down, until they become violent and one of the disputants ends up dead. Because women prefer to mate with men of high status and good reputation (Buss, 1989), men's status and reputation correlate directly with their reproductive success. Men are therefore highly motivated to protect their honor, and often go to extreme lengths to do so, compelled by their evolved psychological mechanisms. Daly and Wilson thus explain homicides between men in terms of their (largely unconscious) desire to protect their status and reputation in their attempt to gain reproductive access to women.

One can easily extend this analysis to other forms of interpersonal violence among men. Less serious violent crimes, such as assault and battery, can have the same underlying motive to protect one's status and reputation in an effort to gain reproductive access. Whether the violence results in a death (making the crime homicide) or an injury (making the crime serious assault) is often beyond the conscious control of the offender. It crucially depends on the reaction of the victim and what transpires between the offender and the victim in the course of the conflict, as well as other fortuitous circumstances such as the presence and reactions of others, distance to the nearest hospital and the physical strength of the victim. If men can be driven to kill in order to protect their status and reputation, they can easily be driven to commit less serious acts of violence.

Rape appears to be an exception to this reasoning, because, unlike murder and assault, the victims of rape are women and there is therefore no intrasexual competition for status and reputation. However, the same psychological mechanism that inclines men to gain reproductive access to women can motivate men to rape. Predatory rapists are overwhelmingly men of lower class and status, who have very dim prospects to gain legitimate access to women (Thornhill & Thornhill, 1983). While it is not a manifestation of intrasexual competition and violence, rape might also be motivated by men's psychological mechanism that inclines them to gain reproductive access to women when they do not have the legitimate means to do so.

One can also extend the same analysis to property crimes. If women prefer to mate with men with more resources, then men can increase their reproductive success by acquiring material resources. Material resources in traditional societies, which are usually gerontocratic, however, tend to be concentrated in the hands of elder men. Younger men are often excluded from attaining them through legitimate means and must therefore resort to illegitimate means. One method of doing so is to appropriate someone else's resources by stealing them. Thus the same psychological mechanism that creates the motive for violent crime can also induce men to commit property crimes.

My suggestion that men kill and steal in order to attract women might at first sight appear counterintuitive, because murder, assault, robbery, theft and other forms of interpersonal violence and resource malappropriation are universally condemned in human societies (Brown, 1991). It is quite possible, however, that the psychological mechanisms that incline and predispose men to commit property crimes developed in our ancestors in evolutionary history before the ape–human split (5–8 million years ago), even before the ape–monkey split (15–20 million years ago). In fact, an evolutionary psychological perspective on crime *logically requires* that the key psychological mechanisms emerge before the informal norms against crime did; otherwise, resource accumulated and status attained through criminal behavior would not attract mates and lead to reproductive success for men because they would be ostracized for violating norms (unless, of course, the criminal act goes entirely undetected). I believe that the norms against crime might have developed *in reaction to* the psychological mechanisms that incline men to commit crime. The fact that behavior that would be classified as crime among humans—such as theft—appears to be common among our primate cousins who do not have third-party sanctions against such behavior (de Waal, 1989, 1992; de Waal, et al., 1993) seems to suggest that human tendency to commit crime might have evolved before norms against it.

Note that it is immaterial to an evolutionary psychological perspective on crime that most criminals do not cite reproductive success as a motive for their crimes. For, as noted already, psychological mechanisms usually operate at the unconscious level. My contention is that men under some circumstances commit crimes because they want to (making them highly criminal), and they want to commit crimes because something inclines them to. I contend that that something is the evolved psychological mechanism that predisposes all men to seek reproductive success. The men themselves are often unaware of the evolutionary logic behind their motives.

Empirical Puzzles

In addition to providing a comprehensive explanation of all criminal behavior, an evolutionary psychological perspective on crime can solve some of the persistent empirical puzzles within criminology.

Why Men, not Women?

In every human society, men commit an overwhelming majority of both violent and property crimes (Brown, 1991; Kanazawa & Still, 2000). Worldwide, men commit more than 90 percent of all crimes. Why is this?

One relatively unusual feature of the human mating system can account for the overwhelming male bias toward criminality. Unlike most other species in nature, human males make a large amount of parental investment in the offspring. The unusually high degree of *male parental investment* among humans leads to universal human female mate preference for men with a large amount of resources (Buss, 1989). The more resources a potential mate has, the more parental investment he can make in their joint children. Men's resources increase their children's chances of survival and their future reproductive prospects.

Because women prefer men with greater resources as their long-term mates, men fiercely compete with one another to accumulate resources and attain higher status. The more resources they possess and the higher the status they occupy, the greater the reproductive opportunities they have. Wealthier men of high status have more sex partners and copulate more frequently than poorer men of low status (Kanazawa, 2003a; Pérusse, 1993). Wealth and status do not affect women's desirability as long-term mates (Buss, 1989).

From an evolutionary psychological perspective, this is why men comprise an overwhelming majority of criminals worldwide. Material resources and status improve men's reproductive prospects much more than women's. We would therefore expect men to be much more motivated to accumulate material resources, either through legitimate or illegitimate means, than women. In fact, not only do men commit an overwhelming majority of theft and robberies worldwide, but they also make more money and attain higher status through legitimate means because they are more motivated to do so (Browne, 2002; Kanazawa, 2005a). Men are much more motivated to accumulate resources and attain status, whether through legitimate or illegitimate means, in order to attract mates.

That an overwhelming majority of criminals are men does not mean that women never commit crime; they do, of course. However, an evolutionary psychological perspective on female criminality (Campbell, 1995, 1999, 2002, Chapter 6, this volume) suggests that men and women may commit crime for different reasons.

For example, while men steal, not only to satisfy their material needs for food, shelter, and clothing, but also to compete with other men and gain status, women mostly steal only to satisfy their material needs. Campbell (1999:210) astutely points out that "theft by women is usually tied to economic needs and occurs as part of their domestic responsibilities for their children," whereas "robbery is the quintessential male crime, in which violence is used both to extract resources and to gain status." This is why, when women do steal, they steal much less, and much less frequently, than do men. Women steal what they need, men steal partly to show off.

A personal anecdote illustrates this point well. I moved to the London School of Economics and Political Science in July 2003. Within a month of my arrival in London, someone broke into my office and stole two blank checks, by carefully lifting two nonconsecutive checks in the middle of my new checkbook. When I learned from the bank that the two checks had been cashed for £700 each, I made the (statistically very unlikely to be true) prediction that the thief must have been a woman. As it turned out, it was two women. I later found out their identities from the bank, when they cashed the checks by making them out to themselves *in their real names*, perhaps illustrating another point that criminals are less intelligent than others (see later).[3]

Having read Campbell's work before this incident in 2003, it was immediately obvious to me that the thieves must have been women, because it seemed to me that £700 was rent money, not the kind of money to show off or to attract women. It is the kind of money one *needs*, not the kind of money one *wants*. I felt that a male thief would have made out the check for £700,000. Of course, I do not have that kind of money. However, from the thief's perspective, if there is at least one chance in 1,000 (.001%) that the check clears for that amount, he would still come out ahead by gambling on £700,000 rather than making it out for a safer bet of £700. Given men's much higher propensity toward risk taking, generally, I think a male thief might just have taken that chance.

Why Younger Men, not Older Men?

One of the advantages of an evolutionary psychological perspective on crime is that it can explain the universal **age–crime curve**. In their highly influential 1983 article "Age and explanation of crime," Hirschi and Gottfredson claim that the relationship between age and crime is invariant across all social and cultural conditions at all times. In every society, for all social groups, for all races and both sexes, at all historical times, the tendency to commit crimes and other analogous, risk-taking behavior rapidly increases in early adolescence, peaks in late adolescence and early adulthood, rapidly decreases throughout the 20s and 30s, and levels off during middle age. Although there have been minor variations observed around the "invariant" age–crime curve (Greenberg, 1985; Hirschi & Gottfredson, 1985), the essential shape of the curve for serious interpersonal crimes remains uncontested in the criminological literature. For empirical examples of the invariant age–crime curve, see Campbell (1995: Figure 1), Daly and Wilson (1990: Figure 1), and Hirschi and Gottfredson (1983: Figures 1–8).

While Hirschi and Gottfredson claim that the age–crime curve is invariant and holds in all societies at all times, they provide no explanations for this universal observation. They instead argue that no theoretical or empirical variable then available in criminology (in 1983) could explain it. If the age–crime curve is truly constant across all populations, any factor that varies across such populations cannot explain it. Just as a constant cannot explain a variable, a variable cannot explain a constant. The invariant age–crime curve must be explained by something that is constant across all societies and cultures at all times. An evolutionary psychological perspective suggests just such a constant factor (Kanazawa, 2003b; Kanazawa & Still, 2000; Rowe, 2002:53–55).

There are reproductive benefits for men of intense competition. Those who are highly competitive act violently toward their male rivals. Their violence serves the dual function of protecting their status, honor, and reputation, and of discouraging or altogether eliminating their rivals from competition for mates (Daly & Wilson, 1988, 1990). Their competitiveness also predisposes them to accumulate resources to attract mates by stealing from others (either via theft or robbery). The same psychological mechanism induces men who cannot gain legitimate access to women to do so illegitimately through forcible rape (Thornhill & Thornhill, 1983). Figure 5.2(a) represents a hypothetical curve, depicting the relationship between men's age and their benefit from competition. There are no reproductive benefits from competition (violence and theft) before puberty because prepubertal males are not able to translate their competitive edge into reproductive success. With puberty, however, the benefits of competition skyrocket. Once the men are reproductively capable, every act of violence and theft can potentially increase their reproductive success. The benefits of competition stay high after puberty for the remainder of their lives since human males are reproductively capable for most of their adult lives.

This is not the whole story, however. There are also costs associated with competition. Acts of violence can easily result in their own death or injury, and acts of resource malappropriation can trigger retaliation from the rightful owners of the resources and their family and allies. Men's reproductive success is obviously reduced if the competitive acts result in their death or injury. Figure 5.2(b) presents a hypothetical curve depicting the costs of competition as a function of age. Before men start reproducing (before their first child), there are few costs of competition. True, being competitive might result in death or injury, and they might therefore lose in the reproductive game. However, they also lose by not competing. If they don't compete for mates in a polygynous breeding system (which all human societies are; Daly & Wilson, 1988:140–142), they'll be left out of the reproductive game altogether and end up losing as a result. In other words, young men *might* lose if they were competitive, but they will *definitely* lose if they are not competitive. So there is little cost to being competitive even at the risk of death or injury; the alternative—total reproductive failure—is even worse in reproductive terms.

The cost of competition, however, rises dramatically with the birth of the first child and subsequent children. True, men still benefit from competition (as Figure 5.2(a) shows) because such acts of competition might attract additional mates and mating opportunities. However, men's

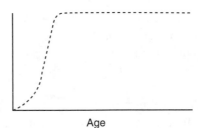

(a) Reproductive benefits of competition

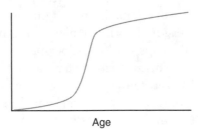

(b) Reproductive costs of competition

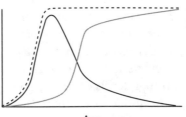

Age

(c) Propensity toward competition
= benefits − costs

Figure 5.2 Benefits and Costs of Competition and the Age–Crime Curve.

Source: Kanazawa and Still (2000). Copyright by the American Sociological Association. Reprinted with permission.

energies and resources are put to better use by protecting and investing in their existing children. In other words, with the birth of children, men should shift their reproductive effort away from *mating effort* and toward *parenting effort*, in the equation: Total reproductive effort = mating effort + parenting effort. If men die or get injured in their acts of competition, their existing children will suffer; without sufficient parental investment and protection, they might starve or fall victim to predation or exploitation by others. The costs of competition, therefore, rapidly increase after the birth of the first child, which usually happens several years after puberty because men need some time to accumulate sufficient resources to attract their first mate. Nonetheless, in the absence of artificial means of contraception, reproduction probably began at a much earlier age than it does today. There is thus a gap of several years between the rapid rise in the benefits of competition, and the similarly rapid rise in its costs.

Figure 5.2(c) depicts a curve that represents the mathematical difference between the benefits and the costs of competition. The curve (in the solid bold line) closely resembles the typical age–crime curve. An evolutionary psychological perspective suggests that male criminality varies as it does over the life-course because it represents the difference between the benefits and the costs of competition. It is important to note, however, that, unlike actors in decision theories in microeconomics (Grogger, 1998), men from an evolutionary psychological perspective do not make these calculations consciously. The calculations have already been performed by natural and sexual selection, so to speak, which then equips men's brains with appropriate psychological mechanisms to incline them to be increasingly competitive in their immediate postpubertal years and to make them less competitive right after the birth of the first child. Men simply do not *feel like* acting violently or stealing, or they just *want to* settle down, after the birth of their first child, but they do not necessarily know why.

Fluctuating levels of testosterone may provide the biochemical microfoundation for this psychological mechanism. David Gubernick's unpublished experiment (discussed in Blum, 1997:116) demonstrates that expectant fathers' testosterone levels fall precipitously immediately after the birth of their child. If high levels of testosterone predispose men to be more competitive, then the sudden drop in testosterone after the birth of their children may provide the biochemical reason why men's psychological mechanisms to commit crime "turn off" when they become fathers. Mazur and Michalek's (1998) finding that marriage decreases and divorce increases testosterone levels in men provide a similar microfoundation for the commonly observed negative effect of marriage on criminality (Kanazawa, 2003b; Laub, et al., 1998). Further consistent with this perspective, McIntyre, et al. (2006) show that married men who actively seek extrapair copulations retain high levels of testosterone characteristic of single men.

Given that human society was always mildly polygynous, there were many men who did not succeed in finding a mate and reproducing. These men had everything to gain and nothing to lose by remaining competitive for their entire lives. However, *we are not descended from these men*. As noted above, all of us are disproportionately descended from men and women who were very successful at reproduction. Contemporary men, therefore, did not inherit a psychological mechanism that forces them to stay competitive and keep trying to secure mates for their entire lives. An evolutionary psychological perspective can thus explain why criminal behavior is largely represented by younger men, not older men.

An evolutionary psychological perspective on crime underscores the nondistinctiveness of criminal behavior. Crime is among a large repertoire of behavior that men engage in to attract mates in order to fulfill their ultimate reproductive goals as biological organisms. In this sense, killing and stealing are no different from anything else men do, from composing music, painting portraits, writing books, and, in fact, producing scientific work (Kanazawa, 2003b).

Why the Poor, not the Rich?

Criminologists debate whether there is an inverse relationship between social class and criminality. Shaw and McKay (1929) were among the first to show, using official crime statistics, that the poor were more likely to commit crime than the rich. However, later studies claimed that this observation was an artifact of a selection bias, whereby lower class criminals were more likely to be arrested, prosecuted, and convicted than upper class criminals and that there were no class differences in self-reported criminality (Short & Nye, 1957). Today some criminologists contend that the negative relationship between social class and criminality is a "myth" (Johnson 1980; Tittle & Villemez, 1977; Tittle, et al., 1978), while others claim that there is a genuine relationship (Braithwaite, 1981; Clelland & Carter, 1980; Elliott & Huizinga, 1983). To make matters worse, the debate appears largely driven by ideological conviction rather than empirical data; some scholars conclude that there is no relationship between social class and criminality even when their own data show that the poor are more likely to commit crime than the rich (Dunaway, et al., 2000). After nearly a century of debate, consensus on whether there is a negative relationship between social class and criminality appears nowhere near sight, and the best criminologists can say today is "it remains unclear whether and in what circumstances this negative relationship exists" (Becker & Mehlkop, 2006:194).

Because some criminologists claim that there are no *theoretical* reasons to expect a negative association between social class and criminality (Tittle, 1983), perhaps a new theoretical perspective may help clear the muddy debate. From an evolutionary psychological perspective, it is a straightforward prediction that lower class men will commit more crimes, particularly property crimes such as theft and robbery, than upper class men. If women are attracted to higher status men with greater resources, then lower class men, who possess and have legitimate access to fewer resources with which to attract women, should be more motivated to acquire such resources through illicit means than upper class men. An evolutionary psychological perspective would therefore predict a negative association between social class and criminality. In this connection, it is important to note that some studies of juvenile and adult men show that the social class of their family of origin does not affect their criminality as strongly as their own social class (Stark, 1979; Thornberry & Farnworth, 1982). This is perfectly consistent with an evolutionary psychological perspective on social class and criminality.

An evolutionary psychological perspective on crime can also suggest new hypotheses that have hitherto been unexamined by criminologists. From this perspective, what matters for men's criminality is not social class per se, or even resources per se, but reproductive opportunities that highly correlate with their social class and resources (Kanazawa, 2003a; Pérusse, 1993). For example, because women find taller men more attractive as mates than shorter men (Gillis & Avis, 1980; Sheppard & Strathman, 1989), shorter men are more delinquent and criminal than taller men (Farrington, 1992:Table 11.2(g), 1994:Table 2). Similarly, because women seek out physically attractive men as short-term mates (Gangestad & Simpson, 2000), physically attractive men in general should be less criminal than physically unattractive men. Further, physical attractiveness (or height) and social class should interact in their effect on criminality. Social class should have a weaker negative effect on criminality among physically attractive (taller) men than among physically unattractive (shorter) men. Physically attractive (taller) men of lower class should be less criminal than physically unattractive (shorter) men of lower class. Since social scientists in general, and criminologists in particular, do not consider physical attractiveness or height to be an important influence on human behavior, these hypotheses are unlikely to be tested by traditional criminologists anytime soon.

An evolutionary psychological perspective can also elucidate the mechanism whereby social class influences men's criminality. From this perspective, less intelligent individuals are expected to commit more crime than more intelligent individuals (see later). And social class is significantly negatively correlated with intelligence (Herrnstein & Murray, 1994; Kanazawa, 2005b:254–255). Thus lower class men may commit more crime, not necessarily or not only because they are poor, but because they are less intelligent. I would therefore predict that controlling for men's general intelligence may attenuate or even eliminate the negative effect of social class on their criminality.

Why the Less Intelligent, not the More Intelligent?

Criminologists have long known that criminals on average have lower intelligence than the general population (Herrnstein & Murray, 1994; Hirschi & Hindelang, 1977; Wilson & Herrnstein, 1985). Juvenile delinquents are less intelligent than nondelinquents (Wolfgang, et al., 1972; Yeudall, et al., 1982), and a significant difference in IQ between delinquents and nondelinquents appears as early as ages 8 and 9 (Gibson & West, 1970). Chronic offenders are less intelligent than one-time offenders (Moffitt, 1990; Wolfgang, et al., 1972), and serious offenders are less intelligent than less serious offenders (Lynam, et al., 1993; Moffitt, et al., 1981). The negative correlation between intelligence and criminality is not an artifact of a selection bias, whereby less intelligent criminals are more likely to be caught than more intelligent criminals, because the correlation exists even in self-report studies that do not rely on official police statistics (Moffitt & Silva, 1988).

Why is this? Why do criminals have lower intelligence than the general population? And why do more chronic and serious criminals have lower intelligence than their less chronic and serious counterparts? A new hypothesis in evolutionary psychology called the **Savanna-IQ Interaction Hypothesis** (Kanazawa, 2005b, 2006a, 2006b, 2007a) suggests one possible answer.

Relying on earlier observations made by pioneers of evolutionary psychology (Crawford, 1993; Symons, 1990; Tooby & Cosmides, 1990), Kanazawa (2004a) proposes what he calls the **Savanna Principle**, which states that *the human brain has difficulty comprehending and dealing with entities and situations that did not exist in the ancestral environment.* For example, individuals who watch certain types of TV show are more satisfied with their friendships, just as they are if they had more friends or socialized with them more frequently (Kanazawa, 2002). This may be because realistic images of other humans, such as television, movies, videos, and photographs, did not exist in the ancestral environment, where all realistic images of other humans *were* other humans. As a result, the human brain may have implicit difficulty distinguishing their "TV friends" (characters they repeatedly see on TV shows) and their real friends, and may tend to respond similarly to both.

In an entirely separate line of research, Kanazawa (2004b) proposes an evolutionary psychological theory of the evolution of **general intelligence**. In contrast to views expressed by Chiappe and MacDonald (2005) and Cosmides and Tooby (2000, 2002), Kanazawa (2004b) suggests that what is now known as general intelligence may have originally evolved as a domain-specific adaptation to deal with evolutionarily novel, nonrecurrent problems. The human brain consists of a large number of domain-specific evolved psychological mechanisms to solve recurrent adaptive problems. In this sense, our ancestors did not really have to think in order to solve such recurrent problems. Evolution has already done all the thinking, so to speak, and equipped the human brain with appropriate psychological mechanisms, which engender preferences, desires, cognitions and emotions, and motivate adaptive behavior in the context of the ancestral environment.

Even in the extreme continuity and constancy of the ancestral environment, however, there were occasional problems that were evolutionarily novel and nonrecurrent, which required our ancestors to think and reason in order to solve. To the extent that these evolutionarily novel, nonrecurrent problems happened frequently enough in the ancestral environment (different problem each time) and had serious enough consequences for survival and reproduction, any genetic mutation that allowed its carriers to think and reason would have been selected for, and what we now call "general intelligence" could have evolved as a domain-specific adaptation for the domain of evolutionarily novel, nonrecurrent problems.

General intelligence may have become universally important in modern life (Herrnstein & Murray, 1994) only because our current environment is almost entirely evolutionarily novel. The new theory suggests, and available empirical data confirm, that more intelligent individuals are better than less intelligent individuals at solving problems *only if* they are evolutionarily novel but that more intelligent individuals are *not better* than less intelligent individuals at solving evolutionarily familiar problems, such as those in the domain of mating, parenting, interpersonal relationships, and wayfinding (Kanazawa, 2007b).

The logical conjunction of the Savanna Principle and the theory of the evolution of general intelligence suggests a qualification of the Savanna Principle. If general intelligence evolved to deal with evolutionarily novel problems, then the human brain's difficulty in comprehending and dealing with entities and situations that did not exist in the ancestral environment (proposed in the Savanna Principle) should interact with general intelligence, such that the Savanna Principle holds stronger among less intelligent individuals than among more intelligent individuals. More intelligent individuals should be better able to comprehend and deal with evolutionarily novel (but *not* evolutionarily familiar) entities and situations than less intelligent individuals.

There has been accumulating evidence for this Savanna-IQ Interaction Hypothesis. First, individuals' tendency to respond to TV characters as if they were real friends, first discovered by Kanazawa (2002), is limited to those with below median intelligence (Kanazawa, 2006a); individuals with above median intelligence do not become more satisfied with their friendships by watching more television.

Second, less intelligent individuals have more children than more intelligent individuals, even though they do not want to, possibly because they have greater difficulty employing evolutionarily novel means of modern contraception (Kanazawa, 2005b). Another indication that less intelligent individuals may have greater difficulty employing modern contraception effectively is the fact that the correlation between the lifetime number of sex partners and the number of children is positive among the less intelligent but negative among the more intelligent. The more sex partners less intelligent individuals have, the more children they have; the more sex partners more intelligent individuals have, the fewer children they have.

Third, more intelligent individuals stay healthier and live longer than less intelligent individuals possibly because they are better able to recognize and deal effectively with evolutionarily novel threats and dangers to health in modern society (Deary et al., 2004; Gottfredson & Deary, 2004; Kanazawa, 2006b). Consistent with the hypothesis, however, general intelligence does not affect health and longevity in sub-Saharan Africa, where many of the health threats and dangers are more evolutionarily familiar than elsewhere in the world. For example, relative to the western society, comparatively more people die of (evolutionarily familiar) hunger and natural diseases, and comparatively fewer from (evolutionarily novel) automobile accidents and gunshot wounds in sub-Saharan Africa. Fourth, more intelligent individuals are more likely to acquire and espouse evolutionarily novel values, such as liberalism, atheism, and, for men, sexual exclusivity, than less intelligent individuals (Kanazawa, 2007a). However, consistent with the hypothesis, intelligence does not affect the acquisition and espousal of evolutionarily familiar values for marriage, children, family, and friends.

Now, what does the Savanna-IQ Interaction Hypothesis have to do with crime? How can it explain the empirical observation that criminals tend to be less intelligent on average than the general population?

From the perspective of the hypothesis, there are two important points to note. First, much of what we now call interpersonal crime today was a routine means of intrasexual competition and resource acquisition and accumulation in the ancestral environment. This is most obvious from the fact that our primate cousins engage in what we call theft and robbery if perpetrated by humans (de Waal, 1989, 1992; de Waal, et al., 1993). More than likely, ancestral men competed with each other for resources and mating opportunities by stealing from each other if they could get away with it. In other words, most forms of criminal behavior are evolutionarily familiar.

Second, the institutions that deter, control, detect, and punish criminal behavior today—CCTV cameras, the police, the courts, and the prisons—are all evolutionarily novel; there was no third-party enforcement of norms in the ancestral environment, only second-party enforcement (by the victims and their kin and allies). In other words, the modern criminal justice system is an evolutionarily novel institution to deal with evolutionarily familiar criminal behavior.

Thus it makes perfect sense from the perspective of the Savanna-IQ Interaction Hypothesis that men with lower intelligence are more likely to resort to evolutionarily familiar means of competition for resources, status, and mating opportunities than to evolutionarily novel means (theft rather than full-time employment in a capitalist economy, forcible rape rather than long courtship), possibly because they are less likely to recognize or comprehend the evolutionarily novel alternatives. It also makes perfect sense from the perspective of the hypothesis that men with lower intelligence fail fully to comprehend the consequences of their criminal behavior imposed by evolutionarily novel entities of law enforcement and the criminal justice system. Hence the Hypothesis can explain why less intelligent individuals are more likely to engage in criminal behavior than more intelligent individuals.

The Savanna-IQ Interaction Hypothesis can also suggest a novel hypothesis with regard to intelligence and criminality. As mentioned earlier, while third-party enforcement (the police and the criminal justice system) are evolutionarily novel, second-party enforcement (retaliation and vigilance by the victims and their kin and allies) is not. Thus the hypothesis would predict that the difference in intelligence between criminals and noncriminals disappears in situations where third-party enforcement of norms is weak or absent, and criminal behavior is controlled largely via second-party enforcement, such as situations of prolonged anarchy and statelessness, in fact, any situation that resembles the ancestral environment.

Conclusion

By focusing on the importance of status and material resources for survival and reproductive success, and by underscoring the ultimate reproductive functions of all human behavior, an evolutionary psychological perspective can shed new theoretical light on crime. In particular, it can simultaneously explain why all interpersonal and property crimes are an overwhelmingly male enterprise; why young men are far more likely to engage in crime than older men (the age–crime curve); why social class and criminality are negatively correlated (the association being far from a "myth"); and why criminals in general tend to be less intelligent than noncriminals. It can also elucidate the causal mechanism behind *why* lower class men are more likely to engage in crime than upper class men, and *why* less intelligent men are more likely to engage in crime than more intelligent men.

At the same time, by focusing on individual characteristics that traditional criminologists and social scientists tend to overlook, such as physical attractiveness, height, and general intelligence, an evolutionary psychological perspective on crime can suggest novel hypotheses. For example, lower class men who are physically more attractive should be less criminal than lower class men who are physically unattractive, and the difference in intelligence between criminals and noncriminals should weaken to the extent that third-party enforcement (characteristic of modern society but not the ancestral environment) is absent. These and other novel hypotheses from an evolutionary psychological perspective on crime await empirical tests.

Notes

1. This is how Darwin originally defined natural and sexual selection, as two separate processes. That's why he wrote two separate books—*On the Origin of Species by Means of Natural Selection* (1859) to explain natural selection, and *The Descent of Man, and Selection in Relation to Sex* (1871) to explain sexual selection. In the 1930s, however, biologists redefined natural selection to subsume sexual selection, and began to contend that differential reproductive success was the currency of natural selection. This is now the orthodox in all biology textbooks.

   I concur with Miller (2000:8–12), Campbell (2002:34–35) and others in the current generation of evolutionary psychologists and believe that we should return to Darwin's original definitions and treat natural and sexual selection as two distinct processes. I am fully aware that this view is still controversial and in the minority, but I firmly believe that the conceptual separation of natural and sexual selection will bring theoretical clarity in evolutionary biology and psychology.

2. Technically, however, the environment of evolutionary adaptedness "is not a place or a habitat, or even a time period. Rather, it is a statistical composite of the adaptation- relevant properties of the ancestral environments encountered by members of ancestral populations, weighted by their frequency and fitness-consequences" (Tooby and Cosmides, 1990:386–387). In other words, the environment of evolutionary adaptedness might be different for different evolved psychological mechanisms.

3. In their defense, however, the thieves were constrained by the insane UK banking laws, which do not allow individuals to cash checks at all; personal checks in the UK must be deposited directly into a bank account.

References

Becker, R. & Mehlkop, G. (2006). Social class and delinquency: an empirical utilization of rational choice theory with cross-sectional data of the 1990 and 2000 German General Population Surveys (ALLBUS). *Rationality and Society*, 18:193–235.

Blum, D. (1997). *Sex on the brain: the biological differences between men and women*. New York: Penguin.

Braithwaite, J. (1981). The myth of social class and criminality reconsidered. *American Sociological Review*, 46:36–57.

Brown, D. E. (1991). *Human universals*. New York: McGraw-Hill.

Browne, K. R. (2002). *Biology at work: rethinking sexual equality.* New Brunswick: Rutgers University Press.

Buss, D. M. (1989). Sex differences in human mate preferences: evolutionary hypotheses tested in 37 cultures. *Behavioral and Brain Sciences,* 12:1–49.

Campbell, A. (1995). A few good men: evolutionary psychology and female adolescent aggression. *Ethology and Sociobiology,* 16:99–123.

Campbell, A. (1999). Staying alive: evolution, culture, and women's intrasexual aggression. *Behavioral and Brain Sciences,* 22:203–252.

Campbell, A. (2002). *A mind of her own: the evolutionary psychology of women.* Oxford: Oxford University Press.

Chiappe, D. & K. MacDonald (2005). The evolution of domain-general mechanisms in intelligence and learning. *Journal of General Psychology,* 13:25–40.

Clelland, D. & T. J. Carter (1980). The new myth of class and crime. *Criminology,* 18:319–336.

Cosmides, L. & J. Tooby (2000). Consider the source: the evolution of adaptations for decoupling and metarepresentation. In Sperber, D. (Ed.). *Metarepresentations: a multidisciplinary perspective.* Oxford: Oxford University Press.

Cosmides, L. & J. Tooby (2002). Unraveling the enigma of human intelligence: evolutionary psychology and the multimodular mind. In Sternberg, R. & J. C. Kaufman (Eds.). *The evolution of intelligence.* Mahwah, NJ: Lawrence Erlbaum Associates, Inc.

Crawford, C. B. (1993). The future of sociobiology: counting babies or proximate mechanisms? *Trends in Ecology and Evolution,* 8:183–186.

Daly, M. & M. Wilson (1988). *Homicide.* New York: Aldine De Gruyter.

Daly, M. & M. Wilson (1990). Killing the competition: female/female and male/male homicide. *Human Nature,* 1:81–107.

Daly, M., M. Wilson, M., & S. J. Weghorst (1982). Male sexual jealousy. *Ethology and Sociobiology,* 3:11–27.

Darwin, C. (1859). *On the origin of species by means of natural selection.* London: John Murray.

Darwin, C. (1871). *The descent of man, and selection in relation to sex.* London: John Murray.

Deary, I. J., M. C. Whiteman, J. M. Starr, L. J. Whalley, & H. C. Fox (2004). The impact of childhood intelligence on later life: following up the Scottish Mental Surveys of 1932 and 1947. *Journal of Personality and Social Psychology,* 86:130–147.

Dunaway, R. G., F. T. Cullen, V. S. Burton, Jr., & T. D. Evans (2000). The myth of social class and crime revisited: an examination of class and adult criminality. *Criminology,* 38:589–632.

Elliott, D. S. & D. Huizinga (1983). Social class and delinquent behavior in a national youth panel 1976-1980. *Criminology,* 21:149–177.

Farrington, D. P. (1992). Explaining the beginning, progress, and ending of antisocial behavior from birth to adulthood. In McCord, J. (Ed.). *Advances in criminological theory, vol. 3. Facts, frameworks, and forecasts.* New Brunswick, NJ: Transaction.

Farrington, D. P. (1994). Childhood, adolescent, and adult features of violent males. In Huesmann, L. R. (Ed.). *Aggressive behavior: current perspectives.* New York: Plenum.

Gangestad, S. W. & J. A. Simpson (2000). The evolution of human mating: trade-offs and strategic pluralism. *Behavioral and Brain Sciences,* 23:573–644.

Gibson, H. B. & D. J. West (1970). Social and intellectual handicaps as precursors of early delinquency. *British Journal of Criminology,* 10:21–32.

Gillis, J. S. & W. E. Avis (1980). The male-taller norm in mate selection. *Personality and Social Psychology Bulletin,* 6:396–401.

Gottfredson, L. S. & I. J. Deary (2004). Intelligence predicts health and longevity, but why? *Current Directions in Psychological Science,* 13:1–4.

Greenberg, D. F. (1985). Age, crime, and social explanation. *American Journal of Sociology,* 91:1–21.

Grogger, J. (1998). Market wages and youth crime. *Journal of Labor Economics,* 16:756–791.

Herrnstein, R. J. & C. Murray (1994). *The bell curve: intelligence and class structure in American life.* New York: Free Press.

Hirschi, T. & M. Gottfredson (1983). Age and the explanation of crime. *American Journal of Sociology,* 89:552–584.

Hirschi, T. & M. Gottfredson (1985). Age and crime, logic and scholarship: comment on Greenberg. *American Journal of Sociology,* 91:22–27.

Hirschi, T. & M. J. Hindelang (1977). Intelligence and delinquency: a revisionist review. *American Sociological Review*, 42:571–587.

Johnson, R. E. (1980). Social class and delinquent behavior: a new test. *Criminology*, 18:86–93.

Kanazawa, S. (2001). De gustibus *est* disputandum. *Social Forces*, 79:1131–1163.

Kanazawa, S. (2002). Bowling with our imaginary friends. *Evolution and Human Behavior*, 23:167–171.

Kanazawa, S. (2003a). Can evolutionary psychology explain reproductive behavior in the contemporary United States? *Sociological Quarterly*, 44:291–302.

Kanazawa, S. (2003b). Why productivity fades with age: the crime–genius connection. *Journal of Research in Personality*, 37:257–272.

Kanazawa, S. (2004a). The Savanna Principle. *Managerial and Decision Economics*, 25:41–54.

Kanazawa, S. (2004b). General intelligence as a domain-specific adaptation. *Psychological Review*, 111:512–523.

Kanazawa, S. (2005a). Is "discrimination" necessary to explain the sex gap in earnings? *Journal of Economic Psychology*, 26:269–287.

Kanazawa, S. (2005b). An empirical test of a possible solution to "the central theoretical problem of human sociobiology." *Journal of Cultural and Evolutionary Psychology*, 3:249–260.

Kanazawa, S. (2006a). Why the less intelligent may enjoy television more than the more intelligent. *Journal of Cultural and Evolutionary Psychology*, 4:27–36.

Kanazawa, S. (2006b). Mind the gap . . . in intelligence: reexamining the relationship between inequality and health. *British Journal of Health Psychology*, 11: 623–642.

Kanazawa, S. (2007a). De gustibus *est* disputandum II: why liberals and atheists are more intelligent. London: School of Economics and Political Science, Interdisciplinary Institute of Management.

Kanazawa, S. (2007b). Mating intelligence and general intelligence as independent constructs. In Geher, G. & G. F. Miller (Eds.). *Mating intelligence: sex, relationships, and the mind's reproductive system*. Mahwah, NJ: Lawrence Erlbaum Associates, Inc.

Kanazawa, S. & M. C. Still (2000). Why men commit crimes (and why they desist). *Sociological Theory*, 18:434–447.

Laub, J. H., D. S. Nagin, & R. J. Sampson (1998). Trajectories of change in criminal offending: good marriages and the desistance process. *American Sociological Review*, 63:225–238.

Lynam, D., T. E. Moffitt, & M. Stouthamer-Loeber (1993). Explaining the relation between IQ and delinquency: class, race, test motivation, school failure, or self control? *Journal of Abnormal Psychology*, 102:187–196.

Mazur, A. & J. Michalek (1998). Marriage, divorce, and male testosterone. *Social Forces*, 77:315–330.

McIntyre, M., S. W. Gangestad, P. B. Gray, J. F. Chapman, T. C. Burnham, M. T. O'Rourke, et al. (2006). Romantic involvement often reduces men's testosterone levels—but not always: The moderating role of extrapair sexual interest. *Journal of Personality and Social Psychology*, 91:642–651.

Miller, G. F. (2000). *The mating mind: how sexual choice shaped the evolution of the human mind*. New York: Doubleday.

Moffitt, T. E. (1990). The neuropsychology of delinquency: a critical review of theory and research. *Crime and Justice: An Annual Review of Research*, 12:99–169.

Moffitt, T. E. & P. A. Silva (1988). IQ and delinquency: a direct test of the differential detection hypothesis. *Journal of Abnormal Psychology*, 97:330–333.

Moffitt, T. E., W. F. Gabrielli, S. A. Mednick, & F. Schulsinger (1981). Socioeconomic status, IQ, and delinquency. *Journal of Abnormal Psychology*, 90:152–156.

Pérusse, D. (1993). Cultural and reproductive success in industrial societies: testing the relationship at the proximate and ultimate levels. *Behavioral and Brain Sciences*, 16:267–322.

Rowe, D. C. (2002). *Biology and crime*. Los Angeles: Roxbury.

Shaw, C. R. & H. D. McKay (1929). *Delinquency areas*. Chicago: University of Chicago Press.

Sheppard, J. A. & A. J. Strathman (1989). Attractiveness and height: the role of stature in dating preference, frequency of dating, and perceptions of attractiveness. *Personality and Social Psychology Bulletin*, 15:617–627.

Short, J. F. & I. F. Nye (1957). Reported behavior as a criterion of deviant behavior. *Social Problems*, 5:207–213.

Stark, R. (1979). Whose status counts? *American Sociological Review*, 44:668–669.

Symons, D. (1990). Adaptiveness and adaptation. *Ethology and Sociobiology*, 11:427–444.

Thornberry, T. P. & M. Farnworth (1982). Social correlates of criminal involvement: further evidence on the relationship between social status and criminal behavior. *American Sociological Review*, 47:505–518.

Thornhill, R. & N. W. Thornhill (1983). Human rape: an evolutionary analysis. *Ethology and Sociobiology*, 4:137–173.

Tittle, C. R. (1983). Social class and criminal behavior: a critique of the theoretical foundation. *Social Forces*, 62:334–358.

Tittle, C. R. & W. J. Villemez (1977). Social class and criminality. *Social Forces*, 56:474–502.

Tittle, C. R., W. J. Villemez, & D. A. Smith (1978). The myth of social class and criminality: an empirical assessment of the empirical evidence. *American Sociological Review*, 43:643–656.

Tooby, J. & L. Cosmides (1990). The past explains the present: emotional adaptations and the structure of ancestral environments. *Ethology and Sociobiology*, 11:375–424.

de Waal, F. B. M. (1989). Food sharing and reciprocal obligations among chimpanzees. *Journal of Human Evolution*, 18:433–459.

de Waal, F. B. M. (1992). Appeasement, celebration, and food sharing in the two *Pan* species. In Nishida, T., W. C. McGrew, & P. Marler (Eds.). *Topics in primatology: human origins*. Tokyo: University of Tokyo Press.

de Waal, F. B. M., L. M. Luttrell, & M. E. Canfield (1993). Preliminary data on voluntary food sharing in brown capuchin monkeys. *American Journal of Primatology*, 29:73–78.

Wilson, J. Q. & R. J. Herrnstein (1985). *Crime and human nature: the definitive study of the causes of crime*. New York: Touchstone.

Wolfgang, M. E. (1958). *Patterns in criminal homicide*. Philadelphia: University of Pennsylvania Press.

Wolfgang, M. E., R. M. Figlio, & T. Sellin (1972). *Delinquency in a birth cohort*. Chicago: University of Chicago Press.

Yeudall, L. T., D. Fromm-Auch, & P. Davies (1982). Neuropsychological impairment of persistent delinquency. *Journal of Nervous and Mental Diseases*, 170:257–265.

Part II

Major Correlates of Crime

Having provided the important background concepts, Part II of this book applies them to major correlates of crime. The first three correlates are the major demographic variables of gender, race, and age. The remaining two correlates are substances that affect the functioning of individuals in various ways: drug and alcohol abuse and testosterone. What we have to be aware of is that correlates are just that—correlates. They are descriptors and predictors, but they assuredly are not explanations. We have to dig much deeper to understand *why* these variables have the effect that they do on criminal offending, and we can only do so with the concepts, tools, and methods of biosocial criminology.

Chapter 6 is an evolutionary analysis of gender differences in crime. Everywhere and always males commit far more crime (and other deviant and antisocial acts) than women. Furthermore, the more violent the act the more males are overrepresented in its commission. The correlations Anne Campbell presents in this chapter show forcefully that female offenders are overwhelmingly found in the same places as their male counterparts i.e., among single-parent families residing in poor, socially disorganized neighborhoods. In other words, although males and females are raised together and are exposed to a similar set of developmental conditions, their rates of offending are vastly different. Additionally, the individual-level correlates of offending such as low self-control, conduct disorder, low IQ, and ADHD are the same for both sexes (Moffitt, et al., 2001).

The typical sociological explanation for gender differences in behavior is gender-differentiated socialization, which many sociologists tend to view as an arbitrary historical accident (Kennelly, et al., 2001). Consistent with this view, sociologically oriented criminologists explain the gender ratio in criminal offending in terms of socialization; i.e., males are socialized to be aggressive and dominant, and women are socialized to be nurturing and conforming. This suggests that if males and females were socialized identically their rates of offending would be roughly the same. Parents in all cultures do socialize males and females differently because they know that they *are* different. As Sanderson (2001:198) points out, socialization patterns "simply represent social confirmation of a basic biological reality that is easily recognized by people in all societies." Diana Fishbein (1992:100) sums up the issue of gender differences in crime by informing us that: "Cross cultural studies do not support the prominent role of structural and cultural influences of gender-specific crime rates as the type and extent of male versus female crime remains consistent across cultures."

For the biosocial criminologist, culture can and does mold masculine and feminine characteristics in many diverse ways, but biological sex places constraints on how malleable gender can be. In other words, gender rests on a foundation of differential neurological organization that reflects the influence of prenatal hormones, which in turn reflect sex-specific evolutionary pressures. These hormones "wire" male and female brains differently, and those differences make the sexes differentially responsive to different patterns of behavior. Sarah Bennett and her colleagues (2005:273) provide us with a thumbnail sketch of the pathways from sex-differentiated brain organization to antisocial behavior:

> Males and females vary on a number of perceptual and cognitive information-processing domains that are difficult to ascribe to sex-role socialization . . . the human brain is either masculinized or feminized structurally and chemically before birth. Genetics and the biological environment in utero provide the foundation of gender differences in early brain morphology, physiology, chemistry, and nervous system development. It would be surprising if these differences did not contribute to gender differences in cognitive abilities, temperament, and ultimately, normal or antisocial behavior.

Campbell's chapter provides us with an ultimate-level explanation of the evolutionary reasons why male and female brains are "wired" differently. The sexes have been subjected to eons of sex-differentiated evolutionary pressures having to do with reproductive success. Campbell's main idea is that the asymmetry in the costs of reproduction (female investment is enormous, while male investment is necessarily only the few minutes spent copulating) has led females to evolve a tendency to be more fearful than males in situations that pose a significant risk of physical injury. It is this tendency to avoid harm, along with other traits tied to nurturance, that is the reason behind why females are far less inclined to commit antisocial acts.

Just as Anne Campbell's chapter could attract accusations of sexism for attempting a naturalistic explanation of gender differences in criminal behavior, John Paul Wright's chapter could just as easily attract accusations of racism. Such ad hominem attacks, of course, have no place in science. Wright points out that the people most likely to benefit from a forthright discussion of crime are those most likely to suffer from it—African Americans.

Just as social scientists claim that there are no "real" differences between the sexes, they also claim that there are no racial differences other than socially constructed differences. This continues to be the mantra despite a cascade of studies showing that geneticists can identify racial and ethnic groups with uncanny accuracy. For instance, Tang and his associates (2005) genotyped 3,636 individuals of varying race/ethnicities and were able to place all but 5 (0.14%) into one of the self-identified major racial/ethnic groups (white, African American, East Asian, and Hispanic). The researchers (2005:268) concluded that: "[A]ncient geographic ancestry, which is highly correlated with self-identified race/ethnicity—as opposed to current residence—is the major determinant of genetic structure in the U.S. population." It is Wright's position that given the impeccable logic of evolutionary biology, variance in the genetic makeup of the races is to be expected since the three major races evolved over many thousands of years in quite different environments (the "ancient geographic ancestry" of Tang, et al.).

In the United States, the difference between blacks and whites in criminal behavior is approximately the same as that between males and females, and this is also true in other countries such as Canada and the United Kingdom (Walsh, 2004). Also like male/female differences, the more serious the crime the more blacks are overrepresented in their commission (e.g., burglary vs. robbery). Indeed, Eric Hickey (2006:143) tells us that between 1994 and 2004 approximately 44 percent of serial killers have been black, a figure that contradicts public stereotypes about serial killers.

Just as Campbell uses evolutionary logic to theorize about gender difference, Wright posits that natural selection in different environments has favored different traits in different racial groups. Africans evolved in warm climates in which food was plentiful; Asians and Europeans evolved in colder climates in which food acquisition was problematic. Consequently, there was a greater need among the latter groups to plan ahead for a number of contingencies, which led to higher "executive functioning" than among those whose ancestors evolved in Africa. We do observe that when the three races coexist in the same environment (for instance, the modern United States), Asians outperform whites, who outperform blacks, in many areas of social organization such as greater family income, less likelihood of divorce, lower rates of sexually transmitted diseases and out-of-wedlock births, and of course, lower crime rates (Walsh, 2004).

The age–crime curve is subjected to biosocial analysis in Walsh's chapter. This is an area in which the writer is safe from ad hominem attacks since we were all once young and will all grow old. As indicated in the chapter, criminologists have been incapable of explaining the age–crime curve using sociological variables and have steadfastly refused to examine the data coming from the neurohormonal sciences. Just before writing this introduction, we examined three of the latest texts on juvenile delinquency, and not one of them mentioned (or at least went into any detail about) the profound hormonal and neurological changes that take place during puberty. These changes, and the evolutionary reasons why they occur, are the focus of Walsh's chapter (8).

In many ways, a biosocial perspective on adolescent offending may be the best entrée into biosocial criminology because examining the goings-on of adolescence, which are things that will pass, does not carry with it the threat of someone stooping to name calling. One of the best arguments for those who resist scientific arguments is the *Roper* vs. *Simmons* case heard by the United States Supreme Court in 2005. In this case, the Court ruled that the juvenile death penalty was unconstitutional. Much of the reasoning behind the Court's decision came not from heart-tugging appeals or the rants of righteous outrage, but from hard science data on the immaturity of the adolescent brain. If the data are good enough to convince the Supreme Court on such an important issue, they should be more than enough to convince criminologists that they are of the utmost importance to understanding why adolescence is accompanied every-where by a large increase in antisocial behavior.

Substance abuse and its relationship to crime is the subject of Michael Vaughn's chapter (9). Vaughn's chapter helps to bring together many of the brain structures and functions mentioned in previous chapters in the context of substance abuse, which is a major risk factor for all kinds of crime. Vaughn points out that substance abuse and crime crosses many disciplinary fields and that not to utilize a cross-disciplinary framework leads to many serious misunderstandings.

The chapter links substance abuse first to the mesolimbic reward system in which he talks about the "go" neurotransmitter dopamine and the "stop" neurotransmitter serotonin. Vaughn shows how these stop/go systems differ in people according to polygenic variations, and how these variations are the same ones linked to syndromes such as conduct dis-order and ADHD, which were examined in the previous chapter as highly associated with antisocial behavior. In other words, some people are sit-ting ducks for substance abuse, and therefore probably for antisocial behavior too.

Vaughn notes that crime and substance abuse are inextricably linked, but we should not fall into the trap of believing that substance abuse causes crime. Research indicates that drug abuse does not *initiate* a criminal career, although it does increase the extent and seriousness of one (Menard, et al., 2001). The reciprocal (feedback) nature of the drugs/crime connection is explained by Menard, et al. (2001:295) as follows: "Initiation of substance abuse is preceded by initiation of crime for most individuals (and therefore cannot be a cause of crime). At a later stage of involvement, however, serious illicit drug use appears to contribute to continuity in serious crime, and serious crime contributes to continuity in serious illicit drug use."

The final chapter in Part II is Allan Mazur's chapter on testosterone. Mazur takes pains to emphasize that testosterone is not the "raging bull" substance that turns gentle Dr. Jekylls into violent Mr. Hydes as the popular press sometimes makes out. In human beings, testosterone drives **dominance**, not aggression because by far the majority of **dominance contests** for status among humans are not aggressive. Readers who tend to think of biosocial explanations as "biological determinism" should pay special attention to Mazur's discussion of reciprocal causation. He emphasizes that not only does testosterone affect dominance, but dominance also affects testosterone. In other words, engaging in dominance contests increases testosterone levels in participants.

Much of what Mazur writes further clarifies at a very basic molecular level the gender, race, and age effects discussed in previous chapters. For instance, he points out how androgens (testosterone being the most important of these) masculinize the XY brain by organizing it in a way that will activate male-typical behavior during puberty. This adds to the discussion of gender in Campbell's chapter and to Walsh's discussion of puberty. Mazur's discussion of dominance contests among young black males in so-called "honor subcultures" adds considerably to Wright's chapter by pointing out how environmental factors can affect biological factors. Note that Mazur indicates that black/white differences in testosterone levels tend to be only found when one compares whites with blacks who are younger, poorer, and involved in the highly violent dominance contests that occur in inner city honor subcultures.

References

Bennett, S., D. Farrington, & L. Huesman (2005). Explaining gender differences in crime and violence: the importance of social cognitive skills. *Aggression and Violent Behavior*, 10:263–288.

Fishbein, D. (1992). The psychobiology of female aggression. *Criminal Justice and Behavior*, 19:99–126.

Hickey, E. (2006). *Serial murderers and their victims.* Belmont, CA; Wadsworth.

Kennelly, I., S. Mertz, & J. Lorber (2001). What is gender? *American Sociological Review*, 66:598–605.

Menard, S., S. Mihalic, & D. Huizinga (2001). Drugs and crime revisited. *Justice Quarterly*, 18:269–299.

Moffitt, T., A. Caspi, M. Rutter, & P. Silva (2001). *Sex differences in antisocial behavior: conduct disorder, delinquency and violence in the Dunedin Longitudinal Study*. Cambridge: Cambridge University Press.

Roper vs. *Simmons* (2005). 543 U.S. 551.

Sanderson, S. (2001). *The evolution of human sociality: a Darwinian conflict perspective*. Lanham, MD: Rowman & Littlefield.

Tang H., T. Quertermous, B. Rodriguez, S. Kardia, X. Zhu, & A. Brown (2005). Genetic structure, self-identified race/ethnicity, and confounding in case-control association studies. *American Journal of Human Genetics*, 76:268–275.

Walsh, A. (2004). *Race and crime: a biosocial analysis*. New York: Nova Science Publishers.

6

Gender and Crime: An Evolutionary Perspective

Anne Campbell

Although crime rates may rise and fall across nations and time, some facts remain constant. These invariances can provide clues as to the most appropriate theoretical approach to understanding sex differences in criminal behavior.

First, the crime rate of men, as a sex, everywhere and at all times exceeds that of women. At a theoretical level, those who wish to argue that crime rates are a product of the socialization of boys and girls must explain how and why societies everywhere and throughout history have reached such consistent convergence in their differential treatment of the sexes. At an empirical level, they must also address data on the similarity of parents' socialization of sons and daughters. Lytton and Romney's (1991) meta-analysis revealed no differences in parents' style of interaction, encouragement of achievement or dependency, warmth, restrictiveness, discipline, and use of reasoning. Although developmental psychologists have repeatedly raised objections to the results, none have yet presented a reanalysis or replication.

Second, ecological factors that drive up male crime drive up female crime rates also (Steffensmeier & Haynie, 2000). The correspondence between the two sexes' rates is staggeringly high. Over 48 US states, the correlation between male and female rates is r = .95 for violent crime and r = .99 for property offences (Campbell, et al., 2001). Similarly high correlations appear over nations using data from the International Criminal Police Organization: murder (r = .98), assault (r = .99), minor theft (r = .96) and fraud (r = .95). These data strongly suggest that the men and women respond in a similar way to local social and economic circumstances, but that the threshold for engagement in criminal behavior is lower for men than for women.

Third, this threshold model is further supported by the finding that the risk factors for delinquent behavior are not only depressingly clear to the person in the street—poor academic achievement, lack of supervision, and appropriate discipline by parents, low socioeconomic neighbor-hood—but identical for boys ands girls (Fergusson & Horwood, 2000; Moffitt, et al., 2001). Girls and boys respond to the same adversities in development, but girls have a higher threshold for criminal involvement.

Fourth, when women do become criminally active their involvement is concentrated in non-confrontational crimes, such as prostitution, fraud, larceny, embezzlement, and forgery (see Figure 6.1). Again this raises questions for socialization or enculturation explanations of sex differences. Can it be the case that parents, whose views on the position of women may vary from liberal to oppressive, all choose to communicate to girls that prostitution is more acceptable than assault, and to boys that burglary is more acceptable than fraud?

In summary, girls and boys differ in their threshold for engaging in crime. And when adverse circumstances drive them across that threshold, boys engage in riskier acts than girls. To address the reasons for this, we must make a brief digression to some basic facts of reproductive biology that have provided the background to evolutionary psychologists' explanations of the sex difference in crime.

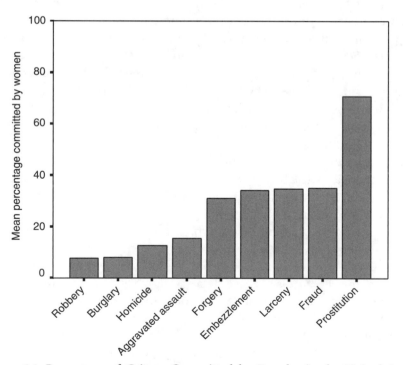

Figure 6.1 Percentage of Crimes Committed by Females in the United States 1964–2004 (Average of 5-year Intervals).

Parental Investment and Reproductive Success

In mammalian species, mothers make a higher parental investment in their offspring than do fathers. At a biological level, this sex difference is reflected even before conception in **anisogamy**—the relative time and cost of gamete production. Men produce an average of 150 million sperm per ejaculate (and can do this several times a day) while women take 28 days to mature and deliver an ovum. Once fertilized, a woman's body will commit her to 9 months of gestation and, in times past, 3 or 4 years of lactation. Lactation is even more costly to sustain in terms of calories than pregnancy. During breastfeeding the mother releases **prolactin**, which inhibits ovulation and makes it unlikely that she will become pregnant during this time. **Oxytocin**, which triggers labor, is also released during breastfeeding and is implicated in the strong calming bond between mother and infant (Campbell, 2008). Women are limited in the number of offspring they can produce (by gestation, lactation, and menopause) and each child represents a massive investment of time and energy. In cold economic terms, a woman's replacement cost per offspring is much higher than a man's. Everywhere, mothers are the chief carers of their children—feeding, cleaning, supervising and ensuring their safety and survival. Throughout the thousands of years of human evolution, when life was fragile and there were no state services to intervene: "Desertion by one's mother means almost certain death, whereas desertion by one's father generally means only a reduction of resources" (Mealey, 2000:341).

In nonhuman primates, the sex that takes primary responsibility for raising offspring (usually but not always the female) has a longer survivorship than the parent whose contribution is lower (Allman, et al., 1998). Among humans, studies from 17th-century Germany to the contemporary Gambia attest to the more serious consequences to an infant of losing a mother rather than a father (Campbell, 2002). Females are in reproductive competition with their own sex and females who were careless with their lives left fewer surviving children than their more cautious peers.

Females in many species act as a limiting resource for males. The Bateman principle affirms that, for a female, mating with multiple males does not increase her reproductive output although for a male multiple sexual partners confer a significant reproductive advantage over male rivals. Polygyny benefits males and contemporary men show a number of characteristics that are suggestive of a prehistory of polygyny. Polygyny is strongly associated with sex differences in size and strength: Because males compete with one another to gain access to extra female partners, there is selection for larger and stronger males over the generations.

Australopithecus males were between 50 and 100 percent larger than females (Geary, 2000). Although the size of the sex difference has diminished—probably as a result of less intense male competition consequent on an increase in paternal investment—it has remained relatively constant over the last 300,000 years with males being about 20 percent larger than females. Men have larger skeletal muscles, a greater capacity for carrying oxygen in the blood and for neutralizing the chemical products of physical exercise.

In polygynous species, puberty occurs earlier in females than in males. The bigger a male is when he enters the ferocious male-male contest for mating opportunities, the greater his chance of success. In humans, boys reach puberty at the age of about 13–14, approximately 2 years later than girls (Tanner, 1978). Males in polygynous species also tend to die earlier than females. The Y chromosome instructs the formation of testes and consequent testosterone production, which energizes youthful sexual and competitive behavior—but at a cost. In the long term, it compromises the immune system leading to men's earlier death relative to women. Despite increases in human longevity, women's life expectancy remains 5–10 percent longer than that of men. Another biological characteristic associated with polygyny is testes size (Harcourt, et al., 1981). Any male who mates with many females must produce copious quantities of sperm to compete with those of other males. Admittedly, human testicles look rather undersized in comparison with our promiscuous chimpanzee cousins but they are considerably more impressive than those of the gorilla. A final requirement of the successfully polygynous male is a strong sex drive and this seems to be a marked feature of human males. In a review of 177 data sources (Oliver & Hyde, 1993), men had a far more positive attitude toward casual sex than did women, they had intercourse more frequently, and the biggest difference of all was in incidence of masturbation—often as a substitute for sex with a partner. Men experience sexual fantasies and sexual arousal about once a day (compared to about once a week in women), and they more often fantasize about someone with whom they have not yet had sex.

If there has been a history of polygyny in our species, how can we explain the widespread biparental care in humans? Remaining with one woman means that a man's reproductive output is entirely constrained by that of his partner—which as we have seen is low. Why do men stay? The mathematical answer is straightforward: If the number of surviving children a man can produce from multiple females each raising his child alone is lower than the number of surviving children from a single mate, he should stay with one partner (Clutton-Brock, 1991). This equation points to two critical variables: The first is a male's ability to attract multiple partners. If a woman is to receive no material or emotional assistance from a mate but only his genes, then she should ensure that they are of exceptionally high quality. Male genetic quality is manifested in facial and bodily symmetry. (Asymmetry results from gene mutation, errors in gene translation, and disease-reflecting immune system failure.) Women experience this pleasing symmetry as attractiveness. Attractive men are best placed to pursue a pure "cad" strategy. The rest are better served by recognizing their limitations and opting for one partner in the hope of producing at least some progeny. However, where men are in short supply, market forces may mean that even less attractive males are able to recruit multiple short-term partners.

The second variable is the marginal value of male support. If the presence of a male helper makes no difference to the likely survival of the offspring then a male is "wasting" his time and resources by staying. In humans, a father's presence can reduce offspring mortality, morbidity, stress levels and problem behaviors, and increase economic and emotional resources associated with children's social, academic, and employment success (Geary, 2000). This "paternal advantage" is most evident at the economic and ecological margins where survival is precarious and a second parent can make a real difference between life and death, between food and starvation (Gangestad & Simpson, 2000).

Crime: Evolutionary Accounts

Evolution is about the differential transmission of genes. Evolutionary psychologists are interested principally in the phenotypic effects of those selected genes—the kinds of body and mind they produce, and, in terms of the present argument, how males and females differ as a result of different selection pressures. What psychological mechanism might lie behind the sex difference in crime?

As Table 6.1 shows, most answers have resulted from posing the question with male behavior as the object of explanation: Why do men show higher rates of aggression and other risky behaviors compared to women? Daly and Wilson's (1988) answer, the most comprehensively argued in terms of evolutionary biology and the forerunner of later proposals, hinges on the human legacy of polygyny and its implications for intrasexual aggression and violent crime. Polygyny can be operationalized as the relative variance in male and female reproductive success. Under absolute monogamy the variance is equal but, under polygyny, males' fitness variance increases in line with the greater gap between the most and least reproductively successful men. Even in contemporary "monogamous" societies, men's fitness variance is slightly greater because a minority of men attract more than their fair share of reproductive opportunities while

Table 6.1 Summary of Evolutionary Accounts of Sex Differences in Crime

Theorist	Focus of argument	Crimes addressed	Evolutionary selecting factor	Psychological mediators of sex difference	Focus of special interest
Daly & Wilson (1988)	Males	Violent crimes	Male intra-sexual competition	Competitiveness 'Taste for risk'	Male violence escalation and the concept of 'honor'
Cohen & Machalek (1988)	Males	Property crime (extended to all crime by Vila, 1994)	Resource acquisition via cultural evolution and learning	Aggressiveness Risk taking (chiefly through social transmission, biology as 'indirect effect')	Frequency-dependent strategies in relation to resource holding and resource value asymmetries
Kanazawa & Still (2004)	Males	Violent and property crimes	Female choice: Preference for males with status and resources	Competitiveness Testosterone	Age–crime relationship
Ellis (2004)	Males	Violent and property crimes	Female choice: Preference for males with status and resources	Status striving Testosterone Learning difficulties	Social class–crime relationship
Campbell (2002)	Females	Violent and property crimes	Reproductive success more closely tied to maternal than paternal survival	Fear Harm avoidance	Exigencies of mothering

others fail to attract a mate at all. This engenders intra-sexual competition among men resulting in the fact that male-on-male attacks are the most common form of violence. Men are not consciously competing for women—they are competing for status and dominance over other men. This bellicosity extends to other forms of risk taking under the principle of honest advertising: To demonstrate that one poses a credible threat to others it is necessary to demonstrate a reckless disregard for personal safety. The psychological mediator of sex differences in crime is young men's "taste for risk" (Wilson & Daly, 1985). This is more marked in neighborhoods where other means of demonstrating rank (academic achievement, employment prestige, surplus wealth) are out of reach.

Others have followed Daly and Wilson in emphasizing men's stronger need to establish status relative to other members of their sex but have extended the argument to encompass property as well as violent crime. This has been achieved by introducing the concept of intersexual competition (sometimes called **epigamic display** or female choice): Whichever sex makes the lesser parental investment (males in our species) must advertise the qualities that are most preferred by the higher investing sex (females). Women's ability to rear children is enhanced by male provision of resources (which are associated with social status) and this emerges as an important factor in surveys of mate choice. Women place a higher value on status, resources and ambition in selecting a mate than do men (Buss, 1989). For this reason, men should be particularly concerned with acquiring resources and, where they are unable to obtain them legitimately, should resort to riskier criminal means. The key variable mediating the sex difference in expropriative crime is greater male competitiveness and status striving, which some argue derives from prenatal and circulating testosterone levels (Ellis, 2004; Kanazawa & Still, 2000). Ellis (2004) contends that young men with high testosterone but poor ability to learn and plan are most likely to be involved in street crimes such as robbery and mugging. Vila (1994) extended Cohen and Machalek's ecological analysis of theft and property offenses to encompass all forms of crime. They argue that through cultural learning (itself an evolved human ability) the disadvantaged employ a range of criminal strategies by which to garner resources, power, and hedonistic experiences in impoverished environments.

There is a broad consensus that the motivation to achieve status and surplus resources is more critical for male than for female reproductive success and that there has been sexual selection for a willingness (even eagerness) to take criminal risks in pursuit of these goals where conventional avenues are closed. Because Kanazawa and Mazur (Chapters 5 and 10, this volume) scrutinize this approach to male crime in detail, I will concentrate on the female side of the equation. The male-centered approach has dominated evolutionary psychology and perhaps the reason for this is captured by Alexander's (1979:241) remark that "the entire life history strategy of males is a higher-risk, higher-stakes adventure than that of females." Men's adventures, especially centered on sex and violence, are more engaging than the long and mundane road of childrearing taken by women.

In male-centered explanations, women are implicitly treated as a default option: Women commit less crime because, as the limiting sex, they have no need to compete for copulations (or for the status and resources that bring mating success). A female-centered approach ("Why do women lag behind men in crime commission?") puts females centre stage and treats them as the object of sexual selection just as much as males. True, females have no need to compete with one another for copulations, but in evolutionary terms, they are in competition to successfully raise their limited number of offspring. As Hrdy (1999:69) so eloquently expressed it: "For species such as primates, the mother is the environment, or at least the most important feature in it during the most perilous phase of any individual's existence. Her luck plus how well she copes with her world—its scarcities, its predators, its pathogens, along with her conspecifics in it—are what determine whether or not a fertilization ever counts." Her most important proximate goal is to stay alive because it is she who, given 100 percent maternal certainty, limited reproductive years and high replacement costs, has most to gain by ensuring that her offspring survive.

Let me pose an evolutionary-minded reverse engineering question: If you had to tinker with the brain to ensure that an organism was especially averse to exposing itself to danger, what would you do? A good candidate might be to decrease the threshold for experiencing fear.

Sex Differences in Fear and Self-control

Fear is an evolutionarily conserved system of motivation and affect that is "designed to detect danger and produce responses that maximize the probability of surviving" (LeDoux, 1996:128). The amygdala in the temporal lobes plays a central role in coordinating immediate response to fear-provoking stimuli. Once activated, the amygdala's connections to a variety of other brain structures cause increases in heart rate, blood pressure, respiration, ACTH secretion, vigilance, and cortical arousal. Behaviorally, it triggers freezing "to suppress approach responses that might lead the organism into a harmful situation" (Derryberry & Rothbart, 1997).

There are pervasive sex differences in the experience of fear. Developmentally, girls express fear earlier than boys and show more hesitation and greater distress in approaching novel objects (Gullone, 2000). Among adults too, women report more intense fear than men and this is true cross-culturally (Brebner, 2003; Fischer & Manstead, 2000). Physiologically, women show greater increases in skin conductance and a more marked startle reflex to physically threatening scenes (McManis, et al., 2001). While women are superior to men in accurately identifying emotions, they show an even greater accuracy for decoding fear than other emotions (Hall, et al., 2000). Women are much more likely than men to suffer from specific phobias and generalized anxiety. Men make riskier decisions than women and this sex difference is especially marked when the risks are physical or life threatening. After a comprehensive review, Byrnes, et al. (1999:378) conclude that: "[F]ear responses may explain gender differences in risk taking more adequately than the cognitive processes involved in the reflective evaluation of options."

Sex differences in fear have been empirically identified as mediators of the sex differences in aggression. Eagly and Steffen (1986) had 200 judges rate 63 experimental studies of aggressive behavior on a 15-point scale in terms of "How much danger you would face if you enacted this behavior?" Female judges rated the danger higher than male judges and sex differences in aggression were significantly larger to the extent that women estimated that they would face more danger than males. In a further meta-analysis, Bettencourt and Miller (1996) also found significant sex differences in danger judgments and again effect sizes for aggression were larger where female judges perceived greater danger than males. Faced with the same low level of objective danger (a university laboratory), women found the situation more dangerous and this predicted their lower level of aggression relative to men. In summary, evidence from a variety of disciplines and methods suggest that there are sex differences in fear. These are evident self-reports, psychometric inventories, reactions to real or hypothetical events, and vulnerability to pathological fear. The sex difference in fear accounts for a considerable portion of the differences observed in aggressive behavior.

Developmentally, fear also forms the infrastructure for the child's acquisition of self-control, also called behavioral inhibition or effortful control. In infancy, fear "automatically" drives attentional processes, such that highly anxious individuals show enhanced attention to threats. This "reactive control" acts as a platform for the later development of "effortful control"—a form of response inhibition that is stronger in those with higher levels of fear. Weak effortful control is associated with externalizing problems and aggression (Fox, et al., 2005). The effect size for the sex difference in studies of children's effortful control, $d = -1.01$, is one of the largest ever reported (Else-Quest, et al., 2006). Boys outnumber girls in psychopathologies deriving from poor inhibitory control such as attention deficit hyperactivity disorder, conduct disorder, oppositional defiant disorder, and **psychopathy**.

Criminologists have also been interested in what they term "low self-control" operationalized as a combination of impulsivity, risk seeking, present orientation, temper, and carelessness (Gottfredson & Hirschi, 1990). The effect size, d = .41, for the impact of low self-control on delinquency over 21 studies ranks as "one of the strongest known correlates of crime" (Pratt & Cullen, 2000:952). The impulsivity and risk-seeking subscales are almost as predictive as the full scale and sex differences in self-control are especially pronounced for these two subscales. Self-control eliminates or significantly reduces the effect of sex on general and violent adolescent offending (e.g., LaGrange & Silverman, 1999).

To the extent that impulsivity represents the obverse of self or effortful control, we would expect to see sex differences in adult community samples. However, whether these are found depends on the psychometric measure employed. Many impulsivity inventories pose general statements about impulsive behavior where no explicit danger is likely to result from the action e.g., "I often act without thinking," "Do you often do things on the spur of the moment?" Such inventories tend to produce weak, inconsistent, or null sex differences (Campbell, under review). Other impulsivity inventories incorporate items that carry an element of risk or danger (e.g., "I have sometimes done things just for kicks or thrills," or "I sometimes like doing things that are a little frightening") and here sex differences are apparent. Women score lower than men on measures of excitement seeking, thrill and adventure seeking, boredom susceptibility, disinhibition, venturesomeness, and impulsive sensation seeking, and higher on harm avoidance. While women may be impulsive in retail purchasing or expressing emotion, they are much less likely than men to act impulsively where there is an element of risk involved, for example, running amber lights or experimenting with drugs. Impulsive sensation seeking completely mediates the relationship between gender and a composite measure of six risky behaviors: drinking, smoking, drug use, sex, driving, and gambling (Zuckerman & Kuhlman, 2000). A measure of "risky impulsivity" completely mediates the relationship between gender and both physical and verbal aggression (Campbell, under review).

In summary, fear and effortful control have emerged as important correlates of aggression and antisocial behavior in the domains of developmental, clinical, and criminological psychology. Because they show robust sex differences, they are also strong contenders as evolved psychological mediators of the sex difference in crime. If women experience fear at a lower threshold than men and inhibit risk-taking behavior accordingly, the pattern of sex differences found in criminal statistics becomes interpretable. Women, as a sex, will be less involved in crime generally, but they will show particular reluctance to engage in high-risk crimes that carry an element of danger. We can now examine specific crimes in light of the evolutionary principles of sexual selection and parental investment.

Women and Their Crimes

Women are underrepresented in crimes of violence generally, but especially so in robbery where only 9 percent of offenders are female. What marks this out as a quintessentially male crime? Of course, it is a means of getting money—but so are larceny, burglary and a range of non-confrontational expropriative crimes. The essence of robbery is a face-to-face confrontation between offender and victim in which the threat or use of force is employed to establish the offender's control of the situation and to intimidate the victim. As others have noted: "[T]he robbery setting is the ideal opportunity to construct an 'essential' toughness and 'maleness' " (Messerschmidt, 1993:107) and "unless it is given sense as a way of elaborating, perhaps celebrating, distinctively male forms of action and ways of being . . . stickup has almost no appeal at all" (Katz, 1988:247). What is this masculine appeal?

Robbers use physical intimidation to dominate their victim. The male preoccupation with hierarchical dominance relations is interpretable from the intra-sexual competition that goes with men's greater fitness variance (see Kanizawa, Chapter 5, & Mazur, Chapter 10, this volume). In consequence, men show particular sensitivity to behaviors that directly challenge their status (slights and putdowns) and to attempts to control or diminish their autonomy. Masculine dominance relationships are apparent from childhood. While girls establish friendship networks in which the impression of equality is paramount and "popular" girls are paradoxically disliked, boys form dominance hierarchies that are often based on physical prowess and athleticism. Boys' rough-and-tumble play from infancy onward is a form of apprenticeship for later aggressive interchanges. In tough urban communities, boys later play at "yoking": One runs up behind another, locks his arms around the victim's neck and effectively incapacitates him. Later still, they turn to mugging—a crime dependent on youthful speed and agility but which lacks the face-to-face confrontation that demonstrates courage and provides the thrill of robbery. At the moment when the robber demands that the victim "give it up" or "hand it over," he is talking as much about status and autonomy as about money. The aim is to dominate the victim, to completely delimit his options and control the unfolding events. The "mark" has been reduced to a "chump" or "fool."

Robbers themselves are deeply conscious of the humiliation of victim-hood and seek to preemptively avoid it: "You know when people are going to rip you off. You know when somebody is up to something . . . The amount of money don't make no difference: you can't let people get out on you. It don't matter who you are or what you are; they'll try and you gotta stop them. At all times you gotta stop them" (Allen, 1978:181). Robbery, to the perpetrators, is about the experiential thrill of demonstrating fearlessness, dominance, and masculinity by creating submission and humiliation in the victim.

But wait. The facts of robbery belie the actual danger that robbers face. Over half of robberies are committed by a team of offenders, half involve the use of a gun against an unarmed victim and two out of three robberies are against a woman, a child under 15 or someone aged over 50. The average robbery lasts less than 1 minute and while the robber has the advantage of deciding and declaring the moment of attack, the victim is taken wholly by surprise with no time to mount an effective defense. Two-thirds of robbery victims who are injured do not resist in any way. Contrast this with robbers' statements that they use violence only as a last resort and that they do not rob from their own community, the poor, women, or children (Lejeune, 1977). The disparity between what robbers do and what they say they do is stark. The descriptions given by robbers function to enhance the degree of risk that they face and, hence, the kudos that they can derive from the act. The rhetorical enhancement of danger confers a reputation as a "hardman," which enhances the robber's status and deters challenges from other men.

Robbery—and its embellished rehearsal in social talk—forms part of a "street" lifestyle that is enjoyed by considerably more men than women. Urban streets are an overwhelmingly male environment where unemployed youth escape the confines of the maternal home and adult dealers, pimps and hustlers go about their business, pausing to talk the fine line between mutual support and competition. On these neighborhood streets, which often delimit the inhabitants' social worlds, local reputations are won and lost. Respect is accorded not only to hardmen but to high rollers—men who spend lavishly and generously, creating indebtedness in the beneficiaries. The robbery lifestyle is one of "earning and burning" in which spoils are rapidly spent on drugs, alcohol, party-ing, and the purchase of designer clothes, cars, and electronic toys. Funds depleted, another mark has to be found. The ostentatious consumption of luxury goods impresses men and causes women to take notice. Men with surplus resources are an attractive proposition.

For homicide also, the gender imbalance is again striking. In 2002 men committed 90 percent of all homicides in which the relationship between offender and victim was known. But if we examine the distribution of male and female killers' victims, we see a clear and surprising pattern (Greenfeld & Snell, 1999). Of all victims killed by men, 10.7 percent were a spouse or a girlfriend. Of all victims killed by women, 42.3 percent were a spouse or boyfriend. Women as a sex kill much less often than men but, if they do kill, they are much more likely than men to victimize intimate partners.

Statistics must be handled with care because they can easily distort our understanding. Daly and Wilson (1988) used homicide data—specifically the fact that the absolute number of wife killings is considerably larger than the number of husband killings—to argue their evolutionary thesis of male proprietary violence toward women. They proposed that such wife killings flow from men's sense of ownership of their female partners and are precipitated by the wife's perceived infidelity or threat to abandon the home. These suspicions trigger a male sexual jealousy module argued to have evolved (with a low threshold) in order to minimize cuckoldry and wasted investment in another man's offspring. Daly and Wilson elide this individual-level male proprietary psychology with societal-level chauvinistic treatment of women embedded in civil and criminal law, proposing that both are built on the evolutionary foundation of paternal uncertainty and consequent cuckoldry. But their argument is vulnerable on a number of counts. Statistically, it fails to recognize that men—regardless of who the victim is—kill more often than women. When this is taken into account, as we have seen, male killers are less likely to victimize their partners than are women killers. It also proposes that proprietary jealousy is felt more strongly by men than women. Although jealousy is a major cause of intimate homicide, a meta-analysis of 20 homicide studies concluded that the association between jealousy as a motive and gender was not statistically significant (Harris, 2003). At a sub-lethal level also, there is little evidence that men's attacks are motivated by jealousy more than women's. Finally, the elision between a husband's sexual jealousy as a motive for violence and a society's patriarchal norms or laws confuses not only levels of analysis but also of motives. Male jealousy as an emotional response is argued to have evolved as a result of the damaging fitness consequences for men of misattributed paternity. Societal-level customs and practices that have controlled and subordinated women may indeed derive from the equation of women with property—even sexual property—but they are products of culture not a manifestation of situated male "jealousy." It is more parsimoniously explained as the state's instantiation of male social control.

So, when baseline rates of aggression are taken into account, it is women not men who are more likely to kill their partners. What motivates them? Female spousal killers more often than males kill in self-defense and in response to a physical attack by the partner. Females, as both offenders and victims, are much less likely than equivalent males to have a history of violence (Felson & Messner, 1998). The chief difference between women who kill versus women who assault their partners is in the degree of violence that their male partner has inflicted on them (Browne, 1987). These women are on the receiving end of a special class of domestic relationships, characterized as "intimate terrorism," in which physical violence is used to control and intimidate. The vast majority of these extremely controlling partners are male and this accounts for why, in surveys taken from women's shelters, from police statistics, and accident and emergency rooms, women consistently appear to suffer rates of domestic victimization that are higher than men.

When we examine self- and partner-reported acts of intimate violence in national random samples, the picture is dramatically different. These surveys pick up "common couple" violence, in which occasional episodes of physical aggression arise out of mundane domestic arguments, often fuelled by alcohol. Here the frequency of attacks by women slightly exceeds that of men (Archer, 2000), although in terms of injury women fare worse by virtue of their lesser strength. And this poses a real question for a comprehensive explanation of sex differences in aggression and violence. The theory must explain not just why women are less aggressive on average but why they equal men in their rate of partner-directed aggression. If fear is the proximate mechanism that restrains women from aggression, as I have argued, then the clear implication is that in intimate relationships women's fear is diminished. There is some evidence that this may be the case. A study that examined self-defense as a motive for women's aggression anticipated a positive correlation between a woman's fear of assault by her partner and her own use of violence. Contrary to this hypothesis, there was a negative correlation between fear and attack frequency—women who attack their husbands are *less* fearful of them (Graham-Kevan & Archer, 2005). This echoes other studies that have found low fear of counteraggression in women who assault their partners (Archer, 2000; Fiebert & Gonzalez, 1997).

Why should sexual intimacy be associated with fear reduction? Evolutionary biologists have established that copulation constitutes a greater threat to females' safety and survival than to males'. A **male–female genetic arms race** is underway in which females must evolve defenses around the lethal potential of the male sex drive (Lew, et al., 2006). In humans, there are immediate and long-term dangers posed by men's eagerness for sex: Injury due to men's greater size and strength, rape, jealousy-precipitated partner violence, infertility from sexually transmitted diseases, and post-copulatory mate desertion. This may explain women's preference for a longer association prior to sexual intercourse. The increase in trust and diminution of fear necessary for a woman's agreement to a sexual relationship may also diminish her fear of employing aggression.

But lest we become too focused on women's intimate aggression, criminal statistics tell us that women select same-sex victims in 75 percent of their assaults (compared to about 70 percent same-sex victims among men). In fact, given the low prevalence of women offenders in the population, women commit simple or aggravated assault against same-sex victims more than would be expected by chance (O'Brien, 1988). Nearly three-fourths of attacks by women are simple rather than aggravated assaults, compared to half among men. About 62 percent of women know their victims before the attack, compared to only about 36 percent among men. Women are much less likely to use a gun or knife and their victims are less likely to be seriously injured or to need hospital treatment. What lies behind women's low-level attacks on their own sex?

Biparental care and paternal investment improve the life chances of offspring in terms of survival and success. But monogamy creates **two-way sexual selection** because males become considerably choosier in terms of mate choice when they must tie their reproductive output to a single woman. Women are thus forced into competition with one another to attract the most valuable mates—those with abundant resources that they are willing to share. This competition is usually managed intersexually through epigamic display. Women compete in terms of the qualities most sought by the opposite sex: facial and bodily attractiveness, and youth. The millions spent by women on cosmetics and even surgical procedures attest to this. In benign economic conditions, competition rarely goes further than this since the majority of men are employed and the difference between them in earnings is not vast. Women have little to gain and much to lose by escalating the contest.

But in conditions of economic deprivation, female competition becomes more intense. First, in such circumstances, the advantage of a providing male becomes more critical (Gangestad & Simpson, 2000). Second, the operational sex ratio in some poor urban areas can be strongly skewed as a result of the high rate of young male death and imprisonment. There are simply too few men to go around. Third, the variance in male resource holding is much greater. Unemployment is high and some potential mates may be more of an economic liability than an asset, spending their partner's and children's state benefits on drugs, alcohol, or gambling. By the same token, "high rollers" or "players" in the marginal economy such as pimps and drug dealers control very substantial amounts of cash. A fourth factor is that these men are in a buyer's market and as result can impose their preferred mating strategy on women. Their preference is rarely for long-term emotional commitment so women suitors may have to settle for short-term sexual relationships during which they attempt to extract what resources they can. The over-supply of women means that even these relationships are not immune to attempted takeovers by female rivals. Studies which have investigated the reasons for female–female assaults, in various parts of the world, report that jealousy over men and sexual rivalries are major motives (Burbank 1987; Mullins, et al., 2004; Schuster 1983). The proximate triggers that can precipitate assaults are verbal attacks on a rival's sexual reputation (casting her as a "slut" or "whore") and by attacks on her physical appearance (Campbell, 1995). By undermining her fidelity and desirability as a long-term partner, women seek to decrease her attractiveness to men to their own advantage. The same male/female demographics and dynamics lie behind the high rates of prostitution. If men effectively control the sexual market in their own terms, a woman's transition from a short-term, profitable relationship with a robber on a temporary "spree" to explicitly charging for sex is one more of degree than of kind. Regardless of societies' "moral" evaluation of such an exchange, it is far from uncommon among nonhuman primates.

But it is in the offenses of larceny, embezzlement and fraud that women begin to approach the rates of men.[1] Some years ago, this was taken to be symptomatic of women's increasing equality in the workplace, an unfortunate side effect of women's "liberation." Yet the image of a female executive "fiddling the books" could not be further from the truth. These are petty offences encompassing welfare fraud, credit card fraud, defrauding an innkeeper, other thefts of services, stealing from an employer, passing bad checks, and shoplifting. A high proportion of offenders are undereducated, unemployed, receiving welfare benefits, and supporting dependent family members—usually children. Opportunities for committing these petty offences arise naturally in their daily lives and the take from these crimes is small, leading to sporadic but high-frequency offending in times of need. Women offenders' description of their lives paints a chaotic picture of hectic lives complicated by broken relationships, children, pregnancy, and unemployment (Alarid & Cromwell, 2006). Temporary increases in strain arising from unsafe neighborhoods and life stressors significantly predict changes in women's property offending (Slocum, et al., 2005).

The rise that occurred in women's criminal involvement between 1960 and 1990 was confined almost exclusively to these minor property crimes and this period also saw rises in illegitimacy and divorce rates, creating a population of mothers and children living in poverty. Cross-sectional and time series studies of the percentage female arrests for property offences confirm that this increase was a function of adverse economic circumstances affecting females including rises in female-headed households, illegitimate births, female unemployment, and occupational segregation (Steffensmeier & Streifel, 1992).

When women cannot depend on male economic support, they must fend for themselves in terms of resource provision. In deprived areas, unskilled work for women is poorly paid and mothers must incorporate year-round childcare with traditional working hours. Many rely instead on welfare assistance, existing from one check to the next with the help of short-term loans from friends and female kin. In such circumstances, the attractions of welfare or credit card fraud, shoplifting, and prostitution are not hard to see. The proceeds of such offences do not provide the conspicuously consumerist lifestyle of the earn-and-burn male robber. Neither do the crimes themselves lend themselves to rhetorical "bravado" exaggerations. These crimes exist unremarkably in the twilight world of the marginal economy. They are driven by immediate need born of an inability to accumulate sufficient capital to achieve an economic breathing space. They are also low-risk offences where the likelihood of injury or death is as small as the likely "take".

It is hard to avoid the obvious parallel with patterns of sex differences in food provision among hunter–gatherer societies. Here, as in the urban underclass, wealth (surplus resource) is hard to accumulate and life is lived on a day-to-day basis. The bulk of daily calories consumed are provided by women's foraging, a mundane and unremarkable activity that can be done relatively close to home with the children in attendance. Men, meanwhile, direct their attention to hunting, which takes them away from the settlement and involves a degree of risk. Hunting success is boasted about and celebrated; it confers status and attracts women (Hawkes, 1991). Across cultures, it seems, men embrace risk and aggrandize it in social talk while women prioritize the "mere" survival of themselves and their children.

Conclusions

From a biological viewpoint, females are the "first" sex. A fetus will develop as female unless a Y chromosome diverts it from this default path. (Ironically, the fetal testosterone that crosses the blood brain barrier to channel brain development into a masculine mode does so by being converted to the female hormone estrogen.) Mammalian species need women far more than men. A mind experiment—if you had to choose 100 people to restart the species in the event of a global catastrophe, how many of each sex would you select? More women than men, I suspect, given men's modest biological effort in reproduction. As biologist George Williams (1996:118) put it: "A sperm is not a contribution to the next generation; it is a claim on the contributions put into an egg by another individual.

Males of most species make no investments in the next generation, but merely compete with one another for the opportunity to exploit investments made by females."

It is then surprising how large males have loomed as a focus of theorizing in evolutionary psychology—including explanations of crime. "Why do men do it?" has been the chief question. And the answer has been: Men do it in order to take a free genetic ride on women's higher investment and to achieve this they will risk assaults, robberies, and homicides that garner status and resources. They may die in the process, but if copies of their genes now reside in offspring they can rely on the mother to do the rest.

But there is another way of posing the question: "Why do women avoid risks to their life?" This answer deserves equal weight: Their offspring rely on them for survival, and men, with their risky sexual and aggressive lifestyles, cannot be depended upon. Unlike fathers, every mother knows that her offspring carry copies of her genes, and she is their temporary protector and caretaker. A woman's evolutionary task may be less exciting, it seems, but it is surely no less important than a man's.

Note

1. The association between drug use and women's property crimes merits attention (Denton & O'Malley, 2006). The effects of drug use on criminality are discussed by Vaughn (this volume).

References

Alarid, L. F. & P. Cromwell (2006). *In her own words: women offenders' views on crime and victimization.* Los Angeles: Roxbury.

Alexander, R. D. (1979). *Darwinism and human affairs.* Seattle, WA: University of Washington Press.

Allen, J. (1978). *Assault with a deadly weapon: the autobiography of a street criminal.* New York: McGraw-Hill.

Allman, J., A. Rosin, R. Kumar, & A. Hasenstaub (1998). Parenting and survival in anthropoid primates: caretakers live longer. *Proceedings of the National Academy of Science,* 95:6866–6869.

Archer, J. (2000). Sex differences in aggression between heterosexual partners: a meta-analysis. *Psychological Bulletin,* 126:651–680.

Bettencourt, B. A. & N. Miller (1996). Gender differences in aggression as a function of provocation: a meta-analysis. *Psychological Bulletin,* 119:422–447.

Brebner, J. (2003). Gender and emotions. *Personality and Individual Differences,* 34:387–394.

Browne, A. (1987). *When battered women kill.* New York: Free Press.

Burbank, V. (1987). Female aggression in cross-cultural perspective. *Behavioral Science Research,* 21:70–100.

Buss, D. M. (1989). Sex differences in human mate preferences: evolutionary hypothesis tested in 37 cultures. *Behavioral and Brain Sciences,* 12:1–49.

Byrnes, J. P., D. C. Miller, & W. D. Schafer (1999). Gender differences in risk taking: a meta-analysis. *Psychological Bulletin,* 125:367–383.

Campbell, A. (1995). A few good men: psychology and female adolescent aggression. *Ethology and Sociobiology*, 16: 99–123.

Campbell, A. (2002). *A mind of her own: the evolutionary psychology of women*. Oxford: Oxford University Press.

Campbell, A. (2008). Attachment, aggression and affiliation: the role of oxytocin in female social behavior. *Biological Psychology*, 77:1–10.

Campbell, A. S. (under review). Can "risky" impulsivity explain gender differences in aggression?

Campbell, A., S. Muncer, & D. Bibel (2001). Women and crime: an evolutionary feminist approach. *Aggression and Violent Behavior*, 6:481–497.

Clutton-Brock, T. H. (1991). *The evolution of parental care*. Princeton, NJ: Princeton University Press.

Cohen, L. E. & R. Machalek (1988). A general theory of expropriative crime: an evolutionary ecological approach. *American Journal of Sociology*, 94:465–501.

Daly, M. & M. Wilson (1988). *Homicide*. New York: Aldine de Gruyter.

Denton, B. & P. O'Malley (2006). Property crime as it relates to women drug dealers. In Alarid, A. F. & P. Cromwell (Eds.). *In her own words: women offenders' views on crime and victimization*. Los Angeles: Roxbury.

Derryberry, D. & M. K. Rothbart (1997). Reactive and effortful processes in the organization of temperament. *Development and Psychopathology*, 9:633–652.

Eagly, A. H. & V. Steffen (1986). Gender and aggressive behavior: a meta-analytic review of the social psychological literature. *Psychological Bulletin*, 100:3–22.

Ellis, L. (2004). Sex, status and criminality: a theoretical nexus. *Social Biology*, 51:144–160.

Else-Quest, N. M., J. S. Hyde, H. H. Goldsmith, & C. A. Van Hulle (2006). Gender differences in temperament: a meta-analysis. *Psychological Bulletin*, 132:33–72.

Felson, R. B. & S. F. Messner (1998). Disentangling the effects of gender and intimacy on victim precipitation in homicide. *Criminology*, 36:405–423.

Fergusson, D. M. & L. J. Horwood (2000). Male and female offending trajectories. *Development and Psychopathology*, 14:159–177.

Fiebert, M. S. & D. M. Gonzalez (1997). College women who initiate assaults on their male partners and the reasons offered for such behavior. *Psychological Reports*, 80:583–590.

Fischer, A. H. & A. S. R. Manstead (2000). Gender and emotions in different cultures. In Fischer, A. H. (Ed.). *Gender and emotion: social psychological perspectives*. Cambridge: Cambridge University Press.

Fox, N. A., H. A. Henderson, P. J. Marshall, K. E. Nichols, & M. M. Ghera (2005). Behavioral inhibition: linking biology and behavior within a developmental framework. *Annual Review of Psychology*, 56:235–262.

Gangestad, S. & J. Simpson (2000). The evolution of human mating: trade-offs and strategic pluralism. *Behavioral and Brain Sciences*, 23:573–644.

Geary, D. (2000). Evolution and proximate expressions of human paternal investment. *Psychological Bulletin*, 126:55–77.

Gottfredson, M. & T. Hirschi (1990). *A general theory of crime*. Stanford, CA: Stanford University Press.

Graham-Kevan, N. & J. Archer (2005). Investigating three explanations of women's relationship aggression. *Psychology of Women Quarterly*, 29:270–277.

Greenfeld, L. A. & T. L. Snell (1999). *Women offenders*. Washington, DC: Bureau of Justice Statistics.

Gullone, E. (2000). The development of normal fear: a century of research. *Clinical Psychology Review*, 20:429–451.

Hall, J. A., J. D. Carter, & T. G. Horgan (2000). Gender differences in nonverbal communication of emotion. In Fischer, A. H. (Ed.). *Gender and emotion: social psychological perspectives*. Cambridge: Cambridge University Press.

Harcourt, A. H., P. H. Harvey, S. G. Larson, & R. V. Short (1981). Testis weight, body weight and breeding system in primates. *Nature*, 293:55–57.

Harris, C. R. (2003). A review of sex differences in sexual jealousy, including self-report data, psychophysiological responses, interpersonal violence, and morbid jealousy. *Personality and Social Psychology Review*, 7:102–128.

Hawkes, K. (1991). Showing off: tests of an hypothesis about men's foraging goals. *Ethology and Sociobiology*, 12:29–54.

Hrdy, S. B. (1999). *Mother nature: natural selection and the female of the species.* London: Chatto & Windus.

Kanazawa, S. & M. C. Still (2004). Why men commit crimes (and why they desist). *Sociological Theory,* 18:434–447.

Katz, J. (1988). *Seductions of crime: the moral and sensual attractions of doing evil.* New York: Basic Books.

LaGrange, T. C. & R. A. Silverman (1999). Low self-control and opportunity: testing the general theory of crime as an explanation for gender differences in delinquency. *Criminology,* 37:41–72.

LeDoux, J. E. (1996). *The emotional brain.* New York: Simon & Schuster.

Lejeune, R. (1977). The management of a mugging. *Urban Life,* 6:123–148

Lew, T. A., E. H. Morrow, W. R. & Rice (2006). Standing genetic variance for female resistance to harm from males and its relationship to intralocus sexual conflict. *Evolution,* 60:97–105.

Lytton, H. & D. Romney (1991). Parents' differential treatment of boys and girls: a meta-analysis. *Psychological Bulletin,* 109:267–296.

McManis, M. H., M. M. Bradley, W. K., Berg, B. N., Cuthbert, & P. J. Lang (2001). Emotional reactions in children: verbal, physiological and behavioral responses to affective pictures. *Psychophysiology,* 38:222–231.

Mealey, L. (2000). *Sex differences: developmental and evolutionary strategies.* London: Academic Press.

Messerschmidt, J. W. (1993). *Masculinities and crime.* Lanham, MD: Rowman & Littlefield.

Moffitt, T. E., A. Caspi, M. Rutter, & P. A. Silva (2001). *Sex differences in antisocial behavior: conduct disorder, delinquency and violence in the Dunedin longitudinal study.* Cambridge: Cambridge University Press.

Mullins, C. W., R. Wright, & B. A. Jacobs (2004). Gender, streetlife and criminal retaliation. *Criminology,* 42:911–940.

O'Brien, R. M. (1988). Exploring the intersexual nature of violence crimes. *Criminology,* 26:151–170.

Oliver, M. B. & Hyde, J. S. (1993). Gender differences in sexuality: a meta-analysis. *Psychological Bulletin,* 114:29–51.

Pratt, T. C. & F. T. Cullen (2000). The empirical status of Gottfredson and Hirschi's general theory of crime: a meta-analysis. *Criminology,* 38:931–964.

Schuster, I. (1983). Women's aggression: an African case study. *Aggressive Behavior,* 9:319–331.

Slocum, L. A., S. S. Simpson, & D. A. Smith (2005). Strained lives and crime: examining intra-individual variation in strain and offending in a sample of incarcerated women. *Criminology,* 43:1067–1110.

Steffensmeier, D. & D. Haynie (2000). Gender, structural disadvantage and urban crime: do macro-social variables also explain female offending rates? *Criminology,* 38:403–438.

Steffensmeier, D. & C. Streifel (1992). Time series analysis of female-to-male arrests for property offences 1960–1985: a test of alternative explanations. *Justice Quarterly,* 9:78–103.

Tanner, J. M. (1978). *Fetus into man: physical growth from conception to maturity.* Cambridge, MA: Harvard University Press.

Vila, B. (1994). A general paradigm for understanding criminal behavior: extending evolutionary ecological theory. *Criminology,* 32:311–359.

Williams, G. C. (1996). *Plan and purpose in nature.* London: Phoenix.

Wilson, M. & M. Daly (1985). Competitiveness, risk-taking and violence: the young male syndrome. *Ethology and Sociobiology,* 6:59–73.

Zuckerman, M. & D. M. Kuhlman (2000). Personality and risk taking: common biosocial factors. *Journal of Personality,* 68:999–1029.

7

Inconvenient Truths: Science, Race, and Crime

John Paul Wright

Criminology remains in a self-imposed scientific quarantine when it comes to understanding the possible connection between race and behavior. So too are other "social" sciences. The American Sociological Association (ASA), to which many criminologists belong, made its position on race clear when it issued its "official statement on race" (2003). In short, the ASA claims that "biological research now suggests that the substantial overlap among any and all biological categories of race undermines the utility of the concept for scientific work in this field"; that "it is important to recognize the danger of contributing to the popular conception of race as biological"; and that "race is a social construct (in other words, a social invention that changes as political, economic, and historical contexts change)."

Other social sciences have taken similar positions. Echoing the ASA, the American Anthropological Association's official statement on race states that "physical variations in the human species have no meaning except the social ones that humans put on them." The group's president-elect, Alan H. Goodman, was quoted in an article in the *Baltimore Sun* as saying: "Race as an explanation for human biological variation is dead," and compared the race concept to a gun in the hands of racists (www.world-science.net, 2005). And finally, in a special issue of the *American Psychologist*, the editors wrote: "New and sophisticated methods for studying the relationship between human genetic differences, the environment, health and behavior, all made possible by the completion of the Human Genome Project, have made traditional race-based measurements of human differences obsolete" (www.word-science.net, 2005).

Race is an undoubtedly complex subject that remains on the fringes of acceptable discussion in civil society. Race becomes an even more sensitive topic when it is connected to biology, and especially when biologically based racial differences are connected to differences between races in human traits and behaviors. Linking race to biology is risky business, but linking race to criminal behavior runs the risk of public repudiation, professional exile, and even career death. If social security is the holy grail of politics, race and crime is the holy grail of criminology. Touch it and you expose yourself to wrath and fury. For this reason, many criminologists are loath to examine the connection between race and crime outside the modern sociological paradigm that holds that race is a mere social construct—that is, something defined by any given society. Or, as the ASA notes, race is just a "social invention."

The views of professional organizations aside, it remains an open, scientific question if race is a "social invention" or a "dead" organizing concept. As this chapter will discuss, there are solid empirical reasons why races should exist and why races should vary in key attributes. Science is about what "is." It is not about what we want or desire. If races exist then empirical data will show this. If races differ in important traits and behaviors, empirical data will show this too. And if there are no races, no biological variables that distinguish races from one another, or no differences between races in behaviors and traits, well, data will also show this.

There is a disagreeable tendency to label those who do not follow the party line with respect to race as racists, which has led to "an unproductive mix of controversy and silence" (Sampson & Wilson, 2000:149). The racist label can stick like hot tar and may severely burn a career, so most scholars avoid the race issue. However, I agree with LaFree and Russell (1993:279) when they argue that the crime/race connection should be studied honestly and courageously because, "no group has suffered more than African-Americans by our failure to understand and control street crime." The corollary of this is that no other group can benefit more from a candid examination of race and crime.

In this chapter, I examine the inconvenient truths concerning race and the global patterns of racial adaptation and maladaptation. I begin by outlining what is known about the origins of human and racial differences and then examine the evidence that reveals races still exist. Afterwards, I examine the evolutionary links between race and problem behaviors. The overarching focus of this paper, however, has little to do with race. Instead, the paper is actually a defense of science and of the pursuit of truth. Science does not evolve from pronouncements of organizations, neither do important insights emerge from the declarations of committees. Instead, science advances when scientists are free to investigate their subject matter, when they are free to discuss the complexities of their subject matter, and when they are free to look at the accumulated evidence and make up their own mind. Unfortunately, when it comes to the study of race, obfuscation is frequently favored over scientific truth.

Race and Evolution

In the strictest biological sense, race refers to human breeding populations that evolved in relative isolation over the course of human evolution. However, a strict definition of race is not necessary to understand that for most, race refers to the place of origin, such as Africa (Negroid), Europe (Caucasoid), and Asia (Mongoloid). In this sense, populations differ visibly based on skin color, cranial structure, hair texture, orbital orientation, physical size, and a host of other phenotypes, but these phenotypes do not constitute a race—they are merely visible markers that individuals use to identify another's place of origin (Levin, 2005).

Why is this important? As Figure 7.1 shows, various species of the genus

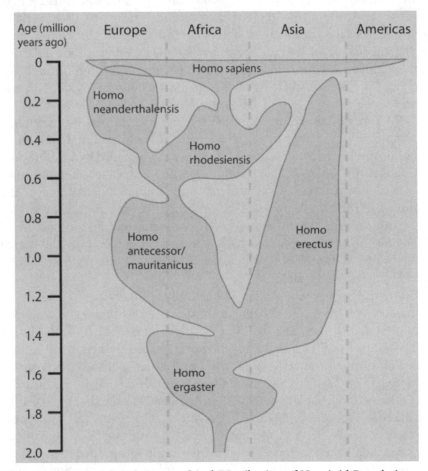

Figure 7.1 Temporal and Geographical Distribution of Hominid Populations.

Source: Reed, D. L., Smith, V. S., Hammond, S. L., Rogers, A. R., & Clayton, D. H. (2004). Genetic analysis of lice supports direct contact between modern and archaic humans. *PLoS Biology*, 2, 11; e340 doi:10.1371/journal.pbio.0020340.

Homo evolved in Africa, with some, such as Homo neanderthalis and Homo erectus, migrating to the rest of the known world. What is worth noting is that the evolution of Homo appeared as a series of gradual advancements. Homo habilis, which lived 2.4 to 1.4 million years ago (MYA) eventually gave way to Homo erectus (1.8 MYA to 70,000 years ago), and, finally, to Homo neanderthalis (250,000 to 30,000 years ago). Each successive evolution brought with it larger brains (600 cm^3 habilis to 1,200–1,700 cm^3 for neanderthalis), which may help to explain why earlier waves of humans eventually vanished from existence—they simply could not compete with other species, neither could they adapt to unique environmental constraints.

Modern H. sapiens evolved in Africa about 250,000 years ago and began to migrate out of Africa roughly 50,000 years ago. H. sapiens had a high brain to body ratio and the largest forebrain known to date. Perhaps owing to its large brain or to a genetic mutation in the **FoxP2** gene, H. sapiens also developed the use of oral language. Yet evolution also took place within the continent of Africa. Scientists know this through the study of **mitochondrial DNA**, or mtDNA. Mitochondria exist in cells and provide energy for cell metabolism. Unlike nuclear DNA, however, mtDNA is passed down only through females and it does not recombine as strands of nuclear DNA do when maternal and paternal DNA mix. These properties allow geneticists the ability to study mtDNA evolution.

Changes in mtDNA that group together are called **haplogroups**. Haplogroups represent differences between human populations in the evolution of mtDNA or nuclear DNA. While there are currently 39 known haplogroups, only three dominated Africa during the Pleistocene: L1 in the south, L2 in the west, and L3 in the east. However, only the macro haplogroups M and N, originally from L3, migrated out of Africa (Sarich & Miele, 2004; Wade, 2006).

Contemporary genetic studies indicate that initially only a handful of Homo sapiens from the M haplogroup departed Africa, with some estimates placing the number at 150. H. sapiens moved north into Europe and east into Asia. Their migration, however, placed tremendous selection pressures on the groups. As usual, food and water had to be located and obtained, but H. sapiens also encountered something new to their experience: the cold. H. sapiens migrated out of lush grasslands of east Africa during the Pleistocene period, when most of Europe and Asia were covered in ice. Brawn and aggression, which gave tremendous evolutionary advantage to those who stayed in Africa, no longer helped to guarantee survival in an area covered by ice. Instead, thinking, planning, and creativity suddenly became prized characteristics. Individuals with these abilities increased their survival likelihood and also increased the likelihood that they would pass on their genes to the next generation.

It would take another 50,000 years, which also saw the evolution of other haplogroups, but eventually H. sapiens would populate the planet. No other hominid would survive. With their large brains, capable of abstract reasoning, planning, and problem solving, as well as the capacity for spoken language, humans eventually displaced neanderthalis in Europe and erectus in Asia and Australia. The migrating H. sapiens were more intelligent than their counterparts, which allowed for better social organization, the creation of more sophisticated tools, as well as the use of verbal commands and directions.

The evolutionary pathways that led a few hundred early humans out of Africa to eventually dominate the world as we know it fostered considerable adaptation. The forces of natural selection, **genetic drift**, and **genetic mutations** often combined to produce humans uniquely adapted to their environment. Over time, adaptations to local environmental circumstances would produce differences between groups, primarily those in Africa, Asia, and Europe. The Homo sapiens who colonized Europe faced varied and uniquely different evolutionary obstacles than did those who would colonize Asia or those who would cross the Bearing Strait and eventually colonize the Americas. The morphological differences we see today between Europeans, Asians, and Africans provide us a visual glimpse into that past.

From an evolutionary point of view, which is strongly supported by genetic and archeological findings, human races were almost destined to emerge. It would, in other words, defy all that is currently known about the evolution of mankind if races did *not* exist, and if races did not differ in fundamental ways. Yet is there current evidence that shows, despite enormous human progress and interbreeding, that races still exist in modern times?

Do Races Exist?

Imagine a test in which scientists collected the genes of individuals from across the world. In this test, they clustered genotypes with greater similarity together, so that the gene clusters were relatively homogenous—that is, the clusters were relatively genetically similar. Now imagine if these scientists could classify, with about 100 percent accuracy, any given set of genes into these clusters. What I have just described is called a **structure analysis** and the clusters are actually "population groups" that correspond directly to African, Asian, and European races (Jorde & Wooding, 2004). With sufficient genetic information, traditional racial categories can be detected and classified with 100 percent accuracy. With a little bit more genetic information, differences between closely related groups, such as the Japanese and Chinese and between specific African tribes, can even be accurately categorized (Shriver, et al., 2004). As if that were not sufficient, individuals' self-classification, such as African American, correspond almost perfectly with their genetically classified lineage (Risch, et al., 2002).

Sociologists are fond of stating that genetic differences between individuals are so small they are unimportant. Bill Clinton once famously stated publicly that we are 99.9 percent genetically similar to each other. Unfortunately, contemporary estimates of genetic differences between individuals, derived from the Human Genome Project (the same project the APA pointed to), indicate that there is much more genetic variation between individuals than ever imagined. Findings from a genetic analysis of 270 people with Asian, African, and European ancestry (Redon, et al., 2006) revealed that over 2,900 genes, or over 12 percent of the genes in the human genome, varied in the number of copy number variations—that is, the number of genes that have been deleted or duplicated in the genome. So convincing were these findings that Craig Venter, the founder of the company that first mapped the human genome and the first person in history to have his entire genotype published, changed his opinion on the degree of variation between humans.

If humans differ genetically by 10 percent or more, do races also differ? Again, many sociologists argue that any genetic differences between races are so small as to be inconsequential. They are, again, incorrect. However, they also make the point that there is greater genetic variation within "races" than between "races." On this point, they are correct. Once more, modern genetic studies have found that genetic differences between traditional racial categories range from 10 to 15 percent, but increase to 20 percent when mtDNA data are used (Melton, et al., 2001). These differences are large and show substantial genetic variation based on ancestry. However, it is also important to point out that 80 to 85 percent of the genetic variation occurs within a race (Lewontin, 1972). Indeed, individuals with an African origin have the greatest degree of genetic variation, for no other reason than African populations have existed for a longer period of time and mutations have thereby had longer to occur. Once more, Craig Venter, an outspoken critic of "race science" had to concede that data supported the notion that races exist within the human race.

Humans are highly mobile, and, while they tend to breed mostly within their own race, they will also breed outside their race. This is referred to as "admixture," or the mixing of maternal and fraternal genes from different genetic backgrounds (races). Admixture should have the effect of blending racial differences, which critics point to as an important reason why races should no longer exist. This logic is used commonly to nullify race differences between African Americans and those of European descent. While admixture should genetically "merge" races, evidence consistently points out that admixture rates for African Americans range from a low of 3.5 percent for a sample from Gullah, South Carolina, to a high of 22.5 percent for a sample from New Orleans. The average level of admixture among African Americans is 15 percent, which means that 85 percent of African American genes originated in Africa (Mielke, et al., 2005; Parra, et al., 1998, 2001).

Understanding human evolution and human genetics gives us the ability to scientifically determine whether or not races exist. Given the studies reviewed, plus a range of others not mentioned, it appears completely compatible with evolutionary theory and with modern genetic science that races exist and that races vary genetically. In short, the morphological differences we see between individuals are reliable indicators of their ancestral origins and their evolutionary pathway. Moreover, systems of self-described racial classification are just as accurate as genetic tests in determining one's ancestry; and genetic tests are about 100 percent accurate. Hence the idea that race is a social artifact, a contrived construct, or just part of our collective imagination is clearly wrong. Unfortunately, science by committee or by fiat rarely provides sound findings capable of standing up to empirical scrutiny.

Race, Behavior, and Maladaptation

Crime rates in the United States are typically higher than in other parts of the world. This is particularly true for rates of violence, but, especially, murder. While many explanations have been offered for why America is unique among other industrialized nations, none has adequately accounted for this empirical regularity. While it is politically incorrect to say this, the strongest, most consistent predictor of the crime rate in an area is the number of blacks who live in that area (Walsh, 2004). The relationship between race and criminal conduct can be seen in neighborhood studies, in studies at the county level, in studies across states, and in studies that compare industrialized nations. The relationship is stronger than the relationship between poverty and crime and between measures of social status and class and crime. Indeed, if the volume of crime committed by blacks were removed from the crime rates of the United States, then U.S. rates would equal those found in Europe and Canada (Levin, 2005).

The relationship between race and crime has been consistent over time and place. Virtually all studies find that blacks have the highest crime rates, especially rates of murder and violence, followed by Caucasians and then Asians. Of course, criminal behavior is not restricted to one race and there is tremendous variation within races, yet the undeniable fact is that blacks commit more crime than any other group; and they commit more violent crime than any other group.

The data on this fact could not be any clearer. Using highly restrictive criteria to establish a "universal correlate of crime," Ellis (1988) found that over 60 studies on race and crime "indicate that blacks are more prone toward criminal behavior than whites, and that whites are more so than Orientals, the more serious and clearly victimful the offenses being considered, the stronger the racial differences (p.531)." Data from the Federal Bureau of Investigation converge on this point. For example, blacks commit 85 percent of all interracial crimes. Over 45 percent of violent crimes involve blacks on whites while 43 percent involve blacks on blacks. Whites, by contrast, select black victims only 3 percent of the time. Blacks are thus 39 times more likely to commit a violent crime against a white, and they are 136 times more likely to commit a robbery against a white. Blacks are seven times more likely to commit murder than are whites and they are almost three times more likely to use a gun in the commission of a violent felony. Black youth, while 15 percent of the population, account for 26 percent of all juvenile arrests and 45 percent of all detention cases. Black youth are also overrepresented in arrest statistics for every violent crime recorded, such as murder, rape, and armed robbery.

Critics will be quick to point out that these patterns might also be produced by America's past involvement in slavery, segregation, and Jim Crow laws. This viewpoint, espoused frequently by sociologists, needs to be taken seriously. It is, after all, difficult to argue that decades of government enforced discrimination and brutality did not have some effects on the upward mobility and behavior of black Americans. Even so, this theoretical explanation has to be tempered with at least two other facts of equal import: First, the African slave trade existed for thousands of years prior to the importation of slaves into America. The capture and selling of humans was common business within Africa for millennia. Within Africa, would be slaves were captured from warring tribes or were sold because of their criminal behavior, their mental defects, or because they found themselves out of favor with the local warlord. African slaves were traded first to Arabs of North Africa and then were sold throughout the Middle East. Eventually, Europeans would become involved in the slave trade, and, finally, after thousands of years of the selective capture, selective breeding, and the exchange of African slaves, slavery was imported into the United States.

The evidence already mentioned shows that those who stayed in Africa varied genetically from those who left. Moreover, those who left encountered many selection forces and thus underwent substantial evolutionary change. This was documented recently in studies of the ASPM gene (*abnormal spindle-like microcephaly*) and the microcephalin gene (Bond, et al., 2002; Evans, et al., 2004; Zhang, 2003). These genes have been under strong selection forces and, subsequently, allowed for the development of larger brains in humans. These studies also found, however, that the mutation leading to larger brains occurred in the haplotype group (D) that departed Africa. The mutation swept through Europe and Asia, showing that it provided substantial benefit to those populations, but there is no evidence of the mutation in African samples.

This is important because brain size is highly heritable, above .9 (Holden, 2006), correlates with IQ at .44 (Rushton & Jensen, 2005; Thompson, et al., 2001; Vernon, et al., 2000), and follows traditional racial categories (Lynn, 2006). Asians have an average brain size of 1,425 ccs; Europeans have an average brain size of 1,369 ccs; and Africans have an average brain size of 1,280 ccs. Differences in brain sizes correspond to differences in the average number of cortical neurons: Asians average 13,767 billion cortical neurons, Whites average 13,665 billion, while blacks average 13,185 billion cortical neurons. As Evans and his coauthors (2005) noted, if selection pressures "acted on a brain-related phenotype," it could affect "brain size, cognition, personality, motor control or susceptibility to neurological/psychiatric diseases" (p.1720). Similarly, according to Zhang (2004): "Big brains are related to strong social bonds, high levels of intelligence, intense parenting, long periods of learning, and ability to deal with volatile environments." This casts doubt on the idea that American slavery, in isolation from all other evolutionary forces, caused the pattern of black maladaptation.

Second, the problems experienced by blacks in America are very similar to the problems experience by blacks in other countries. Blacks are overrepresented in arrest and confinement in Britain (Kalunta-Crumpton, 2006), in Canada (Wortley, 2003), and throughout Europe (Rushton, 1997). In Britain, for example, blacks represent only 2.8 percent of all citizens yet they account for 9 percent of all arrests. Blacks are also three times more likely to be arrested than whites (Kalunta-Crumpton, 2006). Moreover, according to Home Office data, the imprisonment of blacks increased 138 percent from 1993 to 2003. These patterns hold true for black youth between the ages of 10 to 17, which make up only 2.7 percent of England's society. Black youth "constitute 6% of all youth court disposals, 20% of all the young people given orders for long-term detention and 11% of all custodial disposals" (Kalunta-Crumpton, 2006:3). And in Canada, where blacks are only 2 percent of the population, they account for 18 percent of the prison population (Trevethan & Rastin, 2004). Overrepresentation has also been found in New Zealand (Country Reports on

Human Rights Practices, 2004) and Australia (Australian Bureau of Statistics, 2006).

The pattern of black overrepresentation in criminal involvement is well documented. What is also interesting is how crime data also follow racial categories. INTERPOL statistics on homicide, rape, and serious assault consistently show that Orientals have the lowest involvement in serious crime, followed by Caucasians, and then blacks. In 1984 the corresponding rates per 100,000 were 48.8 (Orientals), 72.4 (Caucasians), and 132.3 (blacks). In 1986 the corresponding rates were 38.4, 76.4, and 153.3. Ten years later, in 1996, they were 35, 42, and 149 per 100,000 (Rushton, 1997). Clearly, the universal pattern of black over involvement in crime and disrepute casts doubt on the notion that racism and America's history with slavery are solely responsible.

Finally, criminal behavior is not the only social problem where blacks are the predominate actors in the United States and other advanced countries. Black youth are more likely to qualify for special education (Osher, et al., 2002), they are more likely to drop out of school (National Center for Educational Statistics, 2000), and they are more likely to score substantially lower on all measures of intellectual ability (Rushton & Jensen, 2005). Black children are overrepresented in the child welfare system (Casey Family Programs, 2006), and they are significantly more likely to be born premature, with low birth weight, or to die than are white or Asian youth (Centers for Disease Control, 2002). Blacks are also over-represented in the military judicial system (Verdugo, 1998), they are more likely to have low credit scores (Fellowes, 2006), to die early in life, and to undergo an abortion (Centers for Disease Control, 2004). Blacks also have higher self-reported levels of self-esteem (Zeigler-Hill, 2007), a positive correlate to crime, and they watch significantly more television than do any other group (Childtrends, 2004). Finally, blacks are overrepresented in every measure of reliance on government aid, whether it is receipt of food stamps, Section 8 housing, or transportation (Administration for Children and Families, 2004).

Possible Mechanisms Linking Race to Behavioral Problems

The nexus between race and problem behavior has generated a plethora of theories and studies. There is, perhaps, no topic more studied in the United States than race and its assorted outcomes. Most of the theories that inform these studies attempt to link race to structural aspects of society, such as poverty or neighborhood influences. Other theories point to the lack of access to societal opportunities, while still others emphasize institutional and individual racism. In this section, I offer two possible reasons for the pattern of the findings detailed here. These reasons are highly couched in an evolutionary understanding of race differences and, as such, overlap with one another.

Executive Functioning

Executive functions refer to a range of brain-based abilities housed in the frontal, prefrontal, and orbital frontal cortex. These abilities are highly heritable and provide humans with their unique abilities to plan, organize their lives, and control their emotions. Self-control, which incorporates the abilities to focus, to delay gratification, and to resist impulses, is a major predictor of a range of life outcomes, including dropping out of school, drug use, criminal behavior, and being unemployed for a pro-longed period of time (Pratt & Cullen, 2000; Wright & Beaver, 2005). Experimental studies on the ability to delay gratification and to control internal impulses show substantial differences between black and white youths (Rushton & Jensen, 2005).

While self-control is an important executive function, so, too, is intelligence. Indeed, there is no other individual variable as studied as intelligence. While hotly debated, thousands of studies of millions of individual intelligence scores indicate that IQ follows traditional racial categories (Rushton & Jensen, 2005). Asians have an average IQ of 106, Caucasians 100, and Blacks 85 (Lynn, 2006; Sarich & Miele, 2004). These findings have been corroborated in meta-analytic reviews and in experimental studies of cognitive reaction times (Rushton & Jensen, 2005). IQ, as modern studies have recently found, reflects the brain's ability to process information, to accurately categorize information, to store information, and to recall specific information to solve problems. IQ is also strongly correlated with self-control (Thompson, et al., 2001) and highly depend-ent on the volume of gray matter in the frontal regions of the brain (Thompson, et al., 2001). Gray matter volume, moreover, is strongly heritable.

Self-control and IQ covary, so that individuals with low self-control are also more likely to have a low IQ. These deficits are potent enough to predict many of the negative life-course factors that afflicted indi-viduals will experience. Longitudinal analyses of cohorts of individuals demonstrate that these individuals will face multiple problems across their life-course and that their self-limiting choices will show a high degree of continuity. Most will fail at their education and will then encounter problems in employment, including prolonged unemployment (Shover, 1996). They likely will live a fluid existence, relocating from place to place but often within the same economic stratum (Wright & Decker,

1997). Finally, their relationships will frequently be marred by conflict, unfaithfulness, and unreliability. This pattern holds for anyone with deficits in executive control functions, black, white, or Asian, but due to the distribution of low IQ and low self-control found in black populations, it is more often reflected in the lives of blacks.

Ability to Organize Socially

Deficits in executive functions and their associated problems tend to cluster socially and geographically. Criminologists have long known that crime patterns vary tremendously by neighborhood and that neighborhoods marred by crime show a diverse array of other social pathologies. Criminologists, however, almost always ascribe causation to factors that differentiate neighborhoods—that is, they view neighborhood variables such as poverty as causing crime.

There are at least two problems with this viewpoint: First, despite a wealth of data, advanced statistical techniques, and over 100 years of theoretical pursuit, contemporary studies frequently fail to find "neighborhood effects," and, if they do, they are typically minor in magnitude (Kling, et al., 2005; Sobel, 2006). Second, and more importantly, neighborhood variables are usually measured by aggregating individual-level measures. A neighborhood's poverty rate, for example, is derived by knowing how many *individuals* in a neighborhood live at or below established poverty guidelines. Unfortunately, this measurement strategy automatically confounds the *processes* that have generated these patterns with the outcome of interest (Sobel, 2006). How, for example, someone finds themselves in poverty, the choices they made that led them to their economic position, are hidden when analysts aggregate upwards measures taken at the individual level.

Process, however, is important because it is here, at the level of individual development, where the dynamic unfolding of lives can best be understood. Individuals make choices, and while these choices are circumscribed by a range of factors, they tend to make the same types of choice across their lifetime (Clausen, 1993). It should be expected that individuals with similar traits and abilities, who have made many of the same choices over their life-course, should tend to cluster together within economic and social spheres (Cleveland & Crosnoe, 2004). In other words, a certain degree of homogeneity should exist within neighborhoods, within networks within those neighborhoods, and within families within those neighborhoods. The process of self-selection should naturally lead to greater social similarity, not to less (Cleveland, et al., 2000).

With this in mind, neighborhoods often stand in stark contrast to one another. Those composed of criminals, of large single-parent households, of drug abusers, of the mentally ill, and of individuals of limited intelligence are visibly different than those composed by the educated, the intelligent, and the prosocial. Unfortunately, these factors also tend to cluster on race. Areas afflicted by crime and other social pathologies are more frequently black than white, and even less frequently Oriental. Part of the reason for these visible and dramatic differences may have to do with the differential abilities of races to organize socially.

Collective social behavior is an evolved ability and set the stage for the beginning of the complex societies we see today (Wade, 2006). It entails individuals making a choice to sacrifice or risk something they value personally for the overall good. This process can occur at the level of the individual, the neighborhood, or the nation. For instance, the choice for fathers to stay with their offspring represents, at least from an evolutionary framework, a sacrifice made for the possible betterment of his genetic legacy. Otherwise, he would be free to produce as many offspring with as many mates as he would desire. Marriage thus represents one mechanism of collective social behavior that passes advantage on to the next cohort.

At another level, the regulation of moral norms for behavior within a neighborhood rests on the willingness of others to enforce those norms when challenged or violated. When residents place themselves or their families at risk by confronting drug dealers or prostitutes, they are acting in a collective fashion. When individuals call the police for assistance with a problem in their neighborhood, or they call other authorities to enforce local ordinances or regulations, they typically are acting collectively. What differentiates neighborhoods is not always the total absence of collective social behavior, but the mass necessary to enforce basic social norms. In other words, there are individuals within high-risk neighborhoods who will act for the betterment of the collective, but there simply are not enough to make a difference.

To place these differences in context, we must keep in mind that the majority of neighborhoods in the United States, Canada, and Europe have no need for collective social behavior because the overwhelming number of individuals in those neighborhoods do not violate social norms or laws—itself a hallmark of evolutionary change (Wade, 2006). When a problem is encountered, for instance when a house is used for drug sales, a sufficient number of individuals with social and personal capital exist to have the occupants of the house arrested and the home resold. Yet the ability and willingness to act collectively appears to vary by race. In many black neighborhoods, but especially in inner cities and ghettos, there are too few individuals with the ability to act collectively and there are too many who violate basic social norms and laws. And the undeniable fact is that individual differences in IQ and other executive functions, which tend to cluster within neighborhoods by race, is intimately tied to the lack of collective social behavior, to the lack of informal social control (Sampson & Laub, 1993), and to the violation of rudimentary norms of appropriate social conduct.

Conclusions

Science advances when ideas are discussed openly and when data converge from multiple sources to confirm or disconfirm hypotheses. As it applies to race, however, the rules are different. What started out as a way to convey the dignity and respect for individuals of any race has given way to a radical form of political correctness whereby the mere suggestion that races vary biologically is now tantamount to actually being a racist. Nature, and to a lesser degree science, are not as sensitive, however. Neither should they be. The question on the existence of races is empirical, as is the connection between race and the distribution of any trait or behavior in a society. Fear of what this knowledge may unmask, which advocates of the "no such thing as race" mantra point to, is not a sufficient scientific reason to avoid the discussion or to limit empirical research. Instead, it is an act of betrayal to science and ultimately to any truth that may be uncovered.

The implications of imposed ignorance are often overlooked but we need only examine how medicine is dealing with the issue of race and racial differences in disease and pharmaceutical effectiveness. Recently, the Food and Drug Administration (FDA) approved the drug BiDil for use by those with heart disease. The surprise, however, is that BiDil works only on African Americans and is thus prescribed only to African Americans. Heart disease is a very serious and prevalent problem in African Americans, afflicting over 750,000 lives annually. BiDil was approved for use among blacks only after two studies showed no overall net reduction in mortality in mixed race samples. Those studies, however, strongly hinted at the possibility that blacks were more responsive to the drug than were whites. With this information at hand, another study was initiated, only this time of an all black sample. The study was stopped for ethical reasons after it was found that the drug significantly reduced mortality among blacks. Had the questions not been asked, had the research not been done, thousands of black lives would be lost yearly.

From the available data, it would seem ludicrous to continue to argue that "race" is a construct devoid of a biological or evolutionary backdrop. That evolutionary forces have produced biological variance across races is now scientifically undeniable. That many of the characteristics that define races appear to be universal and time stable is also undeniable. Evolution can produce many forms of adaptation, but it cannot produce equality.

The connection between race and criminal behavior is clearly complex and involves a range of historical, social, psychological, and individual variables. Evolution, however, provides a powerful mechanism to understand the development of human races and the distribution of traits and behaviors within and across races. It helps to explain why races would appear and under what conditions races would appear. It helps to explain why certain traits would be beneficial and why these traits, such as a higher IQ, would be unequally distributed across races. Moreover, evolutionary theory helps to explain why race-based patterns of behavior are universal, such as black over-involvement in crime. No other paradigm organizes these patterns better. No other paradigm can explain these inconvenient truths.

Any effort to divorce evolution from an understanding of race runs the risk of substituting imagination and political agendas as a convenient truth that stands apart from the scientific truth. Fortunately, social convenience is not a scientific or evolutionary principle. Instead of hiding our collective heads in the sands of ignorance, it may benefit humanity if we continue to purse knowledge on our origins, our differences, and our similarities. While this chapter has focused on evolutionary differences, it goes without saying that the vast majority of people desire the same things out of life: safety, security, and a chance to improve on their own condition. A science free to pursue all avenues of inquest, free of self-censorship, and free of political obstacles to uncovering scientific facts is one way, maybe even the best way, to help ensure that people from all races lead a fulfilling life.

References

Administration for Children and Families. (2004). *Temporary assistance for needy families (TANF): fifth annual report to congress.* Washington, DC: US Department of Health and Human Services.
American Anthropological Association. (1998). *Statement on "race".* Arlington, VA: American Anthropological Association.
American Sociological Association. (2003). *The importance of collecting data and doing social scientific research on race.* Washington, DC: American Sociological Association.
Australian Bureau of Statistics. (2006). Retrieved on 05/04/2007.
Bond, J., E. Robert, G. H. Mochida, D. J. Hampshire, S. Scott, J. M. Askham, et al. (2002). ASPM is a major determinant of cerebral cortical size. *Nature Genetics,* 32:316–320.
Casey Family Programs. (2006). www.casey.org.
Centers for Disease Control. (2002). www.cdc.gov.
Centers for Disease Control. (2004). www.cdc.gov.
Childtrends. (2004). *Statistical abstracts.* www.childtrends.org.
Clausen, J. A. (1993). *American lives: looking back at the children of the Great Depression.* New York: Free Press.
Cleveland, H. H. & R. Crosnoe (2004). Individual variation and family-community ties: a behavioral

genetic analysis of the intergenerational closure in the lives of adolescent boys and girls. *Journal of Adolescent Research*, 19:174–191.

Cleveland, H. H., R. Wiebe, van den Ord, E. J. C. G., & D. C. Rowe (2000). Environmental and genetic contributions to behavior problems of children from different families: the influence of genetic self-selection. *Child Development*, 71:733–751.

Country Reports on Human Rights Practices. (2004). Released by the Bureau of Democracy, Human Rights, and Labor, 28 February, 2005.

Ellis, L. (1988). The victimful–victimless crime distinction, and seven universal demographic correlates of victimful criminal behavior. *Personality and Individual Differences*, 9:525–548.

Evans, P. D., J. R. Anderson, E. J. Vallender, S. S. Choi, & B. T. Cahn (2004). Reconstructing the evolutionary history of microcephalin, a gene controlling human brain size. *Human Molecular Genetics*, 13:1139–1145.

Evans, P. D., S. L. Gilbert, N. Mekel-Bobrov, E. J. Vallender, J. R. Anderson, L. M. Vaez-Azizi, et al. (2005). *Microcephalin*, a gene regulating brain size, continues to evolve adaptively in humans. *Science*, 309:1717–1720.

Fellowes, M. (2006). *Credit scores, reports, and getting ahead in America*. Washington, DC: The Brookings Institute.

Holden, C. (2006). Human behavior and evolution society meeting: an evolutionary squeeze on brain size. *Science*, 312:1867.

Jorde, L. B. & S. P. Wooding (2004). Genetic variation, classification and "race". *Nature Genetics*, 36:S28–S33.

Kalunta-Crumpton, A. (2006). A fair hearing? Ethnic minorities in the criminal court. *British Journal of Criminology*, 46:774–776.

Kling, J. R., J. B. Liebman, & L. F. Katz (2005). Bullets don't got no name: consequences of fear in the ghetto. In Weisner, T. S. (Ed.). *Discovering successful pathways in children's development: mixed methods in the study of childhood and family life*. Chicago: University of Chicago Press.

LaFree, G. & K. Russell (1993). The argument for studying race and crime. *Journal of Criminal Justice Education*, 4:273–289.

Levin, M. (2005). *Why race matters: race differences and what they mean*. Oakton, VA: New Century Foundation.

Lewontin, R. C. (1972). The apportionment of human diversity. *Evolutionary Biology*, 6:381–398.

Lynn, R. (2006). The intelligence of East Asians: a thirty-year controversy and its resolution. *Mankind Quarterly*, 46:435–441.

Melton, T., S. Clifford, M. Kayser, I. Nasidze, M. Batzer, & M. Stoneking (2001). Diversity and heterogeneity in mitochondrial DNA of North American populations. *Journal of Forensic Sciences*, 46:46–52.

Mielke, J., L. Konigsberg, & J. Relethford (2005). *Human biological variation*. New York: Oxford University Press.

National Center for Educational Statistics. (2000). Drop out rates in the United States. www.nces.ed.gov.

Osher, D., D. Woodruff, & A. E. Sims (2002). Schools make a difference: the overrepresentation of African-American youth in special education and the juvenile justice system. In Losen, D. J. & G. Orfield (Eds.). *Racial inequality in special education* Cambridge, MA: Harvard Education Press.

Parra, E. J., R. A. Kittles, G. Argyropoulos, C. L. Pfaff, K. Hiester, C. Bonilla, et al. (2001). Ancestral proportions and admixture dynamics in geographically defined African Americans living in South Carolina. *American Journal of Physical Anthropology*, 114:18–29.

Parra, E. J., A. Marcini, J. Akey, J. Martinson, M. A. Batzer, R. Cooper, et al. (1998). Estimating African American admixture proportions by use of population-specific alleles. *American Journal of Human Genetics*, 63:1839–1851.

Pratt, T. C. & F. T. Cullen (2000). The empirical status of Gottfredson and Hirschi's general theory of crime: a meta-analysis. *Criminology*, 38:931–964.

Redon, R., S. Ishikawa, K. R. Fitch, L. Feuk, G. H. Perry, T. D. Andrews, et al. (2006). Global variation in copy number in the human genome. *Nature*, 444:444–454.

Risch, N., E. Burchard, E. Ziv, & H. Tang (2002). Categorization of humans in biomedical research: genes, race and disease. *Genome Biology*, 3:1–12.

Rushton, J. P. (1997). *Race, evolution, and behavior: A life-history perspective.* New Brunswick, NJ: Transaction.

Rushton, J. P. & A. R. Jensen (2005). Thirty years of research on race differences in cognitive ability. *Psychology, Public Policy, and Law*, 11:235–294.

Sampson, R. J. & J. H. Laub (1993). *Crime in the making: pathways and turning points through life.* Cambridge, MA: Harvard University Press.

Sampson, R. & W. Wilson (2000). Toward a theory of race, crime, and urban inequality. In Cooper, S. (Ed.). *Criminology.* Madison, WI: Coursewise.

Sarich, V. & F. Miele (2004). *Race: the reality of human differences.* Boulder, CO: Westview.

Shover, N. (1996). *Great pretenders: pursuits and careers of persistent thieves.* Boulder, CO: Westview Press.

Shriver, M. D., G. C. Kennedy, E. J. Parra, H. A. Lawson, V. Sonpar, J. Huang, et al. (2004). The genome distribution of population substructure in four populations using 8,525 SNPs. *Human Genomics*, 1:274–286.

Sobel, M. (2006). What do randomized studies of housing mobility demonstrate? Causal influence in the face of interferences. *Journal of the American Statistical Association*, 101:1398–1407.

Thompson, P. M., T. D. Cannon, K. L. Narr, T. van Erp, V. P. Poutanen, M. Huttunen, et al. (2001). Genetic influences on brain structure. *Nature Neuroscience*, 4:1253–1258.

Trevethan, S. & C. J. Rastin (2004). *A profile of visible minority offenders in the Federal Canadian Correctional System.* Ottawa, ON: Research Branch, Correctional Service of Canada.

Wortley, S. (2003). Hidden intersections: research on race, crime and criminal justice in Canada. *Canadian Ethnic Studies Journal*, 35: 99–117.

Wright, R. T. & S. H. Decker (1997). *Armed robbers in action: stickups and street culture.* Boston, MA: Northeastern University Press.

Verdugo, N. (1998). Crime and punishment: Blacks in the army's criminal justice system. *Military Psychology*, 10:107–125.

Vernon, P. A., J. A. Wickett, G. Bazana, & R. M. Stelmack (2000). The neuropsychology and psychophysiology of human intelligence. In Sternberg, R. J. (Ed.). *Handbook of intelligence.* Cambridge: Cambridge University Press.

Wade, N. (2006). *Before the dawn: recovering the lost history of our ancestors.* New York: Penguin.

Walsh, A. (2004). *Race and crime: a biosocial analysis.* New York: Nova Science Publishers.

Wright, J. P. & K. M. Beaver (2005). Do parents matter in creating self-control in their children? A genetically informed test of Gottfredson and Hirschi's theory of low self-control. *Criminology*, 43:1169–1202.

Zeigler-Hill, V. (2007). Contingent self-esteem and race: implications for the Black self-esteem advantage. *Journal of Black Psychology*, 33:51–74.

Zhang, J. (2003). Evolution of the human ASPM gene, a major determinant of brain size. *Genetics*, 165:2063–2070.

Zhang, J. (2004). Quoted from http://genome.wellcome.ac.uk/doc_wtd020880.html.

8

Crazy by Design: A Biosocial Approach to the Age–Crime Curve

Anthony Walsh

The sudden upsurge in antisocial behavior that occurs among children entering the second decade of their lives has long been a source of sorrow and consternation among parents and of puzzlement and debate among those who philosophize about such matters. Four hundred years before the birth of Christ, Plato and Aristotle were condemning the impulsive and obnoxious behavior of Athenian teens, and fast forwarding to Elizabethan England, William Shakespeare wrote in *The Winter's Tale*: "I would there be no age between ten and three-and-twenty, or that youth would sleep out the rest; for there is nothing in the between but getting wenches with child, wronging the ancientry, stealing, fighting" (Act III, Scene III).

These ancient commentators alert us to the fact that serious juvenile misbehavior occurs everywhere and at all times. Figure 8.1 presents four graphs showing crime rates by age in various countries during various modern time periods. Although the heights of the peaks in the graphs indicate that the proportion of the population committing crimes will change across time periods and across cultures, the same sharp rise beginning around puberty and rising steadily until the mid-teens and then falling off is constant. In 2005 youths under age 18 accounted for 16 percent of all violent crime arrests and 26 percent of all property crime arrests (FBI, 2006). According to the United States Census Bureau (2007), the percentage of the population between the age of responsibility aver- aged across all states (10) and age 17, inclusive, was about 11.5 percent in 2005. Juveniles were thus overrepresented by about 38 percent in violent offenses and by about 226 percent in property offenses. But the good news is that: "[B]y the early 20s the number of active offenders decreases by over 50 percent; by age 28 about 85 percent of former delinquents desist from offending" (Caspi & Moffitt, 1995:493).

Criminologists using social science models (i.e., biology free) have been unsuccessful in explaining why we consistently see this age–crime curve. In fact, Hirschi and Gottfredson have stated that "the age distribution of

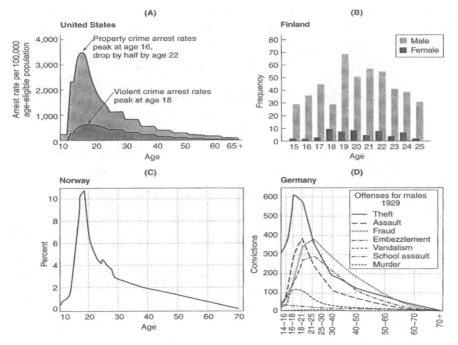

Figure 8.1 Illustrating the Age–Crime Curve in Different Countries.

Source: Ellis & Walsh (2000).

crime cannot be accounted for by any variable or combination of variables currently available to criminology" (1983:554). Shavit and Rattner (1988:1457) share this opinion when they write that delinquency remains "unexplained by any known set of sociological variables."

David Greenberg (1985) does not agree and offers a *strain theory* interpretation of the effect indicating that pocket money provided by parents is insufficient to provide for the perceived needs of many adolescents. This says only that the financially and morally challenged will steal to meet their needs, which is an observation not an explanation. The gap between the "pocket money" provided to many adults from legitimate employment and the perceived needs of adults with mortgages, spouses, and children is objectively greater, yet shortchanged adults are proportionately less likely to steal to satisfy their needs. Thus we arrive back where we started—why are *teens* more likely to behave antisocially than *adults*? Greenberg's observation also ignores the fact that most delinquency is motivated by short-run hedonism and status striving and is malicious and destructive rather than instrumental (Anderson, 1999).

Ronald Akers (1998:338) insists that: "Age-specific [crime] rates differ because individuals are differentially exposed to the learning variables at different ages." From this point of view, the only thing that matters is "exposure to learning variables." Reflect for the moment on the fact that newly pubescent children have had a dozen years or so of socialization in which, at least for the great majority, prosocial conformity and compliance with parental demands were rewarded and the opposite punished. "Definitions favorable" to prosocial behavior have enjoyed priority, frequency, duration, and intensity over their opposite for most of the entire lives of most children, but we are expected to believe that all of a sudden this learning counts for naught as teenagers turn to different sources of reward and punishment. Yes, they are exposed to "different learning variables," but the question begged is why so many youths are so receptive to them after a decade or more of contrary "learning variables."

Finally, after Mark Warr (2002:92) tells us that the age–crime curve is "lawlike," and that trying to explain it is "daunting," he attempts to do so by centering on the increase in peer associations during adolescence to explain the **onset** and increase in delinquency. He then appeals to the decrease in peer associations in early adulthood and the increasing influence of girlfriends, wives, children, and employers to explain its decrease. Again, this merely describes situations that *correlate* with the onset and the desistence of offending; it does not explain *why* the period between these events is so filled with antisocial conduct, *why* the influence of peers suddenly becomes more powerful than that of parent, or *why* associations with peers so often lead to negative behavior. After all, if social influences shorn of evolved developmental patterns were all that mattered, surely we would have accounts of some cultures and some times when the age–crime curve did not exist, or was even reversed, but we do not.

Age is an index of a series of developmental stages from prenatal to senescence that we all go through if we live long enough, with each having its own characteristic physiology. There must be something special requiring its own explanations going on during adolescence that dramatically, albeit temporarily, greatly increases the probability of antisocial behavior.

Puberty, Adolescence, Hormones, and Evolution

Puberty is the developmental stage that marks the onset of the transition from childhood to adulthood and which prepares us for procreation. The onset of puberty occurs around 11 years of age for girls and 12 for boys in the modern western world. Puberty begins with the release of growth hormones when a series of permissive signals, such as when sufficient body weight is achieved, and initiates a cascade of physical, hormonal, and neurological changes that often have profound influences on behavior. When undergoing these changes, many happy and loveable children suddenly morph into malcontents acting like they should be in diapers rather than pants. They revel in their newly acquired independence from parental authority; they rebel against the generation that reared them while simultaneously being consummate conformists with the fads and fashions of their own generation.

For developmental scientists, "puberty refers to the activation of the hypothalamic–pituitary–gonadal axis that culminated in gonadal maturity" and "**adolescence** refers to the maturation of adult social and cognition behaviors" (Sisk & Foster, 2004:1040). Thus, whereas puberty is a defined biological *event* (or series of events), adolescence is a *process* of maturation that begins at puberty and ends sometime during adulthood. The term *adulthood* is both vague and variable because it is a socially defined status. The legally defined adult age of 18 rarely matches socially defined adulthood today. Socially defined adulthood typically means taking on socially responsible roles such as acquiring a steady job and starting one's own family, roles that mark one as an independent member of society.

Adolescence is thus a period of limbo in which individuals no longer need parental care but are not yet ready to take on the roles and responsibilities of adulthood. If teens are to become individuals capable of adapting to new situations it is crucial that they temporarily rupture the close emotional bonds with parents and relatives that served their purpose so well in childhood, but which would stifle their development as independent beings if continued unabated. Adolescence is a time of fission and fusion, a kind of "out with the old and in with the new." Adolescents must bond and mate with their own generation and to explore their place in the world. To do this, however, they must leave the nest and become independent. Leaving the nest is a risky business, but it is an evolutionary design feature of all social primates as males seek out sexual partners from outside the rearing group. Fighting with parents and seeking age peers "all help the adolescent away from the home territory" (Powell, 2006:867). As Caspi and Moffitt (1995:500) put it: "[E]very curfew broken, car stolen, joint smoked, or baby conceived is a statement of independence."

For all its alleged "storm and stress," then, adolescence is a normal and necessary period in the human lifespan (Rosenfeld & Nicodemus, 2003). There is much to learn about being an adult, and adolescence is a time to experiment with a variety of social skills before having to put them into practice in earnest. To encourage all this experimentation, natural selection has provided adolescents with the necessary tools. The first of these important tools is the huge increase in testosterone that accompanies puberty (Felson & Haynie, 2002). Figure 8.2 illustrates the ebb and flow of testosterone across the lifespan for both sexes. Testosterone organizes the male brain during the second trimester of pregnancy so that it will respond in male typical ways when the brain is activated in that direction

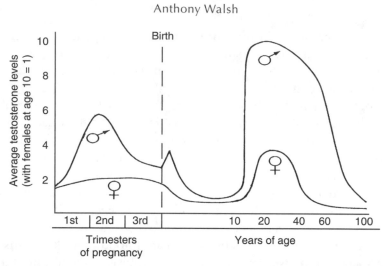

Figure 8.2 Testosterone Levels of Human Males and Females from Conception to Old Age.

Source: Ellis & Walsh (2000).

by the pubertal surge. Note that after sex-specific brain organization takes place, there is little difference in levels of male and female testosterone until puberty, at which time male levels dramatically exceed female levels. Testosterone is most responsible for the development of male characteristics, including behavioral characteristics such as aggression and dominance seeking (see Mazur, this volume).

The evolutionary "purpose" of this testosterone surge is to facilitate the very behaviors—risk taking, sensation seeking, sexual experimentation, dominance contests, self-assertiveness, and so on—that generates so much annoyance, disgust, and trepidation among those who forget that they went through the stage themselves. None of these facilitated behaviors is necessarily antisocial or criminal per se: risk taking could mean joining the marines, sensation seeking could be bungee jumping, sexual experimentation could mean consensual safe sex, dominance contests could be sport participation, and self-assertiveness simply demands to be treated fairly. They could, however, become something quite other, especially in so-called honor subcultures, which Mazur and Booth (1998:362) describe as "communities in which young men are hypersensitive to insult, rushing in to defend their reputations in [violent] dominance contests."

No one attributes a causal role for testosterone in these risky behaviors; it is only one of a concatenation of interacting biological and social variables, which, together, affect behavior. Testosterone is like the gas in your car: it doesn't make you want to take the trip to lover's lane, rather it helps you to get there once you've decided that's where you want to go. For instance, a longitudinal study of 1,400 boys found that testosterone levels were unrelated to conduct problems for boys with "non-deviant" or "possibly deviant" friends, but conduct problems were greatly elevated among boys with high testosterone who associated with "definitely deviant" peers (Maughan, 2005). Testosterone also appears to reduce fear (van Honk, et al., 2005) which explains why high testosterone levels are found in high sensation seekers (see Zuckerman, 2007, for a review). Although testosterone levels are highly heritable, at least 40 percent of the variance is attributable to environmental factors (Booth, et al., 2006). Testosterone levels rise and fall to help organisms meet the challenges present in their environments. The "need" to conform to risky deviant behavioral patterns, to seek dangerous sensations, and to engage in dominance competitions with other males certainly qualifies as challenges that would require raising testosterone levels to meet them (Mazur, 2005).

Risk taking does not occur because teenagers lack logical reasoning abilities to sort out the ratio of costs to benefits of engaging in it. The logical reasoning of 15 year olds, contrary to the stereotype, is on par with that of adults and they are able to perceive risk and estimate vulnerability to it just as well (Reyna & Farley, 2006). The problem is that they tend to discount their perceptions and estimates of risk because of poor impulse control, poor emotional regulation, and strong peer influence. Logical decisions can be undermined by emotion and peer pressure even among very mature adults; it is so much easier undermined among adolescents when emotions are in the driver's seat and similarly emotion-driven peers occupy the passenger seats. Teens can act like adults under non-stressful conditions, but when under stress they fall back on emotions and on cues from their peers. They do so because they are not yet able to access areas of the brain that allow adults to react to stress in a more controlled way.

Puberty, Adolescence, and the Brain

Ernst, et al. (2006:299) explain adolescent risk taking in terms of the lack of balance between certain areas in the brain associated with approach/avoidance behaviors: "The propensity during adolescence for reward/novelty seeking in the face of uncertainty or potential harm might be explained by a strong reward system (nucleus accumbens), a weak harm-avoidance system (amygdala), and/or an inefficient supervisory system (medial/ventral prefrontal cortex)." This is augmented by Aaron White's (2004:4) summation of the key messages from the 2003 conference of the New York Academy of Sciences:

1. Much of the behavior characterizing adolescence is rooted in biology intermingling with environmental influences to cause teens to

conflict with their parents, take more risks, and experience wide swings in emotion.

2. The lack of synchrony between a physically mature body and a still maturing nervous system may explain these behaviors.

3. Adolescents' sensitivities to rewards appear to be different than in adults, prompting them to seek higher levels of novelty and stimulation to achieve the same feeling of pleasure.

4. With the right dose of guidance and understanding, adolescence can be a relatively smooth transition.

At the same time that adolescents are being juiced up by testosterone they are experiencing profound changes in their neurobiology. Functional magnetic resonance imaging (fMRI) studies show that adolescents have exaggerated nucleus accumbens (NAcc) activity relative to activity in regions of the prefrontal cortex (PFC) relative to children and adults (Eshel, et al., 2007; Galvan, et al., 2006). Because the NAcc is implicated in reward-seeking behaviors and the PFC is an inhibitor of impulse, findings such as these reveal mechanisms behind the adolescent propensity to favor short-run hedonism over more reasoned long-term goals.

Adolescence is also accompanied by changes in the ratios of excitatory and inhibitory neurotransmitters; the excitatory transmitters dopamine and glutamate peak while the inhibitory transmitters gamma-aminobutyric acid and serotonin are reduced (Collins, 2004; Walker, 2002). Having all the biological tools needed to increase novelty seeking, sensation seeking, status seeking, and competitiveness, it seems as though the behaviors manifested in adolescence were "meant to be;" that is, they are adaptations forged by natural selection (Spear, 2000; White, 2004). Evolutionary biologists stress that natural selection favors the most adventurous and dominant males because such characteristics typically result in more mating opportunities, and thus to greater reproductive success. Mid-adolescence and early adulthood is a period of intense competition among males for dominance and status among many primate species aimed ultimately at securing more mating opportunities than the next male. As Martin Daly (1996:193) put it: "There are many reasons to think that we've been designed to be maximally competitive and conflictual in young adulthood."

In addition to all these chemical changes, the adolescent brain is also going through an intense period of physical resculpting: "Significant changes in multiple regions of the prefrontal cortex [occur] throughout the course of adolescence, especially with respect to the processes of myelination and synaptic pruning" (Steinberg, 2005:70). The pubertal hormonal surges prompt the increase of gene expression in the brain, which then play their parts in slowly refining the neural circuitry to its adult form (Walker, 2002). Magnetic resonance imaging studies reveal that the PFC (the modulator of emotions from the limbic system) undergoes a wave of synaptic overproduction just prior to puberty, which is followed by a period of pruning during adolescence and early adulthood (Giedd, 2004; Sowell, et al., 2004). The selective retention and elimination of synapses relics crucially on experience-dependent input from the environment because the developing brain physically "captures" these inputs in somatic time the way that natural selection seizes on advantageous alleles in evolutionary time.

The adolescent PFC is also less completely myelinated (myelin is the fatty substance that coats and insulates axons) than the adult PFC (Sowell, et al., 2004). Because the more complete the myelination of the axons the faster the message, a less myelinated brain will result in a larger "time lapse" between the onset of an emotional event in the limbic system and a person's rational judgment of it in the PFC. MRI studies (e.g., Nelson, et al., 2003) have shown that adolescents exhibit greater brain activation in response to angry and fearful faces than to happy and neutral faces whereas adults show the opposite.

In other words, there are *physical* reasons for the greater ratio of emotional to rational responses evidenced by many teens. The physical immaturity of the adolescent brain combined with a "supercharged" physiology facilitates the tendency to assign faulty attributions to situations and the intentions of others. In other words, a brain on "go slow superimposed on a physiology on fast forward" explains why many teenagers "find it difficult to accurately gauge the meanings and intentions of others and to experience more stimuli as aversive during adolescence than they did as children and will do so when they are adults" (Walsh, 2002:143). As Richard Restak (2001:76) so well put it: "The immaturity of the adolescent's behavior is perfectly mirrored by the immaturity of the adolescent's brain."

Several studies show generally that the earlier the onset of puberty the greater the level of problem behavior for both girls and boys (Cota-Robles, et al., 2002; Felson & Haynie, 2002). Juveniles who enter puberty significantly earlier than their peers must confront their "raging hormones" with a brain that is no more mature than those of their age peers. In one study, testosterone level predicted future problem behavior, but only for boys who entered puberty early (Drigotas & Udry, 1993). Felson and Haynie (2002) found that boys who experience early onset of puberty were more likely to commit a number of delinquent and other antisocial acts than other boys, but that they were also more autonomous, better psychologically adjusted, and had more friends.

What about when adolescence is over and adulthood is attained? We talk about "aging out" of crime, but this is just as empty of explanatory power as saying adolescence "ages in" crime: we need to know what the mechanisms are. In terms of brain mechanisms, we know that around about the age of 20, the "go get it" neurotransmitters start to decrease, and the "stop it" inhibitory transmitters start to increase, the brain is more fully myelinated, and the connections between areas associated with emotions and cognition become more fully integrated (Sowell, et al., 2004; Steinberg, 2007). With a more mature brain on board, more adult-like personality traits emerge. McCrae (2000:183) and his colleagues report findings from five different countries showing age-related decreases in personality traits positively related to antisocial behavior and increases in personality traits positively related to prosocial behavior: "From age 18 to 30 there are declines in neuroticism, extraversion, and openness to experience, and increases in agreeableness and conscientiousness; after age 30 the same trends are found, although the rate of change seems to decrease." The fine-tuning of neurological and endocrine systems occurs across the lifespan and thankfully results in personality traits in adulthood conducive to prosocial behavior for the great majority of individuals. These changes lay the foundations for the acquisition of responsible social roles that help us stay on the straight and narrow.

Risk Factors for Serious Delinquency: The Terrible Twins, ADHD and CD

Some individuals go beyond the normal adolescent hell raising to commit serious crimes. One of the major predictors of which individuals will continue to commit crimes after adolescence is the comorbidity of attention deficit with hyperactivity disorder (ADHD) and **conduct disorder (CD)**. These separate but often linked syndromes are neuropsychological and temperamental deficits that can lead to criminal offending long after adolescence. For those who are afflicted with both, ADHD symptoms usually appear first, followed by CD.

ADHD is a chronic neurological condition that is behaviorally manifested as constant moving and restlessness, low levels of inhibitory control, impulsiveness, difficulties with peers, frequent disruptive behavior, short attention span, academic underachievement, risk-taking behavior, and proneness to extreme boredom. As with any other syndrome, the symptoms vary widely in their severity and frequency of occurrence. Most healthy children will manifest some of these symptoms at one time or another, but they cluster together to form a syndrome in ADHD children (8 out of 14 symptoms are required for diagnosis) and are chronic and more severe than simple high spirits (Durston, 2003). A virtual cascade of brain imaging studies finds many differences (albeit small ones) in brain anatomy and physiology between ADHD and non-ADHD children (Raz, 2004; Sanjiv & Thaden, 2004).

ADHD affects somewhere between 2 and 9 percent of the childhood population and is four or five times more prevalent in males than in females (Levy, et al., 1997). Although the precise cause of ADHD is not known, it is known that genes play a huge role (Coolidge, et al., 2000). Compared to other behavioral disorders, the heritability of ADHD is exceptionally high (in the .75 to .91 range). These heritability values are consistently found regardless of whether ADHD is considered to be a categorical or continuous trait (Levy, et al., 1997). Environmental features that have been identified as playing a role in the etiology of ADHD are fetal exposure to drugs, alcohol, and tobacco, perinatal complications, and head trauma (Durston, 2003). Subsequent environmental factors such as family, school, and peer variables appear not to have any causal impact on it, although they can exacerbate its symptoms (Coolidge, et al., 2000). ADHD symptoms generally decline in their severity with age, although about 90 percent of ADHD sufferers continue to display some impairment into adulthood (Willoughby, 2003).

Neurological deficits associated with ADHD include suboptimal arousal and frontal lobe dysfunction. Some, but not all, children diagnosed with ADHD show EEG patterns of under-arousal (slow brain waves) similar to those found in adult psychopaths (Lynam, 1996). Such a brain wave pattern is experienced subjectively as boredom, which motivates the person to seek or create environments containing more excitement. ADHD behavior can be normalized temporarily by administering **methylpheni-date** (Ritalin). The efficacy of Ritalin and other such stimulants gave researchers their first clues to the underlying neurochemical basis for the disorder (Durston, 2003). We know that although stimulant drugs have the effect of *increasing* activity for non-ADHD individuals, they have a calming or normalizing effect on suboptimally aroused individuals by raising the activity of the brain's sensory mechanisms to normal levels. This relieves feelings of boredom because the brain is now able to be more attentive to features of the environment that it could not previously capture. When on medication, ADHD children are less disruptive, become less obnoxious to peers, and can focus more on schoolwork.

Given the range of symptoms associated with ADHD, it is not surprising that it is consistently found to be related to a wide variety of antisocial behaviors. A review of 100 studies conducted prior to 1999 found that 99 of them reported a positive relationship between ADHD and various antisocial behaviors (violent and property crimes, delinquency, drug abuse) while only one (for drug offenses) was found not to be significant (Ellis & Walsh, 2000).

ADHD delinquents are more likely than non-ADHD delinquents to persist in their offending as adults, but this probability rises dramatically for ADHD children also diagnosed with conduct disorder (CD). CD is defined as the "persistent display of serious antisocial actions [assaulting, stealing, setting fires, cruelty to animals] that are extreme given the child's developmental level and have a significant impact on the rights of others" (Lynam, 1996:211). ADHD and CD are found to co-occur in 30 to 50 percent of cases in most clinical and epidemiological studies (reviewed in Lynam 1996). Conduct disorder has an onset at around 5 years of age. It remains at a steady rate for girls (about 0.8% of all girls) and rises to about 2.8 percent at age 15, but rises steadily in boys from about 2.1 percent at age 5 to about 5.5 percent at age 15 (Maughan, et al., 2004). Conduct disorder also appears to be a neurological disorder, and there are substantial genetic effects on the syndrome, with heritability estimates reported to range between .27 and .78 (Coolidge, et al., 2000).

Terrie Moffitt (1996) has proposed that verbal deficits are what place children at risk for CD. If this is true, then the reported heritability estimates for CD may actually be heritability estimates of verbal IQ. Moffitt indicates that neurological evidence suggests that the left frontal lobes contain the mechanisms by which children process their parents' instructions ("No!," "That's naughty," "Please pick up your shoes"). These instructions then become the child's internalized verbally based basis of self-control. Children with deficits in these frontal lobe mechanisms do not profit from their parents' verbal instructions and thus tend to develop a present-oriented and impulsive cognitive style. Lacking normal levels of abstract reasoning, such children may have to learn lessons through the more painful process of trial and error and may thus experience more frequent punishments for their lack of compliance with instructions.

Many of the cognitive and temperamental symptoms of CD and ADHD children are similar. CD children tend to score in the low–normal or borderline range of intelligence and are highly overrepresented in impoverished family environments (Lewis, 1991). As mentioned, the co-occurrence of ADHD and CD represent the greatest risk for serious delinquency and adult criminality. A number of researchers have offered evidence that ADHD is a product of a deficient behavioral inhibition system (BIS) and CD is a product of an oversensitive behavioral activation system (BAS) (Levy, 2004; Quay, 1997) (See Walsh & Beaver, Chapter 1, this volume, for a discussion of the BIS and BAS.) If this is the case, then those afflicted with both ADHD and CD suffer a double disability. First, they are inclined to seek high levels of stimulation because of an over-sensitive BAS, and, second, they are hampered by a faulty BIS, and thus have difficulty putting a stop to their search for pleasurable stimulation once it is initiated.

CD children are most likely to be found in impoverished families and are significantly more likely than children without CD to have parents diagnosed with antisocial personality disorder (ASPD) (Sergeant, et al., 2003). One of the psychiatric requirements for a diagnosis of ASPD is a childhood diagnosis of CD. Thus, if a parent is diagnosed with ASPD it means that he (almost always a he) was diagnosed with CD as a child, and if his offspring is also diagnosed with CD, the cross-generation linkage strongly suggests genetic transmission.

Lynam (1996:22) describes the trajectory from ADHD/CD to criminality in a way that reminds us of the process of reactive gene/environment correlation, stating that the co-occurrence of ADHD and CD: "[M]ay tax the skills of parents and lead to the adoption of coercive child rearing techniques, which in turn may enhance the risk of antisocial behavior. Entry into school may bring academic failure and increase the child's frustration, which may increase his or her level of aggressive behavior. Finally, the peer rejection associated with hyperactivity may lead to increased social isolation and conflict with peers."

I am not suggesting that ADHD represents some form of hopeless pathology that leads its victims down the road to inevitable criminality, particularly in cases where CD is not also present. The ever increasing numbers of children being diagnosed with ADHD most likely reflects a growing intolerance for disruptive classroom behavior than anything else. In other words, environmental changes push more children over the risk threshold for being labeled with the disorder. Perhaps it should not even be called a disorder, but rather a natural variant of human diversity. While acknowledging that ADHD is problematic in modern society, that it has real neurological foundations, and that parents are probably right in the current social context to choose to medicate their ADHD children, Jaak Panksepp (1998) asserts that ADHD-like behaviors are observed in the young of all social species, and it is called "rough-and-tumble" play. ADHD-like behaviors may have even been adaptive in our evolutionary history when restless boldness and curiosity meant exploring beyond known boundaries (Crawford, 1998). If the "true" rate of ADHD is as high as reported, then genes underlying it have survived natural selection, which means that they must have conferred some benefits in evolutionary environments even if they do not in modern, evolutionarily novel, classroom environments.

Many ADHD individuals have above average IQs and are creative, so perhaps the symptoms of ADHD are only problematic in the modern context in which children are expected to sit still for long periods learning subjects that they find boring. Panksepp's suggestion that we as a society provide far more opportunities in schools for the young (especially boys) to indulge in their biological need for rough and tumble play is sound

—*more recess, less Ritalin* sounds like a good rallying cry for a drug-free delinquency reduction program.

Patterns of Serious Delinquency

Figure 8.3 presents the developmental pyramid model of offending from Thornberry, et al. (2004). This model focuses on the escalation of seriousness of delinquent acts being committed as boys age. The model is based on three longitudinal studies—the Denver Youth Survey, the Pittsburgh Youth Study, and the Rochester Youth Developmental Study—and includes over 4,000 subjects followed since 1987. Their model presents three theoretically distinct offending pathways that represent patterns of behavior; it says *nothing* about individual characteristics.

The *authority conflict* pathway is the earliest pathway (starting before the age of 12) and begins with simple stubborn behavior, followed by defiance and authority avoidance. Note that the base of the triangle represents the earliest stage and contains the most boys. Some boys in this pathway move into the second stage (*defiance/disobedience*), and a few more into the

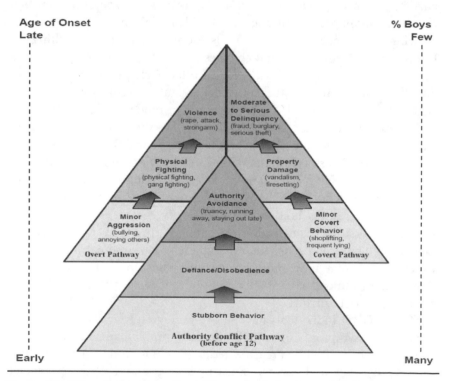

Figure 8.3 Three Pathways to Boys' Disruptive Behavior and Delinquency.

Source: Thornberry, et al. (2004).

authority avoidance stage. At this point, some boys progress to one of the other two pathways, but many will go no further than authority avoidance. The *covert* pathway starts later and involves minor offenses in stage 1 that become progressively more serious for a few boys who enter stage 3 on this pathway. The covert pathway would consist overwhelmingly of boys who were not diagnosed with CD. The *overt* pathway progresses from minor aggressive acts in stage 1 to very serious violent acts in stage 3. The more seriously involved delinquents in the overt and covert pathways may switch back and forth between violent and property crimes, with the most serious probably fitting the criteria for ADHD/CD comorbidity. The take-home lesson of this model is that as boys get older their crimes become more serious, but happily there are far fewer of them.

Terrie Moffitt's Dual Pathway Theory

Whereas the Thornberry, et al. (2004) model is concerned with behavioral pathways, Terrie Moffitt's theory is concerned with individuals' developmental pathways. Based on findings from an ongoing longitudinal study of a New Zealand birth cohort, it has become a robust empirically supported theory and has been described as the "most innovative approach to age-crime relationships" in the literature (Tittle, 2000:68).

It had long been known that the vast majority of youth who offend during adolescence desist, but that there are also a small number of them who continue to offend into adulthood. Moffitt calls the former group **adolescent limited (AL)** offenders and the latter group **life-course persistent (LCP)** offenders and charts the life-course trajectories of both. The AL/LCP dichotomy is simply a convenient typology and it is not meant to imply that all offenders fit snugly into one category or the other. Differences among offenders are quantitative rather than qualitative, reflecting varying levels of antisocial propensity. Also, the phrase *life-course persistent* is simply a convenient and descriptive phrase; and is not meant to imply that these offenders commit crimes across the entire life course—we rarely see 60-year-old muggers. Despite the qualifiers, Moffitt's typology has great heuristic value for exploring similarities and differences between low-rate offending/early desisting delinquents and high-rate offending/late desisting offenders.

Life-course persistent offenders are individuals who begin offending prior to the onset of puberty and continue well into adulthood. Studies differentiating between prepubescent and postpubescent starters have consistently found that early starters are the most frequent and serious offenders in all age categories (Farrington, 1996). Moffitt's theory states that LCP offenders are saddled with neuropsychological and temperamental deficits that are manifested in low IQ, hyperactivity, inattentiveness, negative emotionality, slow heart rate, and low impulse control. These problems arise from a combination of genetic and environmental effects on central nervous system development. Environmental risk factors include being the offspring of a single teenage mother, low SES, abuse/neglect, and inconsistent discipline (Moffitt & Walsh, 2003). These related individual and environmental impairments initiate a cumulative process of negative person/environment interactions that result in a life-course trajectory propelling individuals toward ever hardening antisocial attitudes and behaviors.

Moffitt describes the antisocial trajectory of LCP offenders as one of: "[B]iting and hitting at age 4, shoplifting and truancy at age 10, selling drugs and stealing cars at age 16, robbery and rape at age 22, fraud and child abuse at age 30; the underlying disposition remains the same, but its expression changes form as new social opportunities arise at different points of development" (1993:679). This age-consistent behavior is matched by cross-situational behavioral consistency. LCP offenders "lie at home, steal from shops, cheat at school, fight in bars, and embezzle at work" (Moffitt, 1993:679). Given this antisocial consistency across time and place, opportunities for change and for legitimate success become increasingly unlikely for these individuals.

Although LCP offenders constituted only 7 percent of the studied cohort, they were responsible for more than 50 percent of all delinquent and criminal acts committed by it (Henry, et al., 1996). These figures are consistent with other cohort data indicating that serious and frequent offending is concentrated among a very small percentage of offenders, the majority of whom began offending prior to puberty (Walsh, 2002). Moreover, whereas AL offenders tend to commit relatively minor offenses such as public drunkenness and petty theft, LCP offenders tend to be convicted of more serious crimes against the person such as assault, robbery, rape, domestic violence, and carrying concealed weapons (Moffitt & Walsh, 2003).

Adolescent limited offenders have a different developmental history that places them on a prosocial trajectory that is temporarily derailed at adolescence. They are not burdened with the neuropsychological problems that weigh heavily on LCP offenders, and they are adequately socialized in childhood by competent parents. AL offenders are "normal" youths adapting to the transitional events surrounding adolescence and whose offending is a social phenomenon played out in peer groups, and does not reflect any stable personal deficiencies (Moffitt, 1993:692).

According to Moffitt, many more teens than in the past are being diverted from their prosocial life trajectories by biological, social, and economic vectors that are increasingly diverging. Better health and nutrition

has lowered the average age of puberty while at the same time technological advances have increased the average time needed to prepare for
participation in the economy. These changes have resulted in about a 5- to
10-year "maturity gap" between puberty and entry into the job market.
Thus, "adolescent-limited offending is a product of an interaction between age and historical period" (Moffitt, 1993:692). Filled with youthful
energy, strength, and confidence, and a strong desire to shed the restrictions
of childhood, AL offenders are attracted to the excitement of antisocial
peer groups, which are typically led by antisocially "experienced" LCP
youths. Once initiated into the group, juveniles learn the attitudes and
techniques of offending (as differential association theory asserts) through
mimicking others, and gain reinforcement (as social learning theory
asserts) in the form of much desired group approval and acceptance for
doing so.

Moffitt maintains that adolescent antisocial behavior is adaptive because
it offers those engaging in it opportunities to gain valuable resources they
could not otherwise obtain. The most valuable of these resources is peer
group status. Teenagers who are still dependent on their parents for so
many things turn their envious eyes on LCP offenders, who, while no
older than they, already have many of the things that signal independence
and mature status, such as cars, nice clothes, and access to sex partners.
It is no accident that disruptive and belligerent antisocial youths who are
in school become "central members of prominent classroom cliques"
(Rodkin, et al., 2000:21). In the eyes of their admirers, the behavior of LCP
offenders brings them positive results, and many see no reason why similar behavior on their part cannot bring them the same results. LCP and AL
youths reinforce one another for their antisocial behavior; LCP youths are
rewarded with the admiration of their AL peers, and AL youths receive
reinforcement by being accepted by LCP youths as their peers.

Figure 8.4 compares the life-course trajectories for LCP and AL offenders. Note the role of association with delinquent peers in the two trajectories. In the case of LCP offenders, *stable* antisocial characteristics precede
association with delinquent peers. This exemplifies the principle of active
rGE that like seeks like (see Chapter 1 for a discussion of rGE). For AL
offenders, by way of contrast, association with delinquent peers precedes
the development of *temporary* antisocial characteristics. This suggests that
association with delinquent peers may be necessary to initiate delinquency
for most AL offenders, and that there is little or no genetic influence on
AL delinquency. Teens have a limited ability to choose their environments,
so even those at low risk for delinquency may succumb to it under the
influence of their more daring peers whom they temporarily admire and
seek to emulate at a time in life when peer influence is of such tremendous
importance.

Life-course persistent: Applicable to congenitally predisposed youths

Temperamental and neuropsychological deficits combine with → inept parenting (passive G/E correlation)	Antisocial characteristics, negative interaction with others (evocative G/E correlation) →	Association with delinquent peers (active G/E correlation) →	Delinquency, crime, and numerous other antisocial behaviors (active G/E correlation)

Adolescent limited: Applicable to many "normal" youths during adolescence

Early puberty, no real social role, desire for → independence. Long wait for adult roles	Association with delinquent peers. Antisocial behavior mimicked and reinforced →	Temporary antisocial characteristics →	Delinquency. Will desist with neurological and social maturity

Figure 8.4 Moffitt's Dual Developmental Pathways.

Desisting

As AL offenders mature neurologically and socially, they begin to realize that an adult criminal record will severely limit their future options. They also begin to realize that they are freer now to structure their environments consistent with their innate preferences. For some AL offenders, **desistance** from antisocial behavior is abrupt, for others it is a slower process. Much depends on a combination of how well they were integrated into the antisocial peer group, what prosocial opportunities become available to them, and on personal characteristics. By definition, offenders who limit their offending to adolescence have accumulated a store of positive attachments (they elicit positive responses from prosocial others) and academic skills (they stayed in school and did reasonably well) before they started offending, and even while they were offending. These attachments and skills can be called on to provide them with prosocial opportunities such as a good marriage and a good job. In Moffitt's (1993:690) words, AL offenders desist from offending because they are "psychologically healthy," and "healthy youths respond adaptively to changing contingencies."

Other life-course theories (Sampson & Laub, 1999) have also shown that obtaining a stable job and attachment to a prosocial spouse are important protective factors for preventing continuing criminal behavior (interestingly, testosterone levels among men have been found to fall with marriage and rise with divorce (Mazur & Michalek, 1998). Sampson and Laub did not differentiate between LCP and AL offenders (they explicitly deny such a dichotomy), but report that positive social bonds represent **social capital**, and are the result of prior "social investment" that only AL offenders seem to accumulate. Given that LCP offenders essentially burn their prosocial bridges early in life, we may assume that Sampson and Laub are referring only to AL offenders, who, of course, constitute by far the biggest group of adolescent offenders. If LCP offenders do acquire jobs, girlfriends, wives, the problem, according to Gottfredson and Hirschi (1990:141): "[I]s that the offender tends to convert these institutions into sources of satisfaction consistent with his previous criminal behavior." In other words, they expand their antisocial repertoire into domestic abuse and workplace crime.

We also know from the **assortative mating** (like seeking like in dating and mating) data for antisocial behavior and characteristics (Krueger, et al., 1998; Quinton, et al., 1993) that the likelihood of persistent offenders securing the support of a non-deviant spouse is slim. Only 15 percent of the boys in the New Zealand cohort with early onset of offending had escaped all adjustment problems by the age of 26 (Moffitt & Walsh, 2003). Given the many differences between late- and early-onset boys discovered in numerous longitudinal studies, it is difficult to disagree with C. Ray Jeffery's statement that the early-onset persistent offender is "biologically different from the adolescent offender who stops at age 18– 21" (1993:494).

Adolescents who Abstain from Delinquency

Because experimenting with antisocial behavior is normative behavior for adolescents, those who abstain altogether are unusual. Consistent with many other studies, the New Zealand cohort contained only a small group of males who avoided virtually any antisocial behavior during adolescence. Examining the personality profiles at age 18, it was determined that abstainers were extremely self-controlled, fearful, interpersonally timid, socially inept, and most were virginal at age 18. Subsequent studies at age 26 confirmed that abstainers had not become late-onset offenders (Moffitt, et al., 2002). They retained their self-constrained personality as adults, were mostly settled into marriage, had delayed having children, were likely to be college educated, held high-status jobs, and expressed optimism about their futures.

Cohort abstainers fit the personality profiles found in other studies for youths who abstain from drug and sexual experimentation in a historical period when such experimentation is normative: i.e., they were over-controlled, not curious, not active, not open to experience, socially isolated, and lacking in social skills. By way of contrast, frequent users and the sexually permissive were alienated, deficient on impulse control, and were less attached to parents than either the experimenters or abstainers (Shedler & Block, 1990; Walsh, 1992).

The kind of inhibited and introverted personality characteristic of abstainers is consistent with studies of autonomic nervous system (ANS) arousal and criminality. Individuals with a hyperarousable ANS are easily conditioned (socialized), and those with a hypo-arousable ANS are conditioned with difficulty. Given the personality profiles of abstainers, it is probable that they are individuals located at the "hyper" tail of the ANS arousal distribution, and thus have excessive guilt feelings and excessive fear of the negative consequences of nonconformity (Moffitt & Walsh, 2003).

What Role do Genes Play in Delinquency?

Genes are obviously responsible for initiating all the physical changes accompanying puberty, but what role do they play beyond that? Numerous studies have found large heritability coefficients (ranging from .20 to .82) for the various traits associated with delinquent and criminal behavior such as fearlessness, aggressiveness, sensation seeking, impulsiveness, and low IQ (Moffitt & Walsh, 2003). High estimates for these traits contrast with the rather low heritability estimates from meta-analyses of between .40 and .58 for adolescent and adult antisocial behavior noted in Chapter 2. Although we must keep in mind the distinction between LCP offenders (probably high genetic contribution) and AL offenders (low to non-existent genetic contribution), we may still ask why the heritability for delinquent and criminal behavior is so small compared with the traits that are its constituent parts. One reason is that the constituent parts are *traits* whereas criminality is *behavior* expressing those traits. Parents potentially have a greater deal of control over their offspring's behavior, but little or none beyond the genes they bequeathed them over their personality traits. This is why the heritability of all forms of antisocial behavior is less than the basic psychological traits that are its constituent parts. In other words, behavior is more subject to environmental influences than are personality traits. Parenting matters, and that is what the last of the four key messages from the 2003 conference of the New York Academy of Sciences ("With the right dose of guidance and understanding, adolescence can be a relatively smooth transition") conveys (White, 2004:4).

References

Akers, R. (1998). *Social learning and social structure: a general theory of crime and deviance*. Boston, MA: Northeastern University Press.

Anderson, E. (1999). *Code of the street: decency, violence, and the moral life of the inner city.* New York: W.W. Norton.

Booth, A., D. Granger, A. Mazur, & Katie Kivligan (2006). Testosterone and social behavior. *Social Forces,* 85:167–191.

Caspi, A. & T. Moffitt (1995). The continuity of maladaptive behavior: from description to understanding in the study of antisocial behavior. In Ciccheti, D. & D. Cohen (Eds.). *Manual of developmental psychology.* New York: John Wiley & Sons.

Colligan, R., D. Osborne, W. Swenson, & K. Oxford (1989). *The MMPI: a contemporary normative study.* Odessa, FL: Psychological Assessment Resources.

Collins, R. (2004). Onset and desistence in criminal careers: neurobiology and the age—crime relationship. *Journal of Offender Rehabilitation,* 39:1–19.

Coolidge, F., L. Thede, & S. Young (2000). Heritability and the comorbidity of attention deficit hyperactivity disorder with behavioral disorders and executive function deficits: a preliminary investigation. *Developmental Neuropsychology,* 17:273–287.

Cota-Robles, S., M. Neiss, & D. Rowe (2002). The role of puberty in violent and nonviolent delinquency among Anglo American, Mexican American, and African American boys. *Journal of Adolescent Research,* 17:364–376.

Crawford, C. (1998). The theory of evolution in the study of human behavior: an introduction and overview. In Crawford, C. & D. Krebs (Eds.). *Handbook of evolutionary psychology: ideas, issues, and applications.* Mahwah, NJ: Lawrence Erlbaum Associates, Inc.

Daly, M. (1996). Evolutionary adaptationism: another biological approach to criminal and antisocial behavior. In Bock, G. & J. Goode (Eds.). *Genetics of criminal and antisocial behaviour.* Chichester: John Wiley & Sons.

Drigotas, S. & Udry, J. (1993). Biosocial models of adolescent problem behavior: extensions to panel design. *Social Biology,* 40:1–7.

Durston, S. (2003). A review of the biological bases of ADHD: what have we learned from imaging studies? *Mental Retardation and Developmental Disabilities,* 9:184–195.

Ellis, L. & A. Walsh (2000). *Criminology: a global perspective.* Boston, MA: Allyn & Bacon.

Ernst, M., D. Pine, & M. Hardin (2006). Triadic model of the neurobiology of motivated behavior in adolescence. *Psychiatric Medicine,* 36:299–312.

Eshel, N., E. Nelson, R. Blair, D. Pine, & M. Ernst (2007). Neural substrates of choice selection in adults and adolescents: development of the ventrolateral prefrontal and anterior cingulated cortices. *Neuropsychologia,* 45:1270–1279.

Farrington, D. (1996). The explanation and prevention of youthful offending. In Hawkins, J. (Ed.). *Delinquency and crime: current theories.* Cambridge: Cambridge University Press.

Federal Bureau of Investigation. (2006). *Crime in the United State: 2005.* Washington, DC: U.S. Government Printing Office.

Felson, R. & D. Haynie (2002). Pubertal development, social factors, and delinquency among adolescent boys. *Criminology,* 40:967–988.

Galvan, A., T. Hare, C. Parra, J. Penn, H. Voss, G. Glover, et al. (2006). Earlier development of the accumbens relative to orbitofrontal cortex might underlie risk-taking behavior in adolescents. *The Journal of Neuroscience,* 26:6885–6892.

Giedd, J. (2004). Structural magnetic resonance imaging of the adolescent brain. *Annals of the New York Academy of Science,* 1021:77–85.

Gottfredson, M. & T. Hirschi (1990). *A general theory of crime.* Stanford, CA: Stanford University Press.

Greenberg, D. (1985). Age, crime, and social explanation. *American Journal of Sociology,* 91:1–21.

Henry, B., Caspi, A., Moffitt, T., & Silva, P. (1996). Temperament and familial predictors of violent and non-violent criminal convictions: from age 3 to age 18. *Developmental Psychology,* 32:614–623.

Hirschi, T. & M. Gottfredson (1983). Age and the explanation of crime. *American Journal of Sociology,* 89:552–584.

Jeffery, C. R. (1993). Obstacles to the development of research in crime and delinquency. *Journal of Research in Crime and Delinquency,* 30:491–497.

Krueger, R., T. Moffitt, A. Caspi, A. Bleske, & P. Silva (1998). Assortative mating for antisocial behavior: developmental and methodological implications. *Behavior Genetics,* 28:173–185.

Levy, F. (2004). Synaptic gating and ADHD: a biological theory of comorbidity of ADHD and anxiety. *Neuropsychopharmacology*, 29:1589–1596.

Levy, F., D. Hay, M. McStephen, C. Wood, & I. Waldman (1997). Attention-deficit hyperactivity disorder: a category or a continuum? Genetic analysis of a large-scale twin study. *Journal of the American Academy of Child and Adolescent Psychiatry*, 36:737–744.

Lewis, D. (1991). Conduct disorder. In Lewis, M. (Ed.). *Child and adolescent psychiatry: a comprehensive textbook*. Baltimore, MD: Williams & Wilkins.

Lynam, D. (1996). Early identification of chronic offenders: who is the fledgling psychopath? *Psychological Bulletin*, 120:209–234.

Maughan, B. (2005). Developmental trajectory modeling: a view from developmental psychopathology. *Annals of the American Academy of Political and Social Science*, 602:118–130.

Maughan, B., R. Rowe, J. Messer, R. Goodman, & H. Meltzer (2004). Conduct disorder and oppositional defiant disorder in a national sample: developmental epidemiology. *Journal of Child Psychology and Psychiatry*, 43:609–621.

Mazur, A. (2005) *Biosociology of dominance and deference*. Lanham, MD: Rowman & Littlefield.

Mazur, A. & A. Booth (1998). Testosterone and dominance in men. *Behavioral and Brain Sciences*, 21:353–397.

Mazur, A. & J. Michalek (1998). Marriage, divorce, and male testosterone. *Social Forces*, 77:315–30.

McCrae, R., P. Costa, F. Ostendorf, A. Angleitner, M. Hrebickova, M. Avia, et al. (2000). Nature over nurture: temperament, personality, and life span development. *Journal of Personality and Social Psychology*, 78:173–186.

Moffitt, T. (1993). Adolescent-limited and life-course-persistent antisocial behavior: a developmental taxonomy. *Psychological Review*, 100:674–701.

Moffitt, T. (1996). The neuropsychology of conduct disorder. In Cordella, P. & L. Siegel (Eds.). *Readings in contemporary criminology*. Boston, MA: Northeastern University Press.

Moffitt, T. E., Caspi, A., Harrington, H., & Milne, B. (2002). Males on the life-course persistent and adolescence-limited antisocial pathways: follow-up at age 26. *Development & Psychopathology*, 14:179–206.

Moffitt, T. & A. Walsh (2003). The adolescence-limited/life-course persistent theory of antisocial behavior: what have we learned? In Walsh, A. & L. Ellis (Eds.). *Biosocial criminology: challenging environmentalism's supremacy*, Hauppauge, NY: Nova Science Publishers.

Nelson, E., E. McClure, C. Monk, E. Zahran, E. Leibenluft, D. Pine, et al. (2003). Developmental differences in neuronal engagement during implicit encoding of emotional faces: an event-related fMRI study. *Journal of Child Psychology and Psychiatry and Allied Disciplines*, 44:1015–1024.

Panksepp, J. (1998). Attention deficit hyperactivity disorders, psychostimulants, and intolerance of childhood playfulness: a tragedy in the making. *Current Directions in Psychological Science*, 7:91–98.

Powell, K. (2006). How does the teenage brain work? *Nature*, 442:865–867.

Quay, H. (1997). Inhibition and attention deficit hyperactivity disorder. *Journal of Abnormal Child Psychology*, 25:7–13.

Quinton, D., A. Pickles, B. Maughan, & M. Rutter (1993). Partners, peers and pathways: Assortative pairing and continuities in conduct disorder. *Development and Psychopathology*, 5:763–783.

Raz, A. (2004). Brain imaging data of ADHD. *Neuropsychiatry*, August:46–50.

Reyna, V. & F. Farley, F. (2006). Risk and rationality in adolescent decision making: implications for theory, practice, and public policy. *Psychological Science in the Public Interest*, 7:1–44.

Restak, R. (2001). *The secret life of the brain*. New York: Dana Press/Joseph Henry Press.

Rodkin, P., T. Farmer, R. Pearl, & R. Van Acker (2000). Heterogeneity of popular boys: antisocial and prosocial configurations. *Developmental Psychology*, 36:14–24.

Rosenfeld, R. & B. Nicodemus (2003). The transition from adolescence to adult life: physiology of the transition phase and its evolutionary basis. *Hormone Research*, 60:74–77.

Sampson, R. & J. Laub (1999). Crime and deviance over the lifecourse: the salience of adult social bonds. In Scarpitti, F. & A. Nielsen (Eds.). *Crime and criminals: contemporary and classical readings in criminology*. Los Angeles: Roxbury.

Sanjiv, K. & E. Thaden (2004). Examining brain connectivity in ADHD. *Psychiatric Times*, January: 40–41.

Sergeant, J., H. Geurts, S. Huijbregts, A. Scheres, & J. Ooserlan (2003). The top and bottom of ADHD: a neuropsychological perspective. *Neuroscience and Biobehavioral Reviews*, 27:583–592.

Shavit, Y. & A. Rattner (1988). Age, crime, and the early lifecourse. *American Journal of Sociology*, 93:1457–1470.

Shedler, J. & Block, J. (1990). Adolescent drug use and psychological health. *American Psychologist*, 45:612–630.

Sisk, C. & D. Foster (2004). The neurobiology of puberty and adolescence. *Nature Neuroscience*, 7:1040–1047.

Sowell, E., P. Thompson, & A. Toga (2004). Mapping changes in the human cortex throughout the span of life. *Neuroscientist*, 10:372–392.

Spear, L. (2000). Neurobehavioral changes in adolescence. *Current Directions in Psychological Science*, 9:111–114.

Steinberg, L. (2005). Cognitive and affective development in adolescence. *Trends in Cognitive Sciences*, 9:69–74.

Steinberg, L. (2007). Risk taking in adolescence: new perspectives from brain and behavioral research. *Current Directions in Psychological Science*, 16:55–59.

Thornberry, T., D. Huizinga, & R. Loeber (2004). The causes and correlates studies: findings and policy implication. *Juvenile Justice*, 9:3–19.

Tittle, C. (2000). Theoretical developments in criminology. *National Institute of Justice 2000, vol. 1. The nature of crime: continuity and change*. Washington, DC: National Institute of Justice.

U.S. Census Bureau (2007). *The population of the United States*. Washington, DC: U.S. Census Bureau.

Van Honk, J., J. Peper, & D. Schutter (2005). Testosterone reduces unconscious fear but not consciously experienced anxiety: implications for the disorders of fear and anxiety. *Biological Psychiatry*, 58:218–225.

Walker, E. (2002). Adolescent neurodevelopment and psychopathology. *Current Directions in Psychological Science*, 11:24–28.

Walsh, A. (1992). Drug use and sexual behavior: users, experimenters and abstainers. *Journal of Social Psychology*, 132:691–693.

Walsh, A. (2002). *Biosocial criminology: introduction and integration*. Cincinnati, OH. Anderson.

Warr, M. (2002). *Companions in crime: the social aspects of criminal conduct*. New York: Cambridge University Press.

White, A. (2004). *Substance use and the adolescent brain: an overview with the focus on alcohol*. Durham, NC: Duke University Medical Center.

Willoughby, M. (2003). Developmental course of ADHD symptomology during the transition from childhood to adolescence: a review with recommendations. *Journal of Child Psychology and Psychiatry*, 43:609–621.

Zuckerman, M. (2007). *Sensation seeking and risky behavior*. Washington, DC: American Psychological Association.

9

Substance Abuse and Crime: Biosocial Foundations

Michael G. Vaughn

Reliable data indicate that alcohol and drug use is present in the majority of violent crimes both in the United States and Europe. Many of these violent offenses comprise homicides. Alcohol abuse has been consistently associated with crime. For example, 1998 data from the Arrestee Drug Abuse Monitoring (typically referred to as ADAM) program, which collects biomarker data on drugs in the systems of persons arrested found that the rate of testing positive across 35 cities ranged between 40 and 80 percent (Arrestee Drug Abuse Monitoring Program, 1999). Figure 9.1 shows the trends in arrests by type of drug law violated from 1982–2005.

A 2004 survey by the Bureau of Justice Statistics indicated that approximately 33 percent of inmates committed their offense while under the influence of drugs and over half were using drugs in the month prior to their offense. The percentage of offenders reporting that they committed their offense in order to obtain money for drugs was 17 percent of state inmates and 18 percent of federal inmates. The most common drugs of

Figure 9.1 Number of Arrests, by Type of Drug Law Violation, 1982–2005.

Source: FBI, Uniform Crime Reports, *Crime in the United States*, annually.

abuse were marijuana and cocaine/crack. Importantly, these figures are relatively similar to data from 1997 thus indicating stability in these trends. Approximately half of both state and federal inmates met criteria for a diagnosis of substance abuse/dependence. According to a nationally representative survey (National Epidemiological Survey of Alcohol and Related Conditions) the proportion of those in the general population meeting criteria for abuse and dependence in 2002 was 2 percent. This remarkable difference underscores the close relationship that exists between substance abuse and criminal offending.

Most of the costs associated with drug abuse involve relationships to crime and criminal justice. These costs include government crime control (e.g., law enforcement and police protection), incarceration, social services, and loss of productivity of victims and drug use careers. Also, there are costs related to emergency room care and ongoing medical care for injuries sustained during violent encounters where alcohol or drug intoxication was a precipitating factor. Although estimates vary, the economic costs are clearly well over 100 billion annually. Furthermore these costs are expected to rise.

Studies of incarcerated youth have shown that drug use and delinquent acts are intertwined. In a study of state wide population of juvenile offenders, Vaughn and colleagues (2007) found that high rates of past drug abuse and property and violent offending clustered together at both the low and high ends of use patterns. Essentially, youth who used the most drugs also possessed extensive criminal histories. Seminal research by Linda Teplin and associates (2002) has shown in a randomly selected sample of 1,829 detained youth in Chicago that approximately half of males and females had a diagnosable substance use disorder. Also, both male and female detainees met criteria for a mental health disorder in excess of 60 percent of cases.

The current chapter will first define drug abuse and dependence, review key mechanisms such as the brains reward pathway, then review the association between substance abuse and crime from the perspective of a general biosocial liability conceptual framework (see Vaughn, 2007; Vaughn, et al., 2007), and, finally, offer comments regarding prevention and treatment for policy and practice.

Definitions of Drug Dependence

Although numerous definitions of drug addiction have been proffered, one contemporary definition that succinctly captures the essence of the disorder has been developed by George Koob (2006:25) who defined drug addiction as follows: "Drug addiction, also known as substance dependence, is a chronically relapsing disorder characterized by (1) a compulsion to seek and take the drug, (2) loss of control in limiting intake, and (3) emergence of a negative emotional state (e.g., dysphoria, anxiety, irritability) when access to the drug is prevented (defined here as dependence)." An additional factor that exacerbates compulsive drug seeking (which often results in crime) is that continued ingestion of a substance often leads to a state of **tolerance** requiring more of the drug to achieve desired effects.

The primary system used to diagnose substance abuse and dependence is the Diagnostic and Statistical Manual (DSM) of the American Psychiatric Association. According to the DSM-IV substance dependence is "a maladaptive pattern of substance use leading to clinically significant impairment or distress, as manifested by three (or more) of the following, occurring any time in the same 12-month period":

1. Tolerance, as defined by either of the following:
   (a) A need for markedly increased amounts of the substance to achieve intoxication or the desired effect *or*
   (b) markedly diminished effect with continued use of the same amount of the substance.
2. Withdrawal, as manifested by either of the following:
   (a) The characteristic withdrawal syndrome for the substance *or*
   (b) the same (or closely related) substance is taken to relieve or avoid withdrawal symptoms.
3. The substance is often taken in larger amounts or over a longer period than intended.
4. There is a persistent desire or unsuccessful efforts to cut down or control substance use.
5. A great deal of time is spent in activities necessary to obtain the substance (such as visiting multiple doctors or driving long distances), use the substance (for example, chain smoking), or recover from its effects.
6. Important social, occupational, or recreational activities are given up or reduced because of substance use.
7. The substance use is continued despite knowledge of having a persistent physical or psychological problem that is likely to have been caused or exacerbated by the substance (for example, current cocaine use despite recognition of cocaine-induced depression or continued drinking despite recognition that an ulcer was made worse by alcohol consumption).

Goldstein's Tripartite Conceptual Framework

In 1985 Paul Goldstein published an influential article that organized the "drugs–violence nexus" as occurring around three levels of phenomenon. He developed this typology inductively as he collected data in New York City on drug abuse and its behavioral effects. The first of these phenomena *psychopharmacological* is related to violence due to the direct effects that drugs have on the brain. According to Goldstein, this type of violence is difficult to measure because "many such instances go unreported and, hence, unrecorded in official records" (1985:495). The second major domain of the drugs–violence nexus is termed *economic-compulsive*. These types of act are simply the result of drug-dependent persons engaging in robberies to provide cash to buy more drugs. Because drug use hijacks the brain's ancient reward system compulsive need to continue to reinforce this pathway is powerful and this combined with the fact that illicit drugs tend to be expensive often elicits violence. As Goldstein (1985:496) points out: "Economically compulsive actors are not primarily motivated by impulses to act out violently. Rather their primary motivation is to obtain money to purchase drugs." The final level is *systemic*. This refers to violence perpetrated as a part of the operation of drug markets and the business of dealing. Goldstein provided several examples of systemic violence and these include "disputes over territory between rival drug dealers," "assaults and homicides committed within dealing hierarchies as a means of enforcing normative codes," elimination of informers," and "punishment for failing to pay one's debts." Although somewhat simplistic, this tripartite framework does provide a useful heuristic for organizing the complexity of violence and drug abuse across the biosocial range. However, the specific mechanisms for understanding the biosocial processes are not well delineated in this model.

Alcoholism and Crime

As previously stated, there is an established association between alcohol use and crime including aggression and violence. Alcohol abuse and dependence are familial in nature meaning that these patterns are often found within the same family. The vulnerability to developing an alcohol use disorder is substantially influenced by genetic factors. Both alcohol use disorders and conduct problems are often comorbid with one another, meaning they co-occur and are intertwined. Thus, the propensity for developing an alcohol use disorder and conduct problems likely share a similar underlying etiology. However, among those diagnosed as alcohol dependent there is often found clinical heterogeneity resulting in subtypes of alcohol-dependent people. The most prominent subtype formulation involves type 1 and type 2 alcoholism developed by Cloninger and colleagues (1981). This framework posits that type 1 is a milder form of alcoholism, occurs more widely in females, and is associated with mood problems while type 2 is more severe. Type 2 alcohol dependence is characterized by an earlier onset, antisocial and criminal behavior during the adult years, chronic relapsing and treatment resistance, and familial alcoholism. Although this typology is widely accepted, recent research is beginning to demonstrate the usefulness of alternative typologies.

The Pivotal Role of the Reward Pathway

In a famous essay appearing in the prestigious journal *Science* (1997), Alan Leshner declared that: "Addiction is a brain disease, and it matters." Leshner, summarizing 20 years of scientific research on addiction, revealed that we now know the neural circuits affected by drugs of abuse and related details of receptor behavior. Major differences in the brains of addicted persons and non-addicted persons are profoundly different. Leshner also recognized that the social contexts that surround the brain (i.e., person) possess an important role in pathogenesis and course of addiction.

The neural circuit that Leshner was discussing is commonly termed the reward pathway. The reward pathway or, more specifically, the **mesolimbic reward system** is of critical importance due to its role in survival. The reward pathway provides the positive reinforcement for eating, drinking, sex, and other functions basic to survival. In the case of abuse and dependence, drugs of abuse flood the reward pathway to an extent above and beyond aforementioned food and sex. Thus, this circuit becomes "hijacked" and compulsive substance seeking follows. The usual inhibitory control associated with **executive governance** is overwhelmed, particularly among those with structural or functional deficits in this area of the brain. After reviewing brain imaging, neuropsychological, and clinical outcome studies, Lubman and colleagues (2004:1491) further specify these relations stating: "The current literature suggests that in addition to the brain's reward system, two frontal cortical regions (anterior cingulated and orbitofrontal cortices), critical in inhibitory control over reward-related behavior are dysfunctional in addicted individuals. These same regions have been implicated in other compulsive conditions characterized by deficits in inhibitory control over maladaptive behaviors, such as obsessive-compulsive disorder."

One useful analogy used to better frame the compulsion brought about by drug abuse and inhibitory control is the "stop" and "go" conceptualization. (The "stop" and "go" analogy is virtually synonymous with the behavioral activating system [BAS] and the behavioral inhibition system [BIS] as discussed by Walsh and Beaver, and Wiebe, Chapters 1 and 12, this volume. The "stop" system corresponds with the BIS and the "go" system corresponds with the BAS.) Childress (2006) suggests that this framework helps us to understand the heterogeneity that exists in the domain of substance abuse. The ancient reward pathway is the "go" system because of its involvement and sensitivity toward motivation related to natural rewards. The "stop" system is responsible for inhibiting behavior when the reward is dangerous or detrimental to survival. Variations in the stop and go systems due to polygenic and neural deficit factors influence the response to drugs of abuse and its consequences for behavior. Not only is there individual variation, there is also developmental variation that has important implications for understanding the covariation between substance abuse and crime. For example, during adolescence, a critical period whereby drug experimentation is common, executive functions responsible for inhibitory control are not yet fully developed or mature thereby creating a situation of a strong reward response coupled with a weak stop system. This situation is thought to account for why the period of adolescence is such a risky developmental period. Adolescent substance abuse is also highly **comorbid** with attention-deficit hyperactivity disorder and conduct disorder—a disorder characterized by aggressive and delinquent acts.

Substances of abuse are known to increase levels of dopamine in the brain. This facilitates increased communication between receptors in the brain associated with heightened states of joy and physiological arousal. The close relations between the reward pathway and dopamine activity has led many to refer to this circuit as the dopaminergic system. Most substances of abuse implicate dopamine and the nucleus accumbens including cocaine and amphetamines, opiates, nicotine, alcohol, and delta-9-tetrahydrocannabinol. Based on brain imaging investigations low numbers of type 2 dopamine receptors (i.e., DRD2) have been found to be associated with heightened vulnerability to substance dependence. Conversely, it has been hypothesized that higher levels may exert a protective benefit or shield from addiction (Childress, 2006). Figure 9.2 displays the area of the brain known as the *ancient reward pathway*.

Neurotransmitters: The Importance of Serotonin

Alcohol and aggressive behavior have been associated with decreases in serotonin activity. The reason for this is that serotonin is a key regulator of aggressive behavior (Nelson & Chiavegatto, 2001). In particular, studies

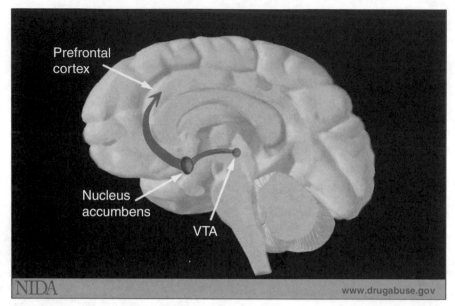

Figure 9.2 Cross-section of the Brain Revealing the Ancient Reward Pathway.

Source: National Institute of Drug Abuse website.

have implicated the low activity short allele polymorphism. These results have been found in western and non-western societies. For instance, in a study of 246 Chinese males, those with the short allele were found to possess convictions for extreme violent offenses compared to none for the control group. However, not all studies have found this link. For example, Amira Brown and colleagues (2007) performed PET scans among patients being treated for alcohol dependence and found no significant variations between patients classified as aggressive or non-aggressive in the densities of the serotonin transporter (5-HTT).

A General Liability Model of Substance Abuse and Crime

One way to conceptualize the reciprocal relations between drug abuse and crime is to employ a general biosocial framework that uses the concept of liability or vulnerability to denote risk across a continuum. Vaughn (2007) has reviewed studies and constructs and has developed a theoretical synthesis that is useful for organizing findings and concepts that range from the biological (dispositional) to the environmental (contextual). Because substance abuse and crime crosses many disciplinary fields a transdisciplinary synthesis is critically needed. Consequences of not utilizing such a framework includes a lack of biological–environment integration leading to isolated studies not linking together, myopic states of explaining substance abuse and crime strictly in terms of a singular disciplinary focus, and associated reductions in new methodologies and findings arising from knowledge fields not communicating with one another.

Dispositional liabilities A large number of twin studies indicate that approximately 50 to 60 percent of the variation in substance use disorders is accounted for by heritability (Hasin, et al., 2006). Several genes and their variants have been found in numerous studies to be associated with behavior control and addiction; specifically, several dopamine (e.g., DRD4) and **GABAergic** (e.g., GABRA1) receptor genes (Kreek, et al., 2005). Further, there is evidence that these gene variants interact to produce associations with antisociality, at least in males (Beaver, et al., 2007).

Much of the recent understanding and conceptualization of addiction as a brain disease has been facilitated by the rise of neuroimaging techniques. There are five of these that have been used in substance abuse research: structural magnetic resonance imaging, functional magnetic resonance imaging, magnetic resonance spectroscopy, positron emission tomography, and single photon emission computed tomography. Each of these techniques possesses different advantages in gathering information on the effects of substance abuse. These techniques allow for direct comparisons to be made between using and non-using individuals. Taken together, findings indicate clear involvement of biochemical, structural, functional, and metabolic processes in the brain that influence decision making, planning, and craving. Persons with genetic or developmental deficits in critical areas of the frontal lobes are already vulnerable to dysregulation in inhibitory control and are likely to be at higher risk for substance-related crime, perhaps even more persistent and severe forms of offending.

As genes code for proteins that comprise the central nervous system this, in turn, provides the building blocks for various **endophenotypes** (see Meyer-Lindenberg & Weinberger, 2006) comprising personality. Certain personality traits are important factors in their relation to substance abuse and crime. In fact, antisocial personality disorder, the psychiatric category most associated with violence, predatory behavior, criminality and substance abuse, is associated with low scores on the personality traits of harm avoidance and reward dependence and high scores on novelty seeking (Cloninger, 2005). Novelty seeking has much in common with other constructs shown to be related to both substance abuse and crime such as sensation seeking. Interestingly, two constructs that have received much research attention by criminologists and psychologists are low self-control and psychopathy. Self-control theory in criminology began with Gottfredson and Hirschi's *A general theory of crime*

(1990). Since its publication, the low self-control construct has garnered much research attention and empirical support (e.g., DeLisi & Vaughn, in press). Psychopathy is a very old construct (see Cleckley, 1941/1976; Vaughn & Howard, 2005) that has been a valuable tool in the prediction of violence among adults and juveniles. Breaking these constructs down into more intermediate endophenotypes reveals that persons with low self-control can be described as low in traits such as harm avoidance and self-directedness and high on novelty seeking. Psychopaths are low on traits such as harm avoidance, cooperativeness, self-directedness and high in novelty seeking. Overall, antisocial personality disorder, low self-control, and psychopathy are highly convergent with one another and typically comorbid with the troublesome use and abuse of psychoactive substances.

Contextual liabilities   A full appraisal of the nexus between substance abuse and crime needs to examine the interplay between aforementioned dispositional liabilities and environmental contextual factors. As such, an operationalized depiction of the socio-cultural system surrounding the individual that is connected to bioecology is **cultural materialism**. Cultural materialism was originally synthesized by anthropologist Marvin Harris. Contextual liabilities follow the tripartite conception of societies conceptualized by cultural materialism and consist of an infrastructure, structure, and a symbolic-ideational sector. Infrastructure represents the domains of production (e.g., subsistence and related technologies) and reproduction (e.g., demographic patterns, childrearing practices). The infrastructure is most closely related to biogeography and the basic survival needs and drives of human organisms. Therefore, infrastructure tends to select for changes in the rest of society. Structure denotes the organization of domestic and political economy as expressed in their attending institutions. The symbolic-ideational sector refers to a society's religious, philosophical, and ideological features.

With respect to substance abuse and crime, it is important to understand that drugs of abuse are manufactured and distributed and involve marketing factors such as formal and informal advertisements, availability of markets, and the political economy surrounding drug production. Simply, an individual cannot become substance dependent if the drug either does not exist or is unavailable. Another important biosocial fact is that certain illicit drugs such as heroin are derived from opium poppies, which thrive in particular habitats around the globe. This is also true of another major drug of abuse, cocaine. The infrastructures of the countries in which these plants are grown are such that technological lag and related poverty decrease participation in global economic exchange. Under these conditions it is fairly easy to understand how a biogeographic plant resource (i.e., coca and opium poppies) can be elevated to a large financial force in the underground economies of these countries. There exists relatively little research, however, into the contextual liabilities surrounding substance abuse and crime. Future research should attempt to connect these contextual factors to the individual liabilities for substance abuse and criminal offending.

Interventions for Substance Abuse and Dependence

Given findings demonstrating the close associations between substance abuse and crime, how might prevention or treatment proceed to reduce both? There are numerous treatment protocols that have been tested under "controlled conditions," meaning that there was random assignment of like individuals to a treatment group and a non-treated or alternative treatment group, termed the control group. These types of experimental study are considered the gold standard for evaluating treatment effects. Although most of these studies did not focus on offending variables on outcomes rather the focus was on reductions in substance abuse they nevertheless allow for strong inferences to be made about substance abuse–crime relations. I will focus on evidence-based treatments that are founded on robust biosocial principles.

Evidence-based treatments can be organized as motivational, behavioral, and pharmacotherapy. First, motivational treatment is a multidimensional construct rooted in neurocognitive process yet highly sensitive to context. Motivational interviewing was developed for drinking problems and is associated with the work of William Miller, a professor of psychology and psychiatry of the University of New Mexico. Numerous clinical trials have supported the efficacy of this approach (see Miller & Rollnick, 2002). Motivational interviewing is a person- and goal-centered approach that is non-confrontational yet is highly structured toward guiding clients towards commitment. It is a cost-effective treatment that is usually executed in one to four treatment sessions.

The second area of treatment involves behavioral interventions. Based on elemental physiological principles of stimulus–response and reinforcement of the organism toward new rewards instead of the rewarding effects of a given substance, behavioral interventions can be quite useful in their application to substance use disorders. According to Carroll and Rounsaville (2006), behavioral treatment principles can be distilled into increased effectiveness by targeting impulse control problems which are at the heart of the "stop" or "brake" system that help to check the drive toward psychoactive substances. As these authors state (2006: 225): "For those individuals whose substance use is severe enough to warrant treatment, we believe many aspects of these behaviors can be characterized as an *impulse control disorder with two general, socially defined dysfunctional elements*: (1) the excessive desire to use or craving for substances, and (2) insufficient impulse control associated with neuroadaptation and neurocognitive impairment." It may well be that these types of intervention are also simultaneously targeting processes that are also highly involved in criminal offending. Another interesting form of behavioral intervention is cognitive remediation treatment. This type of therapy attempts to target and train components of executive function as if it were a muscle. Thus, cognitive remediation or "brain train" protocols are building up the capacity for self-regulation. Research on cognitive remediation treatments are still in their early stages and although preliminary evidence is promising there still needs to be more empirical tests of its utility for substance use disorders.

Finally, recent advances have led to the development of a small number of medications that provide new tools to combat substance dependence. These medications function as **antagonists** and **agonists** in the brain. On the one hand, antagonists bind to receptor sites and block the effects of a substance. On the other, agonists bind to the receptor site and stimulate the site and thus turn it on. Three recent medications are in use for the treatment of alcohol dependence; Naltrexone, Acamprosate, and Topiramate. Naltrexone is an antagonist medication that partially blocks the rewarding effects of ethanol and yields increases in abstinence and risk for relapse. Acamprosate reduces the excitation of neurons that are no longer stimulated by alcohol during withdrawal and this in turn decreases the stress associated with not drinking. Topiramate directly acts to decrease dopamine activity and serves to reduce the rewarding effects of alcohol. Numerous clinical trials have shown the benefit of these medications particularly when combined with additional psychosocial treatment. There are no FDA-approved drugs for central nervous system stimulants such as cocaine and amphetamines; however, recent trials with a medication called Baclofen shows promise.

Although there exists controversy pertaining to how best to manage the drugs–crime problem with respect to allocation of treatment and control strategies, proper screening, assessment, and use of evidence-based interventions are likely to reduce drug-related criminal offending. Of course, any system of treatment needs to be executed within a context of efficient delivery of services that is held accountable for achieving specific outcomes.

Conclusions

Substance abuse and crime are inextricably linked. Both phenomena have a complex causal structure and together form a near bewildering array of behaviors. These behaviors are associated with biological processes that occur at different levels of organization that are contextualized within a given social and ecological habitat. At the individual level, a longstanding issue is which one comes first, substance abuse or crime. This chicken or egg problem is also seen with regard to which one comes first, neurocognitive deficits or substance abuse. Because of the covariation and diversity involved in substance abuse and different types of crime associated with its use, it has been extremely difficult for researchers to disentangle the causal structure of this very fundamental problem. Looking for simple answers is likely not to work because as James Anthony and Valerie Forman state (2003:12.): "There is no single drugs-crime relationship. Rather there are drugs-crime relationships, most of which are complex rather than simple."

Given the complexity of the substance abuse and crime relationship, an explicit biosocial framework is necessary to facilitate systematic study of the various components of this relationship. For example, much research has demonstrated the importance of the effects of substances of abuse on the reward pathway in the brain. However, we do not fully understand the genetic liabilities that make one person more or less susceptible to the reinforcing effects of drugs. On the macrosocietal end of the equation, we have not been very successful at controlling the deleterious effects of drugs of abuse. Further, we know little about the types of environment that modulate drugs–crime relations. In addition to research that investigates the biosocial interplay between substance abuse and crime, it may be fruitful to investigate the convergence between research on career criminals and addictions careers. Given the disproportional involvement in crime among a subset of persons, shedding light on the overlap between substance abuse careers and career criminals would be useful.

The historical evidence with respect to the use of psychoactive agents suggests that the human species seeks to alter consciousness. In other words, the ingestion of natural or synthetic chemicals among human is likely an ever present danger. Therefore, it is imperative to find efficient ways to manage this vulnerability that is closely tied with our evolutionary heritage. Finding effective methods to accomplish this difficult and seemingly intractable problem requires a foundation of sound empirical evidence that is interpretable within a sound biosocial framework.

References

American Psychiatric Association. (2000). *Diagnostic and statistical manual of mental disorders (4th edition, text revision, DSM-IV-TR)*. Washington, DC: Author.

Anthony, J. C. & V. Forman (2003). At the intersection of public health and criminal justice research on drugs and crime. *National Institute on Justice Special Report*, September:11–64.

Arrestee Drug Abuse Monitoring Program. (1999). *1998 annual report on drug use among adult and juvenile arrestees.* Washington, DC: United States Department of Justice, National Institute of Justice.

Beaver, K. M., J. P.Wright, M. DeLisi, A. Walsh, M. G. Vaughn, D. Boisvert, et al. (2007). Gene × gene interaction between DRD2 and DRD4 in the etiology of conduct disorder and antisocial behavior. *Behavioral and Brain Functions*, 3:3–30.

Brown, A. K., D. T. George, M. Fujita, J. Liow, M. Ichise, J. Hibbein, et al. (2007). Pet [^{11}C]DASB imaging of serotonin transporters in patients with alcoholism. *Alcoholism: Clinical and Experimental Research*, 31:28–32.

Carroll, K. M. & B. J. Rounsaville (2006). Behavioral therapies: the glass would be half full if we had a glass. In Miller, W. R. & K. Carroll (Eds.). *Rethinking substance abuse: what the science shows, and what we should do about it.* New York: Guilford Press.

Childress, A. R. (2006). What can human brain imaging tell us about vulnerability to addiction and to relapse. In Miller, W. R. & K. Carroll (Eds.). *Rethinking substance abuse: what the science shows, and what we should do about it.* New York: Guilford Press.

Cleckley, H. (1941/1976). *The mask of sanity*, 5th edn. St. Louis, MO: Mosby.

Cloninger, C. R. (2005). Antisocial personality disorder: a review. In Maj, M., H. S. Akiskal, J. E. Mezzich & A. Okasha (Eds.). *Personality disorders.* New York: John Wiley & Sons.

Cloninger, C. R., N. Bohman, & S. Sigvardsson (1981). Inheritance of alcohol abuse: cross-fostering analysis of adopted men. *Archives of General Psychiatry*, 36:861–868.

DeLisi, M. & M. G. Vaughn (in press). The Gottfredson-Hirschi critiques revisited: reconciling self-control theory, criminal careers, and career criminals. *International Journal of Offender Therapy and Comparative Criminology.*

Goldstein, P. J. (1985). The drugs/violence nexus: a tripartite conceptual framework. *Journal of Drug Issues*, 15:493–506.

Gottfredson, M. R. & T. Hirschi (1990). *A general theory of crime.* Stanford, CA: Stanford University Press.

Hasin, D., M. Hatzenbuehler, & R. Waxman (2006). Genetics of substance use disorders. In Miller, W. R. & K. Carroll (Eds.). *Rethinking substance abuse: what the science shows, and what we should do about it.* New York: Guilford Press.

Koob, G. E. (2006). The neurobiology of addiction: a hedonic Calvinist view. In Miller W. R. & K. Carroll (Eds.). *Rethinking substance abuse: what the science shows, and what we should do about it.* New York: Guilford Press.

Kreek, M. J., D. A. Nielsen, E. R. Butelman, & S. K. LaForge (2005). Genetic influences on impulsivity, risk taking, stress responsivity and vulnerability to drug abuse and addiction. *Nature Neuroscience*, 8:1450–1457.

Leshner, A. I. (1997). Addiction is a brain disease, and it matters. *Science*, 278:45–47.

Lubman, D. I., M. Yucel, & C. Pantelis, C. (2004). Addiction, a condition of compulsive behaviour? Neuroimaging and neuropsychological evidence of inhibitory dysregulation. *Addiction*, 99:1491–1502.

Meyer-Lindenberg, A. & D. R. Weinberger (2006). Intermediate phenotypes and genetic mechanisms of psychiatric disorders. *Nature Reviews Neuroscience*, 7:818–827.

Miller, W. R. & S. Rollnick (2002). *Motivational interviewing: preparing people for change*, 2nd edn. New York: Guilford Press.

Nelson, R. J. & S. Chiavegatto (2001). Molecular basis of aggression. *Trends in Neuroscience*, 24:713–719.

Teplin, L. A., K. M. Abram, G.M. McClelland, M. K. Dulcan, & A. A. Mericle (2002). Psychiatric disorders in youth in juvenile detention. *Archives of General Psychiatry*, 59:1133–1143.

Vaughn, M. G. (2007). Biosocial dynamics: a transdisciplinary approach to violence. In DeLisi, M. & P. J. Conis (Eds.). *Violent offenders: theory, research, public policy, & practice.* Sudbury, MA: Jones & Bartlett.

Vaughn, M. G. & M. O. Howard (2005). The construct of psychopathy and its role in contributing to the study of serious, violent, and chronic youth offending. *Youth Violence and Juvenile Justice*, 3:235–252.

Vaughn, M. G., K. M. Beaver, & M. DeLisi (2007). A general biosocial liability model of antisocial behavior: a preliminary test in a prospective community sample. Manuscript under review.

Vaughn, M. G., S. Freedenthal, J. M. Jenson, & M. O. Howard (2007). Psychiatric symptoms and substance use among juvenile offenders: a latent profile investigation. *Criminal Justice and Behavior*, 34:1296–1312.

10

Testosterone and Violence among Young Men

Allan Mazur

Numerous animal experiments, especially on rodents, show that raising **testosterone** levels increases **aggression**. In interpreting this work, it is important to distinguish aggressive behavior from **dominance** behavior. An individual will be said to act *aggressively* if its apparent intent is to inflict physical injury on a member of its species. An individual acts *dominantly* if its apparent intent is to achieve or maintain high status—i.e., to obtain power, influence, or valued prerogatives—over a conspecific. Rodents typically dominate aggressively, but that is not true among the higher primates.

The distinction between aggression and dominance is particularly important for humans, because we normally assert our dominance without any intent to cause physical injury. Sports, spelling bees, elections, criticism, competitions for promotion, and academic jousting all involve contests for domination without intending physical injury. We understand that there are different motivations for dominance and aggression, although they may sometimes work concurrently.

Until fairly recently, researchers thought that young men with high testosterone were especially aggressive, rather like male rodents. This picture remains in the public mind, including images of body builders on anabolic steroids (chemically similar to testosterone) being prone to violent "'roid rages." In fact, empirical research shows little if any *direct* linkage between testosterone and physical aggressiveness. However, we shall see that testosterone may play an *indirect* role in interpersonal violence.

Without a doubt, the most significant and far reaching function of androgens, among which testosterone is the most important, is their function in differentiating the male body from its inherent female state. In all mammalian species, maleness is induced from an intrinsically female form by a gene on the Y chromosome called the "sex-determining region of the Y" (SRY) gene. The SRY gene first induces the development of the testes from the undifferentiated gonads, the testes then produce androgens that will masculinize (or defeminize) various brain areas and Mullerian inhibiting substance, which causes the atrophy of internal female sex organs (Swaab, 2004). Masculinized versus feminized brains presumably contribute to the higher aggressive and antisocial behavior seen in males relative to females (see Bennett, et al., 2005; Campbell, 2006, for reviews).

A common view among today's researchers is that testosterone is related primarily to dominant behavior among men, not to aggression as such (Archer, 2006; Mazur & Booth, 1998). Nearly all animal studies once interpreted as linking testosterone to aggression may as easily be interpreted as linking testosterone with dominance. On theoretical grounds, dominating mechanisms—whether aggressive or nonaggressive in form—would confer an evolutionary advantage in helping an individual acquire valued resources, especially in competition for mates. This is not simply a matter of a dominant man taking what he wants; women regard men who *look* dominant as attractive.

An important variant of dominant behavior occurs in settings like schools, prisons, the military, families or work groups, where authority figures require behavior to conform closely to rigid standards. In these circumstances, dominant-acting individuals who hold subordinate roles are relatively likely to break restrictive norms and codes of conduct. Such actions, opposed or hostile to social institutions and laws, are conventionally defined by sociologists as *antisocial behavior,* and are labeled by those in authority as rebellious or even criminal. Antisocial actions are often attempts to dominate figures in authority (teachers, policemen) or, more abstractly, to prevail over a constraining environment.

A Primer on Testosterone

Testosterone is the primary *androgen,* a class of steroid hormones that develops and maintains masculine features. Although testosterone is made in the adrenal cortex and ovaries of females, it is produced in far greater amounts by the Leydig cells of the testis.

Many effects that we explain today by testosterone deficiency were obtained since ancient times by castration of men and animals, which was practiced not only to prevent fertility but also to prevent the development of secondary sexual characteristics, produce docility, reduce sex drive, and —in butchered animals—to produce fatter, more tender meat. Castrating a male chick, for example, makes its adult flesh more edible, and the capon fails to develop the rooster's head furnishings (red comb and wattles—markers of reproductive competence), does not crow or court hens, and does not fight other cocks. In Asia, eunuchs were presumed to be safe harem guards because of their lack of both interest and ability to copulate. Male sopranos and contraltos, emasculated to maintain their prepubescent voice range, were prominent in the opera and church music of 17th- and 18th-century Europe.

Our modern understanding began in the 1930s after the isolation and identification of testosterone. Reminiscent of the Curies' heroic extraction of minute amounts of radium from a ton of pitchblende, Fred Koch and his coworkers mashed tons of bull testicles to fractionate ounces of material sufficiently pure to make the combs of capons grow bright red. (Another researcher distilled 25,000 liters of policemen's urine to obtain 15 mg of the androgen androsterone.) Chemical synthesis followed quickly, enabling experimenters to replace or enhance testosterone in animal subjects and human patients. An example is the classic study of hen peck orders by Allee, et al. (1939), who injected testosterone into low-ranking hens. These females became aggressive, and each rose in her status hierarchy, some to the top position. Furthermore, their comb size increased (a male characteristic), egg laying was suppressed, some began crowing (rare in hens), and a few began courting other hens.

Until the availability of radioimmunoassay in the 1960s, the measurement of endogenous testosterone was elusive because it is produced by the body in tiny amounts. Normal men have about one hundred-thousandth gram of hormone per liter of blood; women roughly one-seventh as much. Soon it was practical to measure *free* testosterone in saliva (i.e., testosterone not bound to protein, which is assumed to be the physiologically active portion) with a concentration of about one-hundredth that of total testosterone in blood. Furthermore, collection of saliva has made studies on humans more practical. These improvements in method, plus the recent availability of studies of thousands of men, have expanded our knowledge greatly.

Testosterone in men is secreted into the bloodstream in spurts, so measured levels can change considerably within a few minutes. The hormone has a circadian rhythm in both sexes, highest and most variable in the morning, lower and more stable during the afternoon. Despite what can literally be minute-to-minute variation, each man's testosterone measurements represent short-term fluctuations around his characteristic basal level. By adolescence or shortly afterward, this basal level is more or less consistent from year to year, with reliabilities from $r = .50$ to $.65$ reported for testosterone measurements taken (at the same time of day to control for circadian variation) over periods ranging from days to 6 years (Booth & Dabbs, 1993). Thus, men with relatively high testosterone at one time tend to be relatively high at other times too.

Synthetic modifications of testosterone are pharmacologically more useful than testosterone itself because they are absorbed more easily when taken as pills or have longer lasting effects when injected. Beside its *andro-genic* (masculinizing) effects, testosterone also has *anabolic* (protein tissue building) qualities that have therapeutic value. The anabolic steroids used by athletes to build muscle mass and reduce fat are synthetic derivatives of testosterone, designed to maximize protein synthesis and minimize mas-culinizing effects; however, virilization by anabolic steroids is never wholly eliminated.

Testosterone Works Differently Perinatally, at Puberty, and in Adulthood

It is now clear that testosterone affects human males importantly but differently at three stages of life: perinatally (in utero and shortly after birth), during puberty, and in adulthood. This chapter focuses on the adult stage, but a brief review of earlier effects is worthwhile.

The mammalian fetus of both XX and XY individuals begins with undifferentiated sexual parts. A gene on the Y chromosome causes the asexual gonads to develop as testes; lacking this gene the gonads become ovaries. The sex chromosomes have little more to do with sex differen-tiation which hereafter is driven by hormones produced in the now sex-specific gonads. The testes produce testosterone during gestation, and production peaks again a month or two after birth, then declines by 6 months of age to the low range seen in later childhood. Testosterone and other testicular secretions cause the external genitalia to form into penis and scrotum rather than clitoris and labia, and internal ducts take the male form. The central nervous system is masculinized. The general rule, somewhat simplified, is that early exposure to greater amounts of testosterone will produce more male characteristics and fewer female characteristics, while less exposure to testosterone will produce the reverse. Perinatal manipulation of animal subjects, and developmental abnormal-ities among humans, show convincingly that even genetic females will show male forms if dosed early enough with testosterone, and genetic males will show female forms if deprived of the hormone.

Perinatal testosterone exposure affects behavior in a number of animal species. For example, young male rhesus monkeys normally engage in more threats and rough-and-tumble play than do females, but when testoster-one is administered to pregnant monkeys, their pseudo-hermaphroditic female offspring exhibit male-type play behavior. Furthermore, by limit-ing testosterone administration to the later part of gestation, female offspring are produced who exhibit male-type play but retain female

appearing genitals, showing that behavioral masculinization is independent of genital masculinization.

Many perinatal hormone effects are regarded as *organizing* the architecture of the body and brain, and the distribution of hormone receptors,
into a relatively male-like configuration. When male testosterone increases
later in life, it *activates* these preexisting structures. Thus, behaviors derive
from the interaction of long-term organizational *and* shorter-term
activation effects.

The testes greatly increase production of testosterone at puberty, elevat-
ing prepubescent serum levels 10 or more times. This promotes growth
of the penis, larynx (and deeper voice), muscles, beard and body hair,
and sex interest. Boys who are hypogonadal or castrated before puberty do
not experience these changes, but they can be induced by testosterone
replacement therapy.

It is tempting to assume the testosterone surge in adolescent boys to be
the cause of their seemingly heightened aggressiveness or pugnacity at
that age. However, research has not verified a causal link between the
hormonal and behavioral changes. First of all, physical aggression in boys
does *not* generally rise during adolescence (Tremblay, 2000). It is actually
smaller boys who are more prone to physically assault their peers, although,
lacking muscles or weapons, they do little damage. The well-documented
rise in boys' antisocial behavior with puberty is due mainly to nonviolent delinquency such as vandalism and status violations (Rutter, et al.,
1998).

Attempts to evaluate the contribution of testosterone to adolescent
social behavior have produced mixed findings. These are difficult studies
to conduct because investigators must untangle the direct effect of testosterone from other physical changes in the boy's body at puberty, which
affect how people respond to him. There are important *social* changes
during the early teen years, too—entry into high school, taking a job,
prolonged absence from parents, more dependence on peer approval—
which may affect behavior independently of hormonal effects.

Recent work has overcome some of these methodological problems.
The empirical picture now emerging is that the adolescent rise in testosterone does *not* lead simply and directly to increased antisocial behavior among teenage boys. But once the social context is taken into account,
we *do* see an effect of testosterone on dominance *in a direction consistent
with the behavior of peers*. This was most dramatically shown when Rowe,
et al. (2004) considered whether boys did, or did not, have deviant peers.
Boys with high testosterone committed a large number of "conduct disorders" (usually nonviolent antisocial actions like lying or breaking in) *if*
they had delinquent peers, but there was no testosterone disorder relationship among boys without delinquent peers. As if in mirror image, boys

with high testosterone were more likely to be chosen by other children as team leaders if they did *not* have delinquent peers, but there was no testosterone–leader relationship among boys with delinquent peers.

The primary lesson of this research is that one cannot assess the effect of hormones on behavior without taking into account the social context. An adolescent's behavior is importantly affected by relationships with parents and peers. Rising testosterone might have a different effect on a boy in a delinquent gang than on a member of the boy scouts (Booth, et al., 2006).

Among American males, after testosterone peaks in the late teens and early 20s, it usually declines slowly with age. The hormone decline among middle-aged men does not reliably occur in non-industrial societies. In the United States, it seems a consequence of American men getting fatter as they get older. Among 1,880 Air Force veterans who participated in four medical examinations from 1982 to 1992, testosterone declined only among men who gained more than 10 percent in body fat. For men with slighter increases in fat, testosterone remained essentially level. For men who lost fat over the decade, testosterone actually increased (Mazur, 1998).

By the end of the teenage years, the physical form of a boy has changed into that of a man so testosterone no longer influences behavior through major reorganization of the body. However, the level of testosterone circulating in the bloodstream at any moment may affect dominating behavior by activating receptors in organs or the nervous system. The remainder of this chapter focuses on such post-adolescent effects.

Reciprocal Causation

There is considerable evidence from a variety of settings that in men, circulating testosterone is correlated with dominant behavior and anti-social norm breaking (but not with violence). Correlation does not imply causation, and the question remains: Is high testosterone a *cause* of dominant and antisocial behavior? This could be answered with a double-blind experiment, comparing the behavior of men whose testosterone was raised pharmaceutically with a control group receiving a placebo. If dominant actions increased under the testosterone treatment, the hormone would be implicated as a cause of the behavior. Such controlled experimentation has barely begun, so we do not yet know for sure that testosterone is a cause of dominant behavior.

If there *is* a link between testosterone and dominance, primate studies suggest it is reciprocal. Not only does testosterone affect dominance, but changes in dominance behavior or in social status cause changes in testosterone level. We have strong evidence on this "reverse" effect in humans. By now there have been many reports of testosterone changes in young men during athletic events, which are convenient research settings because they are stylized dominance contests involving face-to-face competition with a clear winner and loser.

Male testosterone varies in predicable ways both before and after competitive matches. First, athletes' testosterone rises shortly before their matches, as if in anticipation of the competition. This pre-competition boost may promote dominant behavior, increasing the chance of victory. Second, for 1 or 2 hours after the match, testosterone of winners is usually high relative to that of losers.

These testosterone effects were first obtained in physically taxing sports. Additional studies show the same pattern of male testosterone responses during nonphysical contests or ritual status manipulations. For example, testosterone rises shortly before chess matches or laboratory contests of reaction time, and in subjects confronted with a symbolic challenge from an insult. Second, testosterone levels of winners are high relative to those of losers following chess matches and contests of reaction time, especially if subjects' mood is appropriately positive or negative. Similar effects occur among sports fans who are not themselves participants in the physical competition. Following the 1994 World Cup soccer tournament in which Brazil beat Italy, testosterone increased significantly in Brazilian fans who had watched the match on television, and decreased in Italian fans (Bernhardt, et al., 1998). Thus, the pattern of testosterone fluctuations appears in nonphysical as well as physical competition, and in response to symbolic challenges and status changes among men. (Whether similar changes occur among women is an as yet unresolved question.)

Dominance Contests

Does testosterone play a role in daily challenges to status, either from strangers or from people well known to us? Like all primates, humans in face-to-face groups form themselves into fairly consistent dominance/ status hierarchies so that more highly ranked members have more power, influence, and valued prerogatives than lower ranked ones. Ranks are allocated either *cooperatively*, by consensus of those involved, or *competitively*, when there is disagreement over who should outrank whom.

To appreciate a person's decision to compete or cooperate, visualize two individuals (Ego and Alter) meeting for the first time. If their interaction is very brief or casual, the notion of ranking may never arise. However, in more extended or serious meetings, each will size up the other and gain some sense of their relative standings. If Ego thinks that Alter's status does or should exceed his own, he may defer to Alter without any dispute. In human terms, Ego may believe that Alter belongs in the higher rank, that Alter deserves it, that Alter could easily take it if Ego resisted, or that Alter would be more competent in the duties of high rank. In any case, ranks are allocated quickly and cooperatively. If Ego and Alter do not agree on their relative standings, then they may either break off the interaction or vie for the contested rank.

Ego's decision to compete or to comply will also depend on his motivation to dominate, which seems related to his testosterone level (among other factors). A man who has experienced a recent rise in testosterone, perhaps from a victory or a symbolic elevation in status, will be unusually assertive and may challenge someone of relatively high status. If both Ego and Alter decide to compete, their relative ranks are then determined by the outcome of one or more short dominance contests between them.

Nonhuman primates are commonly observed to establish and maintain their status hierarchies through a series of short face-to-face competitions between members of the group. Some competitions involve fierce combat; others are mild, as when one animal is obviously the more powerful and assertive or the other appears fearful. In such cases, a simple stare by the powerful animal, followed by the fearful animal's eye aversion or by its yielding something of value (perhaps food or a sitting place), may suffice. Sometimes a single contest is all that is needed to allocate ranks or to verify a preexisting rank relationship, but often the outcome is settled only after a series of contests.

A psychophysiological mechanism operating across this range of competition is the manipulation of stress levels (Mazur, 2005). An exchange of threats or attacks is seen as an attempt by each individual to "outstress" or intimidate the other by inducing fear, anxiety, or other discomfort. Stress is experienced as both a feeling of discomfort and a syndrome of neurological responses. The individual who outstresses his adversary is the winner.

The model becomes clearer if we consider a concrete example. Consider two strangers, Ego and Alter, whose eyes meet, by chance, across a room. Let us say that one of the strangers, Ego, decides to hold the stare. The chance eye contact now becomes a dominance encounter. Ego's stare makes Alter uncomfortable. Alter may then avert his eyes, thus relieving his discomfort while, in effect, surrendering; or he may stare back, making Ego uncomfortable in return. In the latter case, the staredown would continue, with each individual attempting to outstress the other until finally one person succumbed to the discomfort (and the challenger) by averting his eyes. The matter thus settled, the yielder usually avoids further eye contact, although the winner may occasionally look at the loser as if to verify his victory.

In this example, Ego's stare is assumed to elicit feelings of stress in Alter. Alter's eye aversion is assumed to relieve his own felt stress. Staring—the stress-inducing behavior—is a dominant sign associated with high status. Eye aversion is a deferential sign associated with low status. In other words, a dominant act (staring) elicits stress in the recipient; a submissive act (eye aversion) relieves stress in the actor. It is a central assumption of this model that most dominant and deferential acts work this way, inducing or relieving stress, respectively. These acts are the means whereby the adversaries wage their stress contest, each aiming "darts" at the other. Finally, when the stress is too great for one, he switches from dominant to deferential actions, thereby relieving his stress and simultaneously signaling his acceptance of the lower rank.

Within hours of this outcome, we assume Ego (the loser) experiences a drop in testosterone, reducing his assertiveness, diminishing his propensity to display the dominant actions associated with high status, and increasing his display of such submissive signs as stooped posture, smiling, or eye aversion. Faced with a new dominance encounter, Ego is more likely than before to retreat or submit. On the other side, Alter, the winner, experiences the opposite effects: rising testosterone, increased assertiveness, and a display of dominant signs such as erect posture, sauntering or striding gait, and direct eye contact with others. Alter may seek out new dominance encounters and is bolstered to win them. This feedback between high (or low) testosterone and dominant (or submissive) demeanor helps to explain the momentum often associated with strings of triumphs or defeats: success begets a high testosterone response which begets more dominant behavior which begets more success (see Figure 10.1).

Murder

In everyday life, dominance contests are based on the subtle manipulation of psychological and physiological stress, not on causing or even

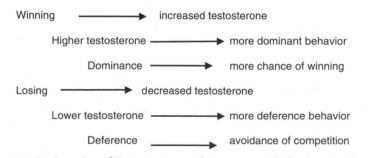

Figure 10.1 Reciprocity of Testosterone and Dominance Behavior, in Theory.

threatening physical harm to one's adversary. Most adult humans experience little violent confrontation. Occasionally, face-to-face competition escalates to a violent stage not originally intended or foreseen. Here is an example from my own city's newspaper:

> Assistant District Attorney Kenneth Rosso said Salgado [age 23] shot Lee [age 21] twice in the right side of the head, then discovered he still had six rounds of ammunition in the handgun, stood over Lee and fired an additional six shots into the left side of Lee's head. Rosso said Lee and Salgado knew each other and the shooting apparently stemmed from an earlier confrontation in a local nightclub where Salgado had bumped into Lee and the two exchanged angry words.
>
> (*Syracuse Post-Standard,* June 8, 2002)

While a killing is rarely the outcome of a violent dominance contest, I focus on murder because it represents an unambiguous endpoint, has good statistics, has been much studied by criminologists, and is so distressing a phenomenon. In the U.S., killers and their victims are disproportionately young adult males. There is a large racial disparity in murder rates. For example, in New York City from 2002 through 2005 there were 1,662 reported murders. Killers were 93 percent male, 76 percent between ages 18 and 40, and 61 percent black (compared to a black population of 25%). Victims were 82 percent male, 69 percent between 18 and 40, and 60 percent black (McGinty, 2006). The reasons for these patterns are not fully understood, but I propose that testosterone plays an indirect role.

Illegal killing occurs for diverse reasons including drug marketing, robbery, jealousy, mental derangement, religious or ideological commitment, and cash payment. Here I focus on what criminologist Jack Katz (1988) calls the most numerous type of criminal homicide, the impassioned killing of someone for what the killer regards as a good moralistic reason, perhaps the defense of his family, his property, or his good name.

Usually these murders of passion occur without premeditation. The episodes Katz had in mind develop quickly, occurring without thought of legal consequences. Often the killers are surprised by the unintended fatality, regarding the outcome as an accident. Reflecting their lack of forethought, many killers do not attempt to escape, or do so ineptly. Police make arrests in roughly 80 percent of homicide cases—usually within 1 day of the crime—compared to arrests in about 25 percent of robberies and 15 percent of burglaries.

Death is not necessarily the desired end point of an impassioned attack so much as hurting or physically punishing the victim. Whether an attack ends as a criminal homicide or an aggravated assault may be incidental, depending on such chance factors as the time to reach an emergency room, the quality of medical service, whether a gun was used, whether the falling victim's head hit concrete, and so on. There is little reason to think such killings differ much from impassioned attacks whose victims survived. Murders are better documented than nonlethal assaults and therefore more amendable to analysis.

Victims are usually relatives, friends, or at least acquainted with their killers. Criminologists have repeatedly replicated Marvin Wolfgang's (1958) classic study of homicide, showing that fatal aggression between men is usually precipitated by a trivial altercation, perhaps an insult, curse, or jostling. This is followed by an escalation of hostile verbal actions that may look no different than many nonfatal arguments, as in the following episode:

> Vice President Cheney . . ., serving in his role as president of the Senate, appeared in the chamber for a photo session. A chance meeting with Sen. Patrick Leahy, D-Vt., the ranking Democrat on the Judiciary Committee, became an argument about Cheney's ties to Halliburton Co., an international energy services corporation . . . The exchange ended when Cheney offered some crass advice.
> "F—yourself," said the vice president.
> Leahy's spokesman, David Carle, Wednesday confirmed the brief but fierce exchange. "The vice president seemed to be taking personally the criticisms that Senator Leahy and others have leveled against Halliburton's sole-source contracts in Iraq," Carle said . . .
> Cheney said Friday he was in no mood to exchange pleasantries with Leahy because Leahy had "challenged my integrity" by making charges of cronyism between Cheney and his former firm . . .
> Tuesday's exchange began when Leahy crossed the aisle at the photo session and joked to Cheney about being on the Republican side . . . Then Cheney, according to Carle, "lashed into" Leahy for the Halliburton remarks.
> (Dewar & Milbank, 2004)

There was no prospect of murder on the Senate floor, but the intensification of hostile remarks is of the kind that often precedes fatal attacks in a bar or on the street.

Often the killer feels provoked by the victim, being the target of an insult, the butt of a joke, or an object of humiliation. "From the killer's perspective, the victim either teases, dares, defies, or pursues the killer . . . That the killer feels compelled to respond to a fundamental challenge to his worth is indicated as well by the frequent presence and the role of an audience" (Katz, 1988: 20).

Extreme anger (rage) heightens the potential lethality of competition by shifting the adversaries' intentions from dominating to damaging the opposition. The red face of anger, with its raised voice and universally recognized facial gestures and body postures, likely entails particular neurophysiological actions. Alcohol may intensify the normal neurophysiological effect of rage.

Dominance Contests among Young Black Men

Nisbett and Cohen (1996) attribute the historically high violence in the American South, compared to the North, to its "culture of honor" whereby Southern men, when challenged by insults to themselves or their families, are required to defend themselves as virtuous warriors or else lose face. Apparently as a result, Southern men are unusually alert to possible insults, reacting dominantly—sometimes violently—to speech or actions that might not be perceived as injurious in other cultures.

Leaving aside the particular historic roots of the South, there may be a general hypersensitivity to insult in *any* subculture that is (or once was) organized around young men who are unconstrained by traditional community agents of social control, as often occurs in frontier communities, gangs, among vagabonds or bohemians, and after breakdowns in the social fabric following wars or natural disasters. When young men place special emphasis on protecting their reputations, and they are not restrained from doing so, dominance contests become ubiquitous, the hallmark of male-to-male interaction.

The leading student of street behavior in America's inner cities, sociologist Elijah Anderson (1994: 88–89), vividly portrays the importance of dominance contests and their constant presence for poor young black men:

> [M]ost youths have ... internalized the code of the streets ..., which chiefly (has) to do with interpersonal communication ..., (including) facial expressions, gait, and verbal expressions—all of which are geared mainly to deterring aggression ...
>
> Even so, there are no guarantees against challenges, because there are always people looking for a fight to increase their share of respect—of "juice," as it is sometimes called on the street. Moreover, if a person is assaulted, it is important, not only in the eyes of his opponent but also in the eyes of his "running buddies," for him to avenge himself. Otherwise he risks being "tried" (challenged) or "moved on" by any number of others. To maintain his honor he must show he is not someone to be "messed with" or "dissed." ...
>
> The craving for respect that results gives people thin skins. Shows of deference by others can be highly soothing, contributing to a sense of security, comfort, self-confidence, and self-respect ... Hence one must be ever vigilant against the transgressions of others or even appearing as if transgressions will be tolerated. Among young people, whose sense of self-esteem is particularly vulnerable, there is an especially heightened concern with being disrespected. Many inner-city young men in particular crave respect to such a degree that they will risk their lives to attain and maintain it.

We know that testosterone rises in men awaiting a contest, regardless of the eventual outcome of that contest. Generalizing to the street, hormone levels should be elevated in young men who are constantly vigilant against challenges to their reputations. Testosterone is also affected by the outcome of the contest, so persistent losers might be hormonally depressed, but most men—those with mixed outcomes or better—are expected to have elevated testosterone.

Data on testosterone from 4,462 U.S. male Army veterans, ranging in age from 30 to 47, permit further exploration of this hypothesis. Among veterans older than the median age of 37 years—too old to be involved in inner city honor cultures—the testosterone of blacks is no higher than that of whites (Figure 10.2). Furthermore, among younger veterans who have gone to college—and thus are unlikely to be inner city residents—there is no significant race difference in testosterone. Only among *younger veterans with little education* do we find testosterone in blacks to be unusually high (Mazur, 2005: 124). These younger black men, poorly educated, most of them urban residents, are most likely to participate in

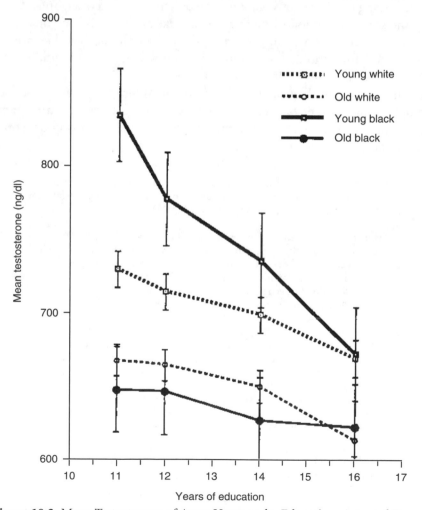

Figure 10.2 Mean Testosterone of Army Veterans, by Education, Age, and Race.

the honor subculture of the street. Their continual defensive posture against dominance challenges would be expected to produce these high hormone levels. High testosterone in turn encourages further dominance contests. Feedback between challenge and testosterone creates a vicious circle, sometimes with lethal effects.

Conclusions

Without diminishing the importance of alleviating social, economic, and environmental deprivations that foster violence, it is worth considering in addition a tactic to reduce testosterone levels among vulnerable young men. This could be accomplished pharmaceutically with androgen antagonists (Maletzky & Field, 2003), but discriminatory medication based on ethnicity or poverty would be morally obnoxious even if it were legal. One shudders to recall that American judges once ordered physical castration of violent sex offenders.

A benign testosterone-reducing tactic would focus on changing the inner city "code of the street" with its hyper emphasis on personal reputation ("juice") and its hair-trigger response to perceived disrespect ("dissing"). A diminution of the honor culture should, ipso facto, reduce testosterone levels of the young men in it, hence reduce the potential for dominance contests to escalate out of control.

Readers should not forget that the association of high testosterone with the violence of honor cultures is hypothetical. It is worthwhile considering the design of a study that would test the hypothesis. A researcher might, for example, compare testosterone levels in the schools of two neighborhoods, one suffering a high murder rate, the other having little criminality. With permission from parents and the students themselves, the researcher would collect saliva from boys at all grade levels, enabling testosterone measurement. The hypothesis predicts little hormone difference between the two neighborhoods at the lowest grades. With increasing grade level, as the two neighborhoods' differing challenge cultures became manifest, one should see a divergence in hormone levels, with higher testosterone in the troubled neighborhood. Absence of this divergence would refute the hypothesis.

References

Allee, W., N. Collias, & C. Lutherman (1939). Modification of the social order in flocks of hens by the injection of testosterone proprionate. *Physiological Zoology*, 12:412–440.
Anderson, E. (1994). The code of the streets. *Atlantic Monthly*, 5:81–94.

Archer, J. (2006). Testosterone and human behavior. *Neuroscience and Biobehavioral Reviews*, 30:319–345.

Bennett, S., D. Farrington, & L. Huesman (2005). Explaining gender differences in crime and violence: the importance of social cognitive skills. *Aggression and Violent Behavior*, 10:263–288.

Bernhardt, P., J. Dabbs, J. Fielden, & C. Lutter (1998). Testosterone changes during vicarious experiences of winning and losing among fans at sporting events. *Physiology and Behavior*, 65:59–62.

Booth, A. & J. Dabbs, Jr. (1993). Testosterone and men's marriages. *Social Forces*, 72:463–477.

Booth, A., D. Granger, A. Mazur, & K. Kivlighan (2006). Testosterone and social behavior. *Social Forces*, 85:167–192.

Burnham, T. (2007). High-testosterone men reject low ultimate game offers. *Proceedings of the Biological Sciences*, 274:2327–2330.

Campbell, A. (2006). Sex differences in direct aggression: what are the psychological mediators? *Aggression and Violent Behavior*, 6:481–497.

Dewar, H. and D. Milbank. (2004). Cheney says he "felt better" after uttering expletive. *Syracuse Post-Standard*, June 26:A7.

Katz, J. (1988). *Seductions of crime*. New York: Basic Books.

Maletzky, B. & G. Field (2003). The biological treatment of dangerous sexual offenders. *Aggression and Violent Behavior*, 8:391–412.

Mazur, A. (1998). Aging and testosterone. *Science*, 279:305–306.

Mazur, A. (2005). *Biosociology of dominance and deference*. New York: Rowman & Littlefield.

Mazur, A. & A. Booth (1998). Testosterone and dominance in men. *Behavioral and Brain Sciences*, 21:353–363.

McGinty, J. (2006). New York killers, and those killed, by numbers. *New York Times*, April 28.

Nisbett, R. & D. Cohen (1996). *Culture of honor*. Boulder, CO: Westview Press.

Rowe, R., B. Maughan, C. Worthman, E.Costello, & A. Angold (2004). Testosterone, antisocial behavior, and social dominance in boys. *Biological Psychiatry*, 55:546–552.

Rutter, J., H. Giller, & A. Hagell (1998). *Antisocial behavior by young people*. New York: Cambridge University Press.

Sanfer, A., J. Rilling, J. Aronson, L. Nystrom & J. Cohen (2003). The neural basis of economic decision-making in the ultimate game. *Science*, 300:1755–1758.

Swaab, D. (2004). Sexual differentiation of the human brain: relevance for gender identity, transsexualism and sexual orientation. *Gynecological Endocrinology*, 19:301–312.

Tremblay, R. (2000). The development of aggressive behavior during childhood. *International Journal of Behavior and Development*, 24: 129–141.

Wolfgang, M. 1958. *Patterns of criminal behavior*. Philadelphia: University of Pennsylvania.

Part III

Serious Violent Criminals and Biosocial Approaches to Crime Prevention

One of the hallmarks of criminological research is that a relatively small percentage of all offenders account for more than half of all offenses committed. These offenders have been tagged with different labels, such as career criminals, life-course persistent offenders, and chronic offenders. Regardless of the label attached to them, there is widespread recognition that they represent the "worst of the worst" criminals (DeLisi, 2005). Psychopaths, who make up a disproportionate number of chronic offenders, represent one of the biggest threats to society (Hare, 1993). Despite the destruction caused at the hands of psychopaths and career criminals, much remains unknown about their etiologies. The biosocial perspective, however, can help to shed some light on the biological, genetic, and neurological underpinnings to serious violent offending. Unfortunately, any insinuation that biological or genetic factors contribute to the development of serious violent offenders and psychopaths is often met with the kneejerk reaction that biology is destiny. As a corollary attack, opponents to biosocial criminology also vehemently argue that since biological factors are immutable, so too are psychopaths and career criminals. This simply is not the case as the three chapters contained in Part III make clear.

Although most adolescents dabble in at least minor forms of delinquency, most discontinue their involvement in these types of behavior by early adulthood. A small pool of all adolescent delinquents, however, engages in acts of serious violence as youths and they persist with their violent behaviors well into adulthood. These offenders typically accrue a lengthy criminal record and spend a considerable amount of time behind bars. They are, in other words, career criminals. Identifying the causes to career criminality is important from a public safety standpoint and also from a prevention/treatment perspective. All too often, research seeking to uncover the correlates to career criminals fails to include a serious examination of biological factors. This is an unfortunate omission because as Michael Ghiglieri (1999:8) explains:

> Nature equipped each of us with a complex brain ruled by chemical neurotransmitters that spur in us instinctive emotional responses to situations, which in turn influence our behavior. This may not be a comfortable way to look at ourselves, but biology tells us that this is the only accurate way and, more to the point, that it is the only way that offers us any real hope of understanding our behavior, including our use of violence.

In Chapter 11, Matt DeLisi employs a biosocial approach to discuss the link between genetics and career criminality. This chapter makes the case that certain personality traits, such as impulsivity, risk taking, and low self-control are antecedent causes to career criminals. It is these personality traits, and *not* the violent behaviors themselves, that are influenced strongly by genetic factors. According to DeLisi, these personality traits can be conceptualized as endophenotypes. Endophenotypes are intermediary characteristics that fall somewhere between genotype and phenotype. In this case, genes do not directly affect career criminality, but rather operate indirectly via their effects on the endophenotypes of self-control, risk taking, and novelty seeking. DeLisi also layers in the different ways in which the environment may contribute to career criminality, such as through gene X environment interactions.

Career criminals impose a tremendous toll on society by inflicting injuries on their victims, by tying up the criminal justice system, and by costing taxpayers a substantial amount of money. These same problems are also created by, and may even be greater for, psychopaths. Psychopaths are people who have a constellation of antisocial traits, such as aggressiveness, impulsivity, sensation seeking, self-centeredness, callousness, and low empathy, among others. Psychopaths commit a disproportionate amount of all violent crimes and they are also overrepresented in the criminal justice system. Although estimates vary somewhat, approximately 25 percent of all inmates meet the diagnostic criteria for psychopathy; however, most psychopaths never enter into the criminal justice system, are not violent, yet still destroy others' lives and prey on people. The costs exacted on society by psychopaths are not known for certain, but are no doubt staggering. Robert Hare (1993:68), the leading expert on issues related to psychopathy, captured the destruction of psychopaths when he notes that:

> Not all psychopaths end up in jail. Many of the things they do escape detection or prosecution, or are on the "shady side of the law." For them, antisocial

behavior may consist of phony stock promotions, questionable business and professional practices, spouse or child abuse, and so forth. Many others do things that, although not illegal, are unethical, immoral, or harmful to others: philandering, cheating on a spouse, financial or emotional neglect of family members, irresponsible use of company resources or funds, to name but a few. The problem with behaviors of this sort is that they are difficult to document and evaluate without the active cooperation of family, friends, acquaintances, and business associates.

Richard Wiebe explores the origins of psychopathy in great detail in Chapter 12 and he ties psychopathy to a host of biological factors, including physiology, genetics, and evolution. Wiebe presents evidence showing that psychopaths have lower fear levels, which probably results from an imbalance between the behavioral activation system (BAS) and the behavioral inhibition system (BIS). Wiebe discusses various other biological processes that appear to be deficient or at least subefficient in psychopaths, such as decoding emotions, startle potentiation, and arousal levels. The ways in which genetic factors and evolutionary forces contribute to psychopathy are also explicated.

The overarching theme of both Wiebe's and DeLisi's chapters is that the causes of violent behaviors are infinitely complex, but are largely governed by biology. This necessarily leads to questions regarding whether violent offending can be prevented or, once it surfaces, whether it can be treated. Although many criminologists who are unfamiliar with biosocial research equate biology with immutability, such a conclusion is unfounded, incorrect, and wrong. Not only can environments blunt the effects of genetic factors, but contrived treatment regimens have been found to alter brain activity level in various regions of the brain, including the prefrontal cortex, among samples of depressed patients (Brody, et al., 2001; Martin, et al., 2001; Thase, 2001). Biological processes can—and indeed are— profoundly affected by environmental conditions.

In Chapter 13, Matthew Robinson helps to dispel the myth that biosocial criminology is unable to guide and inform prevention and treatment efforts by presenting a number of different crime prevention options that flow directly from biosocial research. Robinson's chapter is grounded in the integrated systems theory (IST), which is an interdisciplinary biosocial explanation of crime. By using this theory, Robinson shows that reducing exposure to environmental toxins and increasing nutritional quality (e.g., diets rich in omega-3 fatty acids) promote healthy brain development and prevent neuropsychological deficits from surfacing. This chapter also points out that parenting behaviors matter, but in ways that are often not recognized, such as through structuring exposure to different types of food. (Some parents may force their children to eat healthy, nutritional diets, while other parents may not.) Robinson also underscores the fact that genes do not have effects independent of their environments and genetic effects often only surface when paired with a particular environment. Changing the environment, therefore, will ultimately change genetic expression. In this way, intervention/prevention efforts that target criminogenic environments are also able to alter genetic effects.

References

Brody, A. L., S. Saxena, P. Stoessel, L. A. Gillies, L. A. Fairbanks, S. Alborzian, et al. (2001). Regional brain metabolic changes in patients with major depression treated with either paroxetine or interpersonal therapy. *Archives of General Psychiatry*, 58:631–640.

DeLisi, M. (2005). *Career criminals in society*. Thousand Oaks, CA: Sage.

Ghiglieri, M. P. (1999). *The dark side of man: tracing the origins of male violence*. Reading, MA: Perseus Books Group.

Hare, R. D. (1993). *Without conscience: the disturbing world of psychopaths among us*. New York: Guilford Press.

Martin, S. D., E. Martin, S. Rai, M. A. Richardson, R. Royall (2001). Brain blood flow changes in depressed patients treated with interpersonal psychotherapy or venlafaxine hydrochloride. *Archives of General Psychiatry*, 58:641–648.

Thase, M. E. (2001). Neuroimaging profiles and the differential therapies of depression. *Archives of General Psychiatry*, 58:651–653.

11

Neuroscience and the Holy Grail: Genetics and Career Criminality

Matt DeLisi

Although career criminality has been referred to as the holy grail of criminological research, virtually all the literature centers on its sociological and psychological characteristics. The paucity of biological research is unfortunate given the empirical strength of the effects of genetic and biological factors on antisocial and aggressive behavior. For instance, Walters (1992:604) conducted a meta-analysis of 38 family, twin, and adoption studies on crime and found a consistent and statistically significant association between various indices of heredity and crime. He concluded: "With a mean unweighted effect size of .25, median effect size of .17, and mean weighted effect size of .09, there would appear to be guarded optimism for a genetic interpretation of certain facets of criminal behavior." Since that analysis, "guarded optimism" about the genetic bases of serious antisocial behavior has become significantly more substantial. Moffitt's (2003:54–55) review of the literature indicated that approximately 60 percent of variation in aggression and approximately 40 percent of variation in delinquency is heritable.

If the genetic sources of criminal behavior have been understudied relative to other disciplines, the genetic underpinnings of career criminality have been virtually ignored by criminologists until very recently. The current chapter reviews the molecular genetic research on career criminality including the identification of several candidate genes, examines impulsivity as an important endophenotype (*endo* = "within", *phenotype* = observable characteristics of an individual, determined by genes and environment) that is linked to pathological criminal behavior, and explores environmental conditions that interact with genes to produce antisocial behavioral outcomes.

Career Criminals

Criminologists have commonly utilized family studies to examine the heritability of antisocial behavior. In family studies, index subjects, known as proband, who present the trait or behavior under investigation (e.g., criminality, psychopathy, etc.) are compared to a control group of people who do not present the trait or behavior. From these study groups, the prevalence of the trait is examined among first-degree relatives (children, siblings, or parents) of the proband and control subjects. Genetic effects are inferred or estimated when the trait or behavior is more prevalent among relatives of the proband than control group. Sheldon Glueck and Eleanor Glueck (1930, 1934) used family study designs to examine the heritability of crime among their classic samples of delinquent youth. In their sample of male delinquents, they found that the prevalence of family member arrest was nearly 200 percent greater among proband than controls. For females, the prevalence of family member arrest was about 160 percent higher among proband than controls (Glueck & Glueck, 1934). In short, the Gluecks provided speculative but empirically compelling evidence that crime "runs in the family."

Robert Cloninger, Samuel Guze, and their colleagues produced even stronger evidence for the heritability of crime in their studies of the transmission of sociopathy among families sampled from St. Louis, Missouri. For example, Guze, et al. (1967) studied 519 first-degree relatives of sociopathic males and found that the prevalence of sociopathy among proband subjects was more than *330 percent* higher than among controls. Similarly, Cloninger and Guze (1973) produced stronger effects among female index subjects using arrests and sociopathy diagnosis as outcomes. Arrest prevalence was nearly *700 percent* greater among proband than control subjects and sociopathy diagnosis prevalence was more than *700 percent* greater among proband than controls. Subsequent studies by this research team affirmed the strong familial transmission of serious antisocial behavior (Cloninger, et al., 1975a, 1975b).

For decades, criminologists were confident that antisocial and criminal behavior, especially pernicious forms such as sociopathy had a familial transmission. There was also a general sense that not only was there some amorphous criminal propensity within individuals but also that it might have a genetic origin. What was missing, however, was authoritative evidence of what this pathological group might look like. That evidence arrived in 1972 with the publication of *Delinquency in a Birth Cohort*, a seminal study by Wolfgang, et al., that followed 9,945 males born in Philadelphia in 1945 and who lived in the city at least from ages 10 to 18. Wolfgang and his colleagues found that nearly two-thirds of the population never experienced a police contact and that 35 percent of the population had. Based on this, one can be comforted to know that most people in a population are law abiding to the extent that the police never contact them for deviant behavior. For the minority of persons whom were actually contacted by police, the police contacts were rare occurrences occurring just once, twice, or three times. By the same token, some youth experienced more frequent interaction with police. According to Wolfgang et al. (1972), people with five or more police contacts were chronic or habitual offenders. Of the nearly 10,000 boys, only 627 members, just 6 percent of the population (18% of those arrested), qualified as habitual offenders yet the chronic 6 percent accounted for 52 percent of the delinquency in the entire cohort, 63 percent of all index offenses, 71 percent of the murders, 73 percent of the rapes, 82 percent of the robberies, and 69 percent of the aggravated assaults. Herein was the quantifiable evidence that a small minority of high-rate offenders known as **career criminals** were guilty of perpetrating the majority of all criminal acts in a population.

A second and improved study examined a cohort of 13,160 males and 14,000 females born in Philadelphia in 1958 (Tracy, et al., 1990). Overall, the 1958 cohort committed crime at higher rates than the 1945 cohort and demonstrated greater involvement in the most serious forms of crime, but roughly the same proportion of persons, 33 percent, experienced arrest prior to adulthood. Approximately 7 percent of the population members were habitual offenders, and they accounted for 61 percent of all delinquency, 60 percent of the murders, 75 percent of the rapes, 73 percent of the robberies, and 65 percent of the aggravated assaults.

There are several examples of skewness in the offending distribution indicating that a small percentage of offenders account for the majority of offenses. In a longitudinal sample from Sweden, 5 percent of the subjects recorded 41 percent of all convictions and 62 percent of all arrests (Stattin & Magnusson, 1991). Lyle Shannon (1991) studied the offending patterns of three birth cohorts born in Racine, Wisconsin, in 1942, 1949, or 1955. For the 1942 cohort, 1 percent of the males accounted for 29 percent of the felony offenses; 3 percent of the males in the 1949 cohort were responsible for 50 percent of the felonies; and 6 percent of the males born in 1955 accounted for 70 percent of the felony offenses. Interestingly, this trend persists even when examining offending careers occurring in prison. A study of the infraction records of 1,005 inmates found that a small cadre of inmates accounted for 100 percent of the murders, 75 percent of the rapes, 80 percent of the arsons, and 50 percent of the aggravated assaults occurring in the correctional facilities of a southwestern state in the United States (DeLisi, 2003). In sum, across research designs, analytical methods, and data sources selected from North America, South America, Europe, Asia, and Australia, criminologists have repeatedly affirmed the empirical regularity that a small subgroup of offenders, or career criminals, accounts for the bulk of delinquency occurring in a society (see DeLisi, 2005).

Virtually everything that is known about career criminality strongly implicates at least a partially genetic etiological basis. Career criminals are a small group of offenders, usually less than 10 percent of a population or sample, that accounts for the bulk of crime and the majority of serious violent offenses in that population. Their criminal careers usually have the earliest beginning (onset), continue for longer periods of time (span), are characterized by high offending frequency (**lambda**), include a range of antisocial behaviors (**versatility**) especially for the most serious crimes (seriousness), and take a longer period of time (**persistence**) before they decline (desistance). The end (**termination**) of their criminal career is usually caused by criminal justice system intervention, such as life imprisonment or capital punishment, or the offender's death, which is commonly the result of a lifestyle engaged in risky, illicit activities.

Retrospectively, it is often the case that adult career criminals were chronic delinquents during adolescence and behaviorally problematic youngsters during childhood often to the degree of having diagnosed psychiatric disorders, such as conduct disorder, attention deficit hyperactivity disorder, and oppositional defiant disorder. Conduct disorder (CD) is a clinical disorder characterized by repetitive and persistent patterns of behavior in which the basic rights of others or major age-appropriate societal norms or rules are violated. It is graded on a continuum from mild to moderate to severe, the last diagnosis including behaviors such as forced sex, physical cruelty, use of a weapon, stealing while confronting a victim, and breaking and entering. Attention deficit hyperactivity disorder (ADHD) is a clinical disorder characterized by inattentiveness and poor behavioral control related to hyperactivity and impulsivity (see Walsh, Chapter 9). Oppositional defiant disorder (ODD) is a clinical disorder characterized by a recurrent pattern of negativistic, defiant, disobedient, and hostile behavior toward authority figures. A child with ODD often loses his temper, often argues with adults, often actively defies or is noncompliant, often deliberately annoys others, often blames others for mistakes, is often touchy or easily annoyed by others, is often angry and resentful, and is often spiteful or vindictive (American Psychiatric Association, 2000).

Behaviorally, there are **prodromes** (precursors or early symptoms) in early life that appear to portend a life of crime. For instance, callous–unemotional traits including guiltlessness, lack of consideration of other people's feelings, meanness, disinterest in school and behavioral performance, social isolation, and rare display of feelings or emotion are prodromes of psychopathy and these correlate with the characteristics of career criminals (see Rutter, 2005). Importantly, the early warning signs of severe antisocial behavior are strongly heritable. For instance, a recent study of callous–unemotional traits and antisocial behavior among 3,687 twin pairs indicated that 67 percent of variation in extreme callous–unemotional traits among 7-year-old children was attributable to genetics. When examining extreme antisocial behavior in 7 year olds with psychopathic tendencies, genes accounted for 81 percent of the variation (Viding, et al., 2005). A subsequent study found that 71 percent of conduct problems in boys and 77 percent in girls were attributable to genetic influences (Viding, et al., 2007). In the conclusion of their behavioral genetic research, Viding and her colleagues called on further examination using molecular genetics, in which individual measured genes are used to estimate genetic effects, to specify the genotypic basis of serious criminal behavior. That area of research is explored next.

Molecular Genetics, Career Criminality, and Related Phenotypes

In recent years, behavioral scientists have explored career criminality phenotypes using the National Longitudinal Study of Adolescent Health (Add Health) a dataset in which a subsample were genotyped for five monoamine genes: 5HTT, DAT1, DRD2, DRD4, and MAOA. Thus far, these polymorphisms have been linked to an array of outcomes. A recent study investigated the linkages between self-reported serious and violent delinquency, the *Taq*I polymorphism in the DRD2 gene and the 40-bp VNTR polymorphism in the DAT1 gene using the Add Health data (Guo, et al., 2007a). Both polymorphisms were associated with greater involvement in serious and violent crime among adolescents and adults. In a related study, Guang Guo and his colleagues (2007b) found that all five genes predicted frequency of alcohol use in adulthood accounting for between 7–20 percent of the variation in alcohol consumption. Although alcohol use is itself not indicative of career criminality, problem alcohol use is one of several antisocial behaviors that are comorbid with high-rate criminal activity. Moreover, specific genes, such as DRD2 have been linked to alcoholism (e.g., Cloninger, 1991; Pato, et al., 1993).

Genetic factors have also been linked to specific dimensions of the criminal career. Matt DeLisi and his colleagues (2007) examined the effects of DAT1 and 5HTT on chronicity and dangerousness while controlling for age, sex, cognitive ability, and self-control. They found that genetic effects were conditioned by the delinquent peer network within which adolescents were situated, suggesting a significant gene X environment interaction. The genetic effects were predictive of repeated and dangerous criminal behavior among youths with few delinquent peers.

In a related study, DRD2 and DRD4 were significantly related to police contacts and arrests but only among youths in low-risk family environments (DeLisi, et al., 2008). A gene X environment interaction has also been detected for youths with the DRD2 risk allele and few delinquent peers in predicting criminal victimization which is a phenotype behaviorally related to career criminality (Beaver, et al., 2007b).

The effects of measured genes on career criminality phenotypes sometimes work in interesting ways. To illustrate, Kevin Beaver and his colleagues (2007a) explored the linkages between DRD2, DRD4, adolescent conduct disorder, and adult antisocial behavior across three waves of data. With the exception of DRD2 and conduct disorder at wave 1, no direct effects were detected between the polymorphisms and outcomes. However, the interaction of DRD2 and DRD4, that is subjects with risk alleles for both polymorphisms, was predictive of conduct disorder at all three waves, lifetime conduct problems, and a composite index of antisocial behavior. Their study is noteworthy because it is the first evidence of a gene X gene interaction in the etiology of career criminality occurring during adolescence and adulthood.

Molecular genetic research is also being conducted using diverse samples with multiple genetic polymorphisms and multitudinous behavioral phenotypes. Many of these phenotypes are strongly correlated with life-long criminal behavior. Jonathan Mill and his colleagues (2006) explored the links between the 7-repeat allele of DRD4 and 10-repeat allele of DAT1 on ADHD and intellectual functioning. Their longitudinal epidemiologic investigation examined two birth cohorts: the E-Risk Study of 2,232 children in England and the Dunedin New Zealand birth cohort including 1,037 children. The findings were alarming. Both DRD4 and DAT1 predicted intellectual functioning and ADHD. Respondents in the Dunedin study were followed up to age 26 and evaluated for 10 adult outcomes, including violent conviction, nonviolent conviction, substance abuse diagnosis, psychiatric diagnoses, aggression against partner, aggression against minors, no high school qualification, out-of-wedlock parenthood, government welfare benefits, and long-term unemployment of more than 6 months. Children who had been diagnosed with ADHD were significantly likely to experience multiple negative adult outcomes and the effects were largely accounted for by DRD4 and DAT1.

Danielle Dick and her colleagues (2006a) reported that the high-risk genotype of GABRA2 was related to positively related alcohol dependence, negatively related to likelihood of marrying, and positively related to divorce. Failure at interpersonal relationships and strife in both family of orientation and family of procreation is characteristic of career offenders (DeLisi, 2005; Gottfredson & Hirschi, 1990). Using the same sample, Dick, et al. (2006b) also reported a link between GABRA2 and childhood conduct disorder and a link between GABRA2 and adult onset drug and alcohol dependence. In this way, GABRA2 has pleiotropic effects on antisocial phenotypes at multiple stages of the life-course.

As indicated earlier, diagnoses for CD, ODD, or ADHD are important because although they are not unequivocal precursors to career criminality, they *are* meaningful phenotypes that often show a sustained and stable manifestation of chronic antisocial conduct. As such, by understanding the genetic bases of CD, ODD, and ADHD, we can locate candidate genes for career criminality. David Comings and his colleagues (2000a) explored the predictive value of 20 genes on CD, ODD, and ADHD. The analyses included six dopaminergic genes (DRD1, DRD2, DRD3, DRD4, DRD5, and DAT1), seven serotonergic genes (5HTT, HTR1A, HTR1B, HTR1DA, HTR2A, TDO2, and TRH), and seven noradrenergic genes (DBH, ADRA2A, ADRAB, ADRA2C, PNMT, NET, and COMT). The three strongest dopamine genes contributed to 2.3 percent of the variance, the three strongest serotonin genes contributed to 3 percent of the variance, and the six strongest adrenergic genes accounted for 6.9 percent of the variance in ADHD. Similar predictive effects were found for CD and ODD. A follow-up study included 42 genes including six new neurotransmitter genes: CHNRA4, ADOA2A, NOS3, NMDAR1, GRIN2B, and GABRB3. Comings and his colleagues (2000b) again found that noradrenergic genes were the strongest predictors of ADHD and ODD. By way of contrast, the genes that were most helpful in predicting CD were hormone and neuropeptide genes, such as CCK, CYP19, ESRI, and INS. Overall, the use of multivariate analysis of associations (MAA) with batteries of genes is very useful in determining the genetic underpinnings of serious antisocial conduct. The MAA technique focuses on the additive effect of multiple genes as well as the cumulative effect of functionally related groups of genes. Multiple genes and groupings of genes are associated with behavioral disorders indicating their polygenic etiology.

Endophenotypes and Career Criminality

There is no career criminality gene, just as there are not genes for specific forms of criminal behavior, such as murder, rape, or robbery. As described by Andreas Meyer-Lindenberg and Daniel Weinberger (2006:818): "[A]lmost by definition, the more behavioral the phenotype, the less directly it will be predicted by a genotype." Consequently, geneticists have identified intermediate phenotypes, which are located between genotypes and complex behavioral phenotypes. These intermediate phenotypes are called *endophenotypes*, defined as heritable neurophysiological, biochemical, endocrinological, neuroanatomical, or neuropsychological constituents of behavioral disorders that are assumed to have simpler genetic underpinnings than the disorders themselves (Caspi & Moffitt, 2006:583). Put more simply, endophenotypes relate to psychosocial characteristics that lend themselves to criminal activity.

Endophenotypes refer to the molecular middle ground that exists between genes and the ultimate behavior. Genes encode proteins to perform specific tasks or functions. When genes are suboptimal, the neuronal activity in the brain does not operate correctly—there is some degree of neural dysfunction. In turn, this produces cognitive or behavioral dysfunction, which, in turn, manifests as symptoms of a behavioral disorder. Endophenotypes are important because they illustrate the complexity and sophistication that typifies genetic effects on human behavior. Genes do not run roughshod over the brain in influencing behavior, especially when the behavior is a multifactorial phenomenon, such as crime. Instead, genetic risks factors set into motion an array of neural developments that ultimately result in behavior (see Figure 11.1).

A popular criminological theory that is useful to illustrate the importance of endophenotypes is self-control theory developed by Gottfredson and Hirschi (1990:85). People with low self-control demonstrate a constellation of attitudinal and behavioral characteristics. They tend to (1) have a here-and-now orientation whereby they seek immediate as opposed to delayed gratification; (2) prefer easy and simple tasks and dislike activities that require diligence, tenacity, and persistence; (3) engage in behaviors that are risky and exciting rather than cautious and cognitive; (4) fail to see the longer-term benefits of investing in social institutions; (5) are attracted to endeavors that entail little skill or planning; and (6) are unkind, insensitive, hot tempered, self-centered, and unsympathetic to others.

This profile is not unique to self-control theory, however. For instance, in their research on personality correlates of crime, Donald Lynam and Joshua Miller (2004:320) observed that: "[I]mpulsivity-related traits are consistently related to antisocial outcome variables. Impulsivity appears,

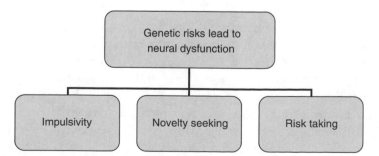

Figure 11.1 The Self-control Theory Endophenotype.

in one form or another, in every major system of personality, often sub-sumed by broader personality dimensions (e.g., conscientiousness, con-straint, impulsive-sensation seeking, novelty seeking). Impulsivity also plays a prominent role in the understanding and diagnosis of various forms of psychopathology." The reason that self-control is important to career criminality is that the set of characteristics described by self-control researchers typifies the personality and behavioral repertoire of the most serious offenders (DeLisi, 2005; Wilson & Herrnstein, 1985).

Mary Kreek and her colleagues (2005:1452–1453) have shown the connections between genes, endophenotypes, such as those implicated in self-control theory, and addiction which is a behavioral outcome pheno-typically congruent with chronic delinquency. For instance, **impulsivity** is a personality trait characterized by behavioral disinhibition, such as acting suddenly in an unplanned manner to satisfy a desire. Impulsivity entails not thinking through the long-term impact of carrying out actions, such as the use of aggression and violence. Impulsivity is an endophenotype clearly linked with the serotonergic system. Serotonin is an inhibitory neurotransmitter that modulates behaviors and acts as the body's natural brake system. When serotonin is released in the brain, neuronal activity is reduced and innate drives, such as aggressive tendencies and primitive impulses are controlled. Research indicates that serotonin levels are lower in persons that commit serious, violent crime (Moore, et al., 2002). Moreover, several serotonergic genes, including TPH1, 5HTT, and MAOA are associated with impulsivity in addition to other candidate genes linked to antisocial behavior, such as DRD4, DAT1, COMT, GABRA1, GABRA6, and GABRB1.

The relevance of impulsivity as an endophenotype that facilitates recurrent antisocial behavior, the serotonergic system as the system that modulates behavior, and the specific import of 5HTT to career criminality are crucial. First, risk alleles for 5HTT as a predictor of ADHD, a pro-drome of career criminality, are among the most replicated findings in a recent 15-year review of ADHD research (Bobb, et al., 2006). Second, 5HTT is also associated with criminal and violent behavior in adulthood as well as personality disorders that co-occur with crime. In this sense, 5HTT is one of likely many genes that contribute to antisocial behavior across the life-course. For instance, Wolfgang Retz and his colleagues explored the effects of 5HTT among 153 male forensic psychiatric patients, 72 of whom were violent offenders. Nearly one in four violent patients had two risk alleles for 5HTT a prevalence estimate that was nearly three times greater than the prevalence among nonviolent psychiatric patients. Nearly 81 percent of violent patients had at least one risk allele and there was a significant overrepresentation of the risk 5HTT genotype among subgroups with personality disorders. Third, recent research reported that

5HTT plays a part in the functioning of the amygdala, bilateral parts of the limbic system of the brain that play a primary role in the processing and memory of emotions in particular the modulation of fear (also, see, Meyer-Lindenberg, et al., 2006). The emotional impairments produced by amygdala dysfunction are at the heart of recent causal explanations for psychopathy (Blair, et al., 2005).

Environmental Conditions, Genes, and Career Criminality Phenotypes

A recurrent finding in the criminal career literature is that habitual offenders are disproportionately likely to be reared in adverse, highly stressful, often abusive home environments with problematic parenting styles. There are many illustrative examples. Shayne Jones and his colleagues studied a sample of incarcerated adolescent offenders and found that most delinquents had parents who weakly supported them. In turn, poor parenting contributed to several negative outcomes among their children including antisocial behavior, low impulse control, and low consideration of others. Carolyn Smith and Susan Stern (1997:383) concluded: "We know that children who grow up in homes characterized by lack of warmth and support, whose parents lack behavior management skills, and whose lives are characterized by conflict or maltreatment will more likely to delinquent, whereas a supportive family can protect children even in a very hostile and damaging external environment." Janna Haapasalo and Elina Pokela (1999) examined several major longitudinal studies of delinquency, such as the Cambridge Study in Delinquent Development, Christchurch Health and Development Study, Dunedin Multidisciplinary Health and Development Study, and the Oregon Youth Study. They found that career criminals experienced harsh, punitive, overly lax, and neglectful types of parenting style, were significantly more likely to be rejected by their parents, and to have suffered more severe forms of child abuse. Indeed, in theorizing the development of life-course persistent offenders, Moffitt (1993:681) claimed:"[V]ulnerable infants are disproportionately found in environments that will not be ameliorative because many of the sources of neural maldevelopment co-occur with family disadvantage or deviance."

From a genetic perspective, privations occurring in the first years of life are especially pernicious because they affect the brain when it is its most pliable. As Walsh and Beaver (Chapter 1, this volume) state: "Because neural pathways laid down early in life are more resistant to elimination than pathways laid down later in life, brains organized by stressful and traumatic events tend to relay subsequent events along the same neural pathways. *A brain organized by negative events is ripe for antisocial behavior because established neural pathways are activated with less provocation than is required to engage less established pathways.*" In recent years, behavioral scientists have examined the ways that early life environmental conditions interact with genetic factors to produce antisocial outcomes. Avshalom Caspi and his colleagues (2002) were the first researchers to examine the interactive effects between a measured environment and a measured gene. Specifically, Caspi and his colleagues hypothesized that a history of childhood maltreatment would interact with MAOA to predict involvement in criminal and violent behaviors. The MAOA gene comes in either a high-activity version or a low-activity version with the latter version conferring an increased susceptibility to antisocial behaviors, but only among those respondents who had been maltreated as children. The high-activity version of MAOA, by the same token, was hypothesized to buffer the criminogenic effects of childhood maltreatment. In short, they expected the MAOA gene to interact with childhood maltreatment in the prediction of antisocial behavior using white males selected from the Dunedin (New Zealand) Multidisciplinary Health and Development Study.

Their analysis revealed three broad findings. First, respondents who were maltreated as a child were significantly more likely to be diagnosed with conduct disorder, to be convicted of a violent offense, to score high on an antisocial personality symptoms scale, to score high on a disposition to violence scale, and to score high on a composite measure of antisocial behavior. All of these are analogs of career criminality. Second, the main effect of the MAOA gene was not a statistically significant predictor of any of the five antisocial outcome measures. Third, and perhaps most importantly, was that childhood maltreatment interacted with MAOA to predict a statistically significant amount of variation in four of the five dependent variables. In substantive terms, this interaction meant that the *low-activity MAOA genotype had an effect only on antisocial behavior among those respondents who had been maltreated as a child.* Although only 12 percent of the sample had been maltreated as a child and had the low-functioning version of the MAOA allele, they accounted for 44 percent of all violent convictions. A recent meta-analysis confirmed the relationship between MAOA, maltreatment, and antisociality (Kim-Cohen, et al., 2006). Moreover, the gene X environment interaction has been supported with recent behavioral genetic research. Sara Jaffee and her colleagues found that the effect of maltreatment on conduct problems was strongest among those at high genetic risk. For children with low genetic risk, maltreatment increased the probability of conduct disorder diagnosis by 2 percent. For children with high genetic risk, maltreatment increased the likelihood of conduct disorder by 24 percent. In other words, there was a 1.2 order of magnitude difference in risk attributable to the interaction between maltreatment and genetic risk.

Caspi and his colleagues (2003) conducted a similar line of research that explored a gene X environment interaction for depression in which the gene was 5HTT and the environmental condition that moderated the genetic effect was stress. They produced two major findings. First, child-hood stress predicted adult depression only among individuals with the short allele of 5HTT. Second, the gene X environment interaction signifi-cantly predicted four phenotypes, including self-reports of depressive symptoms in adulthood, the probability of a major depressive episode, the probability of suicide ideation or attempted suicide, and informant reports of the individual's depression. These recent molecular genetic studies are critically important because they are beginning to identify the environmental conditions that suppress or amplify genetic risk factors to produce antisocial behavior. As shown in Figure 11.2, genetic risks are modulated by environmental conditions that result in psychosocial

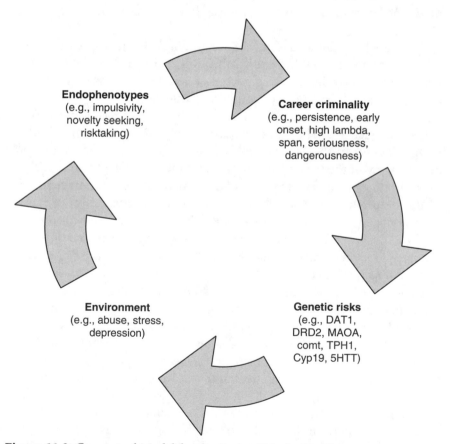

Figure 11.2 Conceptual Model for the Career Criminality Phenotype.

endophenotypes and more complex behaviors. In turn, behaviors recursively affect genetic express and the cycle continues. In this way, the mechanisms of the nature–nurture symbiosis are becoming clearer.

Conclusion

Imagine that the bulk of the incidence of crime was attributable to fewer than 10 percent of offenders. Imagine that this same circumscribed group accounted for an even greater proportion of predatory crimes. Imagine that these empirical regularities were observed across data sources, across cultures, across racial, ethnic, and nationality groups, and across time. Imagine no more: *all of these are true*. Now imagine that a human genome project would identify all 20,000–25,000 genes in human DNA and determine the sequence of the 3 billion chemical base pairs that comprise human DNA. Again, imagine no more: the mapping of the human genome has been accomplished. Because of this marvelous scientific accomplishment, behavioral scientists can now access the role of nature and nurture in determining complex behavioral outcomes via the use of measured genes and measured environmental factors. The misleading black box of "nature or nurture" has been replaced by a transparent understanding of nature and nurture. Consequently, there has never been a more exciting time to be a criminologist.

From an array of disciplines and using an array of phenotypes, criminologists are connecting the conceptual and empirical dots between antisociality occurring from infancy to late adulthood. The scientific understanding of career criminality from a neuroscience perspective is being refined rapidly. Consider research on ADHD. To date, four candidate genes for susceptibility to the disorder have been identified: ADHD1 located on chromosome 16p13 (Smalley, et al., 2002), ADHD2 located on chromosome 17p11 (Ogdie, et al., 2003), ADHD3 located on chromosome 6q12 (Ogdie, et al., 2004), and ADHD4 located on chromosome 5p13 (Ogdie, et al., 2004). How terrific is the progress toward the genetic understanding of complex behavioral disorders such as ADHD than the identification of genes with names like ADHD1, ADHD2, ADHD3, and ADHD4? As the dozens of candidates genes reviewed in this chapter can attest, a firmer understanding of the genetic bases of CD, ODD, and career criminality is likely forthcoming. With insights from molecular genetics, the endophenotypes that connect genotype to phenotype will be more fully understood as will the environmental pathogens that smolder genetic risk factors into recurrent, pathological antisocial behavior.

References

American Psychiatric Association. (2000). *Diagnostic and statistical manual of mental disorders (fourth edition, text revision, DSM-IV-TR)*. Washington, DC: Author.

Beaver, K. M., J. P. Wright, M. DeLisi, L. E. Daigle, M. L. Swatt, & C. L. Gibson (2007a). Evidence of a gene X environment interaction in the creation of victimization: results from a longitudinal sample of adolescents. *International Journal of Offender Therapy and Comparative Criminology*, 51, 620–645.

Beaver, K. M., J. P. Wright, M. DeLisi, A. Walsh, M. G. Vaughn, D. Boisvert, & J. Vaske (2007b). A gene X gene interaction between DRD2 and DRD4 in the etiology of conduct disorder and antisocial behavior. *Behavioral and Brain Functions*, 3:30.

Blair, J., D. Mitchell, & K. Blair (2005). *The psychopath: emotion and the brain*. Malden, MA: Blackwell.

Bobb, A. J., F. X. Castellanos, A. M. Addington, & J. L. Rapoport (2006). Molecular genetic studies of ADHD: 1991 to 2004. *American Journal of Medical Genetics Part B (Neuropsychiatric Genetics)*, 141B:551–565.

Caspi, A. & T. E. Moffitt (2006). Gene-environment interactions in psychiatry: joining forces with neuroscience. *Nature Reviews Neuroscience*, 7:583–590.

Caspi, A., J. McClay, T. E. Moffitt, J. Mill, J. Martin, I. W. Craig, et al. (2002). Role of genotype in the cycle of violence in maltreated children. *Science*, 297: 851–854.

Caspi, A., K. Sugden, T. E., Moffitt, A. Taylor, I. W. Craig, H. L., Harrington, et al. (2003). Influence of life stress on depression: Moderation by a polymorphism in the 5HTT gene. *Science*, 301:386–389.

Cloninger, C. R. (1991). D_2 dopamine receptor gene is associated but not linked with alcoholism. *Journal of the American Medical Association*, 266:1833–1834.

Cloninger, C. R. & S. R. Guze (1973). Psychiatric illness in the families of female criminals: a study of 288 first-degree relatives. *British Journal of Psychiatry*, 122:697–703.

Cloninger, C. R., T. Reich, & S. B. Guze (1975a). The multifactorial model of disease transmission: II. Sex differences in the familial transmission of sociopathy (antisocial personality). *British Journal of Psychiatry*, 127:11–22.

Cloninger, C. R., T. Reich, & S. B. Guze (1975b). The multifactorial model of disease transmission: III. Familial relationships between sociopathy and hysteria (Briquet's syndrome). *British Journal of Psychiatry*, 127:23–32.

Comings, D. E., R. Gade-Andavolu, N. Gonzalez, S. Wu, D. Muhleman, H. Blake, et al. (2000a). Comparison of the role of dopamine, serotonin, and noradrenaline genes in ADHD, ODD, and CD: multivariate regression analysis of 20 genes. *Clinical Genetics*, 57:178–196.

Comings, D. E., R. Gade-Andavolu, N. Gonzalez, S. Wu, D. Muhleman, H. Blake, et al. (2000b). Multivariate analysis of associations of 42 genes in ADHD, ODD, and CD. *Clinical Genetics*, 58:31–40.

DeLisi, M. (2003). Criminal careers behind bars. *Behavioral Sciences and the Law*, 21:653–669.

DeLisi, M. (2005). *Career criminals in society*. Thousand Oaks, CA: Sage.

DeLisi, M., K. M. Beaver, J. P. Wright, & M. G. Vaughn (2007). Genetic antecedents of career criminality: an exploratory empirical assessment with a nationally representative sample of youth. Paper presented at the annual meeting of the Academy of Criminal Justice Sciences, Seattle, Washington.

DeLisi, M., K. M. Beaver, J. P. Wright, & M. G. Vaughn (2008). The etiology of criminal onset: the enduring salience of nature *and* nurture. *Journal of Criminal Justice*, 36:1–25.

Dick, D. M., A. Agrawal, M. Schuckit, L. Bierut, A. L. Hinrichs, C. R. Cloninger, et al. (2006a). Marital status, alcohol dependence, and *GABRA2*: evidence for gene–environment correlation and interaction. *Journal of Studies on Alcohol*, 67:185–194.

Dick, D. M., L. Bierut, A. L. Hinrichs, L. Fox, K. K., Bucholz, J. Kramer, et al. (2006b). The role of *GABRA2* in risk for conduct disorder and alcohol and drug dependence across developmental stages. *Behavior Genetics*, 36:577–590.

Glueck, S. & E. Glueck (1930). *500 criminal careers*. New York: Knopf.

Glueck, S. & E. Glueck (1934). *500 delinquent women*. New York: Knopf.

Gottfredson, M. R. & T. Hirschi (1990). *A general theory of crime*. Stanford, CA: Stanford University Press.

Guo, G., M. E. Roettger, & J. C. Shih (2007a). Contributions of the DAT1 and DRD2 genes to serious and violent delinquency among adolescents and young adults. *Human Genetics*, 121:125–136.

Guo, G., K. Wilhelmsen, & N. Hamilton (2007b). Gene–lifecourse interaction for alcohol consumption in adolescence and young adulthood: five monoamine genes. *American Journal of Medical Genetics Part B (Neuropsychiatric Genetics)*, 144B:417–423.

Guze, S. B., E. D. Wolfgram, J. K. McKinney, & D. P. Cantwell (1967). Psychiatric illness in the families of convicted criminals: a study of 519 first-degree relatives. *Diseases of the Nervous System*, 28:651–659.

Haapasalo, J. & E. Pokela (1999). Child-rearing and child abuse antecedents of criminality. *Aggression and Violent Behavior*, 4:107–127.

Hariri, A. R., V. S. Mattay, A. Tessitore, B. Kolachana, F. Feera, D. Goldman, et al. (2002). Serotonin transporter genetic variation and the response of the human amygdale. *Science*, 297:400–403.

Jaffee, S. R., A. Caspi, T. E. Moffitt, K. A. Dodge, M. Rutter, A. Taylor, et al. (2005). Nature × nurture: genetic vulnerabilities interact with physical maltreatment to promote conduct problems. *Development and Psychopathology*, 17:67–84.

Jones, S., E. Cauffman, & A. R. Piquero (2007). The influence of parental support among incarcerated adolescent offenders: the moderating effects of self-control. *Criminal Justice and Behavior*, 34:229–245.

Kim-Cohen, J., A. Caspi, A. Taylor, B. Williams, R. Newcombe, I. W. Craig, et al. (2006). MAOA, maltreatment, and gene–environment interaction predicting children's mental health: new evidence and a meta-analysis. *Molecular Psychiatry*, 11:903–913.

Kreek, M. J., D. A. Nielsen, E. R. Butelman, & K. S. LaForge (2005). Genetic influences on impulsivity, risk taking, stress responsivity and vulnerability to drug abuse and addition. *Nature Neuroscience*, 8:1450–1457.

Lynam, D. R. & J. D. Miller (2004). Personality pathways to impulsive behavior and their relations to deviance: results from three samples. *Journal of Quantitative Criminology*, 20:319–341.

Meyer-Lindenberg, A. & D. R. Weinberger (2006). Intermediate phenotypes and genetic mechanisms of psychiatric disorders. *Nature Reviews Neuroscience*, 7:818–827.

Meyer-Lindenberg, A.,C. Mervis, & C. Berman (2006). Neural mechanisms of genetic risk for impulsivity and violence in humans. *Proceedings of the National Academy of Sciences*, 103:6269–6274.

Mill, J., A. Caspi, B. S. Williams, I. Craig, A. Taylor, M. Polo-Thomas, et al. (2006). Prediction of heterogeneity in intelligence and adult prognosis by genetic polymorphisms in the Dopamine system among children with ADHD. *Archives of General Psychiatry*, 63:462–469.

Moffitt, T. E. (1993). "Life-course persistent" and "adolescence-limited" antisocial behavior: a developmental taxonomy. *Psychological Review*, 100:674–701.

Moffitt, T. E. (2003). Life-course-persistent and adolescence-limited antisocial behavior: a 10-year research review and a research agenda. In Lahey, B. B., T. E. Moffitt, & A. Caspi (Eds.). *Causes of conduct disorder and juvenile delinquency*. New York: Guilford Press.

Moore, T. M., A Scarpa, & A. Raine (2002). A meta-analysis of serotonin metabolite 5-HIAA and antisocial behavior. *Aggressive Behavior*, 28:299–316.

Ogdie, M. N., S. E. Fisher, M. Yang, J. Ishii, C. Francks, S. Loo, et al. (2004). ADHD: fine mapping supports linkage to 5p13, 6q12, 16p13, and 17q11. *American Journal of Human Genetics*, 75:661–668.

Ogdie, M. N., L. Macphie, S. L. Minnassian, M. Yang, S. E. Fisher, C. Francks, et al. (2003). A genomwide scan for ADHD in an extended sample: suggestive linkage on 17p11. *American Journal of Human Genetics*, 72:1268–1279.

Pato, C. N., F. Macciardi, M. T. Pato, M. Verga, & J. L. Kennedy (1993). Review of the putative association of dopamine D_2 receptor and alcoholism: a meta-analysis. *American Journal of Medical Genetics*, 48:78–82.

Retz, W., P. Retz-Junginger, T. Supprian, J. Thome, & M. Rosler (2004). Association of serotonin transporter promoter gene polymorphism with violence: relation with personality disorders, impulsivity, and childhood ADHD psychopathology. *Behavioral Sciences and the Law*, 22:415–425.

Rutter, M. (2005). Commentary: what is the meaning and utility of the psychopathy concept? *Journal of Abnormal Child Psychology*, 33:499–503.

Shannon, L. W. (1991). *Changing patterns of delinquency and crime: a longitudinal study in Racine*. Boulder, CO: Westview.

Smalley, S. L., V. Kustanovich, S. Minnassian, J. Stone, M. Ogdie, J. McGough, et al. (2002). Genetic linkage of ADHD on chromosome 16p13, in a region implicated in autism. *American Journal of Human Genetics*, 71:959–963.

Smith, C. A. & S. B. Stern (1997). Delinquency and antisocial behavior: a review of family processes and intervention research. *Social Service Review*, 71:382–420.

Stattin, H. & D. Magnusson (1991). Stability and change in criminal behavior up to age 30. *British Journal of Criminology*, 31:327–346.

Tracy, P. E., M. E. Wolfgang, & R. M. Figlio (1990). *Delinquency careers in two birth cohorts.* New York: Plenum.

Viding, E., P. J. Frick, & R. Plomin (2007). Aetiology of the relationship between callous–unemotional traits and conduct problems in children. *British Journal of Psychiatry*, 190:33–38.

Viding, E., R. J. R. Blair, T. E. Moffitt, & R. Plomin (2005). Evidence for substantial genetic risk for psychopathy in 7-year-olds. *Journal of Child Psychology and Psychiatry*, 46:592–597.

Walters, G. D. (1992). A meta-analysis of the gene-crime relationship. *Criminology*, 30:595–613.

Wilson, J. Q. & R. J. Herrnstein (1985). *Crime and human nature: the definitive study of the causes of crime.* New York: Free Press.

Wolfgang, M. E., R. M. Figlio, & T. Sellin (1972). *Delinquency in a birth cohort.* Chicago: University of Chicago Press.

12

Psychopathy

Richard P. Wiebe

We've all hurt somebody. In fact, many of us have caused a great deal of pain to a lot of people–friends, family, strangers–who didn't deserve it. But most of us feel bad about the pain we've caused, at least once we've acknowledged what we've done. What if we didn't feel bad about harming others? What if the only people we cared about, whom we felt anything for, were ourselves? What if we never felt guilt, or remorse, love, or even true hatred? What if we could watch another human writhe in pain with mild interest, as we would watch puppies at play, with no desire to help? What if we didn't learn from our mistakes, but kept repeating behaviors that prompted others to retaliate? What if we lacked the **social emotions**, such as sympathy, guilt, and love that bind us to other people and cause us to account for their interests as well as our own? Then we'd be **psychopathic** (Mealey, 1995).

Psychopathy does not seem to be exclusively a modern phenomenon. Descriptions of individuals who can now be recognized as psychopathic appear in sources from as far back as biblical times (Hare, 1996), and the psychopath's unremitting selfishness and concomitant lack of social emotions have puzzled post-enlightenment thinkers at least as long ago as the 18th century. The French physician Pinel noticed a phenomenon he termed "manie sans délirée"—basically, impulsive behavior apparently unrelated to delusions or hallucinations—while the American physician Benjamin Rush called psychopathy "moral insanity" (Pridmore, et al., 2005). The term "psychopathy" was first applied to this phenomenon by the American psychiatrist Hervey Cleckley (1941), who noted the existence of individuals whose antisocial behavior seemed "inadequately motivated"—persons whose crimes and other antisocial acts appeared arbitrary or random, arising neither out of any particular need nor from the depths of a violent childhood. According to Cleckley, the psychopath was as likely to harm self as others, failing to learn from the aggrieved and sometimes violent reactions they evoked from others as they stubbornly pursued their own narrow interests. This picture of the psychopath—focused on rewards and inured to punishment—has been supported by later research (Lynam, 1996).

Although Cleckley, who worked in a mental hospital rather than a prison, did not emphasize the criminal aspects of psychopathy, a group of modern, mainly Canadian, researchers have recast the psychopath as a supercriminal. According to the author of the most widely used diagnostic tool for psychopathy, psychopaths are:

> [I]ntraspecies predators who use charm, manipulation, intimidation, and violence to control others and satisfy their own selfish needs. Lacking in conscience and in feelings for others, they cold-bloodedly take what they want and do as they please, violating social norms and expectations without the slightest sense of guilt.
>
> (Hare, 1996:26)

This formulation implies that violence and intimidation are central to psychopathy, as vital components of intraspecies predation.

Along with marrying psychopathy to crime, Hare conceptualized psychopathy as a mental disorder, implying that something within the psychopath isn't working correctly and is creating harm. That psychopaths cause harm is undeniable. Although comprising only about 1 to 4 percent of the general population, they make up about 20 percent of the prison population and at least 33 percent of chronic offenders (Mealey, 1995). And research has uncovered significant physiological differences between psychopaths and nonpsychopaths. But biological differences are not necessarily defects.

It might be useful to consider the alternative: What could psychopathy, and the biological features that underlie it, be good for? Clearly not society, but what of psychopaths themselves? One possibility is that psychopathy may be an adaptation that equips the psychopath with physiological and cognitive tools that facilitate coercive sexual relations (Wiebe, 2004b) or the acquisition of economic resources (Mealey, 1995).

In this chapter, I first describe psychopathy and distinguish it from sociopathy, antisocial personality disorder, and low self-control. I then review its biology, examine its heritability, and makes the case for its status as an adaptation, not a disorder. Finally, I discuss possible "cures." As none has been shown to be consistently effective, this section is fairly short.

The Psychology of Psychopathy: How Can We Recognize a Psychopath?

As recently noted by Walsh and Wu (2008), many people use the terms "**sociopathy**" and "psychopathy" interchangeably, although they represent very different concepts. The term "psychopathy" implies an etiology rooted in individual psychology, perhaps with a genetic foundation, while sociopathy is thought to have social causes. A third term, "antisocial personality disorder," or APD, has been proffered by the American Psychiatric Association (APA) as a diagnosis of the persistently antisocial person whose antisociality was evident in childhood (APA, 1994). The diagnostic criteria for APD are purely descriptive—no attempt is made to identify the causes of the antisocial behavior, which makes the diagnosis difficult to use as the basis for treatment. Substantially more people can be diagnosed with APD than either psychopathy or sociopathy, including most prison inmates (Walsh & Wu, 2008).

As Walsh and Wu note, only criminals are eligible for a diagnosis of sociopathy or antisocial personality disorder. Sociopaths are persistent criminals and delinquents whose offending stems mainly a harsh and abusive social environment. Although they may harbor genetic risk factors as well, these are not thought to be as extreme as those of psychopaths (Mealey, 1995). In contrast, psychopaths need not behave in an overtly antisocial manner. Many researchers (e.g., Lykken, 1995; Widom, 1977) have noted the presence of psychopaths in the community, performing their jobs without necessarily committing crimes. Even Robert Hare, in a book intended for the general public (1993), records anecdotes about psychopaths who are trying to "pass"—to live prosocial lives without input from prosocial emotions. Yet the view of the psychopath as a persistent and dangerous offender dominates the popular understanding.

To more clearly distinguish psychopathy from sociopathy, it might be useful to examine the construct of self-control. Self-control has been defined in at least two contrasting ways. The most widely known version among criminologists is that of Gottfredson and Hirschi (1990), who concentrate on *low* self-control, "the tendency to pursue short-term, immediate pleasure" (p. 93). To them, low self-control is a complex construct that combines several traits—impulsivity, sensation seeking, selfishness, and the inability or unwillingness to consider the consequences of one's actions on other people or one's own future—into a single trait claimed to be, "for all intents and purposes, *the* individual-level cause of crime" (p. 232). They further claim that poor parenting is responsible for low self-control. With this connection between inadequate socialization and offending, this version of low self-control, in its extreme, looks like sociopathy.

Another version has been defined by Baumeister and colleagues as "control of the self by the self" (Muraven & Baumeister, 2000:247). Like Gottfredson and Hirschi, Baumeister considers self-control to be the "master virtue" (Baumeister & Exline, 2000:29). Unlike them, he does not consider selfishness to be part and parcel of low self-control.

Hare, like Gottfredson and Hirschi, conflates the two concepts. Empirically, the measure used by Hare to measure psychopathy, the Psychopathy Checklist-Revised (PCL-R; Hare, et al., 1990) generates two separate factors. The first factor can be summarized as self-centeredness, and includes a selfish, manipulative interpersonal style combined with shallow emotions and **solipsism** (the belief that the self is the center of the universe), while the second includes a parasitic lifestyle and antisocial behaviors. Sexual promiscuity correlates with both factors, a fact to which I will return (Harpur, et al., 1989). As Table 12.1 notes, the first factor may be further split into interpersonal (manipulative, chronic lying) and affective (i.e., emotional) dimensions, while explicitly antisocial behaviors can be separated from parasitic and impulsive behaviors within the second factor (Edens, et al., 2006). Interestingly, several of the Factor 2 items themselves involve offending, so it would seem tautological to use the PCL-R to predict crime.

In sum, Factor 1 can be thought of as a measure of the psychopathic personality, or "primary psychopathy" or simply "psychopathy" (Walsh & Wu, 2008), while Factor 2 can be thought of as low self-control without the selfishness included by Gottfredson and Hirschi (Wiebe, 2003). The two higher order factors correlate at about $r = .5$ (Harpur, et al., 1989), meaning that each explains about 25 percent of the variability in the other. The implication, assuming personality influences behavior more than vice

Table 12.1 Factor Structure of the Psychopathy Checklist, Revised (PCL-R)

Factor 1—Selfish, callous, and remorseless use of others (psychopathy)

Interpersonal features	*Affective features*
Glibness/superficial charm	Grandiose sense of self-worth
Pathological lying	Lack of remorse or guilt
Conning/manipulative	Shallow affect
Failure to accept responsibility	Callous/lack of empathy

Factor 2—Unstable, antisocial, and socially deviant lifestyle (low self-control)

Lifestyle	*Antisocial behavior*
Need for stimulation	Poor behavioral controls
Parasitic lifestyle	Early behavior problems
Lack of realistic goals	Juvenile delinquency
Impulsivity	Revocation of conditional release
Irresponsibility	Criminal versatility

Items correlating with both factors

Promiscuous sexual behavior
Many short-term relationships

versa, is that the psychopathic personality increases the risk of antisocial behavior, but does not require it (Blair, et al., 2006).

Thus, psychopaths can have varying levels of self-control. Because low self-control correlates with crime, a high-self-control psychopath is less likely to become a habitual criminal. The lack of concern for others—the absence of the social emotions—and the focus on reward over punishment make a psychopath more likely than a nonpsychopath to victimize others, but a psychopath with high self-control would, at the very least, be less likely to run afoul of the law than one with low self-control, and might even have figured out how to gratify him or herself without breaking very many laws at all.

Compelling evidence for this perspective lies in studies that show that, like crime within the general population (see this volume, Chapter 9), the parasitic and antisocial behaviors of criminal psychopaths decline with time, while the core of their personality remains stable (Blonigen, et al., 2006; Harpur & Hare, 1994).

Before continuing: a point about nomenclature. Throughout this chapter, I have been referring to "psychopaths" as if they were a discrete class. However, it would be more accurate to call them "persons with psychopathic tendencies," because not every psychopath has all of the traits that comprise psychopathy in its pure form (see Table 12.1). These traits vary along continua (Edens, et al., 2006)—for example, persons can vary in the amount of guilt and remorse they tend to suffer—and many have been shown to predict crime and delinquency on their own (Wiebe, 2003). Thus, individuals can be more or less psychopathic than each other, just as one person may be taller than another. However, it may still be useful to retain the label "psychopath" for persons who score substantially higher than average on measures of the most of the traits associated with psychopathy. In fact, this is how the PCL-R is scored. Out of 40 total points measuring 20 separate traits and behaviors, a person need only 28–30 points to be considered a psychopath. Thus far, it has proved impossible to verify that any particular score represents a clear cutoff between two different types of person (Edens, et al., 2006), but this need not be of great concern. It is just as difficult to identify the exact height at which an individual leaps into the category of "tall person." However, this does not keep us from considering some people to be tall.

The Biology of Psychopathy: What Underlies the Psychopathic Personality?

Thus far, psychopathy has been described and its empirical connection to crime noted. But in the biosocial perspective, at least three more steps are needed: describing the biological underpinnings of psychopathy, examining whether it has an underlying genetic component, and inquiring into why it exists in the first place.

How is biology relevant to psychopathy? After all, the most striking feature of psychopathy is emotional in nature: the lack of social emotions that would ordinarily provide internal barriers to antisocial behavior and internal goads toward, and rewards for, prosocial behavior (Mealey, 1995). Further, the most prominent alternate explanation for the foundation of psychopathy also involves the emotions: the "low fear" hypothesis advanced by David Lykken (1995), which has found support in longitudinal research predicting adult psychopathy from childhood temperament (Glenn, et al., 2007). But, like the rest of our psychological processes, emotions are rooted in biology.

Emotions are signals, reactions by our brain to both internal or external stimuli that let us know what's important (Frank, 1988). As such, they are intrinsic to decision making: Without emotions, we could not decide what to do, because everything would appear trivial (Damasio, 1994). Our emotions are housed in a part of the brain called the limbic system, which gets its own input from the sensory organs and sends signals to the frontal lobes for processing by our "rational" selves. It also sends signals to other parts of the brain and body, via neurons and hormones, without waiting for frontal lobe input (LeDoux, 1996). This ability to bypass the frontal lobes can be especially important when the emotion is fear and the danger is mortal.

Several biological differences between psychopaths and nonpsychopaths have been noted in recent research, and they all affect emotional processing. They are now briefly summarized.

Fear

Researchers have associated psychopathy with relatively low levels of fear (Lykken, 1995) and its sibling, anxiety (Harpur, et al., 1989). Fear facilitates learning: Without fear, a person may reenact behaviors that previously brought aversive consequences. A person without fear is insensitive to punishment, focusing instead on potential rewards. The person with low anxiety can approach fear-inducing situations with aplomb, including situations that might bring a hostile reaction from a potential crime victim (Benning, et al., 2005).

Biologically, one of the underpinnings of low fear among psychopaths is thought to be an imbalance between the *behavioral activation system (BAS)* and the *behavioral inhibition system (BIS)* (Walsh & Wu, 2008). The BAS is the brain system, sensitive to the neurotransmitter dopamine, that facilitates goal-directed behavior, while the BIS, sensitive to serotonin, is responsible for risk management, preventing us from blindly seeking gratification no matter what the circumstances. While ideally these systems would be in equilibrium, allowing us to pursue our goals but in a responsible, non-harmful manner, an imbalance in favor of the BAS would cause us to focus on rewards without being afraid of punishment.

Another underpinning of low fear among psychopaths is thought to be an overall low level of arousal of the *autonomic nervous system (ANS)*. The ANS is the part of the nervous system that is outside conscious control, governing such diverse processes as digestion and sensitivity to loud noises. Research consistently shows primary psychopathy—Factor 1 in the PCL-R—to be associated with low autonomic arousal (Benning, et al., 2005). Any stimulation becomes desirable.

Low Fear Leads to Low Empathy: Abnormal Startle Potentiation   One of the most interesting manifestations of low arousal comes from research into startle potentiation. An average person presented with an aversive stimulus—in a psychology lab, it might be a picture of a rotting corpse— would exhibit quicker and stronger involuntary (i.e., autonomic) reactions to subsequent stimuli—perhaps a puff of air to the eye. The startle reflex has been "potentiated," preparing him or her for the flight or fight response. In contrast, a person exposed to a pleasant stimulus experiences involuntary relaxation (Patrick, 1994).

The startle reflex of psychopaths reacts very differently. Psychopaths (as measured by Factor 1 of the PCL-R) do not potentiate when shown aversive stimuli, unless that stimulus appears personally threatening, such as a picture of a gun pointed directly at the camera (Levenston, et al., 2000). This failure to potentiate can inhibit empathy, a seemingly important component of the development of the social emotions. Since emotional empathy occurs when an individual shares the physiological state of another (Levenson & Ruef, 1992), a person who does not feel fear, or is not otherwise discomfited, when another person is endangered or suffering will lack any motive to relieve the danger or suffering. This pattern applies to both low and high self-control (Factor 2) psychopaths (who are high in Factor 1).

Empathy may be further impaired by a phenomenon found in the startle research that psychopaths react to the suffering of others in the same way as they, and nonpsychopaths, react to pleasant stimuli: interested, but not disturbed (Patrick, et al., 1993; Sutton, et al., 2002).

Emotional Perception

The emotional deficits of psychopaths are not all rooted in the fear systems. Psychopaths appear relatively insensitive to many types of social and emotional cue (Damasio, et al., 1990); the work on startle potentiation suggests that they may perceive some of these cues but react abnormally to them. While psychopaths may be able to more readily identify happy and sad faces (Habel, et al., 2002), they react less emotionally to such faces than nonpsychopaths (Blair, et al., 1997). Other research has shown that they fail to react more strongly to emotional than non-emotional words, unlike nonpsychopaths (Lorenz & Newman, 2002), and have less intense emotional reactions to everyday situations than nonpsychopaths (Day & Wong, 1996).

Other specific emotional abnormalities have been found: an enhanced tendency to react to anger (Kosson, et al., 2002), and a reduced ability to recognize the sound of fear in another's voice (Blair, et al., 2002). Psychopaths seem to have a particular deficit relating to the emotion of disgust, both in recognition and autonomic reaction (Kosson, et al., 2002). They also have deficits in their susceptibility to classical conditioning, further inhibiting the development of conscience (Pridmore, et al., 2005).

In sum, psychopaths do not react autonomically to emotional stimuli, perhaps because of a disconnection between words and emotions. Neither do they readily recognize fear and disgust, two emotions that may convey disapproval of the psychopath and his or her behavior (Wiebe, 2004b). They tend to be underaroused and therefore sensation seekers, and have an imbalance between the BAS and BIS in favor of the BAS and therefore focus on rewards while remaining relatively undeterred by punishment or its threat. These characteristics seem to unite in what Donald Lynam (1996) calls the "psychopathic deficit": persistence in goal-directed behaviors even when punished for behaviors for which they were previously rewarded, also known as "response perseveration" or "deficient response modulation" (Lorenz & Newman, 2002). These biological features presumably inhibit the development of a conscience, and allow the psychopath to cold bloodedly pursue selfish interests without distraction from emotional signals (Mealey, 1995), especially the fear or disgust of another person.

It has been suggested that the physiological source of the emotional abnormalities associated with psychopathy lies in the amygdala, a structure within the limbic system (Blair, 2003). Along with facilitating aversive conditioning—ANS changes in response to fear or pain—and instrumental learning—responding consciously and appropriately to pain and pleasure—it responds to fearful and sad facial expressions, important in developing empathy. Researchers have identified a gene in mice that is associated with the failure to produce a particular protein, leading to a smaller amygdala and increased aggression, as well as reduced maternal instincts; whether this research will translate to humans is not yet known (Blair, 2003).

Another area of the brain identified by Blair as abnormal in psychopaths is the region of the frontal lobes just above the eyes, the orbitofrontal cortex (OFC). This area appears important in instrumental learning and response modulation (part of the BIS). Deficits in the OFC might relate to both psychopathy and low self-control.

How Heritable is Psychopathy?

Researchers have begun to investigate whether psychopathy has a genetic component, and have established that it appears to be modestly heritable, with between 29 percent and 67 percent of the variance explained by genes across several studies (e.g., Larsson, et al., 2006; Viding, et al., 2005; see, also, review in Blair, et al., 2006). Perhaps just as importantly, research has failed to find any shared family environmental effects on psychopathy, indicating that, unlike sociopathy, it is not the predictable outcome of harsh and abusive parenting.

What does it mean to say that psychopathy is heritable? For one, it means there is no "gene for psychopathy." Unlike genes governing eye color, which will produce the same color eyes regardless of childhood experience, the genes responsible for the heritability of psychopathy can produce different outcomes in different environments (see Chapter 2, this volume). From the biosocial perspective, there are numerous steps between the genes that make their way into the developing zygote and the mature expression of those genes. For example, a person might discover early on an absence of fear and an insensitivity to punishment, but might seek to become a good person in order to continue to earn the approval of caregivers (Blair, et al., 2006).

While it is generally understood that heritability represents the percentage of variance in a particular trait or characteristic that is explained by the genes, it is not often emphasized that any heritability estimates are relevant only in the context of the environments represented within a particular sample. To generalize from a heritability estimate in a particular study to the population as a whole, it would be necessary to not only claim that the individuals in the sample represent the individuals in the population, but that their *environments*, from uterine to home, from school to neighborhood, represent the environments encountered by the population. And environments, unlike genes, are readily mutable. Therefore, the best that can be said for the generalizability of heritability estimates is that they may be valid for a particular time and place, but do not represent any enduring phenomenon. Change the environment, change the heritability.

An interesting example of the malleability of genetic expression is cited in Chapter 9 of this volume: the heritability of antisocial behavior, as well as aggression (Cleveland, 2003), is substantially higher in advantaged environments than in disadvantaged environments. In disadvantaged environments, there are more reasons for, and routes to, crime and aggression, not all of which require a strong genetic bias.

The Evolutionary Psychology of Psychopathy: What is Psychopathy Good For?

In most of the research cited in this chapter, psychopathy is understood to be a disorder. While it is unquestionable that people suffer because of psychopathy, it is not clear that the psychopath him- or herself suffers. And even if the psychopath felt distress as a result of a lifestyle that left him or her bereft of close emotional relationships, distress by itself does not necessarily represent dysfunction. In a Darwinian sense, if psychopathy equips its host for fitness—reproductive success—then it is doing what it was "designed" to do, and it is an adaptation, not a disorder (Mealey, 1995). Mealey has deemed psychopathy an "ethical pathology" (1997:531): good for the individual, bad for society.

Synergy and Society

Like nearly all other human beings, psychopaths conduct their lives within various social contexts. Society itself exists because individual humans can benefit by collective action and other forms of cooperation (for overviews, see Ridley, 1996; Wright 2000). Through cooperation, more resources become available to the group as a whole than could have been produced by isolated individuals. This phenomenon, where the end product is greater than the sum of the individual contributions to it, is called **synergy**, and, provided the end product is distributed fairly, it benefits each individual as well as the group as a whole.

Cooperation doesn't always result in synergy. Despite our best efforts at working together, we sometimes fail to accomplish our goals, and sometimes would have been better off alone. Further, under some conditions, such as a society that is hopelessly corrupt, under siege, or in violent transition, cooperation is impractical or impossible. But in a well-functioning society, the most important human actions are *inter*actions. For our species in general, it is better to cooperate than to go it alone. Further, our long infancies and childhoods doom us to extinction without someone sharing resources with, and protecting, the young.

To achieve synergy, a well-functioning society requires individuals committed to cooperation over the long term. Skills are acquired, social networks are developed, trust is established. But cooperation brings the temptation to cheat: Trust can be violated (Axelrod, 1984). Most crime is a form of cheating, shortcutting legitimate routes to acquiring resources and mating opportunities, resolving conflicts, and achieving status, each of which can enhance fitness. In addition, crime undermines synergy. In criminal interactions, total resources decrease, because, in almost all cases, the victim loses more—economically, psychologically, temporally— than the criminal gains, a phenomenon called the **magnitude gap** (Baumeister, 1997). A habitual criminal can, therefore, be considered a cheater, a parasite on the host society, or an intraspecies (or intrasocietal) predator.

Fortunately, there is a natural limit to such antisocial behavior, at least within a stable, well-functioning society. Habitual cheating is a **frequency-dependent strategy** for acquiring resources and mating opportunities. Too many cheaters break the system down, but too much trust evokes the temptation to cheat. This means that psychopathy could not be adaptive for everyone. Once psychopaths run out of victims, they start to encounter other psychopaths, and nobody wins. The number of psychopaths will therefore stabilize around a small but significant proportion of the population (Mealey, 1995).

Unfortunately, because psychopaths, though ubiquitous, are scarce, and because it is in their best interests to escape detection, humans have not developed the ability to readily recognize them (Wiebe, 2004a). Instead, we rely on behaviors and reputations.

Adaptive Strategies

A frequency-dependent strategy is a type of **adaptive strategy**, "an organized set of behaviors evolved to maximize individual reproductive success over the life span" (Rowe, 1996:269). As Rowe points out, the amount of effort an individual devotes to successful reproduction can be divided into parenting effort, focused on the care involved in raising children, and mating effort, focused on obtaining mates and fighting off rivals. Generally, as one type of effort increases, the other decreases, because each individual's resources—temporal, emotional, social, and physical as well as economic—are limited. All things being equal, a greater amount of mating effort results in a more diverse set of mates but lower investment in each resulting offspring. Therefore, a person whose adaptive strategy favors mating effort need not be overly concerned with long-term relationships, and may actually be hampered by them. This focus on selfish gratification at the expense of long-term relationships characterizes most crime, as well. Thus, crime can be considered an **epiphenomenon** of a mating effort strategy: a by-product of a strategy that evolved to maximize mating opportunities. After all, sex came before money.

Psychopathy and Mating Effort

Obviously, both resource acquisition and mating opportunities can enhance fitness. The features of psychopathy, individually and collectively, facilitate a selfish approach to each. The individual seeks personal gratification without caring about the well-being of others.

Without anxiety, guilt, remorse, or meaningful ties to other individuals; with low autonomic arousal and high need for stimulation; with relentless selfishness and inflated egos, psychopaths are particularly well suited to pursue a mating effort strategy and are equally unsuited for parenting effort. For different reasons—impulsivity, lack of diligence, and the unwillingness or inability to effectively plan for the future—persons with low self-control are also better suited for mating than parenting effort. Each of these qualities also equips an individual for crime, and makes it more difficult to live an honest life. As noted earlier, both the psychopathic personality and low self-control factors of the PCL-R correlate strongly with promiscuity, illuminating these two broad paths to mating effort (see also, Gottfredson & Hirschi, 1990). It is important to remember, however, that psychopathy is not synonymous with, and does not require, either mating effort or criminality.

Along with the personality characteristics, the biological features associated with psychopathy can facilitate the victimization of others. Previously (Wiebe, 2004b), I have suggested that three specific psychopathic features can be used in the service of an adaptive strategy involving coercive sex: abnormal startle potentiation, response perseveration, and emotionless processing. Unaffected by fear, disgust, punishment, or emotional empathy, the psychopath who wants to have sex but encounters resistance will not be deterred by the victim's reactions. Perhaps only a direct threat to personal safety could prevent the rape. Once the rape has occurred, the psychopath will feel no remorse and will, thus, have no reason not to reoffend.

This model applies to virtually any victimizing behavior. All the psychopath needs is an ignorant or undefended victim, either unable to detect psychopathy directly and unaware of any antisocial reputation, or easy to overpower (Hare, 1993). As long as there are such victims, there will be psychopaths. For this reason, psychopathy may be unusual in small, close-knit communities where reputations are known and people come to each others' aid (Lykken, 1995).

Alternative vs. Conditional Strategies

An adaptive strategy that appears strongly influenced by genetic factors is called an **alternative strategy**, while one that is adopted in response to environmental contingencies is called a **conditional strategy** (Rowe, et al., 1997). An idea of the difference can be seen by examining Figure 12.1, which presents Walsh and Wu's (2008) interpretation of Lykken's diathesis developmental model showing the different contributions of biology and environment for psychopaths, sociopaths, offenders who are neither psychopaths nor sociopaths, and non-offenders. The vertical axis represents a continuum of parental competency. The horizontal axis represents a biological propensity continuum for criminal behavior from high to low. The less extreme the biological propensity, the more likely the individual will pursue a conditional, rather than alternative, strategy.

Because of its heritability and physiological correlates, psychopathy appears to constitute an adaptation that facilitates an alternative strategy—although it is important to remember that psychopathy is not a strategy itself, just a personality type that makes a cheater or mating effort strategy much more likely. Sociopathy, by way of contrast, involves crime by definition, and therefore seems to be a conditional strategy in and of itself. Again: Just because someone has the physiological potential for developing psychopathy, this does not doom the person to life as a psychopath—

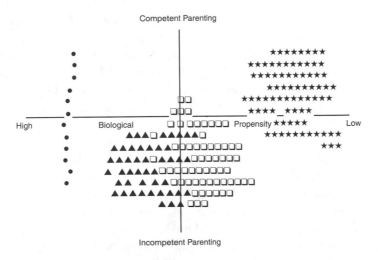

Figure 12.1 David Lykken's Diathesis-developmental Model Illustrating the Role of Biological Propensity and Parental Competency on Different Types of Offender and on Non-offenders.

Source: Walsh and Wu (2008).

s/he might be remorseless but honest, for example, good qualities to find in a manager or judge. And just because someone is a psychopath, this does not mean s/he *must* pursue a mating effort strategy, at least not in a pure form.

There are three alternatives to considering psychopathy as an adaptation that facilitates an alternative strategy rooted in mating effort. The first is, of course, to conceptualize it as a disorder. But its historical and cross-cultural ubiquity, as well as its strong relationship to a cheater or mating effort strategy, would seem to favor the adaptive strategy model.

The second alternative would be to assume that psychopathy is conditional, a product of early experiences acting on an unremarkable genotype that channel the maturing individual into a particular strategy. These experiences—harsh or absent parenting, unstable and dangerous neighborhood, poor schooling and poor school performance, the perception that life is nasty, brutal, and short—can provide cues that antisocial, mating effort behavior will result in greater fitness than prosocial behavior (Caldwell, et al., 2006). But this seems like a better description of sociopathy than psychopathy. Significant biological differences between psychopaths and nonpsychopaths *have* been discovered, psychopathy appears heritable (although the heritability of its individual biological features has not been examined), and these differences appear to relate to the psychopath's personality and behavior. In support of the idea that psychopathy is not conditional, research has not uncovered an exceptional amount of child abuse in the personal history of psychopaths (Blair, et al., 2006).

The third alternative is to consider psychopathy to result from the rational decision by an otherwise average individual to take advantage of opportunities for crime, interpersonal manipulation, and impersonal sexual relations (e.g., Vila & Cohen, 1993). If psychopathy were simply a matter of choice, this would imply that psychopaths would be unremarkable in personality and biology, recognizable only by their behaviors. However, as discussed earlier, this is not the case.

There is one prominent example of the purely rational psychopath: the corporation (Bakan, 2004). Like a human psychopath, the corporation considers the interests of others only when it is in its best interests to do so; it is not bound to prosociality by social emotions. The major contrast between the corporation and the psychopath lies in the comparison group: A psychopath is an abnormal human being, lacking the social emotions that most people have, while a corporation, at least a public corporation, is an entity created by law and directed to maximize shareholder value. There is no contrasting entity that is directed by law to consider the human costs of its actions. Thus, a psychopathic corporation is behaving normally.

Prosocial Psychopaths?

As uncomfortable as it would be for most nonpsychopaths to persistently victimize others, the psychopath would find it equally uncomfortable to live a life full of social obligations and close personal relationships (Cleckley, 1941). Attempting to do so, the psychopath would tend to make the same mistakes over and over again, unintentionally harming others without ever really knowing why, and failing to pick up the early warning signals of distress before destroying relationships and trust (see Hare, 1993). This does not mean that successful, noncriminal psychopaths, or at least successful persons with psychopathic traits, are unknown. Lykken (1995) nominates test pilot Chuck Yeager as an exemplar of a virtually fearless and emotionally detached individual who translated these seeming deficits into a wildly successful career, while Walsh and Wu (2008) discuss the 19th-century British adventurer, Richard Francis Burton:

> If Richard Burton had been the son of a London butcher instead of an army colonel. .. he may have ended up with a rope around his neck rather than the sash of knighthood around his shoulders.
>
> (Walsh & Wu, 2008:6)

Unfortunately, these seem to be the unusual cases. The absence of shared family environmental effects in behavior genetic studies of psychopathy (Blonigen, et al. 2006; Larsson, et al., 2006; Viding, et al., 2005; see also Chapter 2, this volume) supports the conclusion consistently reached by psychopathy researchers: There is no obvious environmental cause of psychopathy (Blair, et al., 2006; Cleckley, 1941; Hare, 1993; Mealey, 1995; Walsh & Wu, 2008).

Conclusion: A "Cure" for Psychopathy?

Because psychopathy has no obvious proximate cause, it has no easy "cure." While psychopaths might lead prosocial lives, they would do so for different reasons from the rest of us. Their adaptations that make it easy for them to cheat and harm others—a lack of anxiety, their persistence in goal-directed behaviors even after punishment—render them difficult to socialize. Yet, it is clearly within society's interest to attempt to prevent or control psychopathy, even if the underlying syndrome cannot readily be changed. Because psychopaths feel little or no guilt, either anticipatory or in response to bad acts, and because there has been no evidence that they can develop a normal set of social emotions in adulthood, it is probably useless to appeal to the conscience, or to confront them with the harm they have wreaked and the suffering of their victims. In fact, in one study, an intervention that placed prison inmates in a "therapeutic community" within the prison was effective in reducing recidivism among nonpsychopaths but actually increased offending among psychopaths (Harris, et al., 1994). Clearly, other interventions may be more appropriate.

Mealey (1995) proposed a solution based in classical criminology (see Gottfredson & Hirschi, 1990): to reduce the rewards, and increase the costs, of crime and cheating. This, of course, fairly describes the goal of the criminal justice system in general, embodied in the concept of deterrence, but deterrence only works among individuals with at least modest levels of self-control. Like other individuals with low self-control, a low self-control psychopath would be undeterred by the threat of future punishment.

Blair and colleagues (2006) suggest a different approach. Citing the work of Kochanska (1997), they say that a fearless child, at risk for psychopathy, can develop a conscience if socialization processes "capitalize on mother–child positive orientation (secure attachment, maternal responsiveness)" (1997:269). This is because the fearless child, like the adult psychopath, is more responsive to rewards than punishment. Lykken (1995) also focuses on the potential for socialization in childhood among fearless children, recommending that they learn skills and engage in activities that satisfy their need for stimulation.

Consistent with the idea that psychopaths respond better to rewards than punishment is a potential intervention that relies on their egotism. This egotism allows psychopaths to feel superior to others, even when they don't deserve to (Campbell & Elison, 2005; see also Baumeister, 1997). Perhaps the way to help psychopaths integrate into conventional society is to appeal to their ego. Overpraise for successful desistance from crime may be uncomfortable to mete out, but if it helps prevent crime, it's better than the alternative.

References

American Psychiatric Association. (1994). *Diagnostic and statistical manual of mental disorders (fourth edition, text revision, DSM-IV-TR)*. Washington, DC: Author.

Axelrod, R. (1984). *The evolution of cooperation*. New York: Basic Books.

Bakan, J. (2004). *The corporation: the pathological pursuit of profit and power*. New York: Free Press.

Baumeister, R. F. (1997). *Evil: inside human violence and cruelty*. New York: W.H. Freeman.

Baumeister, R. F. & J. J. Exline (2000). Self-control, morality, and human strength. *Journal of Social and Clinical Psychology*, 19:29–42.

Benning, S. D., C. J. Patrick, & W. G. Iacono (2005). Psychopathy, startle blink modulation, and electrodermal reactivity in twin men. *Psychophysiology*, 42:753–762.

Blair, R. J. R. (2003). Neurobiological basis of psychopathy. *British Journal of Psychiatry*, 102:5–7.

Blair, R. J. R., L. Jones, F. Clark, & M. Smith (1997). The psychopathic individual: a lack of responsiveness to distress cues? *Psychophysiology*, 34:192–198.

Blair, R. J. R., D. G. V. Mitchell, R. A. Richell, S. Kelly, A. Leonard, C. Newman, et al. (2002). Turning a deaf ear to fear: impaired recognition of vocal affect in psychopathic individuals. *Journal of Abnormal Psychology*, 111:682–686.

Blair, R. J. R., K. S. Peschardt, S. Budhani, D. G. V. Mitchell, & D. S. Pine (2006). The development of psychopathy. *Journal of Child Psychology and Psychiatry*, 47:262–275.

Blonigen, D. M., B. M. Hicks, R. F. Krueger, C. J. Patrick, & W. G. Iacano (2006). Continuity and change in psychopathic traits as measured via normal-range personality: a longitudinal-biometric study. *Journal of Abnormal Psychology*, 115:85–95.

Caldwell, R. M., R. P. Wiebe, & H. H. Cleveland (2006). The influence of future certainty and contextual factors on delinquent behavior and school adjustment among African American adolescents. *Journal of Youth and Adolescence*, 35:587–598.

Campbell, J. S. & J. Elison (2005). Shame coping styles and psychopathic personality traits. *Journal of Personality Assessment*, 84:96–104.

Christie, R. & F. Geis (1968). Some consequences of taking Machiavelli seriously. In Borgotta. E. R. & W. W. Lambert (Eds.). *Handbook of personality theory and research*, Chicago: Rand McNally.

Cleckley, H. (1941). *The mask of sanity*. St. Louis: C.V. Mosby.

Cleveland, H. H. (2003). Disadvantaged neighborhoods and adolescent aggression: behavioral genetic evidence of contextual effects. *Journal of Research on Adolescence*, 13:211–238.

Damasio, A. R. (1994). *Descartes' error: emotion, reason, and the human brain*. New York: G.P. Putnam's Sons.

Damasio, A. R., D. Tranel, & H. Damasio (1990). Individuals with sociopathic behavior caused by frontal damage fail to respond autonomically to social stimuli. *Behavioural Brain Research*, 41:81–94.

Day, R. & S. Wong (1996). Anomalous perceptual asymmetries for negative emotional stimuli in the psychopath. *Journal of Abnormal Psychology*, 105:648–652.

Edens, J. F., D. K. Marchus, S. O. Lilienfeld, & N. G. Poythress, Jr. (2006). Psychopathic, not psychopath: taxometric evidence for the dimensional structure of psychopathy. *Journal of Abnormal Psychology*, 115:131–144.

Frank, R. H. (1988). *Passions within reason: the strategic role of the emotions*. New York: W.W. Norton.

Glenn, A. L., A. Raine, P. H. Venables, & S. A. Mednick (2007). Early temperamental and psychophysiological precursors of adult psychopathic personality. *Journal of Abnormal Psychology*, 116:508–518.

Gottfredson, M. R. & T. Hirschi (1990). *A general theory of crime*. Stanford, CA: Stanford University Press.

Habel, U., E. Kuhn, J. B. Salloum, H. Devos, & F. Schneider (2002). Emotional processing in psychopathic personality. *Aggressive Behavior*, 28:394–400.

Hare, R. D. (1993). *Without conscience: the disturbing world of the psychopaths around us*. New York: Pocket Books.

Hare, R. D. (1996). Psychopathy: a construct whose time has come. *Criminal Justice and Behavior*, 23:25–54.

Hare, R. D., T. J. Harpur, A. R. Hakstian, A. E. Forth, S. D. Hart, & J. P. Newman (1990). The Revised Psychopathy Checklist: reliability and factor structure. *Psychological Assessment*, 2:338–341.

Harpur, T. J. & R. D. Hare (1994). Assessment of psychopathy as a function of age. *Journal of Abnormal Psychology*, 103:604–609.

Harpur, T. J., R. D. Hare, & A. R. Hakstian (1989). Two-factor conceptualization of psychopathy: construct validity and assessment implications. *Psychological Assessment*, 1:6–17.

Harris, G. T., M. E. Rice, & C. A. Cormier (1994). Psychopaths: is a therapeutic community therapeutic? *Therapeutic Communities*, 15:283–299.

Kochanska, G. (1997). Multiple pathways to conscience for children with different temperaments: from toddlerhood to age 5. *Developmental Psychology*, 33:228–240.

Kosson, D. S., Y. Suchy, A. R. Mayer, & J. Libby (2002). Facial affect recognition in criminal psychopaths. *Emotion*, 2:398–411.

Larsson, H., H. Andershed, & P. Lichtenstein (2006). A genetic factor explains most of the variation in the psychopathic personality. *Journal of Abnormal Psychology*, 115:221–230.

LeDoux, J. (1996). *The emotional brain: the mysterious underpinnings of emotional life*. New York: Simon & Schuster.

Levenson, R. W. & A. M. Ruef (1992). Empathy: a physiological substrate. *Journal of Personality and Social Psychology*, 63:234–246.

Levenston, G. K., C. J. Patrick, M. M. Bradley, & P. J. Lang (2000). The psychopath as observer: emotion and attention in picture processing. *Journal of Abnormal Psychology*, 109:373–385.

Lorenz, A. R. & J. P. Newman (2002). Deficient response modulation and emotion processing in low-anxious Caucasian psychopathic offenders: results from a lexical decision task. *Emotion*, 2:91–104.

Lykken, D. T. (1995). *The antisocial personalities*. Hillsdale, NJ: Lawrence Erlbaum Associates, Inc.

Lynam, D. R. (1996). Early identification of chronic offenders: who is the fledgling psychopath? *Psychological Bulletin*, 120:209–234.

Mealey, L. (1995). The sociobiology of sociopathy: an integrated evolutionary model. *Behavioral and Brain Sciences*, 18:523–599.

Mealey, L. (1997). Heritability, theory of mind, and the nature of normality. *Behavioral and Brain Sciences*, 20:527–532.

Muraven, M. & R. F. Baumeister (2000). Self-regulation and depletion of limited resources: does self-control resemble a muscle? *Psychological Bulletin*, 126:247–259.

Patrick, C. J. (1994). Emotion and psychopathy: startling new insights. *Psychophysiology*, 31:319–330.

Patrick, C. J., M. M. Bradley, & P. J. Lang (1993). Emotion in the criminal psychopath: startle reflex modulation. *Journal of Abnormal Psychology*, 102:82–92.

Pridmore, S., A. Chambers, & M. McArthur (2005). Neuroimaging in psychopathy. *Australian and New Zealand Journal of Psychiatry*, 39:856–865.

Ridley, M. (1996). *The origins of virtue*. New York: Viking.

Rowe, D. C. (1996). An adaptive strategy of crime and delinquency. In Hawkins, J. D. (Ed.). *Delinquency and crime: current theories*. Cambridge: Cambridge University Press.

Rowe, D. C., A. T. Vazsonyi, & A. J. Figueredo (1997). Mating effort in adolescence: conditional or alternative strategy. *Personality and Individual Differences*, 23:105–115.

Sutton, S. K., J. E. Vitale, & J. P. Newman (2002). Emotion among women with psychopathy during picture perception. *Journal of Abnormal Psychology*, 111:610–619.

Viding, E., R. J. R. Blair, T. E. Moffitt, & R. Plomin (2005). Evidence for substantial genetic risk for psychopathy in 7-year olds. *Journal of Child Psychology and Psychiatry*, 46:592–597.

Vila, B. J. & L. E. Cohen (1993). Crime as strategy: testing an evolutionary ecological theory of expropriative crime. *American Journal of Sociology*, 98:873–912.

Walsh, A. & H.-H. Wu (2008). Differentiating antisocial personality disorder, psychopathy, and socio-pathy: evolutionary, genetic, neurological, and sociological considerations. *Criminal Justice Studies*, 22:135–152.

Widom, C. S. (1977). A methodology for studying noninstitutionalized psychopaths. *Journal of Consulting and Clinical Psychology*, 45:674–683.

Wiebe, R. P. (2003). Reconciling psychopathy and low self-control. *Justice Quarterly*, 20:297–336.

Wiebe, R. P. (2004a). Delinquent behavior and the five-factor model: hiding in the adaptive landscape? *Individual Differences Research*, 2:38–64.

Wiebe, R. P. (2004b). Psychopathy and sexual coercion: a Darwinian analysis. *Counseling and Clinical Psychology Journal*, 1:23–41.

Wright, R. (2000). *Nonzero: the logic of human destiny*. New York: Pantheon.

13

No Longer Taboo: Crime Prevention Implications of Biosocial Criminology

Matthew Robinson

Crime prevention policies can be derived from any explanation of criminality (Lilly, et al., 2006). Logic suggests that the more complete the theory, the more effective the crime prevention informed by the theory will be (Robinson, 2004). Since biosocial criminology meaningfully integrates perspectives and theories from the biological and social sciences, the approach offers much hope in the area of crime prevention. At the very least, biosocial crime prevention should be far more effective than those strategies currently utilized within agencies of criminal justice, such as mass incarceration and capital punishment, that are based largely on ideological beliefs and "common sense" (Reiman, 2006; Robinson, 2005; Shelden, 2007). This chapter outlines potential crime prevention policies derived from a biosocial theory of crime—the "integrated systems theory" of antisocial behavior—as well as recent studies of risk factors consistent with biosocial criminology. The chapter also attempts to prioritize those crime prevention policies that would likely be the most effective.

Crime Prevention

Crime prevention includes any means to eliminate the causes of crime so that crime does not occur and does not need to be dealt with by criminal justice agencies (Robinson, 1999). It is generally thought to be the most effective way to reduce crime (Lab, 2004). Efforts to stop crime before they occur can be divided into primary crime prevention, secondary crime prevention, and tertiary crime prevention. **Primary crime prevention** is the broadest form of crime prevention and is aimed at preventing crime at all places at all times; it generally consists of large-scale efforts to prevent crime in society by reducing people's exposure to those **criminogenic factors** that promote criminality (e.g., stress, poverty, deviant peers, brain damage). **Secondary crime prevention** is focused on individuals, groups, and communities that have either already been exposed to such crimino-genic factors or who are likely to be. **Tertiary crime prevention** is reactive and better describes efforts to prevent future crimes among those who have already committed them (Faust & Brantingham, 1976). Robinson (2004) suggests that primary crime prevention (aimed at the whole of society) and secondary crime prevention (focused on those people who most need it) offer the most hope for preventing crime.

How Theory can be Used to Prevent Crime

Every **criminological theory** states an **explanation** as to why crime occurs (Akers & Sellers, 2007). Generally, theories posit propositions that relate criminality to some concept(s). **Propositions** are merely sentences that state relationships between various real-world things (such as greed and crime). **Concepts** are those real-world things that are related in the proposition (e.g., greed, crime). An example of a simple proposition is "greed causes crime." Criminologists develop theories and then test them to see if they enjoy **empirical validity**. That is, does real-world evidence support the propositions? When evidence supports the theory, the theory is thought to be **valid** or true. When evidence consistently shows that a theory is false, we can say that the theory has been **falsified**, or that it is disproven.

Unfortunately, virtually every theory enjoys some empirical support, and only a handful have been falsified (Robinson, 2004). The question for criminologists is to determine which theories enjoy the greatest level of empirical validity (that is, which theories are the most supported by evidence). Those theories can be the most useful in crime prevention, assuming they enjoy wide scope. The **scope** of a theory refers to the types of crime that are explained by a theory, as well as how much. Theories that have wide scope are intended to be used to explain multiple forms of crime. For example, Gottfredson and Hirschi's (1990) general theory of crime—commonly referred to as the theory of low self-control—is said to have wide scope, for it supposedly explains all forms of crime including street crime and acts of crime committed by corporations and wealthy individuals.

A theory that can explain a lot of crime can logically be used to prevent a lot of crime, as well. Crime prevention implications can be derived from theories in the form of policies, programs, and projects. **Policies** are a "set of rules or guidelines for how to make a decision." An example is a law passed by Congress aimed at reducing a federal crime such as kidnapping. **Programs** are a "set of services aimed at achieving specific goals and objectives within specified individuals, groups, organizations or communities." An example is an afterschool program for children to reduce the likelihood of antisocial behavior by kids when they otherwise would be unsupervised. **Projects** are essentially time-limited programs (Welsh & Harris, 1999:5–6). Policies are more general than programs and projects and often motivate the development of specific programs and projects aimed at reducing some problem.

Policymakers can develop crime prevention policies, programs, and projects from criminological theories, and/or criminologists can suggest crime prevention strategies based on their theories. Unfortunately, this does not frequently happen in the real world because lawmakers seem uninterested in criminological theory.

An Example: Integrated Systems Theory

Integrated systems theory (IST) is based on the systems perspectives of Whitehead (1925), Lewin (1935), Murray (1938), and especially Miller (1978). Miller (1978) characterized human behavior as a product of factors interacting among seven different living systems. This systems approach was first applied to criminological theory by C. Ray Jeffery (1990) in his book, *Criminology: an interdisciplinary approach*, and subsequently was called in the classroom the "integrated systems perspective" (ISP). ISP is interdisciplinary in nature, meaning it combines the contributions of numerous academic disciplines in order to better understand human behavior. It asserts that various criminogenic factors interact among all levels of analysis—cell, organ, organism, group, community/ organization, and society—to produce antisocial and criminal behavior.

Each **level of analysis** represents a living system that survives on its own and that can be studied independently of the others (e.g., biologists study cells, neurologists study organs, psychologists study individual organisms, sociologists study groups, etc.). ISP assumes that there are things (factors, concepts, or variables) at each of these levels of analysis that influence the likelihood of antisocial behavior. Figure 13.1 shows these levels of analysis.

The levels are connected, meaning that each system above is part of the systems below it and each system below is made up of all the systems above it (e.g., cells make up organs which make up organisms which make up groups, etc.). This means that a change in one level or system leads to a change in all levels or systems. Take, for example, the influence of genes on all levels. Genetic flaws can produce chemical imbalances of the brain (at the organ level). These chemical imbalances can lead to mental illnesses such as depression or schizophrenia (at the organism level), which can lead to antisocial behavior that is likely to strain families (at the group

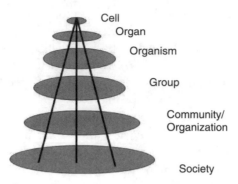

Cell
Organ
Organism
Group
Community/
Organization
Society

Figure 13.1 Levels of Analysis in Integrated Systems Theory.

level), impact neighborhoods and hospitals (at the community/organiza-
tion level), and ultimately affect the entire country in which individuals
with mental illnesses live (at the society level). Robinson (2004) utilized
ISP to develop a theory called the integrated systems theory (IST).

IST is built around a summary of known risk factors that have been
identified by scholars in numerous academic disciplines (e.g., sociology,
psychology, biology, behavioral genetics, neurology, anthropology,
economics, etc.). **Risk factors** are things in the real world that increase
one's risk of committing antisocial behavior on exposure, especially when
exposure is frequent (**frequency**), regular (**regularity**), intense (**intensity**), and occurs early in life (**priority**). **Protective factors** are the opposite of risk factors in that they reduce the likelihood of criminality.

The theory was developed by making a list of propositions that have
already been verified through empirical tests of scores of theories of crime
across many disciplines. True to the interdisciplinary approach of ISP,
these propositions dealt with topics such as genetics, brain structure
(parts of the brain), brain function (levels of neurotransmitters and
enzymes in the brain and hormones levels in the blood), **brain dysfunction** (head injury, exposure to environmental toxins, maternal drug use
during pregnancy), personality traits, intelligence levels, mental illness,
diet and nutrition, drug consumption, family influences, peer influences,
social disorganization, routine activities and victim lifestyles, deterrence,
labeling, *anomie*, strain, culture conflict and subcultures, race, class, and
gender.

IST is similar to what Bernard (2001:337) calls the **risk factor approach**
whereby "risk factors associated with an increased or decreased likelihood
of crime" are identified. Since there "are many such risk factors" every
academic discipline can potentially add something to our understanding
of the etiology of human behavior, including criminality. This approach
assumes that:

- *Some people are more likely than others to engage in crime, regardless of the situation they are in; and*
- *Some situations are more likely to have higher crime rates regardless of the characteristics of the people who are in them.*

(Bernard, 2001:341, emphasis in original)

IST is based on the same assumptions, but specifies how the various risk factors interact to produce antisocial behavior in individuals, including interactive and intervening effects between the numerous risk factors.

According to Bernard (2001:343): "[T]he essential questions should be: which variables are related to crime, and in which ways?" Vila (1994:313) concurs, asserting that the most important question for theorists to answer now is which variables or factors at what level of analysis interact in what ways to produce criminality? "What relationships and processes tend to be fundamentally important for understanding changes over time in the ... behaviors of any social organism?" Miller (1978:1) himself predicted that a systems explanation of behavior would "select, from among different and sometimes opposing viewpoints, fundamental ideas already worked out by others, and fit them into a mosaic, an organized picture of previously unrelated areas." This was one of the goals of IST.

IST asserts that:

- People have choice as to whether or not to commit crime (but choice cannot explain why people behave because choosing is a behavior).
- People's choices are influenced by factors beyond their control.
- The factors that influence people's choices (and hence their behaviors) are risk factors and protective factors.
- These risk and protective factors exist among six different levels of analysis, including cells, organs, organisms, groups, communities/ organizations, and society.
- Exposure to risk factors generally increases the risk of antisocial and criminal behavior, especially when exposure is frequent, regular, intense, and occurs early in life.
- Exposure to protective factors generally decreases the risk of antisocial and criminal behavior, especially when exposure is frequent, regular, intense, and occurs early in life.

IST is a biosocial theory because it asserts that particular risk factors inside and outside of individuals interact to produce behavior. That is, there are well-known biological as well as social factors that interact to increase the likelihood of criminality. The numerous risk factors identified by IST include genetics; brain chemistry (neurotransmitters and enzymes); brain dysfunction (e.g., head injury); levels of hormones in the body; prenatal conditions (including drug use/abuse during pregnancy, unhealthy diet/nutrition during pregnancy, and stress during pregnancy); lower verbal IQ and cognitive deficits; autonomic system (ANS) hypo-arousal; family conditions (such as inconsistent discipline, harsh discipline, and unaffectionate parenting); hanging out with deviant peers; consumption of some legal and illegal drugs (e.g., alcohol, cocaine); nutritional intake; exposure to environmental toxins; severe mental illnesses (e.g., schizophrenia); destructive labeling; perceptions of strain; employment problems and relationship problems; conditions of social disorganization (such as poverty, population heterogeneity, and residential mobility).

IST incorporates the risk factors into a developmental timeline, suggesting greater or lesser import for some factors at different times over the life-course. Although research shows there may be more than one path to antisocial behavior, some risk factors are more likely to impact individuals at different times in their lives. This is consistent with **developmental criminology** (Benson, 2002; Farrington, 2005; Huizinga, et al., 1998; Kelley, et al., 1997; Kumpfer & Alvarado, 1998; Laub & Sampson, 2006; Piquero & Mazerolle, 2001; Sampson & Laub, 2006). Figure 13.2 illustrates this timeline.

Several of the risk factors begin before birth, such as inheriting genetic propensities, maternal drug use/abuse during pregnancy, maternal diet/nutrition during pregnancy, stress during pregnancy, and exposure to environmental toxins during pregnancy. The effects of diet/nutrition, family influences, chemical imbalances in neurotransmitter and enzyme levels, brain dysfunction, environmental toxins, hypoarousal of the ANS, and low verbal IQ/cognitive problems are likely to begin in early childhood. Given the unique demands of adolescence, the risk factors of

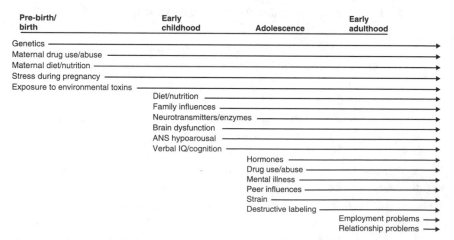

Figure 13.2 A Developmental Timeline of Risk Factors in Integrated Systems Theory.

hormones, drug use/abuse, mental illness, peer influences, general strain, and destructive labeling by criminal justice agencies are most likely to occur during this time period. Finally, employment problems and relationship problems are most likely to occur in early adulthood.

The developmental timeline is not meant as an absolute, it is simply a way of depicting when certain risk factors are most likely to begin to have deleterious effects on individuals. Generally, the earlier risk factors begin to influence people (priority), the greater the likelihood that individuals will commit acts of antisocial behavior. Also, the more risk factors a person is exposed to during any stage of life, the more likely antisocial behavior will occur. That different risk factors are likely to impact people at different times in their lives suggests that crime prevention policies should not be static but rather changing based on the variable influence of different risk factors. That is, this timeline suggests to policymakers that crime prevention policies aimed at individuals at risk for criminal behavior should be focused on different factors at different stages of life.

Preventing Crime Using Integrated Systems Theory

Broadly speaking, two logical crime prevention policies of IST include:

1. Reducing one's exposure to the risk factors that increase the probability that one will behave in an antisocial fashion.
2. Increasing one's exposure to protective factors that reduce the probability that one will behave in an antisocial fashion.

In making efforts to achieve these goals, the goal specifically should be to reduce the frequency, regularity, intensity, and priority of the exposures to risk factors and to increase the frequency, regularity, intensity, and priority of the exposures to their opposites, or protective factors. Of most importance is reducing the **clustering** of disadvantages, for the cumulative effects of exposure to numerous risk factors is far worse than the periodic exposure to one or two risk factors, as predicted by the reality of comorbidity.

This calls for a broader and more sustained effort at crime prevention as opposed to the reactive and largely failing criminal justice policies that we currently pursue. At the one extreme (the most controversial), it involves altering propensities for violent behaviors at the genetic level, and at the other (the more feasible), it involves altering the individual and environmental conditions that produce antisocial behavior. Since IST suggests that risk factors occur at all levels of analysis—from cell to society—prevention implications can be identified at each of these levels of analysis that are focused on the risk factors identified by the theory. The goal is to use our knowledge with regard to these factors in order to prevent criminality before it happens. It really is partial and incomplete to outline policy implications that address only one level of analysis, such as the cellular level of analysis, because human behavior results from the interactions of numerous factors at several levels of analyses. Still, it is possible to do so. Box 13.1 lays out some logical crime prevention strategies justified by integrated systems theory.

Box 13.1   Crime Prevention Implications of Integrated Systems Theory

Beginning at the cell level, there is much speculation that in the very near future it will be possible to alter one's genetic makeup in order to reduce the likelihood that an individual will become antisocial, and/or to replace particular genes in people generally in order to reduce overall rates of antisocial behavior. Such possibilities bring forth thoughts of past efforts to use biological research to control certain segments of the population, including the eugenics movement (Robinson, 2004).

However, recall that genes do not express themselves in the absence of environmental factors; this means that many of the most important crime control and prevention policies will involve alterations to environmental conditions rather than one's genes. In fact, in a cost-benefit analysis, it makes more sense to change the environmental conditions that trigger genes to express themselves in the form of antisocial behavior, given that so many people are exposed to them at one time. Additionally, even when particular genes are identified by scientists as relevant for increasing the probability of antisocial behavior, individuals with these genes may not ever commit repetitive antisocial behaviors. It is not appropriate to assume that just because an individual has a trait found in antisocial populations that the individual will also behave in an antisocial fashion.

Given these important points, there are essentially three possible crime control and crime prevention policy implications of genetics research: alteration of genetics; alteration of environmental triggers and insulators; and the **medicalization of behavior**. First, it is not likely that members of society will ever completely support alterations of genetics for the purposes of preventing crime. Furthermore, it is not called for. The policy implications of genetics studies are typically the same as those made by studies of environmental factors (Herbert, 1997). Walsh (2002: 231) explains: "[W]hatever biological therapies we eventually come up with, they almost certainly will not be genetic. As has been constantly emphasized, there are genes that bias traits in certain directions, but there are no genes that lead directly to any kind of nontrivial behavior. Genes act in concert with other genes, and collectively, they act in concert with the environment." This means that the policy implications of genetic studies point to alterations of the environment. This is especially true given that the same traits that produce many antisocial behaviors also produce many prosocial behaviors. Doing away with one gene that codes for proteins that encourage one trait related to antisocial behavior will wipe out the trait rather than its behavioral manifestations—e.g., aggression will be wiped out in all its forms, including prosocial behaviors.

The medicalization of behavior involves regulating brain chemistry through the admission of legally prescribed drugs. Since genes partially determine levels of neurotransmitter in the brain, genetic abnormalities can lead to unusually high or low levels of brain chemicals that affect behavior. Thus, one way to return brain chemistry to more normal levels is with the administration of drugs under the care of psychiatrists. Such treatment is particularly effective when used in conjunction with traditional treatments such as psychotherapy.

Strategies at the organ level of analysis are aimed at regulating levels of neurotransmitters, **enzymes**, and **hormones**, primarily through eliminating the environmental conditions that produce abnormal levels. In addition, these substances can be regulated with medicine, suggesting the medicalization of behavior. Drugs can be administered to counteract the effects of abnormal brain chemistry and abnormal levels of hormones. These efforts are reactive and thus are less likely to be effective at preventing criminality.

A more promising line of approach entails reducing the conditions that produce organ-level risk factors. For example, stress during pregnancy, drug use or abuse during pregnancy, and unhealthy diet/nutrition are all sources of **brain dysfunction**. Other sources include exposure to environmental toxins, head injury, drug use/abuse, child abuse/neglect, and unhealthy diet/nutrition. Successful crime prevention will address these factors. Finally, treatment is available for people suffering from traumatic brain injuries because of accidents and similar experiences. Never should we rely exclusively on medical treatments, for by themselves they are not as effective at changing behavior as when used in conjunction with other treatments.

Logical policies stemming from organism-level explanations suggest that changes ought to be made to the organism-level factors that increase the likelihood of committing antisocial behavior. Some go as far as to suggest that organism-level factors *must* be specifically considered. For example, Lynam and Moffitt (1995) suggest that any crime prevention policy "that ignores either low IQ or impulsivity as risk factors for delinquency will be ill-informed by social science research." Additionally, it has been claimed that a wide range of medical illnesses have been found to be associated with violent behavior, and, further, that many of these are treatable and reversible.

Again, our two options are thus to either prevent exposure to organism-level risk factors and/or to treat people who have been exposed. Treatment for mental illnesses and poor diet is relatively successful, which is good news for crime control. The most successful approaches to treat mental illness are a combination of medicine and counseling therapies. IQs can be slightly raised through educational programs, but it is not clear that it is possible to change someone's personality once it becomes established early in life. Since personality is the same thing as behavior, this is another way of saying that once a behavioral pattern (or trajectory) becomes established early in life, it is very difficult to change. This means efforts ought to be aimed at preventing the development of antisocial behavior beginning at birth and before. Similarly, once drug use becomes drug abuse, brain damage can occur and make reversing one's behavioral propensities more difficult. If this theory is correct, we must focus our efforts at preventing harmful drug abuse; this can be done by attempting to stop drug use entirely or more realistically to stop people from using drugs in ways that cause harm to others. Efforts should be focused at the very small percentage of users, based on family history, who are at greatest risk for abuse.

The most successful crime prevention strategies will likely be directed at the larger levels of analysis, including the group level, community and organization level, and the society level. Efforts should be made to reduce all individuals' exposure to deviant peers, especially in unsupervised settings, as well as family conflict and disruption, abuse, neglect, and harsh, authoritarian style discipline. These factors increase one's risk of early antisocial behavior, which then increases the risk that individuals will associate with deviant peers, have trouble at school and work, get labeled a troublemaker, and continue on into more serious and sustained antisocial behavior. Efforts should be made to educate parents about the harmful effects of these factors and to encourage good, supportive, loving, egalitarian families who are authoritative (but not physical) and consistent in their use of discipline.

Efforts also need to be directed at reducing conditions of **social disorganization**, especially poverty, an unfettered expansion of urbanization, and residential mobility. A complete antisocial prevention policy will make it possible for people to make a decent living while still being heavily and meaningfully involved in raising their children, monitoring their behavior, and interacting with neighbors and participating in meaningful community organizations. This means businesses must allow and even encourage people to work more flexible schedules, provide affordable, on-site daycare and supervision for children of employees, and permit employees to pattern their lifestyles in ways that reduce their exposure to criminal victimization. Since meaningful and fulfilling employment can be turning points away from deviance, we must do whatever it takes to assure that people find such employment. Such strategies are consistent with what Vila (1994) calls **nurturant strategies**, which are aimed at bettering the lives of people generally.

In neighborhoods, residential heterogeneity can encourage antisocial behavior, but only if people refuse to get to know each other based on their cultural, racial, and ethnic differences. Thus, appreciation of diversity and multicultural tolerance must be promoted and celebrated in the nation's cities. Crime prevention policies must be taken out of the context of politics so that we can invest our money in the programs that work. We must also strive toward **restorative justice** rather than applying negative labels to offenders. Destructive labeling produces more antisocial behavior, not less.

Major emphasis must be placed on addressing employment and relationship problems of all individuals. Healthy and fulfilling marriages are helpful for preventing antisocial behavior in adulthood (but they do not guarantee it). Additionally, two parents are more able than one to provide supervision, and to monitor and correct their children's behavior in a consistent and healthy way. Thus, policies that assure people are ready for marriage will prevent antisocial behavior, as will the prevention of unwanted pregnancies through birth control education programs. All sources of general strain must also be addressed, including discrimination and victimization. People will always experience negative emotions, but in the absence of legitimate means of directing frustration and anger, people will resort to antisocial behavior as a means for coping with strain. Thus, we must give people opportunities to vent when they perceive injustice and experience noxious stimuli. Counseling programs at place of employment are one good example.

Additionally, government and major corporations must stop encouraging antisocial behavior through their policies of crime reduction and business, respectively. Two examples come to mind. A policy of mass incarceration will not only fail to reduce crime in the long run, but is likely to increase it. And mass layoffs by corporations (downsizing) encourage crime in several ways. It is probably time for all government and business executives to consider the implications of their policies and practices for how they may impact crime and antisocial behavior before they are created and initiated. Finally, to the degree that big business harms Americans through fraud, illegal dumping of chemicals, and so forth, they must be held accountable, not only for the sake of justice, but also for the purposes of preventing criminality that results from their harmful behaviors.

Preventing Crime Using Other Biosocial Criminology

In the remainder of this chapter, I utilize examples from some of the most recent scientific research to illustrate how crime prevention might look if it were based on similar biosocial theoretical approaches. The most recent biosocial approaches emphasize factors that have roots in both biological and social sciences; some of the areas stressed in the recent literature are genetic studies, neurological studies, studies of nutrition, and studies of parenting styles. Many of these kinds of study have been discussed in previous chapters of this book.

Genetics Studies

Recent research has demonstrated relationships between genetics and antisocial and violent behavior in children, including callous and unemotional traits in young children (Viding, et al., 2005). Additional research has shown genetic influences on early drinking and alcoholism (Crews, et al., 2006), likelihood of tobacco addiction (O'Loughlin, et al., 2004), and onset of conduct disorder (CD) (Jaffee, et al., 2005).

CD is a condition marked by physical and/or sexual aggression to people and animals, crimes against and destruction of property, deceitfulness or lying, and other serious violations of rules (American Academy of Child & Adolescent Psychiatry, 2004). CD precedes a diagnosis of antisocial personality disorder (APD), a condition characterized by repeated law violations, lying, reckless behaviors, and a demonstrable lack of guilt (Robinson, 2004).

Specific genes have been implicated in such outcomes. For example, a variant of the **COMT gene** is associated with low levels of prefrontal cortical function, a condition that is also related to increased antisocial behavior (Thapar, et al., 2005). Another example is a variant of the **5HTT serotonin transporter gene**, which puts adolescents at risk for substance abuse, novelty-seeking behaviors, school problems, and aggression (Gerra, et al., 2005), and predisposes men to extreme forms of violent behavior (Liao, et al., 2004). Further evidence comes from a variant of the **DRD4 dopamine regulating gene** that is associated with diminished executive function (i.e., poor planning and organization) and symptoms of attention deficit hyperactivity disorder (ADHD) (Froehlich, et al., 2006). ADHD has been associated with an increased likelihood of other outcomes over the life-course, including antisocial behavior, as well as disorders related to addiction, anxiety, and mood (Biederman, et al., 2006).

Reviews of modern genetic studies show clear evidence of significant relationships between genetic makeup and numerous forms of adult criminality (Baker, et al., 2006). There is also clear evidence of genetic contribution to a wide variety of conditions related to antisocial behavior, including but not limited to, impulsivity, hyperactivity, anxiety, depression, risk taking, thrill seeking, drug abuse, IQ, extroversion and introversion, positive and negative emotionality, empathy, conscientiousness, ADHD, mental illness, conditionability to punishment, and aggression (Robinson, 2004).

Studies like those mentioned earlier do not advocate or even call for crime prevention strategies that address or manipulate genes; instead, as already noted, the most logical approach is to modify either the brain chemistry of those who suffer from such conditions (through measures such as medication and mental health therapy) or the environmental conditions that allow the genes to express themselves. The former is an example of secondary crime prevention, whereas the latter is an example of primary crime prevention. Ironically, genetic studies suggest that the most effective crime prevention strategies would be utilized at various levels of social systems (e.g., within families, communities, organizations, and society at large).

Neurological Studies

Recent research has also illustrated relationships between brain dysfunction and antisocial behavior in adults, including brain abnormalities (e.g., traumatic brain injury, brain damage due to illness, epilepsy) associated with sexual murder (Briken, et al., 2005). Further, studies of juvenile murderers have demonstrated clear evidence of neurological impairments caused by premature birth, other birth problems, histories of head injuries, and family abuse victimization (Lewis, et al., 2004). Additionally, right temporal lobe reductions have been implicated in early onset conduct disorder (Kruesi, 2004).

According to Adrian Raine (2004):

> There are . . . 71 brain imaging studies showing that murderers, psychopaths, and individuals with aggressive, antisocial personalities have poorer functioning in the prefrontal cortex—that part of the brain involved in regulating and controlling emotion and behavior. More dramatically, we now know that the brains of criminals are physically different from non-criminals, showing an 11% reduction in the volume of grey matter (neurons) in the prefrontal cortex.

The significance of this reality for crime prevention is summarized by Raine: "Literally speaking, bad brains lead to bad behavior . . . One of the reasons why we have repeatedly failed to stop crime is because we have systematically ignored the biological and genetic contributions to crime causation."

As we find with genetic studies, studies of the brain also tend to have policy implications for social systems. One example is preventing the behaviors that actually cause brain dysfunction, including child abuse, head injury, and unhealthy pregnancies. Such efforts would reduce brain dysfunction and a wide variety of violent acts. Another example would be to make efforts to reduce environmental pollution.

Environmental toxins such as mercury and lead poison the brain and can impair attention, memory, spatial and motor function, and lead to deficits in intelligence as measured by IQ levels (Lamphear, 2005; Murata, et al., 2004; Trasande, et al., 2005). Since unborn babies are exposed to hundreds of harmful chemicals in the womb—many of which are associated with increased antisocial behavior—the prevention implications of a cleaner environment are clear (Houlihan, et al., 2005). Logical crime prevention implications would range from placing regulations on businesses that pollute the environment to encouraging alternative forms of transportation such as trains, subways, and buses.

Nutritional Studies

We have known for quite some time that diet affects behavior in at least two ways. First, unhealthy diets contribute to antisocial behavior (whereas healthy diets reduce it). Second, food additives such as MSG and aspartame can poison brain cells in conjunction with artificial colorings, which can produce conditions such as attention deficit hyperactivity disorder (ADHD) (Lau, et al., 2005). Diets free from pesticides (i.e., organic foods) are associated with decreased likelihood of learning disorders and behavioral problems (Lu, et al., 2005).

Malnourishment at a young age is associated with hyperactivity, lowered IQ, and aggression at later ages (Liu, et al., 2004). This suggests that dietary manipulation should work to alter problematic behaviors. In fact, studies show that dietary manipulation is effective at reducing antisocial behavior of children in schools and adolescents and adults within correctional facilities (Robinson, 2004).

This is logical given the typical diet of American children, which is high in fats, calories, and cholesterol, but low in fruits, vegetables, vitamins, minerals, and whole grains (Robinson, 2004). Deficiencies in fruits, vegetables, vitamins, and minerals (such as iron) are associated with increased risks for ADHD (Konofal, et al., 2004) while vitamins including C, B_6 and manganese can reduce symptoms of ADHD (Joshi, et al., 2005; Mousain-Bosc, et al., 2006). Given the link between ADHD and antisocial behavior, dietary changes will logically reduce antisocial behavior.

Omega-3 fatty acids (e.g., eicosapentaenoic acid or DEA) have been successfully used to reduce symptoms of depression in children (Nemets, et al., 2006), as well as patients suffering from bipolar disorder (Osher, et al., 2005). Deficiencies in this substance (which is not naturally produced in the body) have been associated with attention deficits, depression, lowered IQ, and learning disabilities, as well as impulsive and violent behaviors such as homicide (Daniels, et al., 2004; Hibbeln, et al., 2004; Richardson & Montgomery, 2005). Additionally, zinc supplements administered to teenagers improves attention as well as memory and has been demonstrated to be beneficial to children with ADHD (Penland, et al., 2005).

It would appear that not only is a significant portion of conditions such as ADHD explained by poor diet, but also that dietary changes can help overcome other life disadvantages, such as poverty. However, dietary manipulation must be implemented carefully for too much of a good thing is not always a good thing. For example, excessive manganese levels can interfere with intellectual function in youth (Wasserman, et al., 2006). Further, low cholesterol levels are found to be related to school problems (e.g., suspension or expulsion due to aggression) in some youth (Zhang, et al., 2005). Yet, the fact remains that a proven strategy for reducing antisocial behavior is dietary manipulation.

Parenting Studies

Most criminological research, being sociological in nature, blames delinquency and other forms of childhood and adolescent antisocial behavior on factors such as bad parenting. Risk factors identified in the literature include **child neglect; parental rejection; overly permissive parenting; authoritarian parenting**; harsh, brutal and violent discipline; abuse; **inconsistent discipline; low attachment**, commitment, involvement and supervision of children by parents; parental deviance; single-parent families; and large families (Robinson, 2004).

Yet, recent research shows that there is a two-way relationship between parenting and deviant adolescent behavior (Simons, et al., 2004). That is, while parenting directly impacts childhood behavior, childhood behavior *also impacts parenting*. As an example, good parenting is strained when a child misbehaves, especially in a chronic and repeated way.

Crime prevention policies must include measures intended to increase the tendency of parents to utilize parenting styles that naturally reduce tendencies for antisocial behavior. Examples include encouraging and providing affordable or tax-supported parenting classes or more controversially, parenting licenses.

What is really interesting about the effects of parenting on behavior is that it begins before birth, for reasons related to prenatal conditions. For example, nutritional intake of pregnant women impacts attention levels of infants and toddlers. Studies show that maternal diets rich in omega-3 fatty acids (e.g., docosahexaenoic acid or DHA) are beneficial to young children for years (Colombo, et al., 2004).

One factor that has been implicated in ADHD as well as antisocial behavior (including delinquent behavior in adolescence and criminality in adulthood) is maternal smoking during pregnancy (Button, et al., 2005; Linnet, et al., 2006; Wakschlag, et al., 2006; Yolton, et al., 2005). Another is maternal alcohol use during pregnancy, which at an extreme can produce fetal alcohol syndrome (FAS) and at even mild levels can produce impaired moral reasoning as well as delinquency (Schonfeld, et al., 2005). And after birth, iron deficiencies in new mothers can produce mild forms of child neglect and generally less loving parenting strategies which themselves promote criminality (Perez, et al., 2005).

Educational campaigns—honest and rooted in empirical science—should be designed and implemented to encourage healthy pregnancies and to discourage unhealthy habits such as drug use during pregnancy. Parenting classes are but one way to accomplish this.

Conclusion

As should be obvious based on this review of the integrated systems theory as well as other biosocial approaches, none emphasizes biological risk factors exclusively for purposes of crime prevention; instead, the authors posit that biological factors influence behavior in conjunction with (and sometimes dependent on) social factors. The logic of such interdependence lies at the heart of IST and all biosocial theories of crime. With regard to the four factors discussed in this chapter (i.e., genetics, neurology, nutrition, and parenting), it is rather simple to explain that each not only affects the others, but also that each, in turn, depends on the others.

First, genes influence neurological function (i.e., allelic variation on genes affects levels of neurotransmitters in the brain). This suggests that the genes we inherit from our biological parents at the moment of conception help determine levels of serotonin, dopamine, norepenephrine, and other naturally occurring brain chemicals, each of which is related to the likelihood of antisocial behavior.

Second, genes also influence parenting style (i.e., allelic variation on genes impacts whether an adult utilizes authoritarian, authoritative, or overly permissive parenting approaches). This suggests that the genes we inherit from our biological parents at the moment of conception help determine how adults parent their children; for example, whether they are overbearing, unforgiving, and abusive; or whether they are firm yet respectful and loving; or whether they set down no meaningful rules and allow their children to rule the household. Of course, how people are parented when they are children also matters greatly.

Third, parenting style impacts nutritional intake (i.e., parenting approach affects the kinds of food consumed by children as well as how open children are to trying new foods). This suggests that how adults parent their children significantly impacts not only whether children eat healthy diets but also whether their brains will function properly or will be constrained by conditions such as hypoglycemia, hyperactivity, attention deficits, etc., each of which is related to the likelihood of antisocial behavior.

Fourth, there is a two-way relationship between nutritional intake and neurological function (i.e., levels of neurotransmitters in the brain are directly impacted by the foods consumed by a person, and neurotransmitter levels in the brain impact the foods a person desires to consume). Similar to the proposition stated earlier, this suggests that the food we regularly consume will significantly impact brain function, which is related to the likelihood of antisocial behavior.

Understanding the complex realities of human behavior, as illustrated in the four examples given earlier, allows us to better grasp why it takes the forms it does in given contexts and circumstances. If our goal is to prevent criminal and antisocial behaviors, the more we understand them, the better our chance to prevent them. Since biosocial criminological research helps us better understand the factors that promote criminality, it has great potential to greatly reduce criminality in the United States.

References

Akers, R. & C. Sellers (2007). *Criminological theories: introduction, evaluation, and application.* New York: Oxford University Press.

American Academy of Child & Adolescent Psychiatry (2004). Your child. Conduct disorders. http://www.aacap.org/cs/root/publication_store/your_child_conduct_disorders.

Baker, L., S. Bezdjian, & A. Raine (2006). Behavioral genetics: the science of antisocial behavior. *Law & Contemporary Problems,* 69:7–46.

Barak, G. (1998). *Integrating criminologies.* Needham Heights, MA: Allyn & Bacon.

Benson, M. (2002). *Crime and the life course: an introduction.* Los Angeles: Roxbury.

Bernard, T. (2001). Integrating theories in criminology. In Paternoster, R. & R. Bachman (Eds.). *Explaining crime and criminals.* Los Angeles: Roxbury.

Biederman, J., S. Faraone, T. Spencer, E. Mick, M. Monuteaux, & M. Aleardi (2006). Functional impairments in adults with self-reports of diagnosed ADHD: a controlled study of 1001 adults in the community. *Journal of Clinical Psychiatry,* 67:524–540.

Braithwaite, J. (1995). *Crime, shame and reintegration.* New York: Cambridge University Press.

Briken, P., N. Habermann, W. Berner, & A. Hill (2005). The influence of brain abnormalities on psychosocial development, criminal history and paraphilias in sexual murderers. *Journal of Forensic Sciences,* 50:1–5.

Button, T., A. Thapar, & P. McGuffin (2005). Relationship between antisocial behaviour, attention-deficit hyperactivity disorder and maternal prenatal smoking. *British Journal of Psychiatry,* 187:155–160.

Colombo, J., K. Kannass, D. Shaddy, S. Kunderthi, J. Maikranz, C. Anderson, et al. (2004). Maternal DHA and the development of attention in infancy and toddlerhood. *Child Development,* 75:1254–1267.

Crews, F., A. Mdzinarishvili, D. Kim, J. He, & K. Nixon (2006). Neurogenesis in adolescent brain is potently inhibited by ethanol. *Neuroscience,* 137:437–445.

Daniels, J., M. Longnecker, A. Rowland, & J. Golding (2004). Fish intake during pregnancy and early cognitive development of offspring. *Epidemiology,* 15:394–402.

Elliott, D. (1994). Serious violent offenders: onset, developmental course and termination. *Criminology,* 34:1–22.

Elliott, D., D. Huizinga, & S. Ageton (1985). *Explaining delinquency and drug use.* Beverly Hills, CA: Sage.

Elliott, D., W. Wilson, D. Huizinga, R. Sampson, A. Elliott, & B. Rankin (1996). The effects of neighborhood disadvantage on adolescent development. *Journal of Research in Crime and Delinquency,* 33:389–426.

Farrington, D. (1989). Early predictors of adolescent aggression and adult violence. *Victims Violence,* 4:79–100.

Farrington, D. (1993). Childhood origins of teenage antisocial behaviour and adult social dysfunction. *Journal of the Royal Society of Medicine,* 86:13–17.

Farrington, D. (1994). Early developmental prevention of juvenile delinquency. *Criminal Behaviour and Mental Health,* 4:209–227.

Farrington, D. (1996). The explanation and prevention of youthful offending. In Hawkins, J. (Ed.). *Delinquency and crime: current theories.* New York: Cambridge University Press.

Farrington, D. (2005). *Integrated developmental and life-course theories of offending.* New York: Transaction.

Faust, F. & P. Brantingham (1976). A conceptual model of crime prevention. *Crime & Delinquency,* 22:284–296.

Froehlich, T. and colleagues (2006). Study links ADHD cognitive and behavioral problems to genetic and environmental interactions. News release. Cincinnati Children's Hospital Medical Center, May 1.

Gerra, G., L. Garofano, L. Castaldini, F. Rovetto, A. Zaimovic, G. Moi, et al. (2005). Serotonin transporter promoter polymorphism genotype is associated with temperament, personality traits and illegal drug use among adolescents. *Journal of Neural Transmission,* 112:1435–1463.

Gottfredson, M. & T. Hirschi (1990). *A general theory of crime.* Stanford, CA: Stanford University Press.

Herbert, W. (1997). The politics of biology. *U.S. News & World Report,* April 21:72–80.

Hibbeln, R., L. Nieminen, & W. Lands (2004). Increasing homicide rates and linoleic acid consumption among five Western countries, 1961–2000. *Lipids,* 39:1207–1213.

Houlihan, J., T. Kropps, R. Wiles, S. Gray, & C. Campbell (2005). Body burden: the pollution in newborns. Environmental Working Group, Washington, DC. http://www.ewg.org/reports_content/bodyburden2/pdf/bodyburden2_final.pdf.

Huizinga, D., A. Weiher, S. Menard, R. Espiritu, & F. Esbensen (1998). Some not so boring findings from the Denver Youth Survey. Paper presented to the annual meeting of the American Society of Criminology.

Jaffee, D., A. Caspi, T. Moffitt, K. Dodge, M. Rutter, A. Taylor, et al. (2005). Nature x nurture: genetic vulnerabilities interact with physical maltreatment to promote conduct problems. *Development and Psychopathology,* 17:67–84.

Jeffery, C. R. (1990). *Criminology: an interdisciplinary approach.* Englewood Cliffs, CA: Prentice-Hall.

Joshi, K., S. Lad, M. Kale, B. Patwardhan, S. Mahadik, B. Patni, et al. (2005). Supplementation with flax oil and vitamin C improves the outcome of attention deficit hyperactivity disorder (ADHD). *Prostaglandins, Leukotrienes and Essential Fatty Acids,* November.

Kelley, B., R. Loeber, K. Keenan, & M. DeLamatre (1997). Developmental pathways in boys' disruptive and delinquent behavior. *Juvenile Justice Bulletin.* Washington, DC: OJJDP, U.S. Department of Justice.

Konofal, R., M. Lecendreux, I. Arnulf, & M. Mouren (2004). Iron deficiency in children with attention-deficit/hyperactivity disorder. *Archives of Pediatric and Adolescent Medicine,* 158:1113–15.

Kruesi, M., M. Casanova, G. Mannheim, & A. Johnson-Bilder (2004). Reduced temporal lobe volume in early onset conduct disorder. *Psychiatry Research: Neuroimaging,* 132:1–11.

Kumpfer, K. & R. Alvarado (1998). Effective family strengthening interventions. *OJJDP: Juvenile Justice Bulletin,* November.

Lab, S. (2004). *Crime prevention: approaches, practices, and evaluations,* 5th edn. Cincinnati, OH: Anderson.

Lamphear, B. (2005). Low-level environmental lead exposure and children's intellectual function: an international pooled analysis. *Environmental Health Perspectives,* 113:894–899.

Lanier, M. & S. Henry (2004). *Essential criminology.* Boulder, CO: Westview Press.

Lau, K., W. McLean, D. Williams, & C. Howard (2005). Synergistic interactions between commonly used food additives in a developmental neurotoxicity test. *Neurotoxicology,* 90:178–187.

Laub, J. & R. Sampson (2006). *Shared beginnings, divergent lives: delinquent boys to age 70.* Harvard, MA: Harvard University Press.

Lewin, K. (1935). *A dynamic theory of personality.* New York: McGraw-Hill.

Lewis, D., C. Yeager, P. Blake, B. Bard, & M. Strenziok (2004). Ethics questions raised by the neuropsychiatric, neuropsychological, educational, developmental, and family characteristics of 18 juveniles awaiting execution in Texas. *Journal of the American Academy of Psychiatry and the Law,* 32:408–429.

Liao, D., C. Hong, H. Shih, & S. Tsai (2004). Possible association between serotonin transporter promoter region polymorphism and extremely violent crime in Chinese males. *Neuropsychobiology,* 50:284–287.

Lilly, J., F. Cullen, & R. Ball (2006). *Criminological theory: context and consequences,* 6th edn. Thousand Oaks, CA: Sage.

Linnet, M., C. Obel, E. Bonde, P. Thomsen, N. Secher, K. Wisborg, et al. (2006). Cigarette smoking during pregnancy and hyperactive-distractible preschoolers: a follow-up study. *Acta Paediatrica,* 95:694–700.

Liska, A., M. Krohn, & S. Messner (1989). Strategies and requisites for theoretical integration in the study of crime and deviance. In Liska, A., M. Krohn, & S. Messner (Eds.). *Theoretical integration in the study of deviance and crime: problems and prospects.* Albany, NY: SUNY Press.

Liu, J., A. Raine, P. Venables, & S. Mednick (2004). Malnutrition at age 3 years and externalizing behavior problems at ages 8, 11, and 17 years. *American Journal of Psychiatry,* 161:2005–2013.

Lu, C., K. Toepel, R. Irish, R. Fenske, D. Barr, & R. Bravo (2005). Organic diets significantly lower children's dietary exposure to organophosphorus pesticides. *Environmental Health Perspectives,* 114:260–263.

Lynam, D. & T. E. Moffitt (1995). Delinquency and impulsivity and IQ: a reply to Block. *Journal of Abnormal Psychology*, 104:399–401.

Miller, J. (1978). *Living systems*. New York: McGraw-Hill.

Mousain-Bosc, M., M. Roche, A. Polge, D. Pradai-Prat, J. Rapin, & J. Bali (2006). Improvement of neurobehavioral disorders in children supplemented with magnesium-vitamin B6. I. Attention deficit hyperactivity disorder. *Magnesium Research*, 19:46–52.

Murata, K., P. Weihe, E. Budtz-Jorgensen, P. Jorgensen, & P. Grandjean (2004). Delayed brainstem auditory evoked potential latencies in 14-year-old children exposed to methylmercury. *Journal of Pediatrics*, 144:177–183.

Murray, H. (1938). *Explorations in personality*. New York: Oxford University Press.

Nemets, H., B. Nemets, A. Apter, Z. Bracha, & R. Belmaker (2006). Omega-3 treatment of childhood depression: a controlled, double-blind pilot study. *American Journal of Psychiatry*, 163:1098–1100.

O'Loughlin, J., G. Paradis, W. Kim, J. Difranza, G. Meshefedjian, R. McMillan-Davey, et al. (2004). Genetically decreased CYPA26 and the risk of tobacco dependence: a prospective study of novice smokers. *Tobacco Control*, 13:422–428.

Osher, Y., Y. Bersudsky, & R. Belmaker (2005). Omega-3 eicosapentaenoic acid in bipolar depression: report of a small open-label study. *Journal of Clinical Psychiatry*, 66:726–729.

Penland, J., H. Lusaski, & J. Gray (2005). Zinc supplementation improved mental performance of 7th-grade boys and girls. News release. Federation of American Societies for Experimental Biology, April 4.

Perez, E., M. Hendricks, J. Beard, L. Murray-Kolb, A. Berg, M. Tomlinson, et al. (2005). Mother infant interactions and infant development are altered by maternal iron deficiency anemia. *Journal of Nutrition*, 135:850–855.

Piquero, A. & P. Mazerolle (2001). *Life-course criminology: contemporary and classic readings*. Belmont, CA: Wadsworth.

Raine, A. (2004). Quoted in "Unlocking crime: the biological key," BBC News, December.

Reiman, J. (2006). *The rich get richer and the poor get prison*, 8th edn. Boston, MA: Allyn & Bacon.

Richardson, A. & P. Montgomery (2005). The Oxford-Durham study: a randomized controlled trial of dietary supplementation with fatty acids in children with developmental coordination disorder. *Pediatrics*, 115:1360–1366.

Robinson, M. B. (1999). The theoretical development of crime prevention through environmental design (CPTED). *Advances in Criminological Theory*, 8:427–462.

Robinson, M. (2004). *Why crime? An integrated systems theory of antisocial behavior*. Upper Saddle River, NJ: Prentice-Hall.

Robinson, M. (2005). *Justice blind? Ideals and realities of American criminal justice*. Upper Saddle River, NJ: Prentice-Hall.

Sampson, R. & J. Laub (2005). *Crime in the making: pathways and turning points through life*. Harvard, MA: Harvard University Press.

Schonfeld, A., S. Mattson, & E. Riley (2005). Moral maturity and delinquency after prenatal alcohol exposure. *Journal of Studies on Alcohol*, 66:545–554.

Shelden, R. (2007). *Controlling the dangerous classes*, 2nd edn. Boston, MA: Allyn & Bacon.

Shoemaker, D. (1996). *Theories of delinquency*, 3rd edn. New York: Oxford University Press.

Simons, R., L. Simons, & L. Wallace (2004). *Families, delinquency, and crime: linking society's most basic institution to antisocial behavior*. Los Angeles: Roxbury.

Thapar, A., K. Langley, T. Fowler, F. Rice, D. Turic, N. Whittinger, et al. (2005). Catechol O-methyltransferase gene variant and birth weight predict early-onset antisocial behavior in children with attention-deficit/hyperactivity disorder. *Archives of General Psychiatry*, 62:1275–1278.

Thornberry. T. (1987). Toward an interactional theory of delinquency. *Criminology*, 25:863–891.

Thornberry. T. (1997). Introduction. Some advantages of developmental and life-course perspectives for the study of crime and delinquency. In Thornberry, T. (Ed.). *Developmental theories of crime and delinquency*. New Brunswick, NJ: Transaction.

Thornberry, T., M. Krohn, A. Lizotte, C. Smith, & P. Perter (1998). Taking stock: an overview of the findings from the Rochester Youth Development Study. Paper presented to the annual meeting of the American Society of Criminology.

Thornberry, T., A. Lizotte, M. Krohn, M. Farnworth, & S. Jang (1994). Delinquent peers, beliefs, and delinquent behavior: A longitudinal test of interactional theory. *Criminology*, 32:47–83.

Trasande, L., P. Landrigan, & C. Schechter (2005). Public health and economic consequences of methylmercury toxicity to the developing brain. *Environmental Health Perspectives*, 113:590–596.

Viding, E., R. Blair, T. Moffitt, & R. Plomin (2005). Evidence for substantial genetic risk for psychopathy in 7-year-olds. *Journal of Child Psychology and Psychiatry*, 46:592–597.

Vila, B. (1994). A general paradigm for understanding criminal behavior: extending evolutionary ecological theory. *Criminology*, 32:311–360.

Wakschlag, L., K. Pickett, K. Kasza, & R. Loeber (2006). Is prenatal smoking associated with a developmental pattern of conduct problems in young boys? *Journal of the American Academy of Child and Adolescent Psychiatry*, 45:461–467.

Walsh, A. (2002). *Biosocial criminology: introduction and integration.* Cincinnati, OH: Anderson.

Wasserman, G., X. Liu, F. Parvez, H. Ahsan, D. Levy, P. Factor-Litvak, et al. (2006). Water manganese exposure and children's intellectual function in Araihazar, Bangladesh. *Environmental Health Perspectives*, 114:124–129.

Welsh, W. & P. Harris (1999). *Criminal justice policy and planning.* Cincinnati, OH: Anderson.

Whitehead, A. (1925). *Science and the modern world.* New York: Macmillan.

Yolton, K., K. Dietrich, P. Auinger, B. Lanphear, & R. Hornung (2005). Exposure to environmental tobacco smoke and cognitive abilities among U.S. children and adolescents. *Environmental Health Perspectives*, 113:98–103.

Zhang, J., M. Muldoon, R. McKeown, & S. Cuffee (2005). Association of serum cholesterol and history of school suspension among school-age children and adolescents in the United States. *American Journal of Epidemiology*, 161:691–699.

Glossary/Index

5HTT serotonin transporter gene variant of this gene associated with increased risk for substance abuse, novelty-seeking behaviors, school problems, and aggression among adolescents and violent behavior among adults 213, 215, 217, 255

7-repeat allele 65–6

Acamprosate 186

acetylation an epigenetic process which has the effect of loosening or relaxing histones and thus making the likelihood of genetic expression greater 41

achondroplasia 59

adaptation executors 16

adaptations any anatomical, physiological, or behavioral trait that arose and promoted its own frequency via an extended period of selection because it enabled its possessor to survive and reproduce 14

adaptive criminal behaviors 16–18

adaptive problem a problem of survival or reproduction 90

adaptive strategy an organized set of behaviors that together constitute an adaptation 235–6

admixture 142–3

ADOA2A 215

adolescence a period of fine-tuning post-pubescent individuals' body and physiology to produce maturation of adult social and cognition behaviors 157–62; brain in 114, 159–62; hormones and evolution 157–9

adolescent limited (AL) offenders in Terrie Moffitt's theory, "normal" individuals whose offending is limited to adolescence and which does not reflect any stable personal deficiencies 167–9, 170

adoptive children: brain imaging in 85; evocative gene/environment correlation 37

ADRA2A 215

one another 36–8, 206, 214; active 36, 37, 38; evocative 37, 38; passive 36, 38

gene/environment interaction (G x E) the idea that identical environmental events have different effects on individuals depending upon an individual's phenotype. Also, genetic effects can depend on the environmental background 12, 36–8, 59–60, 65, 67, 68–9

general intelligence the ability to reason, deductively or inductively, think abstractly, use analogies, synthesize information, and apply it to new domains 103–4; longevity and 105; reproduction and 105

generalized anxiety disorder 59

genetic determinism 8

genetic drift random changes in a gene within a population 141

genetic locus 55

genetic mutation any alteration to a gene that may change the expression of a trait 141

genetic polymorphism 56, 64

genetics 51–5

genome an organism's entire genetic information encoded into DNA 50

glial cells cells that support and protect neurons 74

glucocorticoid receptor (GRs) genes 43

glucose a simple sugar that is a major source of energy for the body 81

glutamate 160

gray matter unmyelinated nerve cells 76, 80

GRIN2B 215

haplogroups a group of similar haplotypes, which are a set of genetic markers found on a chromosome. Haplogroups share a common genetic ancestor 140–1

Hebbs' axiom 76

heritability a measure of the extent to which variation in measured phenotypic traits is genetically influenced 10; coefficients 32, 33, 34–6; environment and 32–3; environmentality and 33–6

heroin 184

hippocampus part of the limbic system responsible for memory formation 77

histone acetylation 41

holistic theories 30–1, 45

Holocaust 11

homicide: evolutionary psychological perspective 93–5; gender imbalance 128–30; race and 199; testosterone and 198–200

Homo evolution 139–40

honor subcultures 115, 158, 201–3

hormones a chemical messenger secreted by one cell to have an effect on other cells within the body 8, 251